Production Planning with SAP APO-PP/DS

 PRESS

SAP PRESS is issued by
Bernhard Hochlehnert, SAP AG

SAP PRESS is a joint initiative of SAP and Galileo Press. The know-how offered
by SAP specialists combined with the expertise of the publishing house Galileo
Press offers the reader expert books in the field. SAP PRESS features first-hand
information and expert advice, and provides useful skills for professional deci-
sion-making.

SAP PRESS offers a variety of books on technical and business related topics
for the SAP user. For further information, please visit our website:
www.sap-press.com.

Jörg Thomas Dickersbach, Gerhard Keller, Klaus Weihrauch
Production Planning and Control with SAP
2006, approx. 400 pp., ISBN 1-59229-106-6

Martin Murray
SAP MM—Functionality and Technical Configuration
2006, 504 pp., ISBN 1-59229-072-8

Gerd Hartmann, Ulrich Schmidt
Product Lifecycle Management with SAP
2005, 620 pp., ISBN 1-59229-036-1

Michael Hölzer, Michael Schramm
Quality Management with SAP
2005, 538 pp., ISBN 1-59229-051-5

Jochen Balla, Frank Layer

Production Planning with
SAP APO-PP/DS

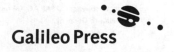

Galileo Press

Bonn • Boston

ISBN   1-59229-113-9

ISBN 13   978-1-59229-113-7

1st edition 2007

Translation Lemoine International, Inc., Salt Lake City, UT
Copy Editor Nancy Etscovitz, UCG, Inc., Boston, MA
Cover Design Silke Braun
Layout Design Vera Brauner
Production Vera Brauner
Typesetting SatzPro, Krefeld
Printed and bound in Germany

Contents at a Glance

Contents

What are the objectives of this book? Which APO releases does it cover? How is the book structured?

Introduction

With SAP Advanced Planning and Optimization (SAP APO) and SAP Supply Chain Management (SAP SCM), SAP has offered a powerful system to support a whole range of processes in supply chain management for many years now. The APO-PP/DS (Production Planning/Detailed Scheduling) component is used for plant-specific production planning and detailed scheduling. The objective of this book is to provide an in-depth introduction to the functions, applications, and customizing of APO-PP/DS.

As of Release 4.0, SAP APO is contained in SAP SCM, along with other applications. This book explicitly refers to the following APO releases:

APO releases

- ▶ SAP APO 3.0
- ▶ SAP APO 3.1
- ▶ SAP SCM 4.0 (containing SAP APO 4.0)
- ▶ SAP SCM 4.1 (containing SAP APO 4.1)
- ▶ SAP SCM 5.0 (containing SAP APO 5.0)

We will refer to the differences between the releases, but this "delta knowledge" will not be in the foreground of the discussion. Unless otherwise indicated, the screenshots in this book are taken from the current release, SAP SCM 5.0 (SAP ERP Central Component (SAP ECC 6.0), respectively).

The large number of processes supported and the basic flexibility of APO-PP/DS make simple and secure access difficult. In addition, the following challenges present themselves:

Challenges associated with advanced planning

- ▶ The concepts and technology behind advanced planning with SAP APO are based on "normal" production planning with SAP ECC.

To fully benefit from using PP/DS, a knowledge of the basic processes is required.

► "Advanced planning," by its very nature, is more complex than standard processes.

► Planning is distributed across more than one system. In addition to SAP SCM or SAP APO, an SAP ECC or SAP R/3 system is required as the executing system.

► Master data and transaction data are exchanged between the systems involved. Knowledge of the relevant interface (the Core Interface, or CIF) is essential.

You can gain this knowledge through the usual channels (the SAP Help Portal, SAP training courses, the SAP Corporate Portal). In addition, many SAP Notes provide detailed explanations of specific functions. However, even with this support on hand, it is still difficult to get a clear overview of the essential functions and understand how to benefit from their use.

Objectives of this book

The goal of this book is to provide an in-depth explanation of the essential functions of PP/DS and how they relate to one another. It will equip you with essential background knowledge, specify the relevant customizing settings, and explain the relationship between PP/DS and SAP ECC. You should note that we have deliberately restricted the scope of the book, so that the focus remains on providing an overall context and an understanding of the core concepts. Furthermore, an extensive index will help you to pinpoint specific information, and the explanations in the book are supplemented by numerous references to other sources of information, as well as several appendices.

In addition, this book will help you to make the essential system settings in accordance with your specific requirements. Numerous screenshots will enable you to reproduce the settings without system support. Finally, a selection of sample processes illustrates how the various functions can be optimally used.

Structure of the book

This book is structured as follows:

Chapter 1 provides an overview of planning with the mySAP SCM solution. Planning with APO-PP/DS is placed in an overall context, and its relationships with other SAP components and concepts are explained.

Chapter 2 begins by explaining the basic features of production planning in SAP, which apply equally to SAP ECC and SAP APO. This part of the chapter is intended for readers who have little or no experience using SAP ECC.

The second part of the chapter examines the special features of planning with SAP APO and focuses on the advantages of planning with APO-PP/DS.

Chapter 3 is devoted to the CIF, which plays an integral role in APO-PP/DS, but is also significant to other applications.

Chapter 4 describes the APO master data required for PP/DS, against the background of transferring this data from ECC.

Since the contents of Chapter 3 and 4 are also relevant for other APO applications (for example, Global Available-to-Promise), they may be of interest to you, irrespective of PP/DS.

Chapter 5 introduces the basic functions in APO-PP/DS and therefore forms a central part of this book.

Chapter 6 describes the main tools for planning and evaluation in APO-PP/DS and their options and practical applications. It therefore provides essential information about the practical work of the planner in the system.

Chapter 7 uses various examples of processes to explain how the individual components interact to create a finite production plan. The examples cited provide insight into how you can get the most out of using APO-PP/DS.

The **Appendix** contains supplementary lists of:

- Menu paths
- SAP Notes that pertain to APO-PP/DS
- Heuristics

Lastly, we should point out that this book *cannot* cover everything you can do with APO-PP/DS. Suffice it to say that APO-PP/DS is extremely flexible and other applications are possible, especially when used with industry-specific enhancements, which will not be addressed here. Nevertheless, the basic and detailed knowledge provided in this book should help you to acclimate to and cope with any PP/DS environment.

Advanced production planning with APO-PP/DS is part of the mySAP SCM solution. This chapter places APO-PP/DS in an overall context.

1 An Overview of Planning with mySAP SCM

Advanced planning with SAP APO is part of the mySAP SCM solution, which supports a whole range of processes in the area of supply chain management.

1.1 mySAP SCM

The mySAP SCM solution uses several different SAP systems. The core logistical processes use the SAP ERP Central Component (SAP ECC) system, which represents an enhancement of SAP R/3 (ECC replaced R/3 after R/3 Enterprise Release 4.7 and the current release is SAP ECC 6.0). SAP ECC handles *Materials Management* (MM) with inventory management and purchasing, *Sales and Distribution* (SD) with sales order processing, production execution with production orders (SFC: Shop Floor Control) or process orders (PI: Process Industries), and other supplementary processes like *Quality Management* (QM). These supply chain management functions can be found under the **Logistics** menu option in the ECC system (see Figure 1.1).

SAP ECC or SAP R/3

Production Planning (PP) is also part of Logistics and can be mapped via SAP ECC. A range of functions is available, covering the entire spectrum from *Flexible Planning* (SOP: Sales & Operations Planning) to the execution of sales forecasts based on historical data, simulative *Long-Term Planning* (LTP), *Material Requirements Planning* (MRP), and *Capacity Requirements Planning* (CRP).

Production planning with SAP ECC

SAP SCM   In addition to SAP ECC, the mySAP SCM solution also comprises the SAP SCM system. SAP SCM supports many additional processes from supply chain management, some of which are completely new, while others represent additions to and enhancements of the processes that are familiar from SAP ECC.

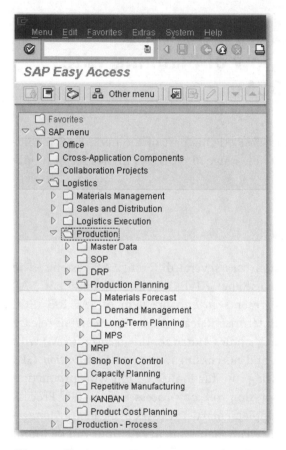

Figure 1.1 The Logistics Menu Structure in the SAP ECC System

The SCM system comprises several different parts:

▸ SAP APO (Advanced Planning and Optimization)

▸ SAP F&R (Forecasting and Replenishment)

▸ SAP ICH (Inventory Collaboration Hub)

▸ SAP EM (Event Management)

▸ SAP EWM (Extended Warehouse Management)

1.2 SAP APO

The SAP APO component is used for *advanced planning* and for the *optimization* of production or procurement plans. Up to and including Release 3.1, APO was a standalone system. With Release 4.0, it was merged with the other systems specified above into a single system—SAP SCM. The current release is SAP SCM 5.0, which includes the component SAP APO 5.0.

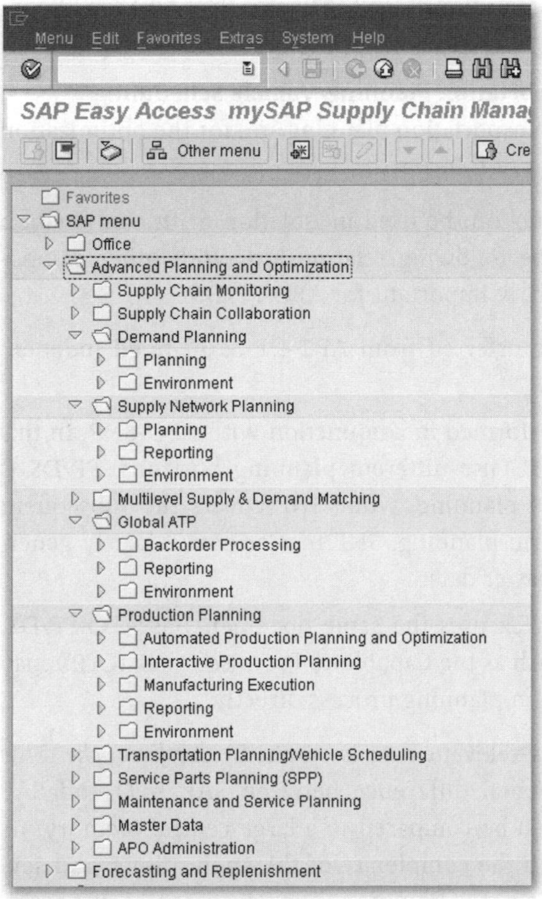

Figure 1.2 The Menu Structure for APO Planning in the SAP SCM System

SAP APO comprises several functions (see Figure 1.2):

▶ **APO-DP: Demand Planning**
  Demand Planning offers extensive options for forecasting based on aggregated historical data.

▶ **APO-SNP: Supply Network Planning**
Supply Network Planning is used for medium to long-term cross-plant procurement planning. Aggregated data is typically used for this purpose (simplified master data, period-based planning).

▶ **APO-PP/DS: Production Planning/Detailed Scheduling**
Production Planning and Detailed Scheduling are used for short-term, plant-specific detailed (capacity) scheduling.

▶ **APO-GATP: Global ATP**
The Global Available-to-Promise (GATP) check in APO enables an availability check across all plants or materials, for example.

▶ **APO-TP/VS: Transportation Planning/Vehicle Scheduling**
TP/VS is used for transportation planning and for the optimization of routes and means of transport.

PP/DS integration with other components

These APO components can be used in isolation or in combination with one another. The following relationships with other components may be particularly important for APO-PP/DS:

▶ Forecasts can be transferred from APO-DP as planned independent requirements.

▶ Planning can be performed in conjunction with APO-SNP. In this case, SNP and PP/DS use different planning horizons. PP/DS is used for short-term planning, while SNP covers the subsequent medium to long-term planning. SNP master data is partly generated from PP/DS master data.

▶ The Global ATP check uses the same documents as APO-PP/DS. Some processes (such as the Capable-to-Promise check (CTP)) may access the production planning process directly.

liveCache

In SAP APO, planning-relevant data is stored in the *liveCache*. This constitutes a fundamental difference between SAP APO and SAP ECC. The liveCache can be compared to a large central memory. Its dimensions depend on the complexity of the applications, and several dozen gigabytes is not uncommon. The advantage of this architecture is that it offers much faster access to data, which means that you can manage even very complex functions that require a large number of master and transaction data records to be read.

The *order liveCache* is used in APO-PP/DS, while the *time series liveCache* is relevant for APO-DP and in part also for APO-SNP.

SAP APO is used exclusively for planning. To execute planning, APO must be integrated with an *Online Transaction Processing* (OLTP) system. The importance of this integration depends on the APO application. APO-DP can be used in relative isolation, with only figures needing to be exchanged. In contrast, integration at document level is essential for APO-PP/DS. PP/DS processes are therefore shaped to a large degree by the need for integration.

Integration with the OLTP system

An SAP ECC system is connected to SAP APO using the Core Interface (CIF, see Figure 1.3). This interface enables the transfer of supply chain master data defined in ECC to APO and also ensures the online integration of transaction data.

SAP ECC and APO CIF

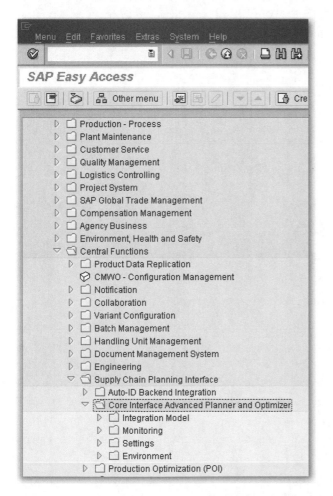

Figure 1.3 The CIF Interface Menu Structure in the SAP ECC System

APO and
industry solutions

In addition to the standard processes that can be executed with a "normal" ECC system (that is, one that has not been enhanced for a specific industry), SAP APO also comprises processes that only come into play when used with one or more industry solutions. For example, integrated Product and Process Engineering (iPPE), which is contained in APO, cannot be used in a core ECC system, but can be used with the *Discrete Industries* industry solution.

Production planning follows the same basic principles in both SAP ECC and SAP APO. This chapter provides an overview of planning with the two systems. This is followed by a discussion of the advanced options available to you with APO.

2 An Overview of Production Planning with ECC and APO-PP/DS

Production planning in APO-PP/DS uses the same processes that are familiar from the SAP ECC system. It is based on master data records, specifically plants, material masters, bills of material (BOM), and routings (PP) or master recipes (PP-PI). Planning results in planned orders, which are converted into manufacturing orders for executing production. These may be either production orders (PP) or process orders (PP-PI).

Repetitive Manufacturing (REM) is also possible, whereby production is executed on the basis of planned orders.

2.1 Production Planning Functions

PP/DS is short for *Production Planning* and *Detailed Scheduling*. Of course, the objectives of this kind of planning did not originate with APO. Production planning in ECC pursues the same objective, that is, consistent, capacity-based planning. In ECC, these functions are found under *Material Requirements Planning* (*MRP*) and *Capacity Requirements Planning* (*CRP*).

PP/DS, MRP, CRP

The basic principles of planning in APO and ECC are outlined below, followed by a discussion of the advanced options in APO.

2.1.1 Material Requirements Planning

The goal of Material Requirements Planning (MRP) is to ensure material availability in good time and in sufficient quantities. Two different procedures can be used:

▶ **Material Requirements Planning**
In this case, procurement planning is controlled by material requirements. The requirements consist of sales orders, planned independent requirements, dependent requirements, and so on. Planning is based on backward scheduling from the requirements date to ensure on-time availability.

▶ **Consumption-Based (Reorder Point) Planning**
In this case, materials planning is based on consumption. Reorder point planning simply checks whether the available stock has fallen below a defined threshold value or reorder point. Whenever this happens, procurement is planned with forward scheduling.

As you can see, the two procedures are essentially different. Consumption-based planning is usually used for only low-value, non-critical materials (consumable material, for example), while MRP is used for precise planning. Consumption-based planning therefore only plays a secondary role in the context of advanced planning in APO-PP/DS.

MRP type
In ECC, you define the MRP procedure in the **MRP type** field in the material master. Typical entries in this field are **PD** for MRP or **VB** for reorder point planning. However, both these entries are irrelevant for planning materials in APO. If a material is planned in APO, it cannot be planned again in ECC. Therefore, you should select the entry **X0** as the MRP type to exclude it from planning in ECC.

There is no MRP type in the APO product master. Planning in APO is essentially "requirement-driven" (i.e., it is based on the MRP procedure described above) unless a different procedure is explicitly chosen by applying a corresponding heuristic.

The starting point for MRP is a requirement for a material in a plant. As a rule, this requirement is in the future. We proceed from the following assumption:

Material A is required in quantity B on date/at time C in plant D.

Think of how this applies to a sales order, for example. However, dependent requirements resulting from in-house production can also be formulated in this way.

Backward scheduling

With backward scheduling for material A in plant D, a suitable procurement element is generated in such a way that the availability date of this element corresponds to the requirements date. The start date of procurement therefore precedes the availability date, and the procurement lead time represents the time interval between these two dates (backward scheduling).

Procurement types

Scheduling of a procurement element depends on the procurement type:

- **In-House Production**
  A routing and a BOM or master recipe is required to produce a material in-house. The in-house production time is the sum total of the durations of the individual operations, plus any additional floats/time buffers.
- **External Procurement**
  If you want to procure a material from an external vendor or to transfer your stock from another location, you must schedule a delivery time.

In the system, these two procurement types correspond to the entries **E** for in-house production and **F** for external procurement on the MRP 2 view of the material master (see Figure 2.1). If you enter **X** here, both procurement types are permitted, but planning initially assumes in-house production.

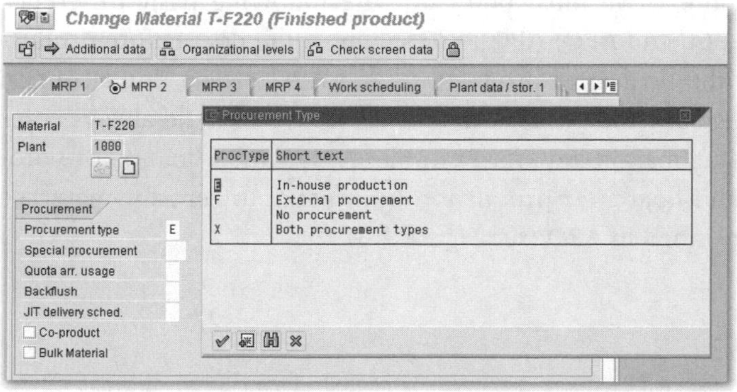

Figure 2.1 ECC Transaction "Change Material Master" (Transaction Code MM02, Material Master View "MRP 2" with Field Selection for Procurement Type)

You can define the procurement type more precisely by specifying the special procurement type (**Special procurement** field). For example, you can configure external procurement as a stock transfer from another production location. With external procurement, you can define a vendor-specific delivery time and factor this in your planning.

Order start and finish dates and production dates

With in-house production, various dates and times can be defined. The ECC manufacturing order contains both production dates and basic order start and finish dates. Floats separate these dates: the float before production separates the order start date and the production start date, while the float after production comes between the production finish date and the order finish date (see Figure 2.2).

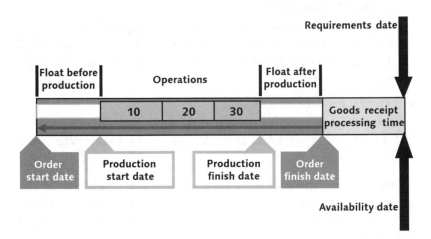

Figure 2.2 Dates in Planned Orders and Manufacturing Orders in ECC

In this context, we must point out the following basic difference between ECC and APO: APO-PP/DS ignores the float before production and the float after production, and APO orders don't contain basic order start and finish dates. Therefore, you should always enter a scheduling margin key (for example, AP1) with a float before production and float after production both equal to zero for materials that are planned in APO (see Figure 2.3).

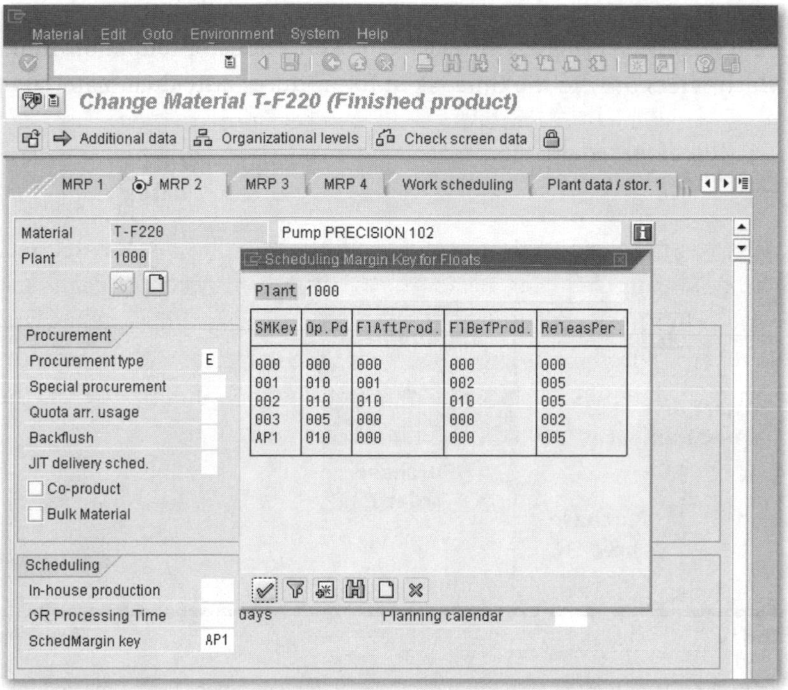

Figure 2.3 ECC Transaction "Change Material Master" (Transaction Code MM02, Material Master View "MRP 2" with Field Selection for Scheduling Margin Key)

2.1.2 Multilevel Planning

With in-house production, you generally use multilevel planning, where the material is produced from other materials that must be available in time for the production process. You can refer to the BOM for information about the required materials. Since a BOM item may be the header of another BOM, planning may encompass several BOM levels. The objective of multilevel planning is therefore to create procurement elements at the right time across all relevant BOM levels (see Figure 2.4). The procurement dates for the assemblies and components are calculated from the BOM structure using backward scheduling from the requirements date of the finished product.

This enables operation-specific material staging.

Multilevel planning uses backward scheduling from the requirements date for the finished product. This means that the start dates for procurement of the required assemblies and components are calculated to ensure that production of the finished product can start on time. The sum total of these times is referred to as the total replenishment lead time. This is distinct from the in-house production time, which refers only to the time taken to produce individual materials.

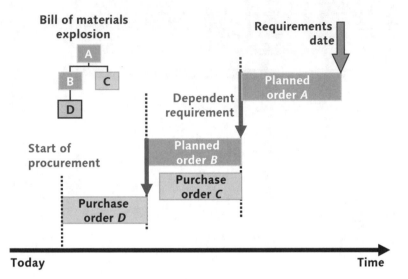

Figure 2.4 Dates in Multilevel Production: Total Replenishment Lead Time and In-House Production Time

Problems may occur with your procurement plan if the requirements date is less than the end of the total replenishment lead time in the future. With backward scheduling, this corresponds to a situation in which the start date for assemblies or components (or even for the finished product itself) would have to be in the past.

Forward scheduling and scheduling delays

Since the system does not create orders in the past, forward scheduling is generally used in this situation. With forward scheduling, the start date of the relevant order is the current date, while the end date is scheduled in the future as the start date plus the lead time of the order. This kind of order is therefore delayed because the requirements date that triggered the order (think of a secondary requirement, for example) cannot be covered in time.

In ECC requirements planning, exception messages normally alert you to this kind of problem. These messages indicate that procurement of a material will be delayed. These delays typically occur in lower-level assemblies, while procurement of the finished product still appears to be on schedule. The exception message is not normally propagated to the relevant finished product. It is the MRP controller's responsibility to identify problematic supply chains using these exception messages and to solve the problem, for example, by changing procurement elements manually or by finding alternatives in the procurement process.

2.1.3 Material Planning and Capacity Planning

In material planning, procurement elements are created with dates that correspond to the requirements situation. This type of planning is based on the individual in-house production times or delivery times of the materials in question.

With externally procured materials, you therefore have to assume that the planned vendor will be able to deliver within the planned delivery time. If in doubt, confirm this with the vendor. You may find that you will need to switch to another vendor with a different delivery time.

The situation is more complex for materials produced in-house. In this case, material planning uses the *MRP II concept*. This means that material planning is initially based on infinite production capacities, with capacity planning following in a second, separate step. When an order is created, there is therefore no check to determine whether the required work centers or resources are available for the relevant period or are already fully occupied by another production process.

MRP II

Capacity planning comprises the following steps: First, the *available capacity* at the work centers (or resources (PP-PI)) is established. For example, it is established that work center A is available for 40 hours each week.

Available capacity

The orders (planned orders or manufacturing orders), on the other hand, have certain capacity requirements, resulting from the routing (or master recipe (PP-PI)). The routing can be broken down into operations. Each operation is assigned a work center, where it can be executed. For example, operation 10 requires work center A for 10 minutes for each piece of the finished product. This means that work center A is required for 50 minutes if you have an order with an order quantity of five pieces. An order therefore contains not only the planned production start and end dates, but also the operations dates, including details of the required production resources, and, in addition, it formulates the corresponding capacity requirement.

Capacity requirement

The goal of capacity planning is to ensure that orders can be executed, in other words, that work centers are available when required. Capacity planning therefore compares the capacity requirement with the available capacity. Since a work center may naturally be required by different orders for completely different finished products, this comparison is normally carried out as work center-specific.

Scheduling

To ensure that a certain order can be executed at a certain time at a specific work center, the order is *scheduled*. A production resource can only be reserved by an order using *scheduling*. Scheduling can be performed interactively in a capacity planning table (or detailed scheduling planning board in APO) for individual orders, or it can be executed automatically as a background job. Problems associated with capacity planning can be extremely complex. For example, orders may involve several operations that require different resources. Successful scheduling of one operation at a resource may conflict with the dates of the other operations, and so on.

Bottleneck
resources

What this means is that capacity planning is restricted to the planning of the *bottleneck resources*. You therefore must assume that no more than one resource from the routing actually needs to be checked for scheduling conflicts, and have to trust that the remaining operations in the order will work. This focus on bottleneck resources is an important principle in capacity planning and is also integral to ensuring an executable production planning process in the context of APO-PP/DS.

Finite and infinite
scheduling

If a check is performed to determine the existing production resource load, that is, to determine whether capacity is available or has already been reserved by another order, this is referred to as *finite scheduling*. The availability checked in this instance is *finite*. If this check is not performed, this is referred to as *infinite scheduling*, whereby the available capacity is assumed to be *infinite*.

Interaction with
requirements
planning

Finite capacity planning generally results in date shifts because time gaps must be found when the bottleneck resources can be scheduled. If a date is brought forward, the availability date of the order is delayed as a result. The deadline of the requirements date of the finished product is missed. If, on the other hand, the order is moved backward in time, the secondary requirements dates for the materials required for production are also delayed, with the result that the receipt elements cannot cover these requirements in time. In short, capacity planning generally impacts the requirements plan (see Figure 2.5). Operation 0020 shown in Figure 2.5 is executed using the bottleneck resource. The total order is based on the bottleneck resource, which means that the availability date and secondary requirements have to be shifted.

You will need to react to these shifts with a new requirements plan, with which any new orders are generated with the scheduled requirement, and so on.

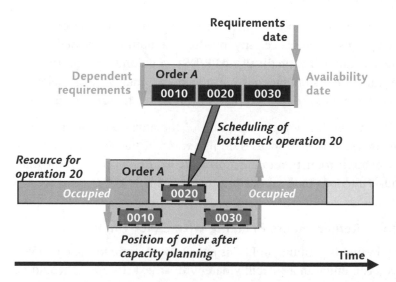

Figure 2.5 Capacity Planning for the Bottleneck Resource of an Order

Material requirements planning and capacity planning are thus closely interwoven. The goal of production planning is to take into account these interdependencies and to create a consistent procurement plan.

To facilitate the planning process, the production plan is often firmed in the short term after capacity planning is completed. Individual orders or all orders can be firmed in a defined *planning time fence*. Firming means that the dates and quantities of the orders cannot be changed automatically; however, they can still be changed manually. The component requirements used for an order can also be firmed. This is useful if the required components are manually changed for an order in a way that deviates from the BOM explosion, with the result that a new BOM explosion is no longer possible.

Firming

2.2   Advanced Production Planning with APO-PP/DS

The previous section discussed the basic principles of production planning with SAP, which apply equally to ECC-MRP and APO-PP/DS. Even if you use APO-PP/DS, you still need to make the basic settings for the production planning process in ECC, so that you can then systematically enhance planning with the functions in APO. This section illustrates the advanced planning options that are available in APO-PP/DS.

APO-PP/DS offers an extremely wide range of additional processes and options. In practice, any one of the points discussed below would be enough to justify using PP/DS—you don't have to use all of the functions simultaneously. Indeed, a gradual and selective enhancement of the core processes is often much more useful.

Note that the following description of the advanced options is not exhaustive. Rather, it focuses on just some of the main features, by way of an introduction to the more detailed descriptions of the individual functions in the following chapters.

2.2.1   Requirements Planning with Exact Times

Requirements planning in ECC is generally accurate to the day. Even if you can enter an availability date with an exact time, as would be done in sales orders, requirements planning still takes into account only the date. Similarly, requirements planning takes into account only the dates of dependent requirements, which are derived from the exact start time of an operation. This means that it is impossible to distinguish between two different requirements that relate to the morning and afternoon of the same date. Orders created to cover requirements in ECC only contain an availability date.

In APO-PP/DS, requirements planning is based on exact times (accurate to the second). Sales orders, dependent requirements, and all other requirements are assigned an exact time. Orders to cover the requirements are scheduled for precisely this time.

If, for example, you need a precise requirement coverage for a just-in-time processing, this can be planned with APO-PP/DS.

2.2.2 Descriptive Characteristics

If you use the *Planning with final assembly* planning strategy, the planned independent requirements are consumed by sales orders, which are generally received at a later stage. In ECC, this consumption is both plant-specific and material-specific.

In APO, you can control consumption more precisely across plants and materials. For example, consumption can be specific to individual customers. For this purpose, planned independent requirements are created with reference to individual customers, that is, they are assigned additional descriptive characteristics. Sales orders that are received then only consume the forecasts for these customers.

2.2.3 Simultaneous Quantity and Capacity Planning

In ECC, quantities and capacities are planned separately. This applies to requirements planning, but the possibility of taking into account capacities is similarly limited when you manually create or move an order. Instead, this must be done in a second step.

In APO-PP/DS, you can plan quantities and capacities *simultaneously*. For example, the capacity situation can also be considered when an additional order is created in a short-term horizon in which capacity planning has already been completed and the production plan is already defined. The order can be created only if periods of available capacity are found for the operations in the order, and it is then automatically scheduled for this period.

2.2.4 Production Planning Runs with Several Steps

In APO-PP/DS, it is easy to construct the automatic production planning process from several steps. The individual steps are simply specified in the production planning run. An example of how individual steps can be placed in a logical sequence is shown below:

1. Requirements planning based on MRP logic

2. Scheduling of capacities for bottleneck resources

3. Requirements planning for the materials for which capacity planning has resulted in shifts in requirements

These steps can be easily defined using procedures referred to as *heuristics*, and can be limited to specific materials or resources (see Figure 2.6). The result of this kind of planning run (which, in practice, often comprises up to 10 steps) is a procurement plan, which allows for as many conditions of planning as possible (capacity bottlenecks, deadlines).

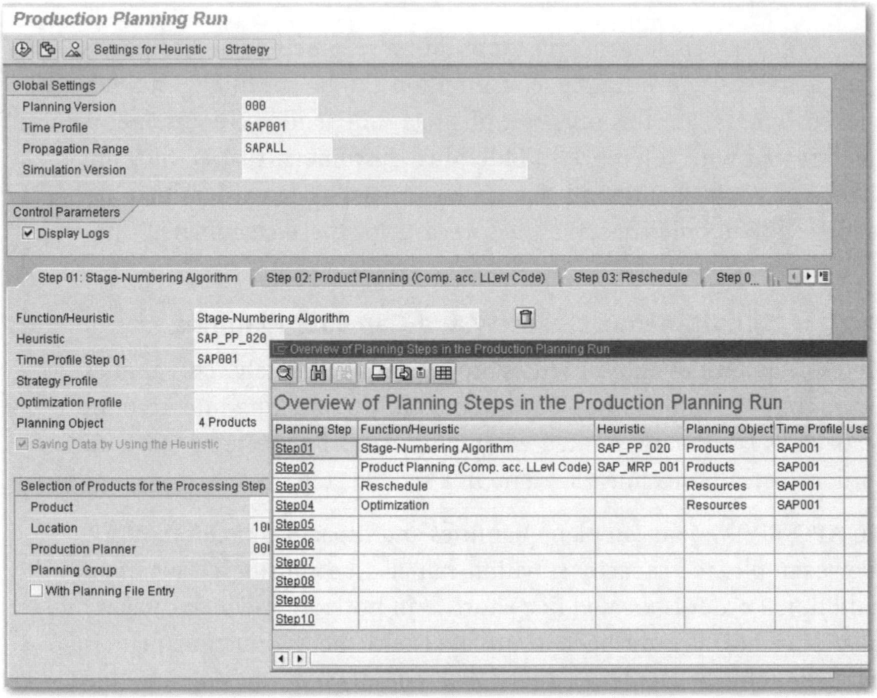

Figure 2.6 APO Transaction "Production Planning Run," Transaction Code /SAPAPO/CDPSB0, Production Planning Run with Multiple Steps

2.2.5 Pegging and Control of the Material Flow

In ECC, dynamic references are created between requirement and procurement elements in order to evaluate requirements planning. These references can be seen in the MRP list or in the current stock/requirements list as part of the Pegged Requirements and Order Report functions, and they can be used to edit the planning result manually. Because these references are generated dynamically and are not stored in the database, they are not available for other transactions or functions.

Pegging   In APO-PP/DS, dynamic references are similarly created between requirements and procurement elements following requirements planning or the generation of orders. In APO, these references are called *pegging relationships*. These relationships are created in multi-level production across all BOM levels. This network of relationships is referred to as a *pegging network*. In contrast to ECC, pegging relationships are stored in the APO database and are therefore available to all applications in APO. The pegging network can be used in capacity planning, for example, to shift the corresponding orders for components whenever an order is shifted.

Dynamic pegging can be influenced by a range of settings, and can be adjusted to suit the specified planning situation (see Figure 2.7). You can also fix pegging relationships so that the relevant orders and requirements remained fixed in a relationship with one another, even if the planning situation changes and new dynamic pegging relationships are created as a result. You can create (and delete) these fixed relationships manually or automatically with the relevant functions or heuristics.

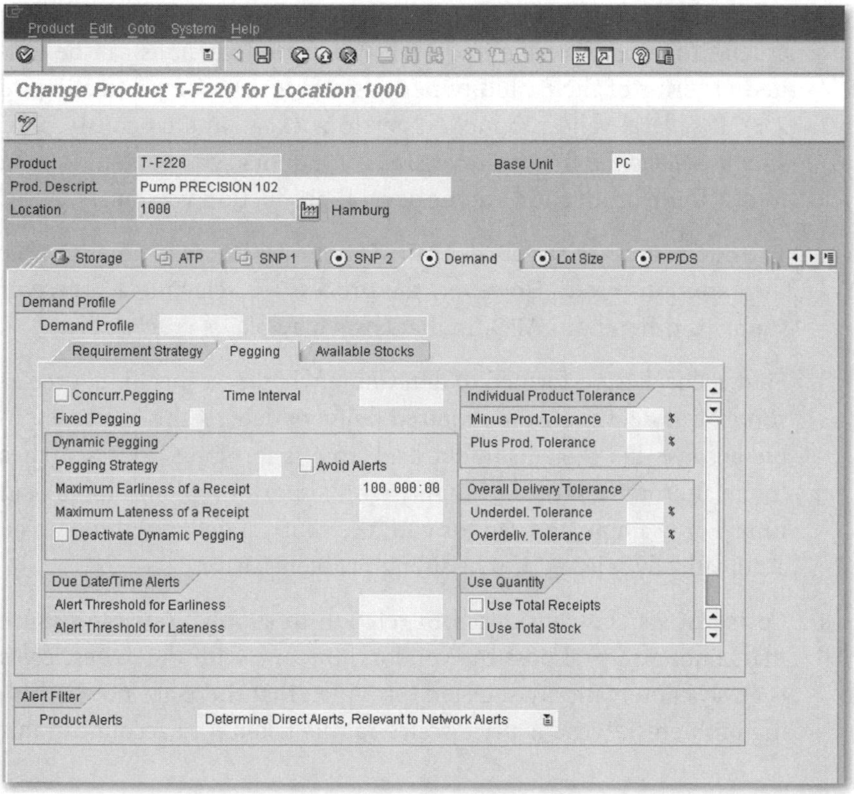

Dynamic and fixed pegging

Figure 2.7 APO Transaction "Product," Transaction Code /SAPAPO/MAT1, Product Master and Pegging Settings

2.2.6 Determining the Source of Supply and Cost-Based Planning

The procedure for selecting a source of supply in ECC is described below.

Source of supply for external procurement in ECC

You may have several different vendors for externally procured materials. If you want one of several vendors to be automatically selected in materials planning, all planning-relevant vendors must first be defined in the purchasing info record, scheduling agreement, or contract in the source list. If several MRP-relevant vendors exist, the selection of a single vendor must be defined using a quota arrangement. In this case, scheduling of the replenishment lead time may be vendor-specific.

Source of supply for in-house production in ECC

Several sources of supply may also exist as alternative production versions for materials produced in-house.[1] Production versions are defined in the material master, and they, in turn, define which manufacturing process is to be used, usually by specifying a routing and a BOM (or master recipe in PP-PI). Production versions can be limited in terms of their validity periods and lot-size range (see Figure 2.8). If several valid production versions exist simultaneously, ECC simply selects the first valid version, or a quota arrangement is used to distribute production among several production versions.

Sources of supply in APO

The ECC sources of supply described above are the same in APO after they are transferred. However, the process for selecting a source of supply is different in APO, in that costs may play a crucial role.

First, a check is performed to determine whether a specific source of supply can deliver by the required delivery date. If this is not possible because the replenishment lead time is too long, APO searches for an alternative source of supply with a shorter replenishment lead time. For example, the vendor with the shortest delivery time can be automatically selected if scheduling problems arise.

Cost-based planning

Costs can also be considered in relation to supply. You can ensure that, among several possible vendors, the one with the lowest costs is always automatically selected (provided that there are no scheduling problems). Various price scales can be taken into account in this

---

1 At this point, we'll focus on using production versions, because only they are relevant to APO.

case, which means that different vendors may be used, depending on the lot size.

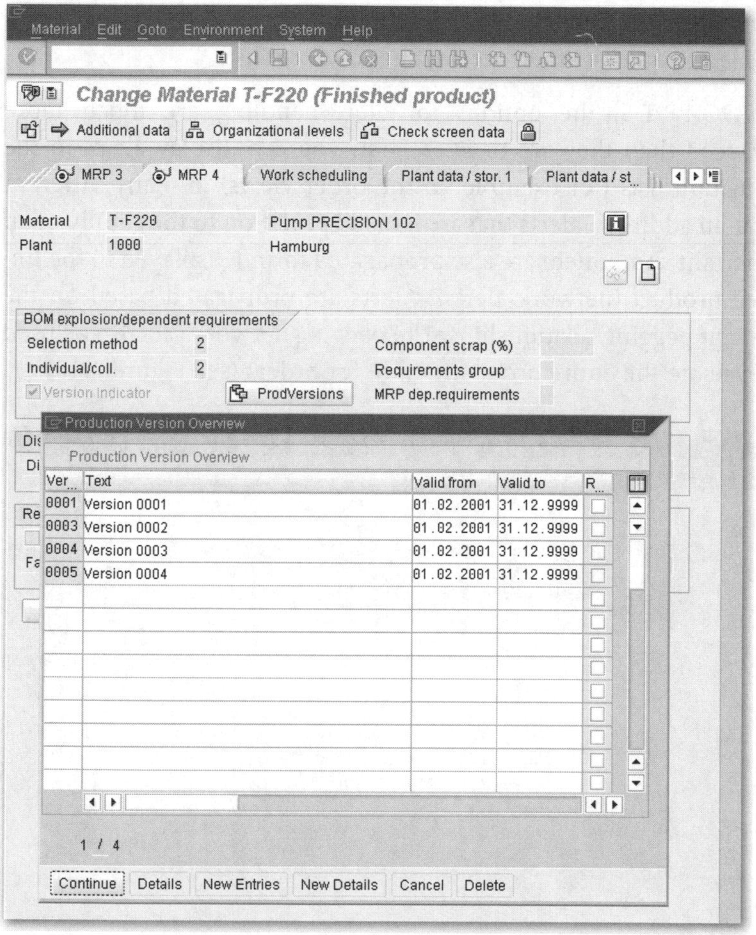

Figure 2.8 ECC Transaction "Change Material Master," Transaction Code MM02, Material Master with Several Production Versions

The process is exactly the same for the planning of in-house production. There may be differences in terms of lead times and production costs in the various production versions (transferred to APO as production process models or production data structures).

2.2.7 Advanced Alert Handling

Exception messages (alerts) indicate problems with planning. In ECC, exception messages are displayed in the MRP list (or in the current stock/requirements list). Collective evaluation is possible if you call up the collective display of all MRP lists. In the material overview, you can display all exception messages that appear in the individual materials, sorted by exception group (see Figure 2.9). To examine a problem, you must then access the individual list.

Alerts   In APO-PP/DS, the options for alert handling are much more advanced than they are in ECC. First, you can display alerts in the evaluation lists (for example, in the order views) in many different ways. In addition, alerts that are issued in relation to the supply of an important component are also propagated to and displayed in the finished product (network alerts). Alerts are propagated based on the relevant pegging relationships. The pegging network can also be used to evaluate the entire order structure for orders (see Figure 2.10).

Light	Material	MRP Area	Material Description	CI	N	1	2	3	4	5	6	7	8	Supply	1stRDS	2nd	MRP date	Plant stock	B	MTyp	PT	S
	T-MD2116	1000	Screw-16		✓	1					1			999,9-	999,9-	999,9-	28.07.2005	0	PC	ROH	F	
	T-MD2117	1000	Screw-17		✓	1					1			999,9-	999,9-	999,9-	28.07.2005	0	PC	ROH	F	
	T-MD2118	1000	Screw-18		✓	1					1			999,9-	999,9-	999,9-	28.07.2005	0	PC	ROH	F	
	T-MD2119	1000	Screw-19		✓	1					1			999,9-	999,9-	999,9-	28.07.2005	0	PC	ROH	F	
	T-MD2120	1000	Screw-20		✓	1					1			999,9-	999,9-	999,9-	28.07.2005	0	PC	ROH	F	
	T-MD2121	1000	Screw-21		✓	1					1			999,9-	999,9-	999,9-	28.07.2005	0	PC	ROH	F	
	T-MD2122	1000	Screw-22		✓	1					1			999,9-	999,9-	999,9-	28.07.2005	0	PC	ROH	F	
	T-MD2123	1000	Screw-23		✓	1					1			999,9-	999,9-	999,9-	28.07.2005	0	PC	ROH	F	
	T-MD2124	1000	Screw-24		✓	1					1			999,9-	999,9-	999,9-	28.07.2005	0	PC	ROH	F	
	T-MD2125	1000	Screw-25		✓	1					1			999,9-	999,9-	999,9-	28.07.2005	0	PC	ROH	F	
	T-MD2126	1000	Screw-26		✓	1					1			999,9-	999,9-	999,9-	28.07.2005	0	PC	ROH	F	
	T-MD2127	1000	Screw-27		✓	1					1			999,9-	999,9-	999,9-	28.07.2005	0	PC	ROH	F	
	T-MD2128	1000	Screw-28		✓	1					1			999,9-	999,9-	999,9-	28.07.2005	0	PC	ROH	F	
	T-MD2129	1000	Screw-29		✓	1					1			999,9-	999,9-	999,9-	28.07.2005	0	PC	ROH	F	
	T-MD2130	1000	Screw-30		✓	1					1			999,9-	999,9-	999,9-	28.07.2005	0	PC	ROH	F	
	101-110	1000-L1000	Slug for spiral casing--cast steel		✓			1		1				999,9-	999,9-	999,9-	28.07.2005	0	PC	HALBF	U	
	100-100	1000	Casing											999,9	999,9	999,9	28.07.2005	881	PC	HALBX		
	100-101	1000	CI Spiral casing (with planned scrap)											999,9	999,9	999,9	28.07.2005	144	PC	HALBX		
	100-110	1000	Slug for spiral casing											999,9	999,9	999,9	28.07.2005	272	PC	ROH	F	
	100-120	1000	Flat gasket		✓									999,9	999,9	999,9	28.07.2005	1.612	PC	ROH	F	
	100-130	1000	Hexagon head screw M10		✓	1					1			999,9	999,9	999,9	28.07.2005	212	PC	ROH	F	

Figure 2.9 ECC Transaction "MRP List Collective Display, Transaction Code MD06," Display of MRP Lists for the MRP Controller with Exception Messages in Various Exception Groups

Alert Monitor   Finally, the Alert Monitor provides a comprehensive tool for the centralized evaluation of alerts. The Alert Monitor provides an overview of all relevant alerts. Alerts can be evaluated across all materials, resources, plants, and so on (see Figure 2.11).

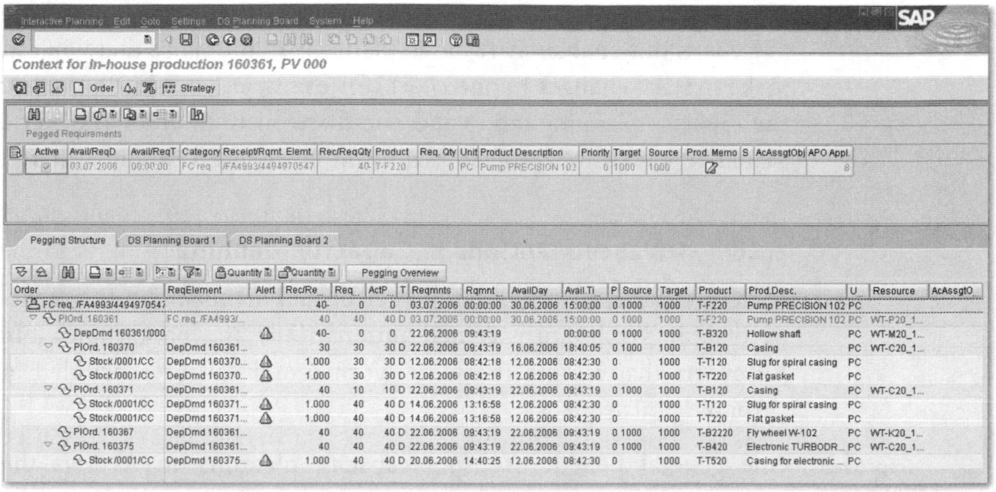

Figure 2.10 APO Transaction "Product View," Transaction Code /SAPAPO/RRP3, Accessing the Context for an Order in Multilevel Production from the Product View

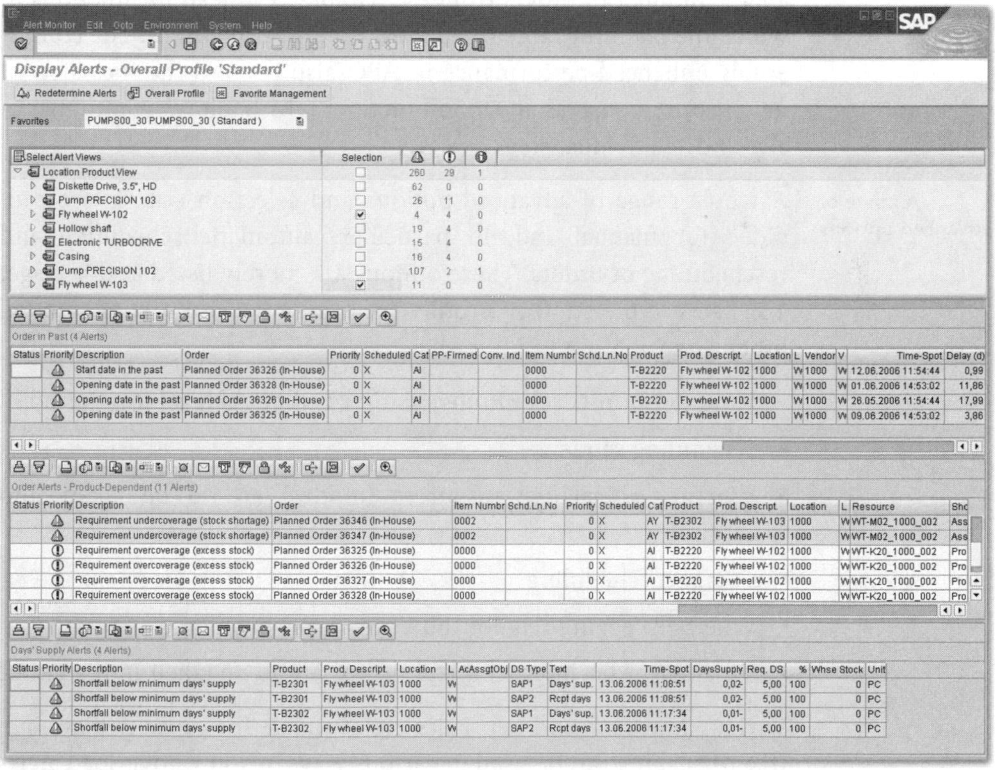

Figure 2.11 APO Transaction "Alert Monitor," Transaction Code /SAPAPO/AMON1, Alert Monitor with PP/DS Alerts

If you incorporate the Alert Monitor into the product planning table as a chart, this enables alert-based planning in the sense that you can make manual changes in one chart (for example, you shift orders in the capacity planning table) and simultaneously monitor the alerts that are triggered or resolved as a result in the Alert Monitor chart.

2.2.8 Advanced Options in Capacity Planning

In ECC, capacity planning can be performed manually (in the capacity planning table), or executed automatically as a background job. All orders that require the same work center can be scheduled in chronological sequence.

Improved performance

One general benefit of using capacity planning in APO is the improved performance. Due to the liveCache architecture, the detailed scheduling planning board in APO can be used for many orders, without affecting runtime (in ECC, the time it takes to import a large number of orders from the database can lead to situations in which the planning table can almost no longer be used). The considerably enhanced performance in APO also enables the inclusion of new features, such as an **Undo** function, which allows you to manually undo individual steps.

A range of advanced options

A whole range of advanced options and selection criteria are provided for manual and, in particular, automatic scheduling and rescheduling of orders. These options are merely listed at this stage. You can use the strategy profile (see Figure 2.12) to define, among other things:

▶ Finite or infinite scheduling, using a finiteness level if required

▶ Scheduling sequence

▶ Whether alternative resources (modes) are to be taken into account

▶ Compact scheduling

▶ Whether pegging relationships are to be considered

▶ Whether order-internal relationships are to be taken into account

Various functions and heuristics are available for capacity planning; (fixed) pegging can be used in various ways; resource overload alerts can be used for troubleshooting; and so on.

APO is ultimately a production planning system, which contains a powerful optimization tool, the PP/DS Optimizer. Optimization is the final step in the production planning process, which can therefore be logically broken down into the following three steps: **Optimizer**

1. Requirements planning (quantity planning)

2. Capacity planning

3. Optimization

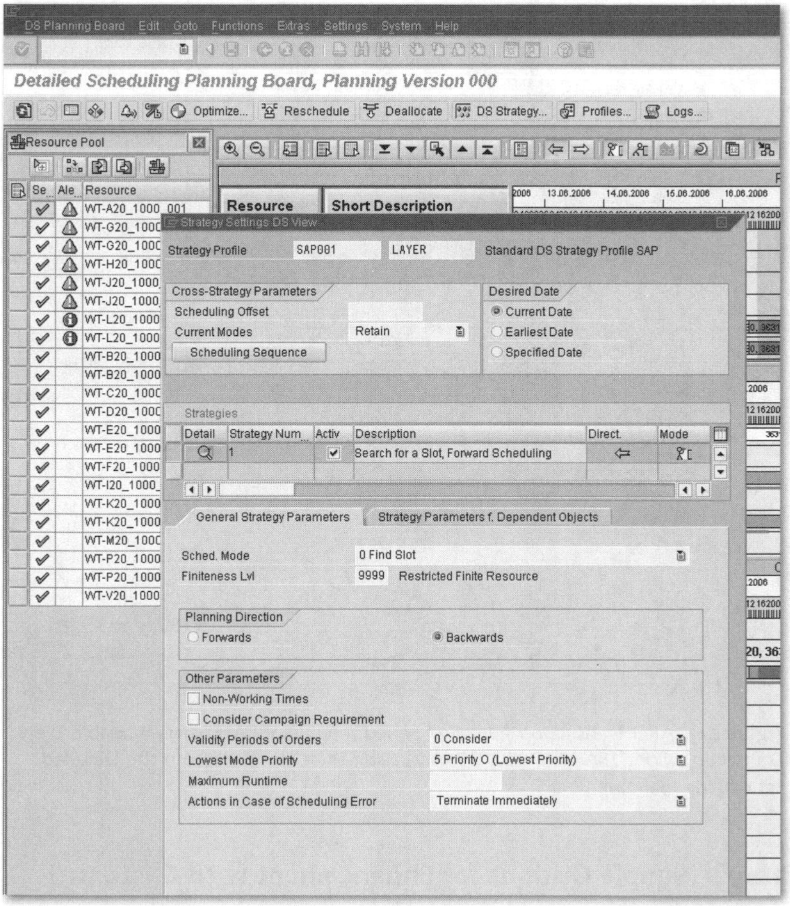

Figure 2.12 APO Transaction "Detailed Scheduling Planning Board—Variable View," Transaction Code /SAPAPO/CDPS0, Detailed Scheduling Planning Board with DS Planning Strategy

Steps 2 and 3 can also be merged and executed by the Optimizer (see Figure 2.13). The Optimizer thus represents the only option for consistently taking into account *all* constraints in a multilevel production plan.

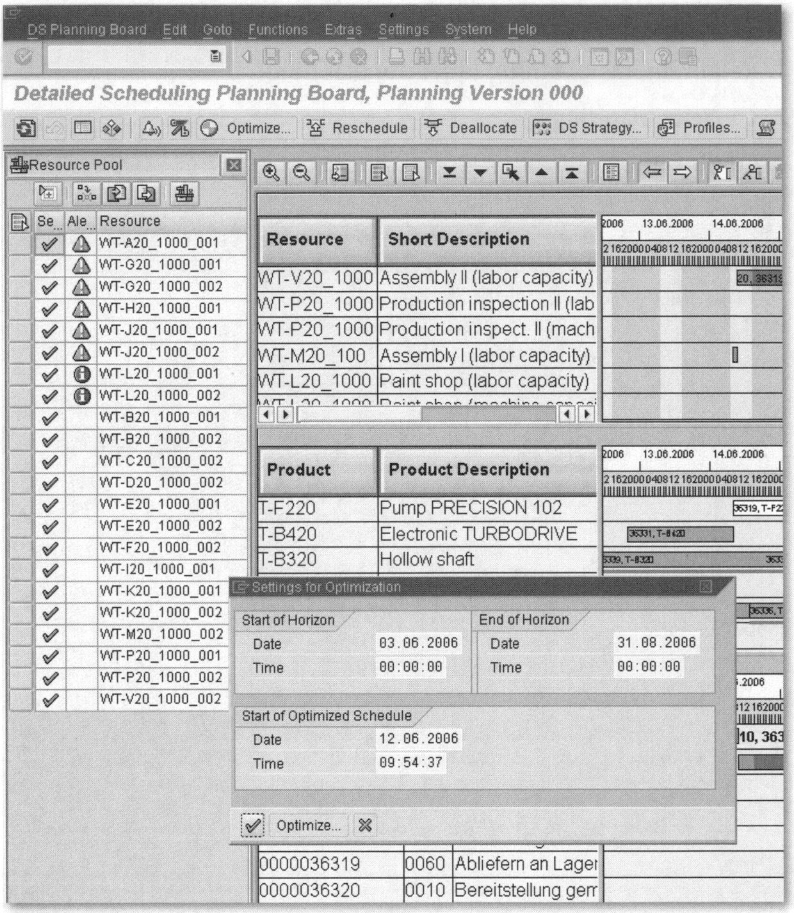

Figure 2.13 APO Transaction "Detailed Scheduling Planning Board—Variable View," Transaction Code /SAPAPO/CDPS0, Accessing the Optimizer from the Detailed Scheduling Planning Board

2.2.9 Simple Options for Enhancement with Custom Functions and Heuristics

In ECC (as in APO), the exact steps involved in planning can be determined by a range of customizing settings. However, if you want to take things a step further and, for example, create special new planning algorithms, a modification of the ECC system is required.

In APO-PP/DS, it is very easy to incorporate new algorithms and processes into the planning process by adding them to the system as additional functions or heuristics. They are then available alongside the standard algorithms (see Figure 2.14) and can simply be used as alternatives in the applications. A system modification is not required.

Heuristic	Short Description	Algorithm
SAP001	Schedule Sequence	/SAPAPO/HEUR_PLAN_SEQUENCE
SAP002	Remove Backlog	/SAPAPO/HEUR_RESOLVE_BACKLOG
SAP003	Schedule Sequence Manually	/SAPAPO/HEUR_PLAN_SEQUENCE_MAN
SAP004	Minimize Runtime	/SAPAPO/HEUR_REDUCE_LEADTIME
SAP005	Schedule Operations	/SAPAPO/HEUR_DISPATCH
SAP_CDPBP_01	Reschedule Blocks	/SAPAPO/MC01_HEU_BLOCKS_SCHED
SAP_CDPBP_02	Adjust and Reschedule Block Limits	/SAPAPO/MC01_HEU_BLOCK_ADJUST
SAP_CDPBP_03	Enhanced Block Maintenance	/SAPAPO/BLRG_HEUR_BLK_MAINT
SAP_CDPBP_04	Block Maintenance, Called Interactively	/SAPAPO/MC01_R05_RES_EDIT_HEUR
SAP_CDS_A01	Admissibility OK Without Check	/SAPAPO/HEU_CDS_ADMI_OK_WO_CHK
SAP_CDS_A02	Tolerance Check	/SAPAPO/HEU_CDS_TOLCHK_LCDDS
SAP_CDS_F01	Confirm Compliance Without Check	/SAPAPO/HEU_CDS_MATCHING_CONF
SAP_CDS_F02	Days' Supply Check	/SAPAPO/HEU_CDS_DSUP_CHK
SAP_CDS_F03	Product Heuristic w. Days' Supply Check	/SAPAPO/HEU_CDS_PHEU_DSUP_CHK
SAP_CHECK_01	Check PDS	/SAPAPO/CULL_PDS_CHECK_HEUR
SAP_DS_01	Stable Forward Scheduling	/SAPAPO/SFW_HEUR_FW_STABLE
SAP_DS_02	Enhanced Backward Scheduling	/SAPAPO/SFW_HEUR_BW_EXT
SAP_DS_03	Change Fixing/Planning Intervals	/SAPAPO/HEUR_REL_FIXINT_MAINT
SAP_DS_04	Activate Seq.-Dependent Setup Activities	/SAPAPO/HEUR_ACTIVATE_SETUPACT
SAP_LEN_001	Length-Based Heuristic	/SAPAPO/EOGL_LENGTH_01
SAP_LEN_002	Manual Creation of LOP Order	/SAPAPO/EOGLM_HEUR
SAP_MLO_BU	Multi-Level, Order-Related - Bottom-Up	/SAPAPO/HEU_MLO_PLANNING
SAP_MLO_TD	Multi-Level, Order-Related - Top-down	/SAPAPO/HEU_MLO_PLANNING
SAP_MMP_HFW1	Model Mix Planning Run 1	/SAPAPO/SEQ_MODELMIX_RUN_01
SAP_MOP_001	Multiple Output Planning Heuristic	/SAPAPO/EOG_HEU_PLAN_MOP
SAP_MOP_002	Manual Creation of MOP Order	/SAPAPO/EOGM_HEUR
SAP_MRP_001	Product Planning (Comp. acc. LLevl Code)	/SAPAPO/HEU_MRP_PLANNING
SAP_MRP_002	Product Planning (Plan Comp. Immdiately)	/SAPAPO/HEU_MRP_PLANNING
SAP_PCM_CRT	Create Production Campaigns	/SAPAPO/HEUR_PCM_CREATE
SAP_PCM_DIS	Dissolve Production Campaigns	/SAPAPO/HEUR_PCM_DISSOLVE
SAP_PCM_ODEL	Delete Setup/Clean-Out Orders	/SAPAPO/HEUR_PCM_ORDERS_DELETE
SAP_PCM_SRVA	Create Setup/Clean-Out Orders	/SAPAPO/HEUR_PCM_SERVICE_ADAPT
SAP_PI_001	Merge Orders (Container Resources)	/SAPAPO/HEUR_MERGE_ORDERS
SAP_PMAN_001	Critical Path	/SAPAPO/PMAN_HEUR_CRIT_PATH
SAP_PMAN_002	Infinite Forward Scheduling	/SAPAPO/PMAN_HEUR_FW_COMPACT
SAP_PMAN_003	Infinite Backward Scheduling	/SAPAPO/PMAN_HEUR_BW
SAP_PP_001	Change Order Manually	/SAPAPO/HEU_ORDER_CHANGE

Figure 2.14 APO Customizing Setting "Change Heuristics," Transaction Code /SAPAPO/CDPSC11, List Showing Some of the Delivered Heuristics

2.3   Planning in APO and Execution in ECC

To fully benefit from using APO-PP/DS, an understanding of the main options for advanced planning is essential. This includes a clear understanding of how an APO function affects the final production plan that is to be executed.

Document flow in production planning

Planned orders and purchase requisitions represent the direct result of production planning in APO-PP/DS. These orders are created based on APO master data, which was transferred from ECC. When they are converted into manufacturing orders or purchase orders, the orders must be transferred to the executing ECC system. The corresponding ECC master data is again essential for this purpose. The ECC master data design is therefore very important in APO planning. Master data should be maintained in a way that both supports the relevant APO process and enables a smooth transfer of the planning result from APO back to ECC.

Executing planning in ECC

The planning steps executed in APO only make sense if the results can have a rippling effect in the manufacturing order or purchase order in ECC. Note also that certain process steps in the ECC manufacturing order must be transferred back to APO (production backflushes result in the reduction of the corresponding capacity requirement in APO, for example). But, it is not useful to exploit all of the options that are theoretically possible in the ECC manufacturing order. For example, you could manually reschedule an operation from the production order by changing the default values. However, the result could not be taken into account in APO because the APO order is based on the APO master data. Therefore, this step is not permitted. The reasoning behind this constraint in this example is that rescheduling is a function of production planning and thus of APO, and therefore should be executed in APO.

It follows that you should therefore verify the integrity of all process steps with APO. These include creating master data, transferring master data to APO and enhancing it there as required, using transaction data, planning in APO, converting orders and transferring them to ECC, and backflushing manufacturing orders.

Planning in APO is based on APO master data, which is transferred from the ECC system. Transaction data must be exchanged between ECC and APO. These functions are provided by the interface between ECC and APO, the APO Core Interface (CIF). This chapter provides a detailed description of the design of the CIF and the required customizing settings.

3 The APO Core Interface

Two systems, SAP ECC and SAP SCM (APO), are used for advanced production planning with APO-PP/DS. Planning in APO is based on APO-specific master data. The master data that lies behind a data transfer between both systems (i.e., APO and ECC) has to be identical in its content; however, because the master data resides in different master data records in both systems, it cannot be truly identical. Therefore, the data consistency is ensured by the transfer of master data from ECC to APO. Since the data has a different structure in the two systems, this transfer involves mapping the ECC data to the corresponding data in APO.

The process is the same for transaction data, although this type of data must be transferred from ECC to APO as well as from APO to ECC.

3.1 Design of the CIF

The Core Interface (CIF) is used for the exchange of data between ECC and APO. This interface performs the following tasks:

- Transfer of master data from ECC to APO
- Transfer of master data changes from ECC to APO to ensure data consistency
- Transfer of transaction data from ECC to APO
- Transfer of transaction data from APO to ECC

The transfer of transaction data includes the transfer of changes in existing documents that have already been transferred.

3.1.1 Plug-In

The CIF is part of a *plug-in*. Up to and including SAP ECC 5.0, this plug-in, which contains the CIF and a range of additional software components, must be installed as an add-on to the ECC system for advanced production planning. As of Release SAP ECC 6.0, the plug-in is contained in the standard ECC system. In other words, it is no longer a separate software component. The complete system landscape for advanced planning therefore comprises the following components:

▶ An ECC system with release status (for example, SAP ECC 5.0) and a plug-in with release status (for example, PI 2004_1_500; see Figure 3.1) or SAP ECC 6.0

▶ An SCM system with release status (for example, SAP SCM 5.0, which includes SAP APO 5.0)

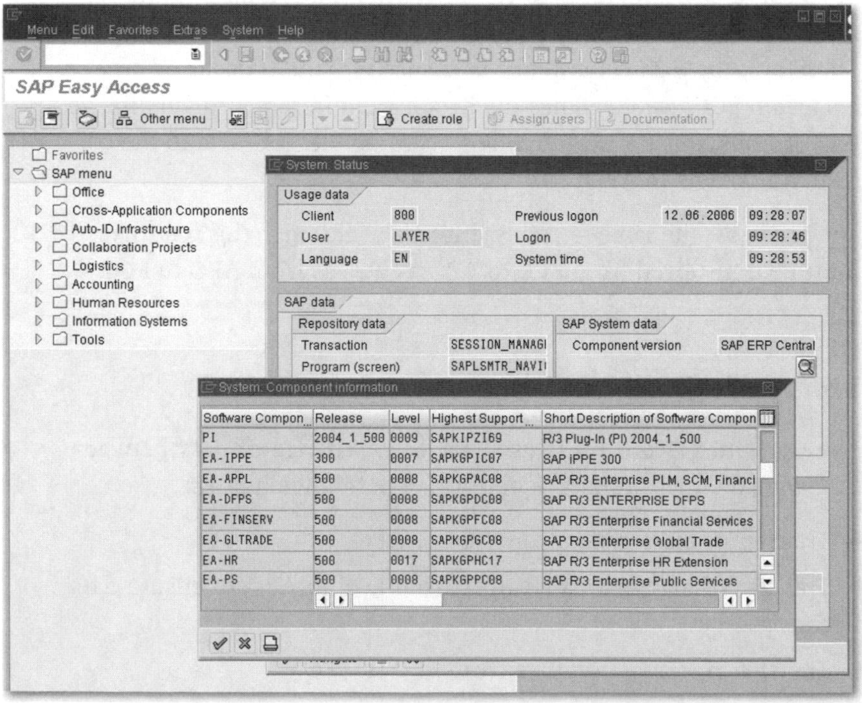

Figure 3.1 System Status of an ECC 5.0 System with PI 2004_1_500

The names of the plug-in releases for the add-on to be installed always specify the year of the release. In recent years, there have been one to two new plug-in releases each year. Different SCM releases require certain minimum plug-in release versions:

- ▶ SCM 4.0 requires PI 2003.1 or higher.
- ▶ SCM 4.1 requires PI 2004.1 or higher.

Up to and including ECC 5.0, the plug-in release is, in principle, independent of the ECC or R/3 release. You should always use the most recent PI. For example, an R/3 Release 4.6C system with PI 2004.1 can be used with SCM 5.0. The plug-ins are downward compatible for both ECC or R/3 and APO.

PI 2004.1 is the last plug-in that is delivered separately. You can then upgrade to SAP ECC 6.0 or, for lower ECC or R/3 releases, import a Support Package for PI 2004.1 (the delivery for 2005 was made available in November 2005 with Support Package 10).[1]

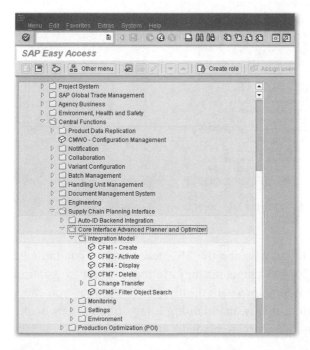

Figure 3.2 "Central Functions" Logistics Submenu in ECC, with the APO Core Interface Menu Expanded

---

1 You can find current information on the installation and the plug-in upgrade in the SAP Service Portal under the /R3-plug-in alias.

CIF transactions

The transactions of the CIF are provided in the plug-in. These include a range of application transactions (for example, Transactions CFM1 and CFM2, shown in Figure 3.2) and additional customizing transactions. You can access the customizing transactions directly from Transaction PIMG. The customizing settings provided allow you to select all required ECC settings for CIF integration (see Figure 3.3).

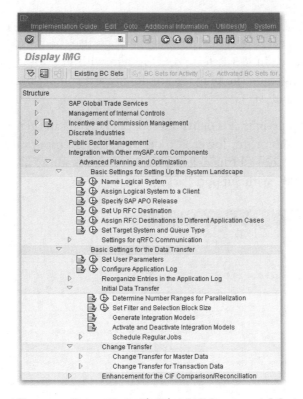

Figure 3.3 "Integration with Other SAP Components" Customizing Menu (Transaction PIMG) in ECC

When you install the plug-in and the CIF, new program components are also added in APO. Various settings are required for integration in both ECC and APO. However, the first basic settings you must select for integration, that is, maintaining integration models or the master data change transfer, are made in ECC.

3.1.2 Connecting the Systems Using RFC

Remote Function Call (RFC) connections are used to exchange data with the CIF. These RFC connections represent a general technique used to connect different SAP systems. With RFC, the relevant function module in the target system for the data transfer is called from outside the system to post the relevant document, and is supplied with data from the source system.

An understanding of this RFC mechanism often facilitates a better appreciation of how the CIF works and the possibilities it offers. If, for example, a material master is transferred from ECC to APO, the function module to create a product master is called in APO (this module and the *Product master* document have a completely different structure than the *Material master* in ECC) and is supplied with data from ECC. Therefore, the material master is not simply copied (which would necessitate the same database structure in both systems). For the transfer to work, the ECC data must be filtered through the CIF and staged to ensure that it can be used by the APO function module. The process is exactly the same for all other master data and for transaction data that is exchanged between ECC and APO.

How RFC works

For CIF integration, RFC connections have to be set up between all ECC and SCM systems that are to be connected. Separate connections are required for transfers from ECC to SCM (this connection is created in ECC) and from SCM to ECC (created in SCM). It is also possible to connect one ECC system to several SCM systems, or one SCM system to several executing ECC systems.

Setting up the RFC connections

In both ECC and SCM, the transactions for maintaining RFC connections are found under ALE customizing and in Transaction SALE. They can also be accessed from Transaction PIMG in ECC. To create an RFC connection, follow the steps below:

1. Name the logical systems (**Name Logical System** setting in customizing):
   The names of the source and target systems must exist, that is, they must be named here. Both an ECC name and an SCM name are required in ECC and in SCM. This step simply generates a list of possible names. We recommend that you use the following naming convention for the logical system names: [*system name*]CLNT[*client name*].

2. Assign the logical systems to a client (**Assign Logical System to a Client** setting in customizing):
   The names are assigned in this step. A unique name must be assigned to the ECC client and to the SCM client.

3. Define the RFC destination for the transfer of data to SCM (**RFC Destination** transaction in ECC, Transaction Code SM59):
Create an RFC destination under the logical SCM name in ECC. Next, enter a **target host** (server) and a **system number** to define how contact is to be made with the SCM system (see Figure 3.4). Finally, enter the user with which the connection to the SCM system is to be created. This user must exist in the SCM system and must have all authorizations required to create and change master data and transaction data in the SCM system.

4. Define the RFC destination for the transfer of data to ECC (**RFC Destination** transaction in SCM, Transaction Code SM59):
Create an RFC destination under the logical ECC name in SCM. Next, enter a **target host** (server) and a **system number** to define how contact is to be made with the ECC system. Finally, enter the **user** with which the connection to the ECC system is to be created. This user must exist in the ECC system and must have all authorizations required to transfer transaction data in the ECC system.

When you are setting up an RFC connection, you can use the **Remote Login** function to check that you can log on to the target system correctly.

RFC user   The user you specify in the RFC connection should be a "normal" dialog (interactive) user.[2] This user must have relevant authorizations (for example, you can assign the **SAP_ALL** authorization profile to the user). The logon language is the language specified in the RFC destination (for the ATP check also).

> **Note**
>
> With a transaction that results in the transfer of data into a target system, the user defined in the RFC destination is used to log on to the target system. All actions in APO that result from a CIF transfer from ECC are therefore technically executed by the RFC user in APO. The same is true if the direction is reversed.

---

2 For the APO-ATP integration in the ECC sales order, it is mandatory that the user be dialog-enabled.

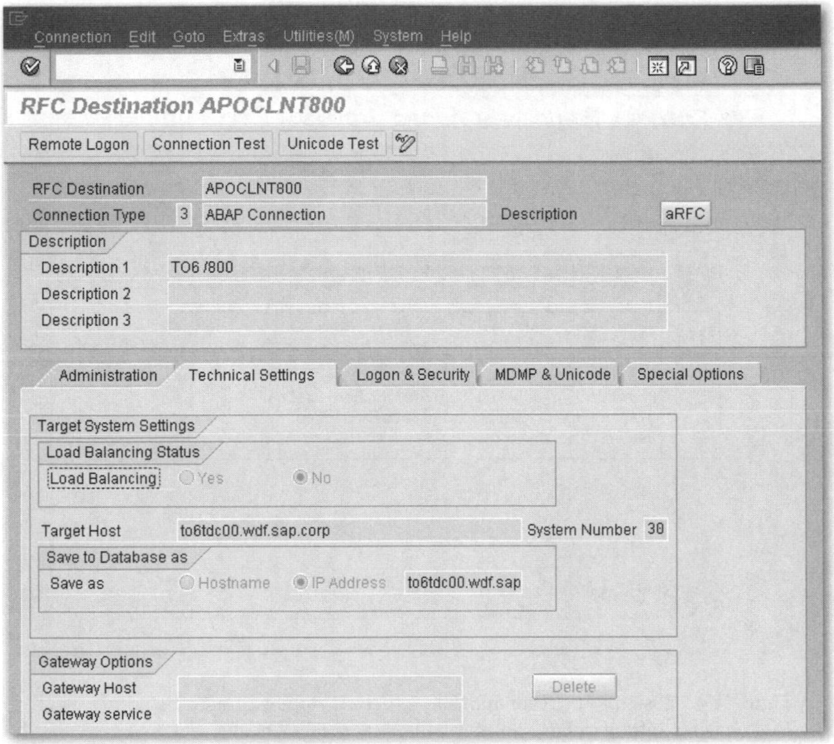

Figure 3.4 "Configuration of RFC Connection" Transaction in ECC, Transaction Code SM59, with RFC Destination "APOCLNT800"

This may result in problems. Take, for example, the case of APO-ATP integration in a sales order. If the ATP check is configured for a material in APO, the ATP screen from APO is displayed when the ATP check is called from the ECC sales order. The user currently maintaining the ECC sales order has not logged on to the APO system, but has instead used the RFC user to access APO. It is then technically possible for this user to access the APO system from this ATP screen. In this case, all transactions that the RFC user has authorization for can be executed in APO.

To avoid these problems, a restricted RFC user can be used in ECC for specific applications (for example, ATP). This user only has the authorizations required to perform a specific task. When an additional, special RFC connection can be set up in ECC for the APO-ATP check, for example, with a user that is only authorized to use ATP in APO (see Figure 3.5). This special RFC connection is then used for the ATP function, while other applications use the basic RFC connection.

RFC for specific applications

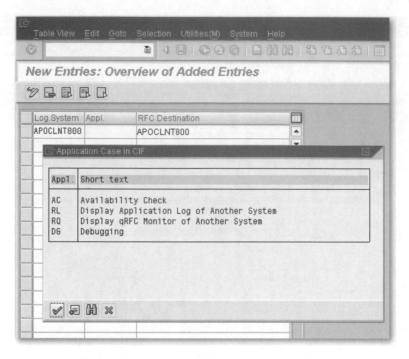

Figure 3.5 "Assign RFC Destinations to Different Application Cases" Customizing Setting in ECC; Selecting the Availability Check

3.1.3 APO-Specific Settings

These RFC connections represent a general technique used to connect two SAP systems, which is not specific to APO. Additional basic settings are required to connect an SCM (APO) system.

APO target systems

> **Note**
>
> For the RFC transfer from ECC to APO, all APO destinations must be defined as APO target systems.

All logical APO systems must be listed in Transaction CFC1 in ECC (see Figure 3.6). The system's underlying operation mode is automatically assigned and does not have to be entered manually. This entry and the specification of the APO release (see Figure 3.7) are prerequisites for successful CIF data transfer.

It is also possible to specify several APO target systems for integration with an ECC system. In the integration model for data transfer from ECC to APO, each target system is then uniquely defined.

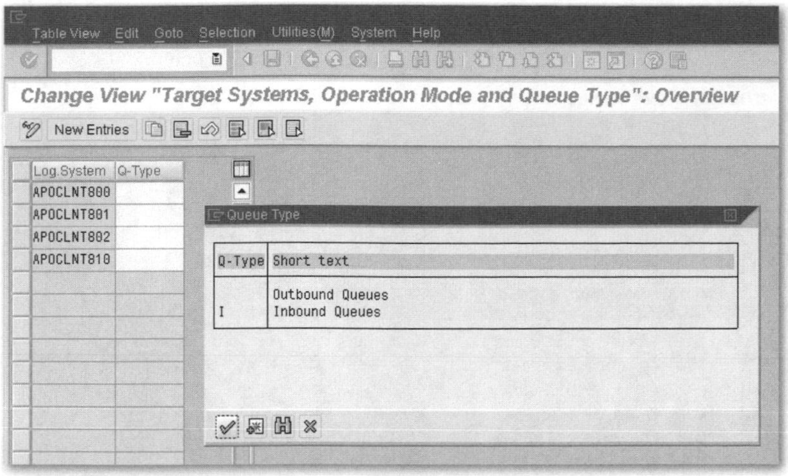

Figure 3.6 "Define Target System and Queue Type" Customizing Setting in ECC , Transaction Code CFC1

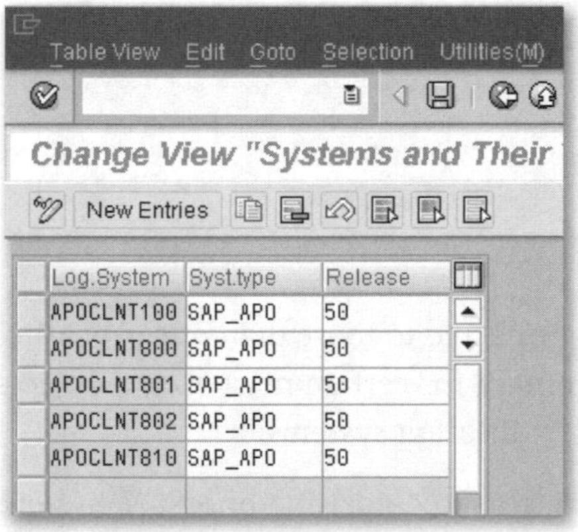

Figure 3.7 "Define APO Release" Customizing Setting in ECC, Transaction Code NDV2

The target system for transferring planning results from APO is defined in APO in accordance with the publication type (for example, external procurement or in-house production) and location. You use the **Maintain Distribution Definition** setting in customizing (see Figure 3.8) for this purpose. Here, the ECC system for the transfer from APO is defined for each publication type and location. The transfer itself is configured in the **Define user parameters** transaction (Transaction Code /SAPAPO/C4; see Section 3.3.3).

Target system for transfer from APO

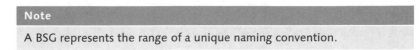

Table View Edit Goto Selection Utilities(M) System Help

Change View "Maintenance View for Distribution Definitions": Overview

New Entries

Maintenance View for Distribution Definitions

Publ. Type	Locatn no.	LogSystem	SAP Rel.
21 External Procurement	CHP2	T90CLNT090	600
21 External Procurement	CHD6	T90CLNT090	600
21 External Procurement	3200	T90CLNT090	600
21 External Procurement	CHD5	T90CLNT090	600
21 External Procurement	3400	T90CLNT090	600
21 External Procurement	3700	T90CLNT090	600
21 External Procurement	2010	T90CLNT090	600
21 External Procurement	CPF4	T90CLNT090	600
21 External Procurement	3300	T90CLNT090	600
21 External Procurement	CHD3	T90CLNT090	600
21 External Procurement	CHD1	T90CLNT090	600
21 External Procurement	1200	T90CLNT090	600
21 External Procurement	CHP4	T90CLNT090	600
21 External Procurement	3000	T90CLNT090	600
21 External Procurement	CHD4	T90CLNT090	600
21 External Procurement	3800	T90CLNT090	600
21 External Procurement	CHD2	T90CLNT090	600
21 External Procurement	3100	T90CLNT090	600
21 External Procurement	3500	T90CLNT090	600
21 External Procurement	3600	T90CLNT090	600
21 External Procurement	CPF3	T90CLNT090	600

Figure 3.8 "Maintain Distribution Definition" Customizing Setting in APO

An SCM (APO) system may be connected to more than one executing ECC system. The number assignment for certain master data objects may not be identical across these different systems.

Take, for example, a system landscape comprising one SCM system with the logical name SCMCLNT800 and two ECC systems with the logical names ECACLNT800 and ECBCLNT800. The same material number, 4711, is used in both ECC systems, but for different physical materials in each case. What name should these materials have when they are transferred to APO for planning?

Business system group (BSG) These kinds of naming conflicts, which may occur with various master data objects, can be resolved using business system groups (BSGs).

> **Note**
>
> A BSG represents the range of a unique naming convention.

BSG is a concept used only in APO, and it has no relevance in ECC. You can define as many BSGs as you require under **Maintain Business System Group** in the basic settings in APO customizing (see Figure 3.9). Each logical system in the system group (including the SCM system itself) must be assigned to a BSG so that it is ensured that naming conflicts can no longer occur within a BSG. This is done in the **Assign Logical Systems and Queue Type** setting in customizing (see Figure 3.10).

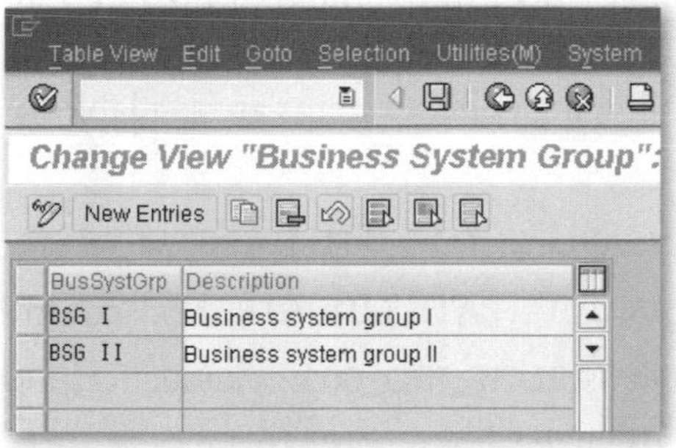

Figure 3.9 "Maintain Business System Group" Customizing Setting in APO

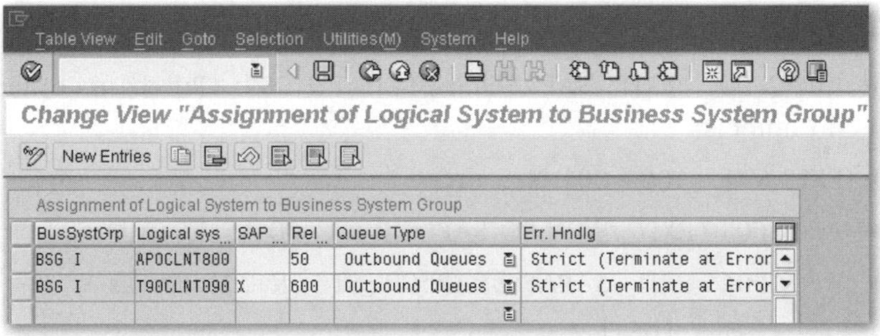

Figure 3.10 "Assign Logical Systems and Queue Type" Customizing Setting in APO

In our example, we require two BSGs: BSGA and BSGB. The ECACLNT800 system is assigned to BSGA, while the ECBCLNT800 system is assigned to BSGB. The SCM system must also be formally assigned to a BSG, for example to BSGA.

If a master data record is then transferred from a logical system to APO, APO recognizes the BSG assignment. In our example, material number 4711 may be transferred from BSGA, while material number 4711 may also be transferred from BSGB.

This information can be used to resolve conflicts. Therefore, you must change the product numbers in APO to ensure that no conflicts occur. For example, material 4711 from BSGA is transferred to APO as product 4711_BSGA, while material 4711 from BSGB is transferred to APO as product 4711_BSGB.[3]

Customer exits and BAdIs for CIF enhancement

A customer exit or a BAdI is required to rename the products. A customer exit or BAdI exists for each master data object and transaction data object in the CIF transfer. These can be used to extend or change the logic. One of these customer exits can be found in the ECC outbound queue, and one can be found in the APO inbound queue in each case. For example, the following enhancements are available for APO inbound processing:[4]

▶ APOCF001 EXIT_/SAPAPO/SAPLCIF_LOC_001: Locations
▶ APOCF002 EXIT_/SAPAPO/SAPLCIF_ATP_001: ATP check control
▶ APOCF003 EXIT_/SAPAPO/SAPLCIF_IRQ_001: Reduction of planned independent requirements
▶ APOCF004 EXIT_/SAPAPO/SAPLCIF_ORD_001: Planned orders and production orders
▶ APOCF005 EXIT_/SAPAPO/SAPLCIF_PROD_001: Products
▶ APOCF006 EXIT_/SAPAPO/SAPLCIF_PU_001: Purchase order documents
▶ EXIT_SAPL_1004_001: Resources
▶ APOCF010 EXIT_/SAPAPO/SAPLCIF_SLS_001: Sales orders
▶ APOCF011 EXIT_/SAPAPO/SAPLCIF_STOCK_001: Stocks

In our example, the following customer exit must be used for APO inbound processing of products in order to change the product numbers when they are posted in APO:

▶ APOCF005 EXIT_/SAPAPO/SAPLCIF_PROD_001

---

3 Our example represents only one type of conflict. You can also assign different material numbers to the same physical material in different ECC systems. This case can also be resolved using BSGs and customer exits.

4 This list is not complete. For more information on customer exits and BadIs, you should refer to the SAP Online Help.

The products are then created in APO with the numbers 4711_BSGA and 4711_BSGB, while the original material number is still visible in the product master as the **External Product Number** (see Figure 3.11).

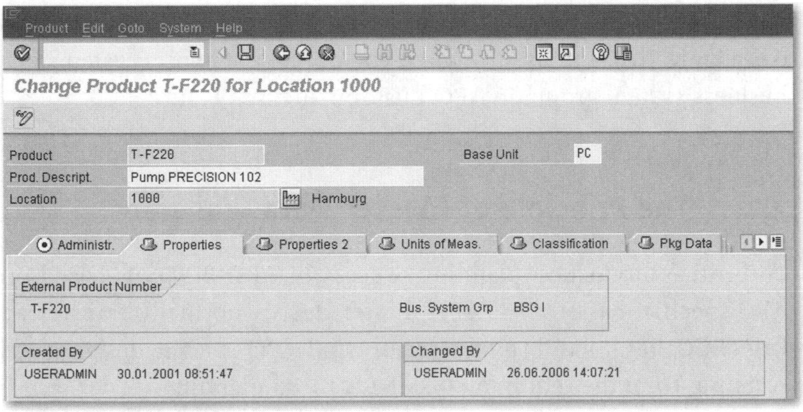

Figure 3.11 "Properties" Tab in the "Product" Transaction in APO

This eliminates all naming conflicts. This step is not required for dependent master data. If the material numbers are unique, this means that the product data structures, for example, are automatically unique as well, because they are identified by their assignment to the product.

Note

Even if no naming conflicts occur and even if your SCM system is only connected with a single ECC system, you must still define at least one BSG in APO, to which all logical systems are then assigned.

Data is transferred using the CIF in the form of *data queues*, which are automatically created with CIF integration. Two processing modes are available for the relevant data queues:

Outbound and inbound queues

▸ **Outbound queue**
The data queue is created by the source system and transferred to the target system. The data is posted in the target system regardless of the system load.

▸ **Inbound queue**
The data queue is sent from the source system to the target system as an inbound queue. This buffering allows the system load to be taken into account when the data is posted in the target system.

Outbound queues are used by default. If, however, you expect a large volume of integration data and there are insufficient work process resources in the target system, it may be useful to switch to inbound queues. You can switch from outbound to inbound queues in ECC when you define the APO target systems (Transaction Code CFC1) (see Figure 3.6), and in APO when you define the logical systems in a business system group (in APO Customizing; see Figure 3.10).

3.2 The Principle of Master Data Transfer

The entire production planning process in APO-PP/DS is based on APO-specific master data. APO master data is normally transferred from ECC, but it has its own structure and APO-specific designations resulting from the requirements of advanced planning.

A consistent data structure | It must not be assumed that all data records in ECC (for example, all material master records) are transferred to APO. As a rule, only a subset of the data is actually relevant for advanced planning in APO (specifically, the materials and resources that are critical to planning), and only this data is transferred. When selecting data for transfer, you must ensure that all dependent data records are also transferred and that a consistent master data structure is created in APO. Take the example of capacity planning: If capacities are to be planned for various resources, you must ensure that any materials produced using these resources are planned in APO.

In addition, the APO data only contains the part of information that is required for production planning. While in the example of material masters, in addition to accounting data, sales and distribution data, and shop floor control data, planning data accounts for only a small part of the data contained in the ECC master record (most of which is contained in the MRP views), the corresponding APO product master only contains information relating to production planning. Only the planning-relevant part of the ECC master data is transferred to APO, and the settings for the remaining steps in the overall process remain in the ECC material master data. The same also holds true for the other master data types.

APO master data | Table 3.1 shows exactly how ECC master data is mapped to APO master data.

ECC Master Data	APO Master Data
Plant, customer, vendor	Location (with location type)
Purchasing info record, scheduling agreement, outline agreement	External procurement relationship, including transportation lane
Special procurement key in material master	Transportation lane or production in another plant
Material master	Product master
Classes and characteristics	Classes and characteristics
Work center, resource (PP-PI)	Resource
Production version with routing and BOM or master recipe (PP-PI)	Production data structure (PDS) or runtime object (RTO), or production process model (PPM)[5]

Table 3.1 Master Data in ECC and APO

We must point out, however, that the APO master data record does *not* come completely from ECC data. Rather, APO data records usually contain two types of data fields:

▶ Data fields that are derived directly from ECC settings and are maintained when data is transferred from ECC

▶ APO-specific data fields, which do not correspond to any settings in ECC and must be maintained in APO

It may be possible and indeed useful to also base APO-specific fields on ECC settings from a logical and technical standpoint, and to transfer them from ECC to APO by extending the logic of the CIF transfer using a customer exit or BAdI. In an ideal scenario, the entire content of an APO document would be maintained in ECC, so that master data maintenance does not have to be divided between two systems.

The CIF has two tasks in relation to master data transfer: Tasks of the CIF

1. **Initial transfer**
   This is the initial transfer of ECC master data to APO.

---

5 As we'll discuss later on in this chapter, you can transfer production versions as production process models or as runtime objects or production data structures (as of SAP APO 4.1) to SAP APO.

2. **Change transfer**

When changes are made to master data in ECC, these changes must be populated to the corresponding APO master data.

To ensure data consistency between ECC and APO, see the following Note:

Note

ECC is the main system for master data. Therefore, APO master data fields that are derived from ECC must not be changed in APO. Instead, they are maintained by a change transfer using the CIF. The only settings maintained in APO are APO-specific settings.

3.2.1 Initial Transfer of Master Data

Master data is transferred using *integration models*, which you use to select the master data that is to be transferred. You will find the transaction for maintaining integration models under **Core Interface Advanced Planner and Optimizer** (referred to below as the *CIF menu*) in the Central Functions submenu of the Logistics menu in ECC. Integration models are used to transfer both master data and transaction data. However, the two data types should be transferred using separate models.

Data transfer sequence

In general, the sequence of transferring data must be considered. The creation of certain master data records in APO may depend on the existence of other master data. For example, the relevant locations must exist in APO before material masters can be transferred. They must either exist in APO already or be included in the integration model. The same applies to the creation of production data structures, which are based on existing resources and may refer to a finished product and several components, and so on. These dependencies must be taken into account when defining an integration model.

The procedure for using integration models comprises the following two steps (see Figure 3.2):

1. Creating the integration model
2. Activating the integration model

Creating the Integration Model

You create an integration model to select master data for transfer to APO. This is done in the **Create Integration Model** transaction (Transaction Code CFM1) in the CIF menu.

First, define an integration model by specifying a **name**, **application**, and the (APO) **target system** to which the data is to be transferred. These three parameters define a unique integration model. This also allows you to group together various related integration models under a single name, while still being able to differentiate between the models based on their application.

Name, application, target system

Next, you use **selection criteria** to select data. The data can be divided into two groups:

Selection criteria

▶ Data that is selected based on its reference to a material

▶ Data that cannot be selected on the basis of a material reference

The first type of data is entered in the top area of the screen, while the second type is specified at the bottom.

For material-dependent master data, you first specify which materials in which plants are to be used as a basis for all selections under **General Selection Options for Materials**. This is a type of preliminary selection filter. Individual material numbers can be entered here. However, it is more common to specify the **MRP type** or **material type** if you have a large number of materials (see Figure 3.12).

Selection options for materials

The **MRP type** is a particularly useful selection criterion. If a material is to be planned in APO, it must be excluded from planning in ECC.[6] This is done by selecting the MRP type in the MRP 1 view of the material master. MRP type **X0** or a similarly defined MRP type must be entered here. When you make this setting, MRP is not executed in ECC. However, a BOM explosion is still possible for the material (see Figure 3.13).[7] If you copy the **X0** MRP type to another identical MRP

MRP type X0

---

6 However, this is not a technical requirement for transferring a material to SAP APO. The MRP type itself is not transferred and is therefore not relevant to SAP APO.

7 MRP type **ND** is not appropriate because it no longer allows for a BOM explosion. If you use an R/3 system that is older than Release 4.0 and the **X0** is not available, you can use MRP type **P4** with a firming horizon of 999 days.

type (such as **X1**, **X2**, etc.), it is very easy to create material groups for selection in integration models.

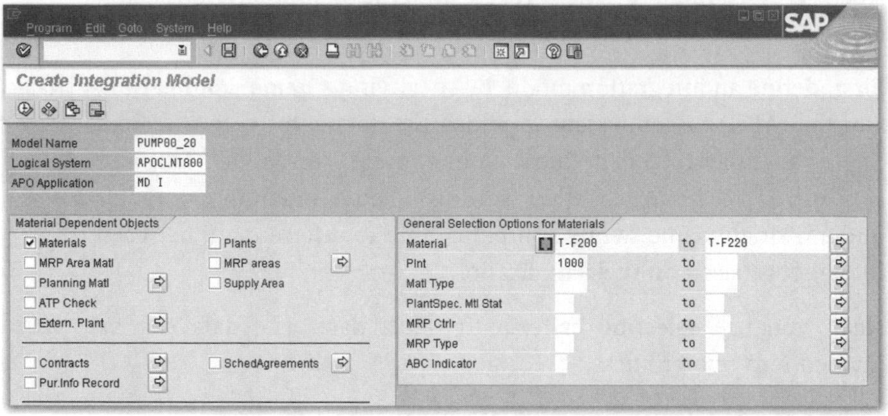

Figure 3.12 "Create Integration Model" Transaction in ECC, Transaction Code CFM1; Integration Model with Name, Application, and Selection Criteria

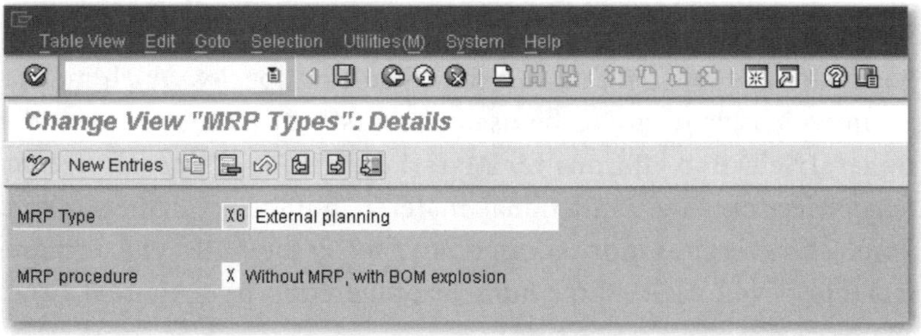

Figure 3.13 "Check MRP Types" Customizing Setting in ECC; Settings for MRP Type "X0"

Selecting
data types

After you specify the general selection options for materials, you select the data types that are to be transferred, for example:

▶ Material master

▶ Plant

▶ Production data structure

Selecting
data records

Finally, you can use the available options to restrict the selection. For example, you can choose to only transfer **production data structures** for a subset of materials and/or restrict the entire selection to production version 0001 (see Figure 3.14). Refer to the transaction itself to see exactly which selections are possible.

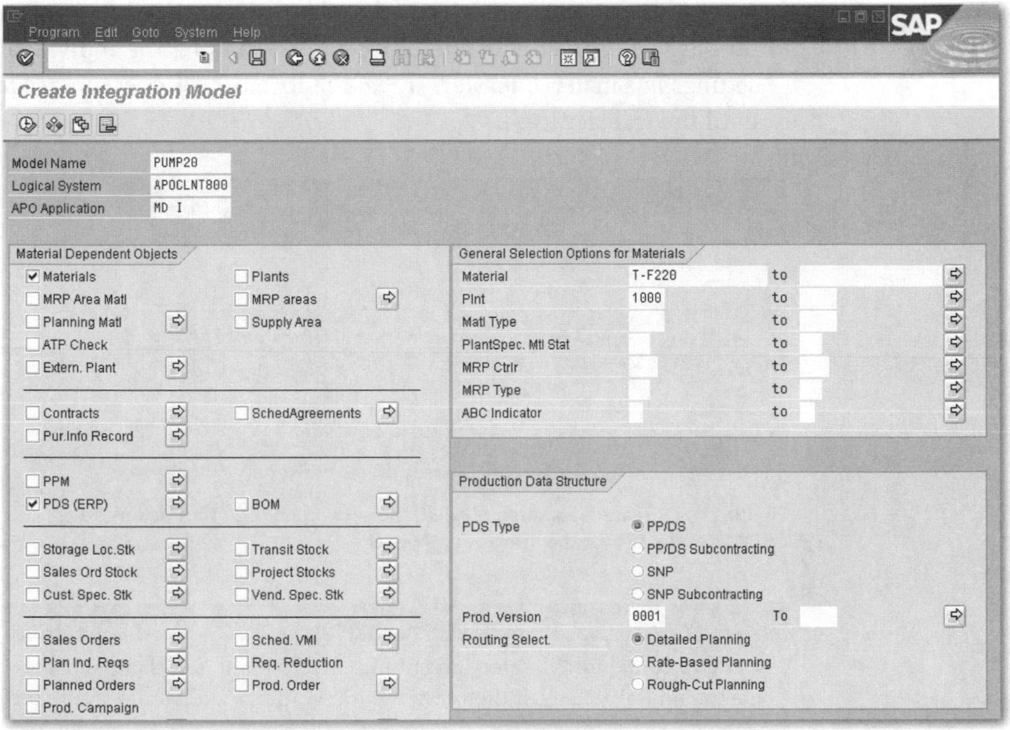

Figure 3.14 "Create Integration Model" Transaction in ECC, Transaction Code CFM1; Integration Model with Material and PDS Selected

After you have specified all the selection criteria, you can execute the integration model. When the integration model is executed, the objects are then selected, and the results of the selection are listed by master data type on the next screen (see Figure 3.15). For example, if you have selected the materials in **plant 1000** by selecting MRP type **X0** and **plants** as your selection criteria, the result of the selection is one plant and a number of material masters. From the result screen, you can display the details of the individual data types and see which individual documents have been selected.

Executing the integration model

The following statements apply to the execution of an integration model and to the steps leading up to execution:

▶ The selection criteria on which an integration model is based are not saved with the integration model, which only contains the list of selected objects. You should therefore use variants, in which the selection criteria can be stored.

63

► Executing an integration model only results in a list of data objects. The contents of the objects, for example, the individual settings in a material master, are *not* imported. This does not occur until the transfer itself.

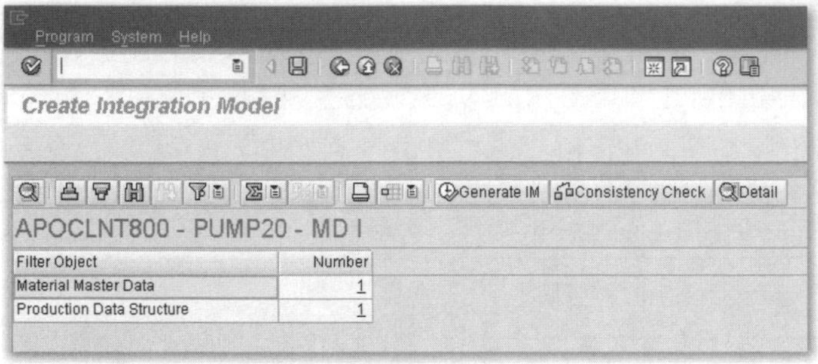

Figure 3.15 "Create Integration Model" Transaction in ECC, Transaction Code CFM1; Results List for the Integration Model

> **Note**
>
> After you configure the selection criteria, save them in a variant, and execute the model, you must then save the integration model (from the result screen).

Saving the integration model

When you save the integration model, your selection of objects is saved in the database in ECC, but no objects are transferred to APO at this point. Figuratively speaking, you have now wrapped and tied up your package of data and put it away for safekeeping, but you have not yet "mailed" it to APO. You do this in the next step by activating the integration model.

Executing an integration model with the same "open" selection criteria (meaning that you select materials using the **X0** MRP type rather than explicitly specifying material numbers, for example) with the relevant variant at different points in time may produce different results. If additional documents correspond to these selection criteria at a later point in time, or if some documents no longer correspond to the criteria (for example, if additional material masters with MRP type **X0** have since been created), the new model differs from the old in terms of the documents it includes. Both models are stored in parallel in the database with the same name and application, but with different generation times. However, only one of these models can be active.

Activating integration models

To transfer the data to APO, you must first *activate* the generated integration models using the **Activate Integration Models** transaction (Transaction Code CFM2) from CIF menu. This transaction is used both to activate inactive models and to deactivate active ones.

After you access the transaction, you first have to enter the name, target system, and application to indicate which integration models are to be activated (see Figure 3.16). It is possible to select several models, for example, which have the same name but contain different applications. The following options are available:

Initial screen

▶ **Log Deactivated Material Masters**
If you select this indicator, materials are logged that are no longer contained in any active integration model (in other words, they are inactive), for example, after a new version of an integration model is activated. With the RCIFMTDE ECC report,[8] these materials can be displayed or "sent to APO," which means that the corresponding APO product masters are marked as being procured and planned outside of APO, so that they are no longer included in planning in APO.

▶ **Parallelized Transfer**
The initial transfer is normally serialized, that is, the objects are selected in sequence in ECC, transferred to APO, and processed there in the same sequence. However, it is also possible to parallelize the initial transfer to improve performance. With a parallelized transfer, you can select a setting to determine whether the selection in ECC, processing in APO, or both are to be parallelized. Parallelization generally occurs within an object type, while the different object types are still transferred in sequence (serialized transfer). With parallelization in ECC, it is also possible to activate several integration models at the same time.

When you execute the selection of the models to be processed, all models that meet these criteria are displayed on the next screen (see Figure 3.17).

Executing activation

---

8 You can, for instance, run a report using Transaction SE38.

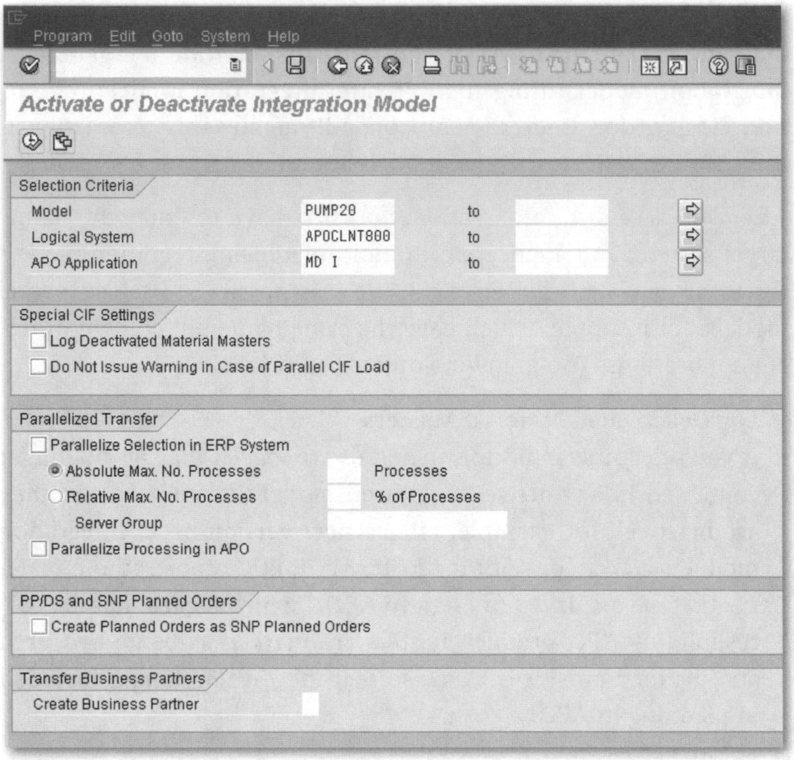

Figure 3.16 "Activate Integration Model" Transaction in ECC, Transaction Code CFM2; Selections and Options

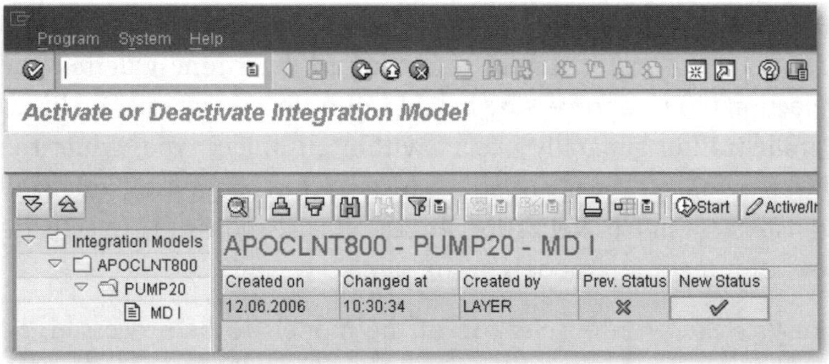

Figure 3.17 "Activate Integration Model" Transaction in ECC, Transaction Code CFM2 (Follow-On Screen)

If you want to activate a new model, set the green checkmark and start the transfer. When you execute this step, the data is transferred to APO. When the data is successfully transferred, the model is assigned the status **active**, and this is indicated by a green checkmark (see Figure 3.18). The transferred master data is then available in APO (see Figure 3.19).

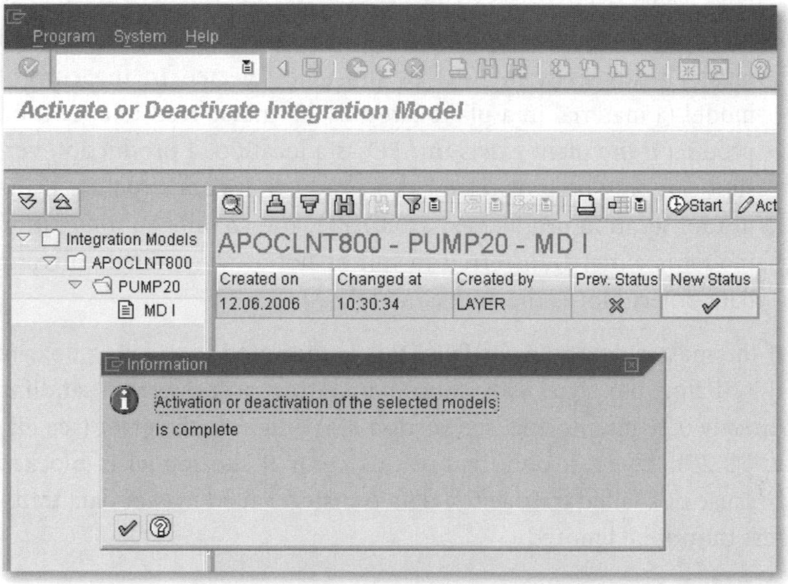

Figure 3.18 "Activate Integration Model" Transaction in ECC, Transaction Code CFM2; Dialog Box Indicating a Successful Data Transfer

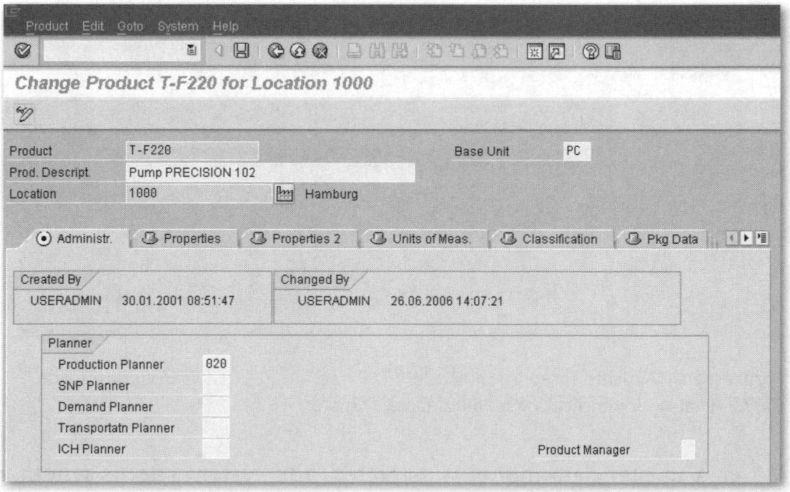

Figure 3.19 "Product" Transaction in APO, Transaction Code /SAPAPO/MAT1; Product Created in APO by the RFC User

Prerequisites for master data transfer There are two prerequisites for the successful transfer of master data:

▶ A previous master data transfer has not failed. When this occurs, a queue is created, which blocks any subsequent master data transfers. If that happens, you must first delete the queue.

▶ All of the APO data required for the master data to be transferred must already exist in APO or must be selected in the current model (a material in a plant can only be transferred as a location product if the plant exists in APO as a location, a production version can only be transferred as a production data structure if the header location product exists in APO, and so on). An integration model is either transferred in full or not at all—a single missing data object blocks the entire model.

If the master data transfer fails, this is indicated in a dialog box. In this dialog box, you can choose to either access error handling directly (CIF monitoring, see Section 3.4) or ignore the error (see Figure 3.20). You can only ignore this error if the model is blocked because of a failed transaction data transfer. Failed master data transfers cannot be ignored.

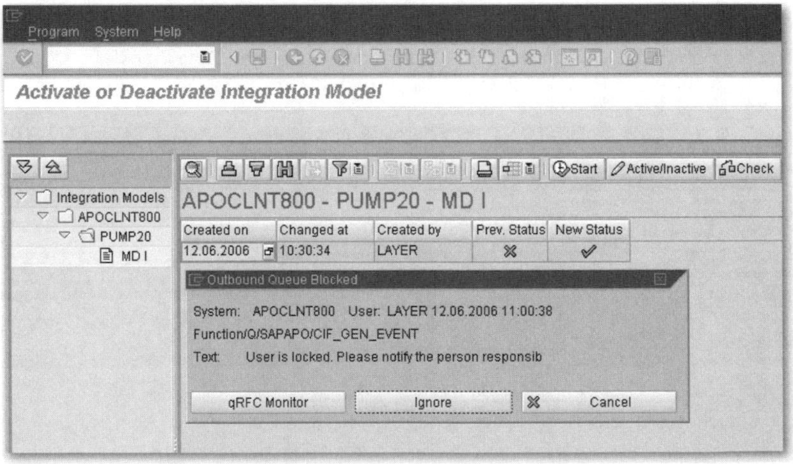

Figure 3.20 "Activate Integration Model" Transaction in ECC, Transaction Code CFM2; Dialog Box Indicating a Failed Data Transfer

Delta comparison When a master data model is activated, the system checks whether the selected data records are already part of another active model. If this is indeed the case, the data is not physically transferred a second time, because it already exists in APO. Instead, the *delta comparison* is used, which only transfers the difference between the new model to be activated and all existing active models.[9]

To speed up this delta comparison, the system uses the *maximum integration model*, which is created in the background from all active integration models for one object type and target system. It is automatically updated each time a new model is activated. You can access the maximum integration model manually with the RCIFIMAX report (see Figure 3.21).

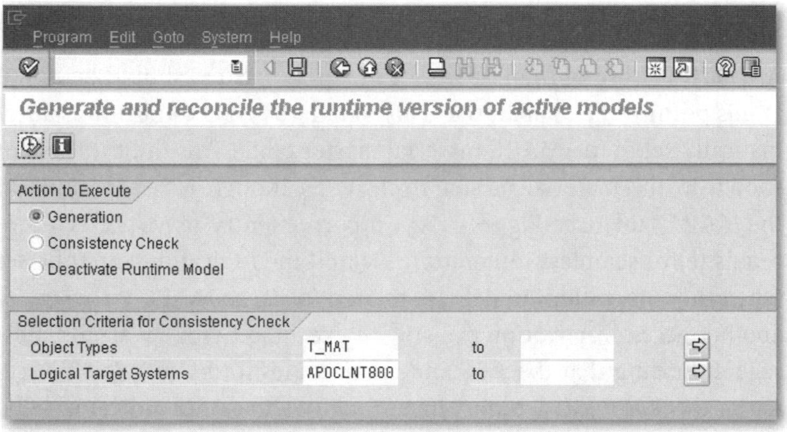

Figure 3.21 RCIFIMAX Report for Generating and Checking the Consistency of the Maximum Integration Model

If an integration model is successfully activated, this indicates that the data has been transferred to APO and is now available there.

Activated models remain active

Note

The master data models must remain active to ensure that the relationships between the ECC and APO master data are preserved. One document may be simultaneously contained in several active models. It remains active as long as it is contained in one active model.

If you deactivate models and certain documents are no longer contained in any active model, the relationships between the data in

---

9 This difference also includes master data changes. Therefore, if ECC master data documents are marked as being changed via change pointers, the documents are transferred once again, even if they are contained in other active documents.

ECC and APO are lost, and, as a rule, the APO data is no longer of any use. The relevant data created in APO by the CIF transfer is *not* deleted or changed as a result. This data must be deleted in APO in a subsequent step.

This process of deleting data is very simple for product masters if you use the **Log Deactivated Material Masters** option mentioned above and set the relevant product masters to being procured and planned outside of APO with the RCIFMTDE report in ECC. You can use these entries in the product masters in APO master data mass maintenance (see Chapter 4) to select the products and set the deletion indicator.

APO indicator in ECC material master table

A special feature of the transfer of material masters should be noted at this point. When a material is activated, the APO indicator is automatically set in the MARC material master table. This indicator is not shown in the material master itself, even though it is contained in the MARC table (see Figure 3.22). A correct entry in MARC is a prerequisite for seamless integration. Even if the indicator cannot be set when the integration model is activated (because MARC is locked by another access), activation can still be executed (with a warning message indicating that the APO indicator could not be set). In this scenario, the RAPOKZFX report in ECC allows the APO indicator to be set consistently for the integration models after activation.

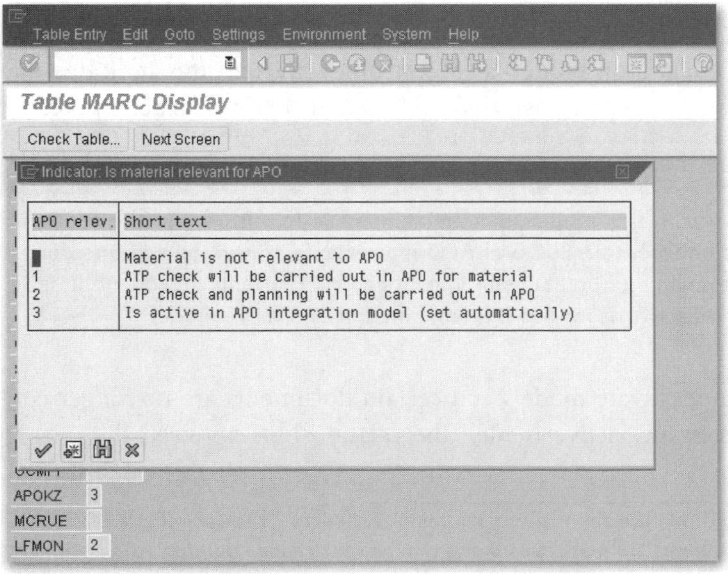

Figure 3.22 Material Master Table MARC in ECC with APO Indicator

How big should the integration model be?

The question of how big an integration model should be is not easily answered. Technically speaking, there is no advantage to using either a large number of small models or a small number of large models.[10] The following criteria provide a starting point for a useful definition of integration models:

- ▶ Master data and transaction data should be contained in separate models.

- ▶ Small integration models facilitate troubleshooting. Several small models can be replaced by one large model at a later stage.

> **Note**
>
> The transfer of setup keys is one example of a special requirement (see Chapter 5). If you want to transfer setup keys from the ECC routing, resources and production data structures or production process models must be transferred in separate integration models. After the resources are transferred, the setup matrixes must be entered in the resources in APO, so that the production data structures or production process models can be transferred with setup keys.

3.2.2 Transferring New APO-Relevant Master Data

If you have already transferred a selection of master data to APO and you now want to transfer new or additional master data to APO for planning, you could simply create and activate additional integration models for this new data. However, this may result in a confusing array of small models, which is particularly undesirable if the new data is closely related to existing models.

The following procedure is preferable in these situations: Use *open selection criteria* that allow you to select all relevant materials for a particular planning area by their MRP type, for example. These selections are defined using corresponding variants. If new APO-relevant data is added, for example, new material masters with the relevant MRP type, create the integration model again with the existing selection. The result is a new version of the same model (with a different

Open selection criteria

---

10 Due to the maximum integration model, which is created in the background, the speed of the delta comparison is not affected by the structure of the integration models. Without the maximum integration model, the delta comparison takes longer for many small models and for models that contain only one type of data.

generation date and time than the old version), which also contains the new master data. When you activate this new model (and deactivate the old model), only the additional data is transferred to APO, while the status **active** is unchanged for the remaining data.

You can execute this procedure manually or schedule it as a regular background job (for example, once each night) to ensure the current data is automatically transferred to APO.

> **Note**
>
> If you want the current master data to be transferred to APO on a regular basis because, for example, new APO-relevant master data is created in ECC on an ongoing basis, you can create and activate integration models with open selection criteria at regular intervals. You can do this automatically by defining and scheduling the relevant jobs.

The following jobs should be scheduled periodically:

1. **Report RIMODGEN** (Generate integration models)
   Use the variant for creating integration models to generate the model.

2. **Report RIMODAC2** (batch-enabled version for activating integration models)
   Create a screen variant for scheduling this step. Activate the most recent version of the integration model in each case. When you select the **Ignore Faulty Queue Entries** indicator, any existing faulty transaction data queues are ignored (in the same way they are ignored for online activation) and do not result in a termination.

3. **Report RIMODDEL** (Delete integration models)
   This function allows you to delete obsolete versions.

4. **Report RCIFIMAX**
   This report ensures consistency between the integration models and the APO indicator in the MARC material master table. This step is only required if material masters may become locked during activation.

5. **Report RCIFMTDE**
   If you have selected the **Log Deactivated Material Masters** option for the activation, you can set any materials or products that are

no longer active to being procured and planned outside of APO immediately after the data transfer. These products are then excluded from planning in APO.

3.2.3 Change Transfer of Master Data

If changes are made to APO-relevant master data in ECC, these changes must also be transferred to the SCM system. A new initial transfer is not normally executed for this purpose. Instead, only the data that is affected by these changes is transferred again to APO using the CIF. A change transfer of this kind is based on the precondition that an active integration model exists for the relevant master data, that is, that the master data is indeed *APO-relevant*.

Note

With a master data change transfer, note that the complete data record is always transferred. For example, if you change one field in a material master record, the complete material master will be transferred again in the resulting change transfer. It is important to note that, as a result, any changes made in APO to fields that are transferred from ECC are overwritten with the original value when a change transfer is performed. Therefore, in general, it doesn't make sense to maintain these fields in APO.

Change Transfer for Material Masters, Customers, Vendors, and External Supply Sources

The change transfer for material masters, customers, and vendors[11] is configured in the **Configure Change Transfer for Master Data transaction in ECC** (Transaction Code CFC9; see Figure 3.23). The change transfer for these objects can be scheduled periodically or can be performed immediately in online mode (or it can also be deactivated).

With online transfers, a check is performed whenever a material master, customer, or vendor is changed, in order to determine whether the change is relevant for APO. This check is based on the APO master data structure. After the change, the new ECC master data document is converted into an APO document, which is com-

Online change transfer

---

11 Customers and vendors are transferred to APO as locations with corresponding location types. For plants that are transferred with the production plant or distribution center location types, no change transfer is possible.

pared with the existing APO document. A new transfer is automatically performed only if differences are found between the two.

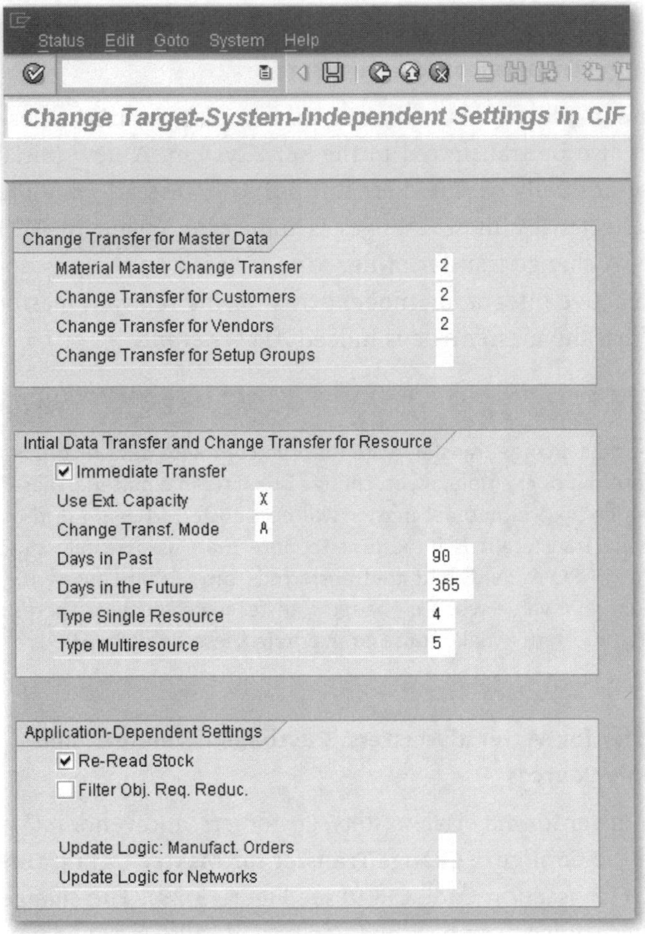

Figure 3.23 "Configure Change Transfer for Master Data" Customizing Setting in ECC, Transaction Code CFC9

Online transfers are recommended for these three object types because they (i.e., the online transfers) don't require much organizational work to be done.

Periodic change transfer

A periodic change transfer comprises two steps. First, all master data that has been changed is logged using (ALE) change pointers. In a second step, this selected master data is transferred to APO using the **Master Data Change Transfer** transaction from the CIF menu (Transaction Code CFP1; see Figure 3.24). This procedure can be used for the three object types listed above, as well as for external supply sources, for example.

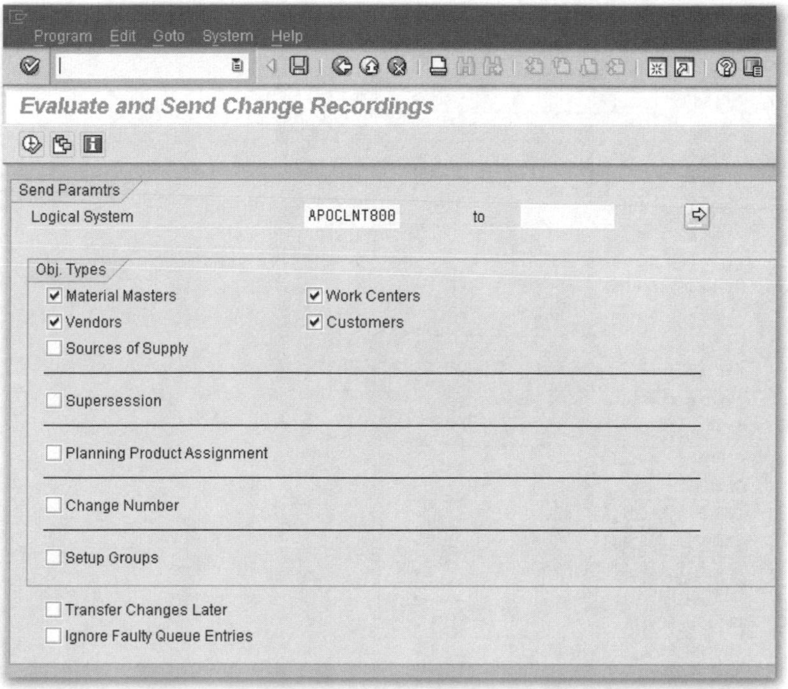

Figure 3.24 "Master Data Change Transfer" Transaction in ECC, Transaction Code CFP1

The corresponding ALE settings for the **CIFMAT** (material master), **CIFVEN** (vendor), and **CIFCUS** (customer) message types are automatically set when you use the **Configure Change Transfer for Master Data** transaction (see Figure 3.23). The **CIFSRC** change pointer must be activated in the **Activate Change Pointers for Message Type** customizing setting (Transaction BD50; see Figure 3.25) for external supply sources. You must first ensure that change pointers are activated generally (**Activate Change Pointers Generally** setting in ALE Customizing, Transaction BD61).[12]

Change pointers

---

12 In addition, you can use ALE Transaction BD52 to define which field changes (e.g., in the material master, message type **CIFMAT**) entail the creation of a change pointer.

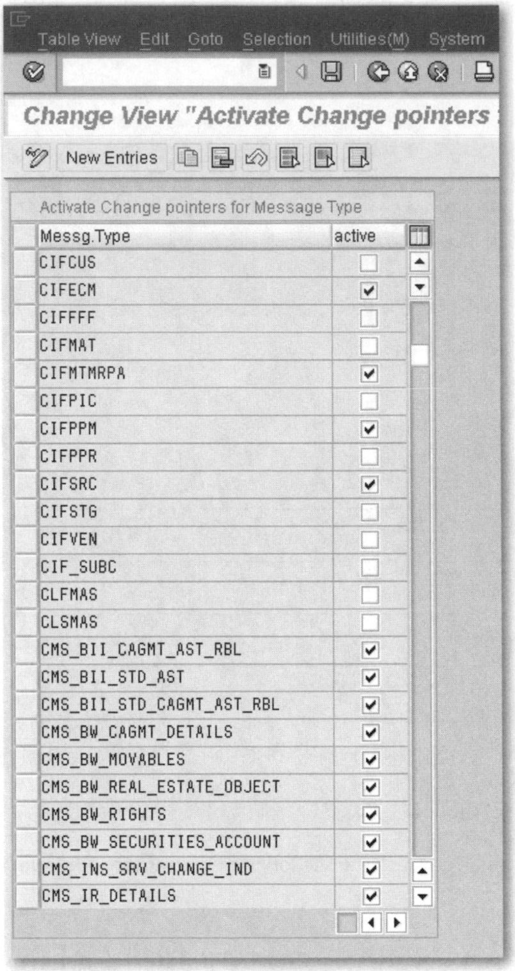

Figure 3.25 "Activate Change Pointers for Message Type" Customizing Setting in ECC, Transaction Code BD50

Executing periodic change transfers

When you execute periodic change transfers with the **Master Data Change Transfer** transaction in the CIF menu (see Figure 3.24), all ALE change pointers are read. These change pointers determine the selection of the master data to be included in the transfer. In this transaction, you enter the logical target systems and the master data objects for which a change transfer is to be executed. You can save your settings for the change transfer as a variant. In addition, you can use the RCPTRAN4 report to schedule the change transfer as a periodic job.

Note the following in relation to executing a periodic change transfer:

You can of course execute an additional change transfer at any time in order to transfer any new changes to APO.

The following additional points apply to change transfers of material masters:

Enhancements to the change transfer of material masters

▶ Creating a new view for an existing ECC material master constitutes a change in terms of CIF transfer. The new settings can therefore be transferred to APO as a change transfer.

▶ A deletion flag for a material is transferred to the corresponding APO product by means of a change transfer.

▶ A change transfer is also possible for MRP area segments that have been transferred to APO as location products. The **CIFMTMRPA** CIF message type is used in this case (see Figure 3.25).

▶ The tables of the ECC material master can be enhanced with customer-specific fields using append structures.[13] This is particularly useful in this context due to the relatively simple structure of ECC material masters and APO product masters. These additional fields can be used to define field contents for functions that do not exist in ECC. The CIF transfer of these fields must then be extended using the customer exits for materials or products in the ECC outbound processing and in the APO inbound processing. Therefore, the complete APO product master can be maintained from ECC.

Models and Planning Versions in APO

We will now provide a brief outline of the concept of models and planning versions in APO, before moving on to the subject of change transfers for resources. As you will see, the assignment of planning versions plays a role in CIF integration in connection with resources.

---

13 See SAP Note 44410 for more on append structures.

In APO, master data is assigned to a model. Of all possible models that can be used, the active model **000** is of particular relevance in this context. Operational planning takes place in the active model. Other models that are not active (such as **Z01, Z02**, and so on) are used for simulated planning. The supply chain can be modified or changed with completely new master data in these models.

> **Note**
>
> The CIF integration of master data is based on active model 000.

Several planning versions can be assigned to the same model. The active planning version **000** plays a key role here. Operational planning takes place in the active planning version. Transaction data is only integrated with ECC for this active planning version. Other planning versions that are not active are used for simulated planning. For example, you can execute alternative planning steps based on the existing master data or use planning-version-specific settings to change some of the master data.

> **Note**
>
> The CIF integration of master data provides master data for active planning version 000. The assignment and use of master data transferred using the CIF in other planning versions depends on the master data type.

Change Transfers for Resources

Resource types ECC work centers or resources (PP-PI) are transferred to APO in the form of their assigned capacities. In other words, in APO, an APO resource is created for each work center capacity. Resources are transferred using a planning-version-independent resource, which is copied to all planning versions of the active model in APO, including, and in particular, planning version 000. Depending on the number of individual capacities and whether multiple operations are allowed for in ECC, these APO resources are either single-activity or multi-activity resources. Resources may also be mixed resources,[14] which can be used in both PP/DS and SNP.

---

14 The use of mixed resources is generally recommended, even if you only use PP/DS.

Up to and including APO Release 3.1, change transfers were not possible for resources.[15] With SAP APO 4.0 and PI 2003.1, a completely new procedure was developed for master data in relation to the transfer of changes to resources. This procedure allows you to maintain all relevant settings (including APO-specific settings) in the ECC document.[16]

The basic settings for the change transfer are found in the **Configure Change Transfer for Master Data** transaction in ECC (Transaction Code CFC9; see Figure 3.23). Here you define:

Basic settings

▶ Whether changes to header data are to be transferred immediately or periodically

▶ Whether external capacities should be used in planning

▶ Which APO resource type is selected (this only has an effect on the initial transfer, and a subsequent change in APO is not possible)

▶ The effect of the change transfer on planning-version-dependent resources

The header data of the ECC work center capacities are enhanced with APO-specific settings, which you can specify using the **APO resource** function in the maintenance transaction for work center capacities (see Figure 3.26). The change transfer also incorporates these additional settings. With a periodic change transfer, you can use the **Change Transfer Master Data** transaction (see Figure 3.24) for this purpose also for resources.

Intervals of available capacity in ECC (for example, shifts) cannot be transferred directly as APO intervals of available capacity. Instead, you must choose one of the following options for this data:

External capacity

1. **Not using the external capacity**
   The available capacity is maintained in APO. Only the header data of the work center capacities (for which a change transfer is possible) are transferred from ECC. Any additional intervals of available capacity above and beyond the overall capacity are maintained in the APO resource.

---

15 Even deactivating the integration model and reactivating it in order to force the transfer of the current data record—which is theoretically possible for master data—did not enable the re-transfer of the resources without a problem, because only the planning-version-independent resource would be transferred.

16 SAP APO 5.0 enables you to proceed in a similar way for routings.

2. **Using the external capacity**

The entire available capacity is maintained in ECC. The header data is also transferred to APO in this case. In addition, the intervals of available capacity that are created in ECC are used for planning in APO ("external capacity"). The available capacity in ECC is stored in APO, but it cannot be maintained in APO (APO uses this data for planning, rather than the data in ECC). You can use Transaction CFC9 to configure the period for which the external resources are defined in APO (see Figure 3.23; the default value is used if no entry is made). Any intervals of available capacity maintained in APO are irrelevant if you use this option. There is one exception to this rule: If downtimes are defined in APO, they are also considered when using the external capacity.

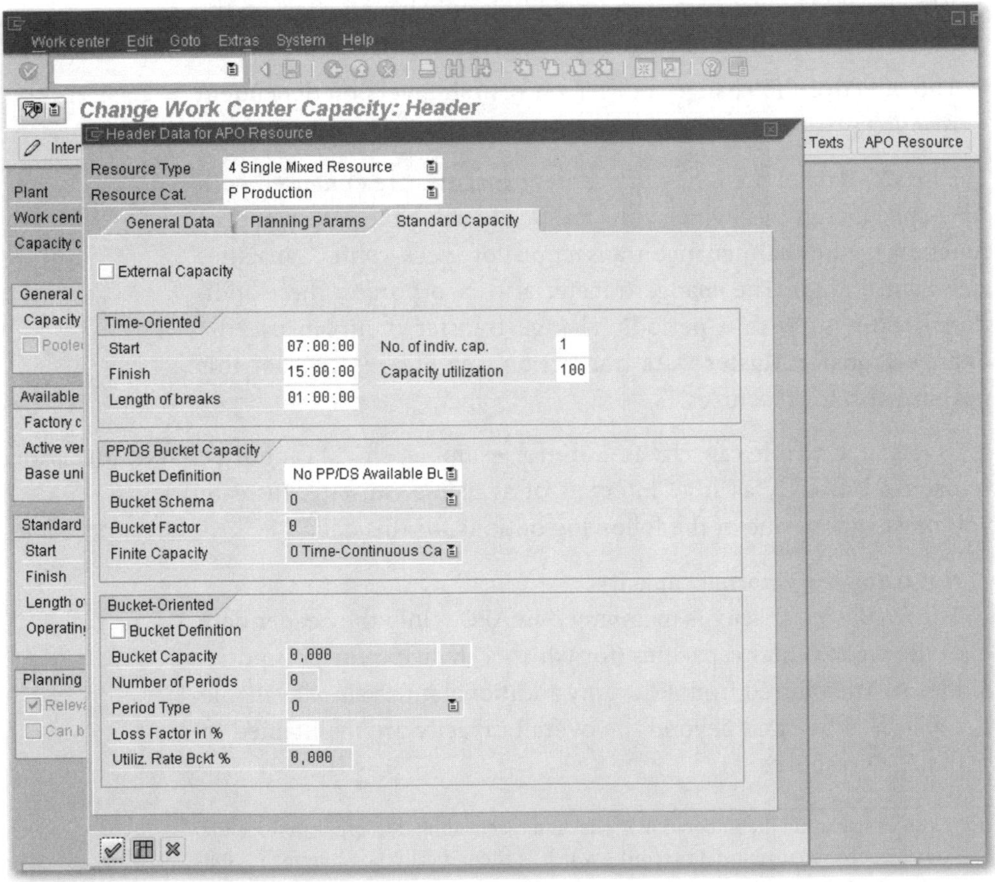

Figure 3.26 "Change Work Center Capacity" Transaction in ECC, Transaction Code CR02; Settings for the APO Resource

> **Note**
>
> The advantage of using the external capacity for the transfer of resources is that all settings for the APO resource can be made in ECC. When you consider that you also have the option of transferring changes to header data immediately, it is clear that this option is very easy to use.

Change Transfers for Production Data Structures and Production Process Models

Change transfers are possible for both production process models (PPM) and production data structures (PDS) (which were called *runtime objects* up to APO 4.0). The change transfers for these two structures are executed using two separate transactions. Changes to ECC production versions, routings, master recipes, and BOMs are taken into account.

The PPM change transfer is executed in the corresponding CIF transaction (Transaction Code CFP3; see Figure 3.27). On the initial screen, you select the PPMs for which changes are to be transferred. The PPMs to be changed are then indicated by automatically generated internal change pointers.[17] If change pointers have been written that do not indicate that a transfer is required (because the changes are now obsolete, for example), they can be deleted in Transaction CFP4.

PPM change transfer

The following restrictions apply to PPM change transfers: No change pointers are written for changes to dummy BOMs, reference operation sets, referenced objects (for example, component scrap in the material master), or changes to an operation by means of classification in the work center.

The change transfer for production data structures or runtime objects is similarly executed in the corresponding CIF transaction (Transaction Code CURTO_CREATE; see Figure 3.28). On the initial screen, you again select the objects that are to be transferred when changes are made to them. In this case also, a change transfer corresponds to the creation of a new document.

Change transfer for PDS and RTO

---

17 These change pointers are not related to the ALE message types described above (also, ALE message type **CIFPPM** in Transaction BD50 is not important here).

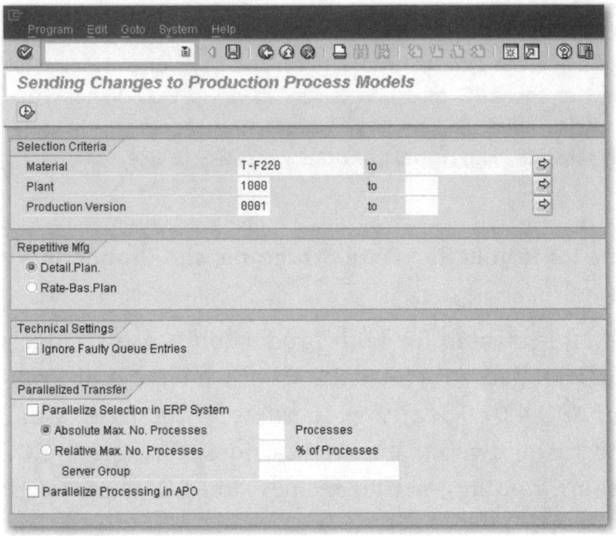

Figure 3.27 "Change Transfer for Production Process Models" Transaction in ECC, Transaction Code CFP3

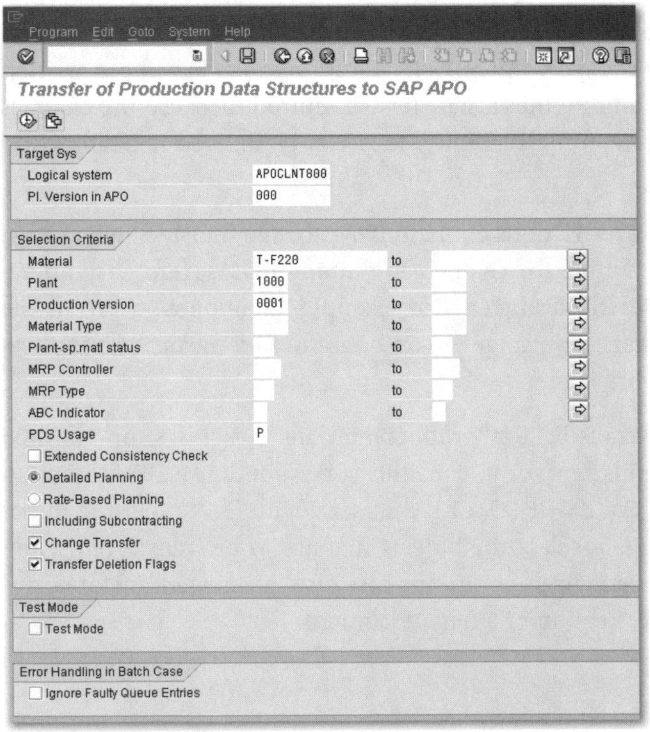

Figure 3.28 "Transfer of Production Data Structures" Transaction in ECC, Transaction Code CURTO_CREATE

Periodic change transfers can be scheduled for production process models and for production data structures or runtime objects.

3.3   The Principle of Transaction Data Transfer

Generally, planning in APO is based on master data that has been transferred from ECC to the SCM system. Planning takes place at the level of transaction data. For example, requirements are received in the form of sales orders, which result in procurement elements. Therefore, in APO, a large amount of initial data must be known to the system, while the planning result must also be returned to ECC so that planning can be executed there.

> **Note**
>
> Active planning version 000 is used for operational planning in APO. Transaction data integration between ECC and APO is based on the active planning version.

3.3.1   Transaction Data in ECC and APO

When transaction data is exchanged between the systems, it is mapped to *similar* data in the target system and is transferred by RFC. In APO, the individual documents generally appear under the name used in ECC, but they are all technically stored as orders in the PP/DS liveCache. The orders have different (ATP) categories[18] (see Table 3.2).

ECC Transaction Data	APO Transaction Data
	Order with category
Order	BF (Pur. Ord.)
Purchase requisition	AG (Pur. Req.)
Sales order	BM (Sales Ord.)
Planned order	AI (Pl. Ord.)

Table 3.2 Transaction Data in ECC and APO

---

18 The order category that's used to define the type and content of the document for all applications is often referred to as the "ATP category" in APO. This can be confusing, especially if the current application has nothing to do with ATP.

ECC Transaction Data	APO Transaction Data
Planned independent requirement	FA (Pl. Ind. Req.)
Reservation	AM (Mat. Res.)
Stock	CC (Stock)
...	...

Table 3.2 Transaction Data in ECC and APO (cont.)

Transaction data may be transferred between APO and ECC in either one or both directions, depending on its category, as illustrated by the following examples:

▶ *Stocks* can only be created in ECC. Therefore, they must be transferred from ECC to APO. They cannot be transferred in the opposite direction.

▶ Similarly, *sales orders* can only be created in ECC and transferred to APO.

▶ *Planned independent requirements* can be created in ECC and transferred to APO. However, they can also be released from APO-DP to PP/DS (or entered manually in PP/DS), in which case they only exist in APO. They cannot then be transferred to ECC.[19]

▶ *Planned orders* are normally the result of planning in APO. They can be transferred to ECC, but they are often not transferred until they have been converted into production orders. However, planned orders and production orders can also be created or changed in ECC (although this is only useful in exceptional cases if APO is also in use) and are then transferred to APO. A consistent planning situation in ECC and APO is important for these documents.[20] The same applies to purchase requisitions.

---

19 A transfer of planned independent requirements from APO-DP to ECC is possible, but it does not occur via the CIF. Instead it is carried out directly from demand planning using the **Transfer to ECC** function. This transfer is especially useful if APO-DP is used exclusively for demand planning, whereas production planning is done in ECC without the use of PP/DS.

20 Another re-transfer of the planning result can be set using APO Transaction /SAPAPO/CP3. These settings are relevant if the quantity of a production order that originates from SAP APO is changed in ECC, for example. The changed quantity is transferred to APO, where the order is rescheduled. The new dates are re-transferred to ECC only if this is configured in Transaction /SAPAPO/CP3.

3.3.2   Initial and Change Transfers for Transaction Data

Like master data, the transaction data to be transferred between ECC and APO must be defined using integration models. Technically speaking, integration models are capable of containing both master data and transaction data in parallel. However, it is usually best to separate the two data types for organizational reasons.

Note
As a prerequisite for transferring transaction data, all master data on which it is based must be contained in active models. For example, stocks are only transferred if the material and location are contained in active models.

To generate an integration model for transferring transaction data, select the transaction data categories that are to be included (for example, storage location stocks) and restrict the data to be transferred (for example, to one group of materials) using the general selection options (see Figure 3.29). Generating this model results in a list of filter objects (for example, stocks for certain materials, as shown in Figure 3.30). We recommend you use open selection criteria and variants here also, to ensure that the set of data to be transferred can be easily (or even automatically) extended by generating and activating the model again.

Generating transaction data models

The question of which transaction data objects to include in the integration models is a complex one. The answer depends on the planning process itself, and various different approaches are conceivable. The following basic rules apply:

▶ All initial data required for planning must be contained in active integration models—e.g., stocks, sales orders, planned independent requirements, and so on.

▶ All documents required for executing planning must be contained in active integration models—e.g., planned orders, production orders, purchase requisitions, purchase orders, ATP checks, and so on.

After you create transaction data integration models, they must be activated. Unlike activating master data, activating transaction data is associated with the following two actions:

Activating transaction data models

1. The transaction data in ECC is transferred to APO.

Create Integration Model

Model Name	PUMP20
Logical System	APOCLNT800
APO Application	TD

Material Dependent Objects

- ☐ Materials
- ☐ MRP Area Matl
- ☐ Planning Matl ⇨
- ☐ ATP Check
- ☐ Extern. Plant ⇨

- ☐ Plants
- ☐ MRP areas ⇨
- ☐ Supply Area

- ☐ Contracts ⇨
- ☐ Pur.Info Record ⇨

- ☐ SchedAgreements ⇨

- ☐ PPM ⇨
- ☐ PDS (ERP) ⇨

- ☐ BOM ⇨

- ☑ Storage Loc.Stk ⇨
- ☐ Sales Ord Stock ⇨
- ☐ Cust. Spec. Stk ⇨

- ☐ Transit Stock ⇨
- ☐ Project Stocks ⇨
- ☐ Vend. Spec. Stk ⇨

- ☑ Sales Orders ⇨
- ☑ Plan Ind. Reqs ⇨
- ☑ Planned Orders ⇨
- ☐ Prod. Campaign
- ☐ POs and PReqs ⇨

- ☐ Sched. VMI ⇨
- ☐ Req. Reduction
- ☐ Prod. Order ⇨
- ☐ Manual Reserv. ⇨

General Selection Options for Materials

			to	
Material	T-F220		to	⇨
Plnt	1000		to	⇨
Matl Type			to	⇨
PlantSpec. Mtl Stat			to	⇨
MRP Ctrlr			to	⇨
MRP Type			to	⇨
ABC Indicator			to	⇨

Figure 3.29 "Create Integration Model" Transaction in ECC, Transaction Code CFM; Selecting Transaction Data

Create Integration Model

⊕Generate IM | ⌐Consistency Check | Detail

APOCLNT800 - PUMP20 - TD

Filter Object	Number
Stocks	1
Planned Indep. Requirements	1
Planned Orders	1
Sales Orders	1

Figure 3.30 "Create Integration Model" Transaction in ECC, Transaction Code CFM1; Next Screen After Execution, Showing the Results List with Transaction Data

2. If new transaction data is created in ECC that belongs to an object type that is contained in an active integration model, these documents are transferred to APO immediately.

In other words, activating a transaction data model results in the continuous, real-time change transfer of active transaction data. If new data is created in ECC or if transferred documents are changed (stock changes, new sales orders, changes to customer orders, etc.), this data is automatically and instantaneously transferred to APO.

In contrast to master data, transaction data does not require a separate change transfer.

Note that the initial transfer does not involve the comparison/reconciliation of data between ECC and APO. If a transaction data integration model is deactivated, only the connection between the documents in ECC and APO is lost. If this model is then re-activated, the data in ECC is transferred again, regardless of which data is in APO. As a result, the data in the two systems is no longer consistent.[21]

3.3.3 Transfer of Transaction Data from APO to ECC

The transfer of transaction data from APO to ECC is configured in APO. As a prerequisite, the relevant objects must be contained in active integration models.

First, you must specify in APO the logical ECC system to which the relevant transaction data is to be transferred. You do this in the basic settings under **Maintain Distribution Definition** in APO Customizing (see Figure 3.8). Here you specify for each publication type (for example, in-house production or external procurement) the ECC system (logical system name) to which the data is to be returned. This table must always be maintained, even if APO is only connected with a single ECC system (the entries can be created collectively in the **Generate Distribution Definition** setting in customizing).

Distribution of data

Finally, you must configure either online or periodic transfers of new or changed transaction data in APO. You do this in the **Set User Parameters** transaction in APO (Transaction Code /SAPAPO/C4; see Figure 3.31), where a distinction is made between SNP and PP/DS data.

Online or periodic transfer

---

21 To resolve a data inconsistency between ECC and APO, you must use the APO Transaction **CIF comparison/reconciliation** function. See the section on eliminating transfer errors.

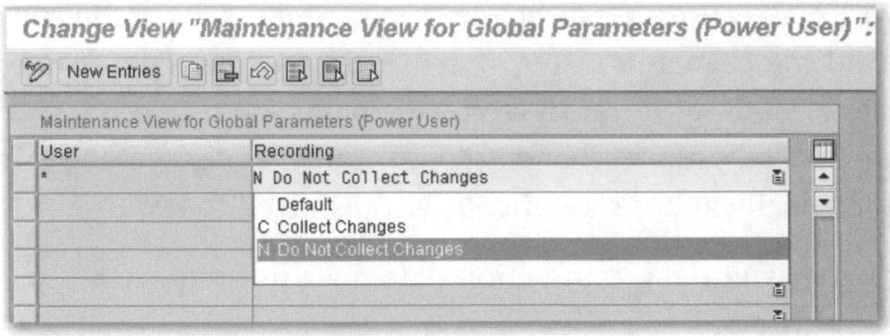

Figure 3.31 "Set User Parameters" Transaction in APO, Transaction Code /SAPAPO/C4; Setting for Transferring Changed Transaction Data

If you want the data to be collected and transferred periodically, you can use the **Process Change Pointers** transaction (Transaction Code /SAPAPO/C5; see Figure 3.32). This step can also be scheduled periodically.

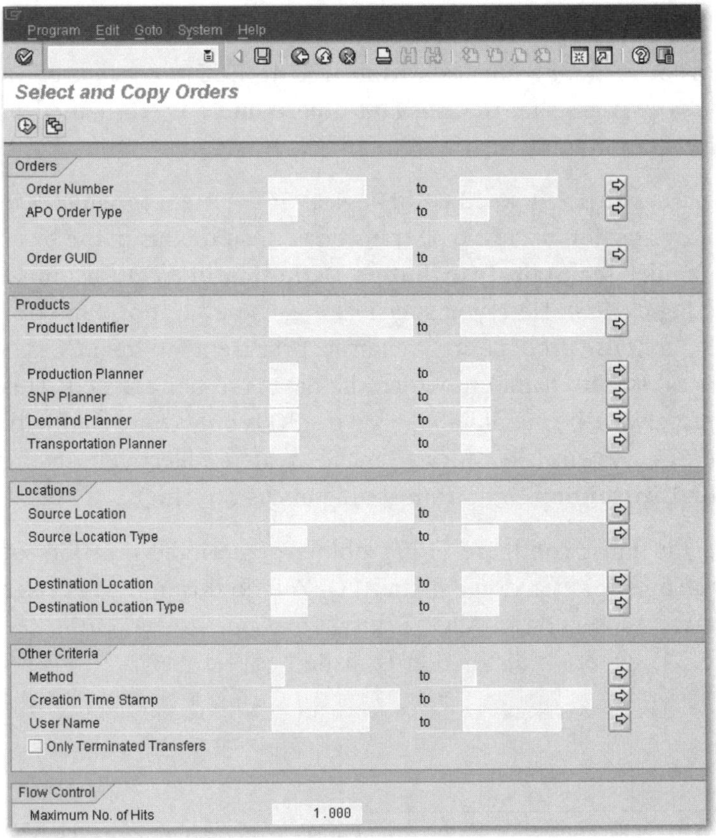

Figure 3.32 "Process Change Pointers" Transaction in APO, Transaction Code /SAPAPO/C5

In addition, you can choose a setting in APO-PP/DS that determines whether planned orders and purchase requisitions created there should be transferred to ECC directly, or whether these documents should first be converted into a production order or a purchase order. This setting is made under **Change Global Parameters and Default Values** in PP/DS Customizing (see Figure 3.33).

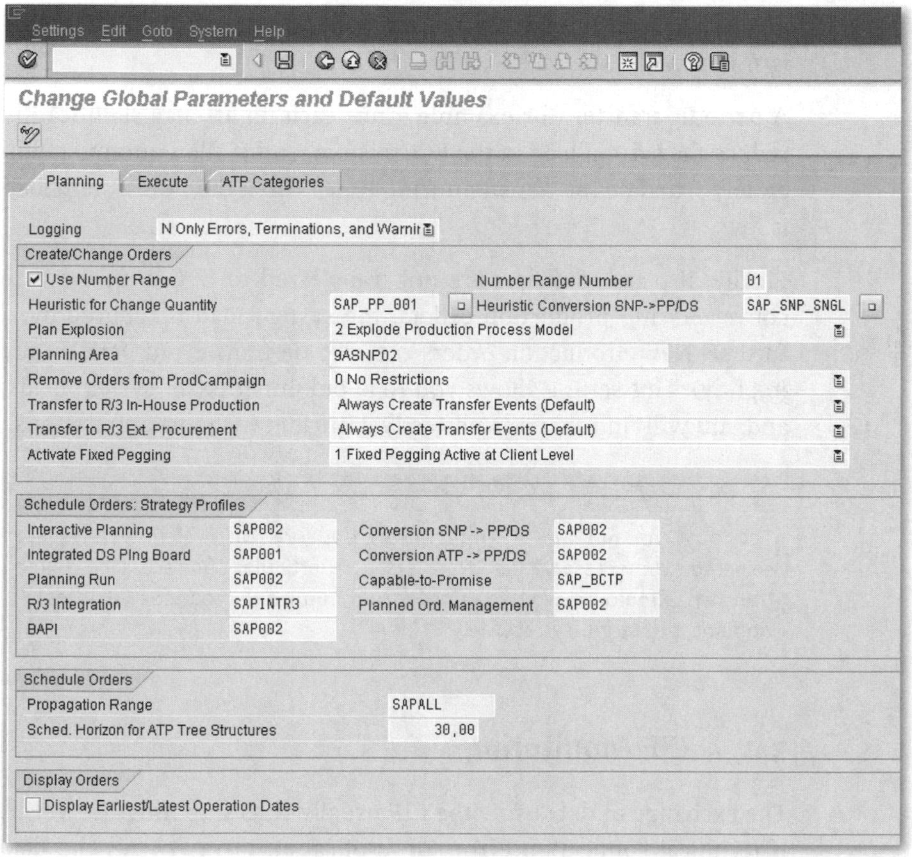

Transfer planned orders and purchase requisitions?

Figure 3.33 "Change Global Parameters and Default Values" Customizing Setting in APO

If data is transferred online, it is sent to ECC immediately after it is posted in APO. This means that a corresponding data queue is created immediately, which must then be posted in ECC. In the case of mass transactions, in particular, which generate large volumes of data to be transferred, the system load in ECC may be high. A check is therefore required to determine which data transfers are required at which point in time.

Data volumes for CIF integration

Consider the following: A large number of new planned orders may be created during production planning in APO. If planning comprises several steps, interim results will be produced. These consist of planned orders, which may be moved in the next step. If planned orders are transferred online, this results in a very high and, to a large extent, unnecessary system load in ECC because all interim results are transferred. An online transfer is therefore only useful if planned orders are urgently and immediately required in ECC, which is almost never the case!

A periodic transfer (for example, once each night) may significantly reduce the system load in the ECC system, and it allows you to deliberately schedule the transfer during times when the ECC system load is low.

Finally, if planned orders are not transferred to ECC until they are converted into production orders, the system load is reduced even further. New production orders can also be transferred periodically (nightly). This setting allows you to avoid unnecessary system loads, and you will find that it is perfectly sufficient for most applications.

> **Note**
>
> The data volume for CIF integration depends on which settings are selected. Unnecessary data transfers (in particular, unnecessary online transfers) should be avoided in order to minimize the load for CIF integration and the target systems.

3.4 CIF Monitoring

The exchange of data using the CIF usually runs smoothly. However, if technical connection errors or application errors occur, the data transfer may fail or may be only partly successful. If this happens, the cause of the transfer error must be detected and eliminated, and the data must be transferred again.

The causes of transfer errors fall into one of two categories:

▶ **Communication errors**
These include network problems, nonexistent RFC destinations, and so on. These communication errors often resolve themselves if the data transfer is repeated periodically. This can be configured for an RFC connection.

▶ **Application errors**
These include program errors, failing to post data in the target system, missing master data for a transaction data record, and so on. Application errors *cannot* be resolved by the system without manual intervention and must be handled by the system administrator.

Therefore, the second category (application errors) usually presents more problems.

3.4.1 The Principle of qRFC

The CIF data transfer is asynchronous and is based on a queued Remote Function Call (qRFC). The data is first processed in the source system and then transferred to the target system with a data queue. The advantage of this approach is that the application that triggers the data transfer is decoupled from CIF integration. On the other hand, however, return parameters cannot normally be delivered in this way, which means that any error messages indicating problems with the CIF transfer cannot be returned to the application. One problem, in particular, with this is that in certain cases, queues may block a data channel, and therefore that channel cannot be used for any further transfers to the target system. The following situations may arise:

The initial transfer of master data uses a channel called CFLD[*logical ECC system*]. This transfer is only performed for the complete integration model. If one data record cannot be transferred, transfer of the complete model fails. In other words, it cannot be activated. A failed activation is immediately detected when you execute the transaction, and a corresponding error message is issued (see Figure 3.34). In addition, a blocked queue is generated, which blocks all subsequent master data transfers. This queue must be corrected and sent or deleted before new master data models can be activated.

Master data transfers

There are no problems associated with deleting these kinds of queues, because they can be created again the next time the model is activated. The change transfer of master data also uses this same master data channel.

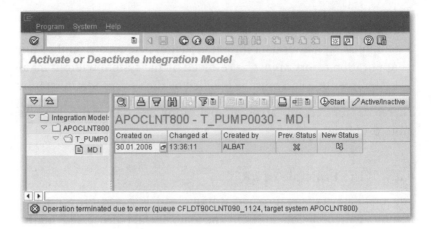

Figure 3.34 "Activate Integration Model" Transaction in ECC, Transaction Code CFM2; Failed Master Data Initial Transfer

Blocking by transaction data queues

Master data transfers can also be blocked by failed transaction data transfers, although this type of problem can be overlooked (that is, ignored). If the **Ignore Faulty Queue Entries** indicator is set in the RIMODAC2 report (for activating integration models as a background job), the initial transfer is not blocked when this occurs. Transaction data queues should only be ignored if you can be sure that the existing queues are not intrinsically related to the pending master data transfer.

Transaction data transfers

The initial transfer of transaction data is very similar to the initial transfer of master data. You can only activate the entire model. If the transfer fails, an error message is issued, the model remains inactive, and the queue must be processed and sent or deleted before a new activation is possible.

Change transfer of transaction data

Successful activation of the transaction data model is followed by the change transfer of transaction data. In contrast to the approach described above, the transfer uses *separate channels.* Normally, each individual document is transferred using a separate channel. The contents of the queue are usually obvious from its name. For example, a queue called CFPLO[*Planned order number*] is generated for the transfer of a planned order from ECC to APO. Usually, a failed transaction data transfer does not block subsequent transfers of other documents.

Transaction data records are connected by logical units of work (LUWs). An LUW is created when data is posted to a transaction. For example, if the planning result is saved in APO after interactive changes are made to a range of orders, all orders are connected by an LUW consisting of several queues (one queue for each new or changed order). This type of LUW can only be transferred in full. If one order has errors or cannot be transferred, all related orders are also blocked. This blocking does not normally affect other LUWs.

LUW

However, LUWs may also block each other simultaneously in certain cases. Some queues (stocks, for example) are only identified by a material number. If, for example, the transfer of a delivery fails because of an application error, the corresponding stock posting is also blocked (both are contained in an LUW). If another (error-free) delivery is then transferred for the same material, and is also connected with a stock posting, the stock encounters the blocked queue. Consequently, the entire LUW is blocked, which means that the second delivery cannot be transferred either.

> **Note**
>
> If a transaction data transfer fails, there is no notification in the source transaction (this applies to all transaction data transfers). The data is posted as usual in the source system, and the queue for the transfer is created. If the queue cannot be transferred, it remains in the system as a blocked queue.

A failed transaction data transfer results in the following:

Do not delete transaction data queues

▶ The source system contains the current planning situation.

▶ The target system contains a different planning situation, which is now obsolete. The planning data in the two systems is no longer consistent.

▶ A (blocked) transaction data queue exists. The information that data should be transferred is associated with this queue.

> **Caution**
>
> The transaction data queue must *not* be deleted in this case. If it is deleted, the information that data was changed and must be transferred to the target system will be lost. To solve this problem, you must find the cause of the application error, eliminate the error, and activate the existing queue (that is, send it to the target system) again.

3.4.2 Tools for Troubleshooting Transfer Errors

Since blocked transaction data queues cannot generally be detected in the application, the data transfer between ECC and APO must be monitored separately. Various analysis functions are available in ECC and APO:[22]

▶ **qRFC monitors** in ECC and APO
All failed transfer queues are displayed in the qRFC monitors. From the monitor, they can be activated again, debugged, or deleted (see Figure 3.35). The qRFC monitors are blank if no transfer errors occur.

▶ **Application logs** in ECC and APO
If logging is activated (Transaction CFC2 in ECC or Transaction /SAPAPO/C41 in APO), logs are written for all data transfers (both successful and unsuccessful), which can be displayed in the application log. This means that you can track when exactly (date/time) which (data objects and integration model) were transferred and by whom (user) (see Figure 3.36). The application log also issues a detailed error message if an application error occurs.

▶ **SCM Queue Manager**
(This can be accessed centrally for both systems in Transaction /SAPAPO/CQ in APO.) The SCM Queue Manager is a tool that enables centralized monitoring and processing of error messages and logs from all systems (that is, APO and the connected ECC system(s); see Figure 3.37). It is therefore ideal for CIF monitoring, because it eliminates the need for parallel monitoring in two systems at the same time.

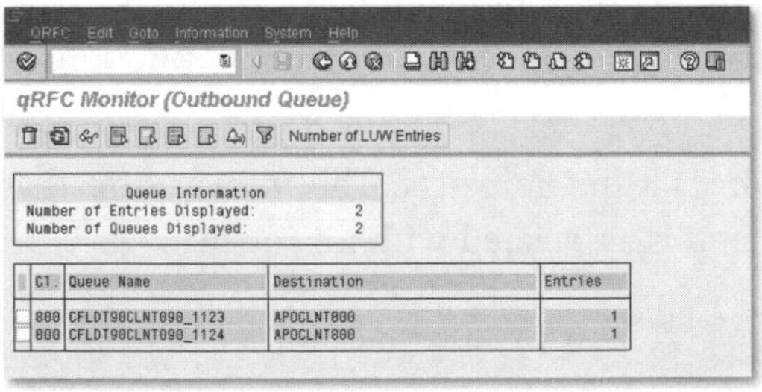

Figure 3.35 "qRFC Monitor" Transaction in ECC, Transaction Code CFQ1, with a Blocked Master Data Queue

---

22 The tools for analyzing and editing the CIF situation are available for both outbound and inbound queues.

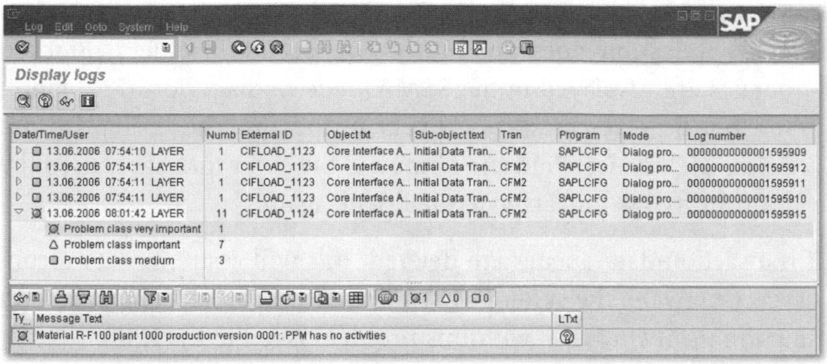

Figure 3.36 "Application Log" Transaction in ECC, Transaction Code CFG1; Log Display

Figure 3.37 "SCM Queue Manager" Transaction in APO, Transaction Code /SAPAPO/CQ

In addition, the CIF Cockpit, a tool that was developed relatively recently, allows you to execute all CIF-relevant actions centrally. It is also possible to configure automatic notifications when errors occur using the qRFC alert.

3.4.3 Eliminating Transfer Errors

If transfer errors occur due to application errors, they must be eliminated by following the instructions below:

▶ **Master data initial transfer failed**
The resulting data queue blocks all subsequent master data transfers. Refer to the error messages (SCM Queue Manager, qRFC monitor, application log) in order to find the error. Then activate (resend) the queue, or delete it and activate the model again.

▶ **Transaction data initial transfer failed**
See the instructions for master data initial transfers.

▶ **Transaction data change transfer failed**
The application does not notify you of this problem. Blocked queues are displayed in the SCM Queue Manager or qRFC monitor, but no error messages appear in the application log. Do not delete the queues! Find and eliminate the error that has caused the transfer to fail, and activate the queue again.

If transaction data queues are deleted, this will result in data inconsistency between the systems. Use the CIF comparison/reconciliation function in APO to deal with this problem (see Figure 3.38).

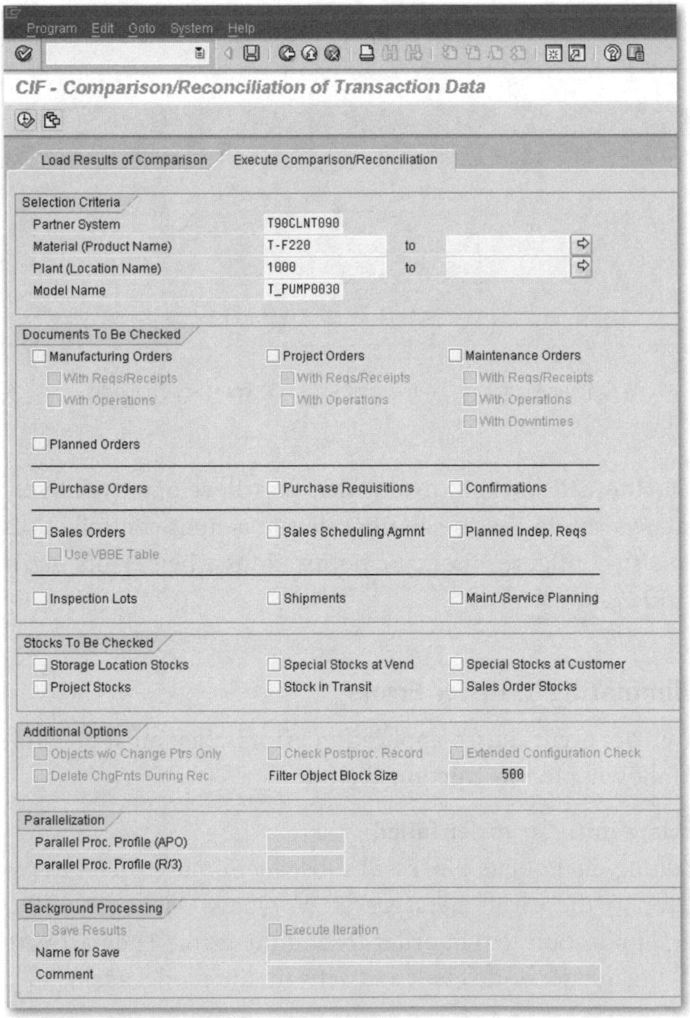

Figure 3.38 "CIF Comparison/Reconciliation" Transaction in APO, Transaction Code /SAPAPO/CCR

This transaction is used to analyze inconsistencies:

▶ Due to missing documents in one of the two systems

▶ Due to differences in content between existing documents

The inconsistencies are listed and can be corrected directly from here.

When you correct errors with the CIF comparison/reconciliation function, data can be transferred in either direction (from ECC to APO, or from APO to ECC) to correct the inconsistency. Here, your only concern is to ensure that the data is consistent in the two systems.

The master data used for planning in APO-PP/DS is normally transferred from ECC, but has different names and a somewhat different structure than the master data that exists in ECC. This chapter, therefore, describes the different types of master data in APO in the context of the CIF transfer.

4   Master Data

4.1   Mapping Principle

In most cases, the master data in APO is not identical to the master data in ECC. For example, material masters in ECC are transferred to APO as product masters, while production versions with routings and BOMs appear in APO as production process models or production data structures, and so on. During the CIF transfer, the settings made in ECC are processed by the CIF and mapped to the corresponding settings in APO.

APO master data generally has a less complex structure than master data in ECC. You maintain APO master data using the **Master Data** menu option in APO, and often only require a single transaction to do so. While ECC has a separate menu for material masters, for example, all settings and actions relating to the product are made in the same transaction in APO.

The CIF transfer of APO master data may include the transfer of ECC customizing settings. For example, a plant (which is typically selected in an integration model) is defined in customizing in ECC and transferred to APO as a master data record.

Transfer of customizing settings

> **Note**
>
> Customizing settings of the ECC basis (such as factory calendars, units of measure, etc.) can be transferred to APO using customizing transport requests, because the settings in the SAP SCM basis correspond to a large degree to those in SAP ECC. ECC application customizing, in contrast, cannot be transferred to APO.

Explicit exceptions to this rule are ATP customizing and various other ECC customizing documents, which can be selected in an integration model.

4.2 Locations

Plants, distribution centers, MRP areas, customers, and vendors in ECC are mapped in APO as locations with different location types (see Figure 4.1). All locations have the same basic structure but differ from each other at a more granular level, based on their location type (for example, additional views are available for certain location types in location maintenance).

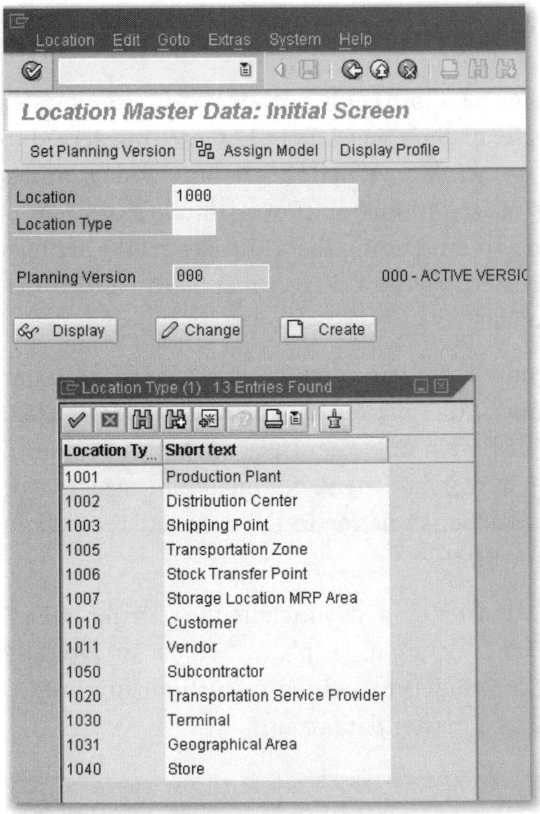

Figure 4.1 "Location" Transaction in APO, Transaction Code /SAPAPO/LOC3, with Field Selection for Location Type

Location types   Table 4.1 shows exactly how ECC master data is mapped to location types in APO during the CIF transfer:

ECC data	APO data
	Location (with location type)
Plant	1001 Production plant
Distribution center	1002 Distribution center
Storage location MRP area	1007 Storage location MRP area
Customer (with transportation zone)	1010 Customer
	1005 Transportation zone
Vendor	1011 Vendor

Table 4.1 Transfer of ECC Data as APO Locations with a Corresponding Location Type

4.2.1 Transferring Plants and Distribution Centers

Plants are defined using the **Define**, **Copy**, **Delete**, **Check Plant** setting in the enterprise structure customizing settings in ECC (see Figure 4.2).

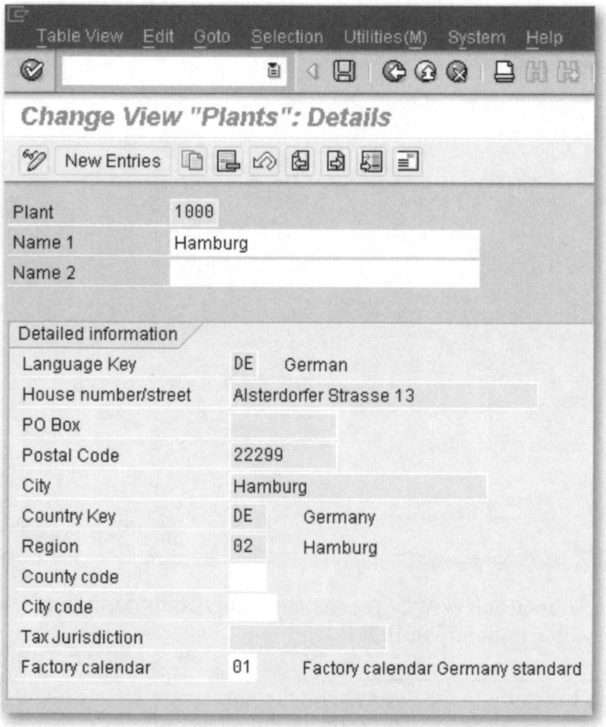

Figure 4.2 "Define, Copy, Delete, Check Plant" Customizing Setting in ECC, Detailed Information for a Plant

Plant If a plant is contained in an integration model, it is transferred to the SCM system as a **Location** with **Location Type 1001 (Production Plant)**. The basic settings for the plant, such as name, address data, time zone, and regional assignment, are transferred (see Figure 4.3).[1] In addition, the APO location contains a range of APO-specific settings, which must be defined in APO. Note also that the short description of locations, unlike those of ECC plants, can be maintained in more than one language.

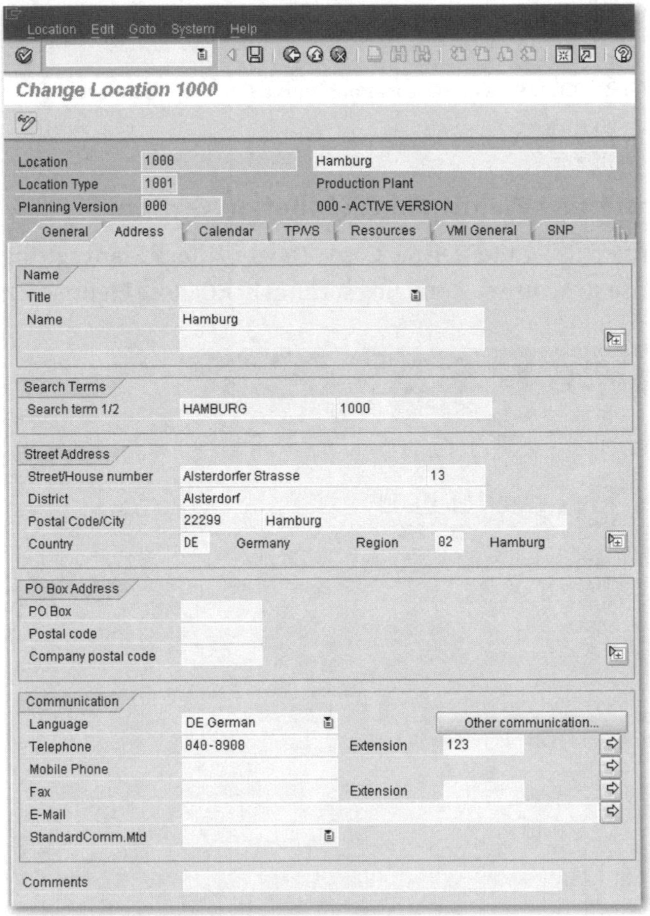

Figure 4.3 "Location" Transaction in APO, Transaction Code /SAPAPO/LOC3, Changing a Location with Location Type 1001

---

1 Note that the data structures in the two systems are not identical. For example, you can define the form of address keys (Mr., Mrs., and so on) in ECC customizing, while these keys are predefined in APO. They can only be transferred if the form of address keys is known in APO.

CIF change transfers are not possible for plants. If APO-relevant data in a plant changes, the changes must be maintained separately in both systems.

A distribution center (DC) in ECC is simply a plant that is assigned the additional attribute **Distribution Center**. This attribute was originally developed with R/3 Release 4.0 for *Distribution Resource Planning* (DRP) functions,[2] and the corresponding setting must therefore be made in DRP Customizing (in the **Maintain Assignment of Node Type – Plant activity** in the basic settings for DRP). The plant is not changed from a functional standpoint (a different icon merely appears in the graphical applications of DRP).

Distribution center

If you transfer plants to APO that are defined in ECC as distribution centers, these plants are transferred to location type 1002 (distribution center). The transfer of the individual ECC plant settings is exactly the same as for production plants.

4.2.2 Storage Location MRP Areas

As of R/3 Release 4.5, ECC has MRP areas that can be used to differentiate planning. Storage location MRP areas (type 2) and subcontractor MRP areas (type 3) can be defined below the plant level in the customizing settings for material requirements planning. If storage location MRP areas are selected in an integration model, they are transferred to APO as location type 1007, and their plant assignment is preserved. The receiving storage location contained in storage location MRP areas is also transferred to APO as a corresponding sublocation (see Figure 4.4).

Subcontractor MRP areas *cannot* be transferred to APO as such. Instead, the vendors themselves are transferred as locations.

The plant MRP data in an ECC material master may include MRP area segments (on the MRP 1 view), which are used for planning with MRP areas. If a material with MRP area segments is included in an active integration model, the MRP area data is also transferred. A location product is then created in APO for each relevant MRP area, in addition to the location product of the plant.

MRP area segments

---

2 Due to its limited functional scope, the ECC functionality of DRP is rarely used in real life. Since R/3 Release 4.0, it hasn't been developed any further in R/3 and ECC. A powerful cross-plant distribution resource planning was not developed until the release of APO-SNP.

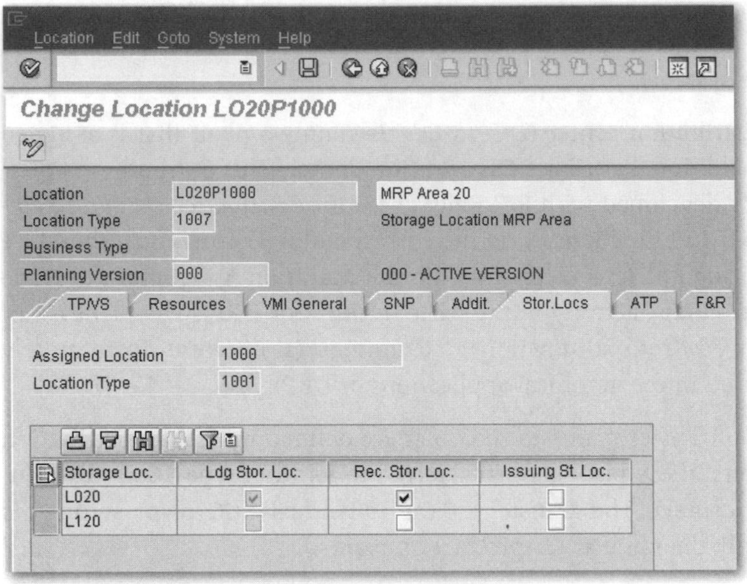

Figure 4.4 "Location" Transaction in APO, Transaction Code /SAPAPO/LOC3, Changing a Location with Location Type 1007, "Storage Locations" View

4.2.3 Customers and Vendors

Customers

Customers are maintained as sales and distribution master data records, which can be transferred to APO for planning as locations with location type 1010. However, this is only necessary if the customer location is explicitly required for planning (for example, for transportation planning for the customer). In normal production planning, this is not usually required, and an ECC sales order can be transferred to APO without the customer.

If the customer contains a transportation zone in ECC, an additional corresponding location with location type 1005 is automatically transferred with the customer.

Customers, like vendors (and unlike plants), are transferred to APO with leading zeros. For example, ECC customer 4711 appears in APO as location 0000004711.

Vendors

Vendors are maintained as purchasing master data records, which can be transferred to APO as locations with location type 1011 (see Figure 4.5). Vendors must be transferred to APO if planning of vendors is explicitly required as part of supply source determination.

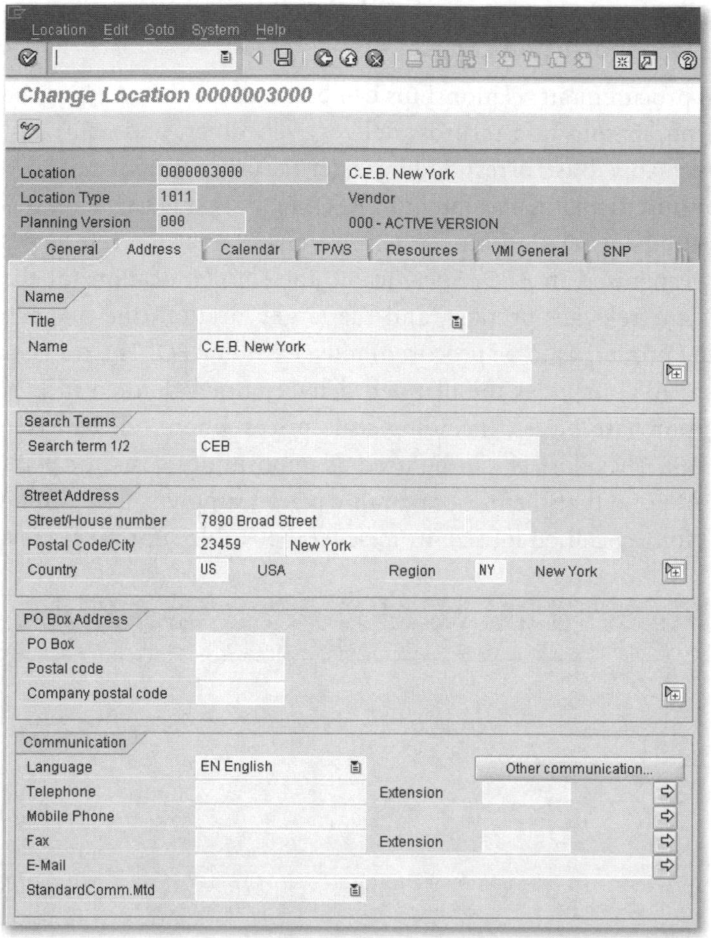

Figure 4.5 "Location" Transaction in APO, Transaction Code /SAPAPO/LOC3, Changing a Location with Location Type 1011, "Address" View

Note	Customers and vendors with identical numbers

The following point is particularly relevant for the transfer of customers and vendors: A location must be identified by a unique name in APO. This also applies if the location types differ. In other words, two locations cannot have the same name in APO, even if they have different location types. This means that if a customer and vendor have the same number in ECC (for example, customer 1000 and vendor 1000), either the customer or the vendor must be renamed in the APO inbound queue using a customer exit (for example, the vendor could be renamed S1000). Conflicts with production plants do not normally occur, because plants are transferred without and customers and vendors are transferred with leading zeros in their names.

4.2.4 External Procurement Relationships and Transportation Lanes

External procurement relationships can be transferred to APO in the form of purchasing info records, delivery schedules, and contracts. They are mapped as corresponding external procurement relationships for purchasing management in APO. Before you transfer external procurement relationships, you must ensure that the references will be recognized in APO. Specifically, the source location (of the vendor), the relevant product, and the target location (the plant in which the product is to be procured) must exist in APO. The transfer of data to APO includes the planned delivery times defined in ECC and the purchase prices, including scale prices where relevant (see Figure 4.6). These prices can be used as opportunity costs for planning in APO, so that the most favorably priced supply source can be selected for a specified lot size from several possible supply sources.

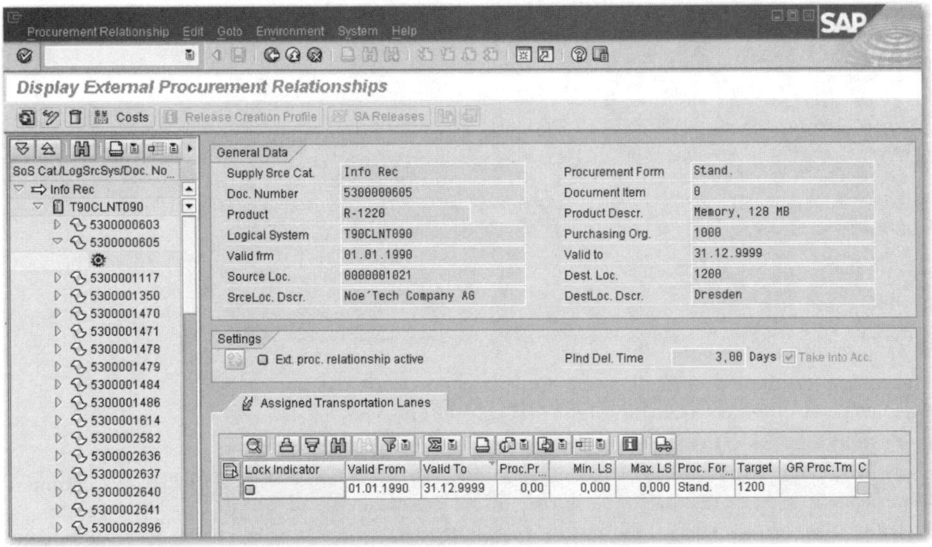

Figure 4.6 "External Procurement Relationships" Transaction in APO, Transaction Code /SAPAPO/PWBSRC1, Displaying a Purchasing Info Record

Subcontracting If you intend to use subcontract procurement processing for procurement, the relevant data can be transferred to APO using the CIF transfer. To do this, you must assign the production version with the subcontracting bill of materials to the supply source in ECC and select the **Subcontracting PPM** or **PDS** object in addition to the supply source in the integration model.

Quota arrangements cannot be transferred from ECC and must be created in APO. APO does not contain source lists. However, individual external supply sources can be deactivated in APO, which will exclude them from automatic supply source determination.

A transportation lane indicates that a product in APO can be procured from another location. It may also contain additional information about the duration of transportation, itinerary, and means of transport, all of which play no role in PP/DS but are relevant for TP/VS or SNP-TLB. The other location may be an alternative internal location (for example, a different production plant), or an external location (for example, an external vendor).

> **Note**
>
> With the CIF transfer of an external procurement relationship, a corresponding transportation lane is automatically created, therefore you usually do not have to maintain any additional data for PP/DS processes.

As of APO 4.0, stock transfers between different plants or distribution centers, as defined with a special procurement key in the ECC material master, can also be automatically transferred to APO as corresponding transportation lanes using the CIF transfer. Any existing transportation lanes that were created manually are not overwritten in this case.

4.3   Products

ECC material masters are transferred to APO as product masters. Provided that they are not renamed using a customer exit, the APO product has the same number as the ECC material.[3] In APO, as in the material master in ECC, the product description can be maintained in multiple languages, and all languages are transferred from ECC. Like the material master in ECC, the product master in APO is divided into several different views. The data in these views falls into one of the following categories:

---

3 The length of the APO product master number can be defined in APO customizing (**Define output display of product number**). By default, an 18-digit product number is used as in ECC.

▶ *Header data* (**Properties**, **Units of Measure**, **Classification** tabs) is of a general nature and is not specific to any one location.

▶ *Planning data* for a product (**Demand**, **Lot Size**, **PP/DS tabs**, and so on) is location-dependent.

A product in a specific location is also referred to as a *location product*. Products are maintained in APO in the **Product** transaction in the APO master data (see Figure 4.7).

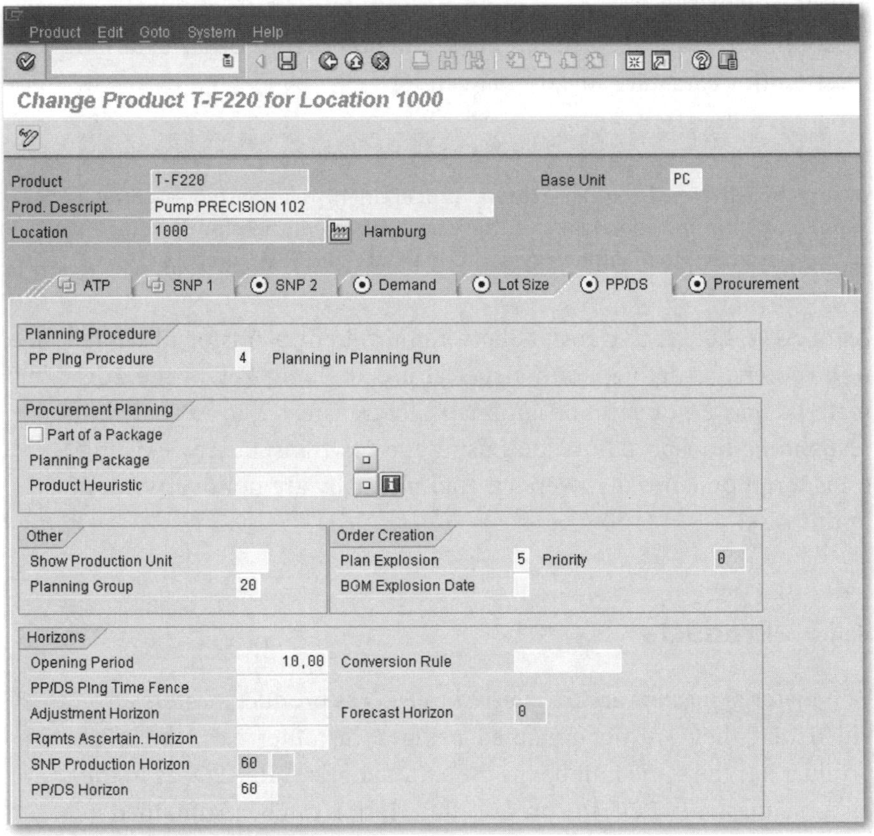

Figure 4.7 "Product" Transaction in APO, Transaction Code /SAPAPO/MAT1, "PP/DS" View

Many fields in the product master are automatically filled when the corresponding material master is transferred from ECC. Other fields are APO-specific and are normally maintained in APO directly (that is, if a customer exit is not used). Therefore, it is very important to check whether a field in an APO product master is maintained in ECC before you change the data in APO.

4.3.1 Header Data

The following general data is transferred from the material master in ECC to the APO product:[4] **Material group**, **gross weight**, and **volume** (**Basic Data view** in ECC), **transportation group** (**Sales: General/Plant Data view** in ECC), and **units of measure** (**Additional Data view** in ECC).

Classification data (**Classification view**) can also be transferred to the APO product. However, classes and characteristics must be transferred to APO first.

Classes and characteristics can be explicitly selected in an integration model and transferred from ECC to APO. In particular, you can transfer the material classification, that is, the class types in the MARA table (001: Material class, ..., 300: Configuration of material variant classes, ...). If you use the classification in APO, you must take a range of restrictions and additional options into account, in particular in relation to industry-specific enhancements. For example, variant configuration is not supported by production process models, while it can, in contrast, be used with production data structures (see Section 4.5).

Classes and characteristics

4.3.2 ATP Settings

Note that if you transfer the ATP settings from the ECC material master to the APO product master, some of the settings only make sense in APO if the ATP customizing settings are also transferred.

ATP customizing can be explicitly selected and transferred in an integration model. In contrast to other master data, the model does not have to be active in the case of ATP customizing. Rather, it is possible and indeed useful to deactivate the model after the ECC settings are transferred, and to complete the settings in APO. To prevent ATP settings from being transferred again from ECC by mistake, you can block imports from ECC in the APO-ATP customizing settings. Table 4.2 shows exactly how the individual objects are mapped:

ATP customizing

---

4 Here and in the following sections, the lists of transferred settings are not complete. Instead, we focus on outlining the central and most important contexts.

ECC-ATP Customizing	APO-ATP Customizing
Checking group	ATP group
Checking rule	Business event
Requirements class	Check mode
Scope of check	Check control with scope of check

Table 4.2 Transferring Various ATP Customizing Objects from ECC to APO

When the data is transferred to the product master, the settings listed in Table 4.3 are automatically copied from the MRP 3 view of the ECC material master.

ECC Material Master	APO Product Master
Availability check group	ATP group
Total replenishment lead time	Checking horizon
Customer requirements class of main planning strategy	Check mode

Table 4.3 Transferring Various ATP Settings from the ECC Material Master to the APO Product Master

ATP check in APO

If the ATP check is to be configured for a material in APO, the **availability check** object must be included in an active integration model for the material in question.

4.3.3 Requirements Settings

Requirements strategies

Requirements strategies are maintained in ECC using a strategy group that contains a main planning strategy in the MRP 3 view. If one of the standard strategies listed in Table 4.4 is entered as the main planning strategy, it can be transferred to APO. Note, however, that the strategy keys may change in some cases. The main planning strategy in the ECC strategy group is always the strategy that is relevant for transfer.

Strategy Description	ECC Key	APO Key
Make-to-stock production	10	10
Planning with final assembly	40	20
Subassembly planning	70	20

Table 4.4 Different Strategy Keys in ECC and APO

Strategy Description	ECC Key	APO Key
Planning without final assembly	50	30
Planning with planning product	60	40
Make-to-order production	20	Blank

Table 4.4 Different Strategy Keys in ECC and APO (cont.)

If other strategies or keys are entered in ECC, the relevant field in the APO product master remains blank.

The settings for consumption, consumption mode, and consumption periods are transferred from ECC to APO. Note that consumption mode 4 does not exist in APO, and that the consumption periods in APO, unlike those in ECC, are specified in calendar days.

Consumption

The ECC settings for individual/collective requirements in the MRP 4 view are also transferred. ECC setting **2** corresponds to the **Always coll. requirement** indicator in APO, while setting **1** or **blank** corresponds to the **Possible indiv. cust. reqt** indicator (see Figure 4.8).

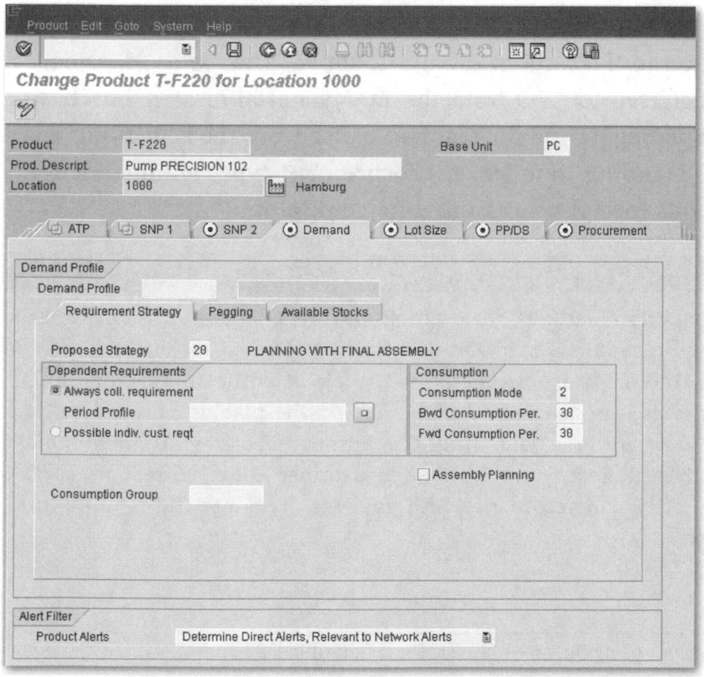

Individual/collective requirements

Figure 4.8 "Product" Transaction in APO, Transaction Code /SAPAPO/MAT1, "Demand" View

4.3.4 Lot Size Settings

The lot size is set in ECC using a lot-sizing procedure, which is defined in customizing (Transaction Code OMI4) and entered in the MRP 1 view of the material master. The procedures for lot-for-lot order quantity, fixed order quantity, and period lot sizes can be transferred to APO (the relevant setting in the lot-sizing procedure is the lot size for the short-term period in each case). Note that the APO product master contains all the settings for lot size. Therefore, when the material master is transferred in a CIF transfer, the ECC customizing is analyzed and transferred to the corresponding entries in the product master. These include special settings, such as the APO period factor or the **Lot size always** indicator, which is transferred from the **Scheduling** or **MTO lot size** indicator in ECC.

The following parameters are also transferred: **Minimum lot size, maximum lot size, assembly scrap,**[5] **rounding value, rounding profile** (the key only, rather than the profile itself), **safety stock, service level, reorder point,** and **maximum stock level**.

4.3.5 Additional Settings

In addition to the settings discussed above, a range of other data is also transferred to APO from the ECC material master: **purchasing group, opening period for planned order** from the **scheduling margin key, planning time fence, procurement type, planned delivery time, goods receipt processing time,** and so on.

APO-specific settings

> **Note**
>
> Other important settings, for example, for pegging and alerts or for the planning procedure, cannot be derived from ECC. If these are required settings, the fields are populated with default entries during the initial transfer. This is occasionally problematic (in the planning procedure, for example). After the initial transfer of a product master, you should therefore analyze all field entries and use a customer exit to correct any problematic settings in accordance with your requirements and for all future transfers.

---

5 The logic for using the assembly scrap is different in ECC and APO: in ECC the procurement quantity = demand + demand * scrap, whereas in APO the procurement quantity = demand * 100 % / (100 %-scrap). Accordingly, the amount of assembly scrap must be converted during the transfer.

Alternatively, you can extend the initial transfer to include product master mass maintenance, which corrects the problematic field contents after they have been transferred.

Finally, additional fields in the APO product master can be activated in the APO customizing settings (the same applies to locations). If necessary, these fields can also be freely defined and filled from ECC using a customer exit in order to derive additional information from ECC materials.

Additional product and location fields

4.4   Resources

ECC work centers or ECC resources (PP-PI) are mapped as **Resources** in APO. Multiple capacities with different capacity categories can be assigned to a work center or a resource in ECC. These individual capacities are transferred to APO along with the work centers (see Figure 4.9).

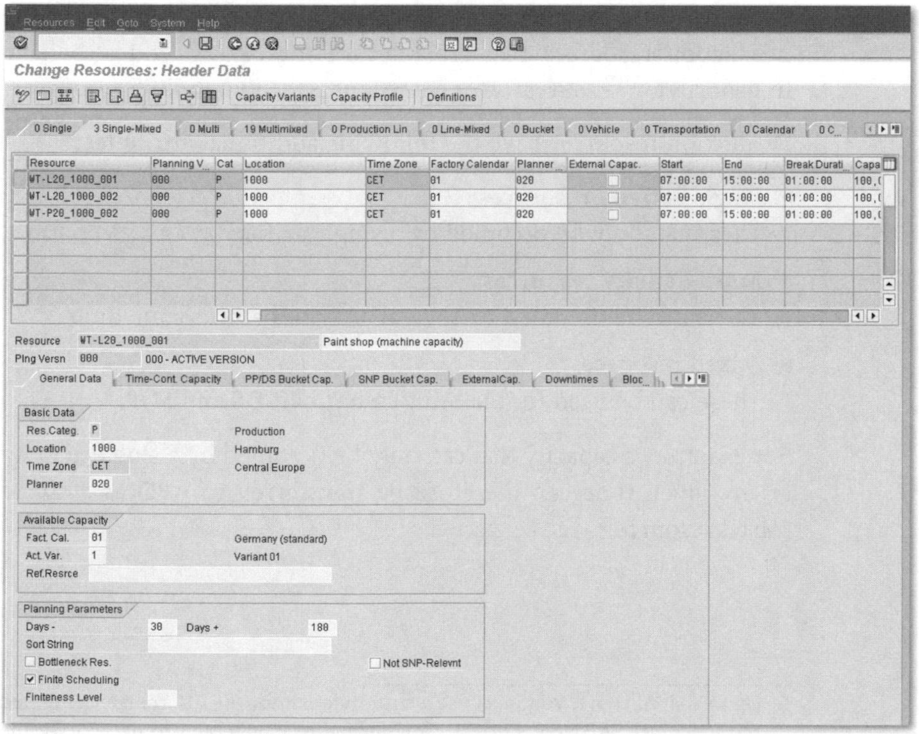

Figure 4.9 "Resource" Transaction in APO, Transaction Code /SAPAPO/RES01

> **Note**
>
> A separate resource is created in APO for each individual work center capacity. The following naming convention is used to assign unique names to the resources in APO: A "W" is placed immediately before the work center name. This is followed by an underscore and the plant ID, which is then followed by an underscore and the capacity category—for example, capacity category 001 of ECC work center T-LACK in plant 1000 appears as **WT-LACK_1000_001 in APO.**

Reference resources and pool capacities can also be transferred. The naming convention is different in this case, in that a "W" is not placed before the name.

As discussed in Chapter 3, the maintenance of resources can be completely confined to the ECC system. APO-specific settings can even be defined in the ECC capacity and transferred from there.

4.4.1 Resources in APO

Resources are used in APO to support a diverse range of processes. Therefore, different resource categories are used. In addition to the production resources that are relevant for PP/DS, you also have transportation resources, storage resources, and handling resources.

Production resources have the following additional attributes:

▶ **Single-activity resources**
These can only be occupied by a single activity at any given time.

▶ **Multi-activity resources**
These can be occupied by several activities at the same time.

▶ **Mixed resources**
These can be used for planning in both PP/DS and SNP.

For example, a capacity that can only be occupied by a single activity at any given time can therefore be transferred to APO as a single mixed resource.[6]

---

6 Up to SAP APO 3.1, you must use a customer exit for the CIF transfer of mixed resources (see SAP Note 329733). You must also activate a customer exit for the PPM (see SAP Note 321474).

The **single** or **multi** and **mixed** attributes and the **resource category** defined when the resource is first created in APO cannot be changed subsequently. The single-activity or multi-activity resource attribute is derived from the settings of the individual capacity categories. The use of mixed resources can be defined for the CIF transfer and is generally recommended.

The resource type to be used for the transfer of a capacity to APO can be defined in the additional APO data of the capacities in ECC (or collectively for all capacities in Transaction CFC9 in ECC customizing). This means that capacities that can only be occupied by a single activity can technically also be transferred as multi-activity resources with only one capacity. The advantage of this is that any additional capacity assigned to the work center at a later stage can also be transferred to APO immediately (otherwise, the APO resource would have to be created again). Note, however, that setup time optimization can only be executed for single-activity resources in APO.

4.4.2 APO Resource Data

When you access the data belonging to an APO resource, you must bear in mind that each planning version has a separate resource. Therefore, to display the operational data, you must specify the planning version (for example, active planning version 000). If you do not specify a planning version, the planning-version-independent resource is displayed.

The settings for the standard available capacity (working time, breaks, rate of capacity utilization, number of individual capacities, etc.) from the header data are transferred from ECC to APO.

Header data

Intervals of available capacity are not transferred, but, as shown in Chapter 3, they can be used as external capacity for planning in APO. If external capacity is not used, intervals of available capacity can be defined in APO directly. External capacity can be configured in the additional APO data of the ECC capacity.

Intervals of available capacity

Other APO-specific settings, such as the finiteness level, or whether the resource is relevant for SNP, are similarly defined in the additional APO data in ECC.

4.5   Production Data Structures and Production Process Models

An ECC production version with a routing and BOM or with a master recipe (PP-PI) can be transferred to APO as a production data structure (PDS) or as a production process model (PPM). Both objects must be selected in the integration model.

4.5.1   PPM, RTO, PDS, and APO Releases

PPM   In older APO releases, the PPM represented the only option for transferring production versions from ECC to APO. The transfer process is the same for PPMs as for other APO master data. PPMs are transferred from ECC and can then be supplemented or changed in APO with APO-specific settings. There are, however, two main restrictions with PPMs:

▸ There is *no* change management in PPMs. Changes can be transferred from ECC to APO with PPM change transfers. However, these changes take effect immediately. As a result, different change statuses with different date/time validities cannot be mapped.[7]

▸ *No* variants can be mapped with PPMs.

RTO   These functions were not implemented in the PPM. Instead an alternative data structure called a runtime object (RTO) was developed. The runtime object is derived from Integrated Product and Process Engineering (iPPE), a complex master data structure used in the automotive field, which incorporates variants and change management. The (iPPE) runtime object is a derivative of iPPE that reduces the runtime for planning (in other words, for the creation of planned orders).

---

7 The only option is to use various production versions with different time validities whose routings or BOMs are resolved at the validity start date.

During the CIF transfer, a runtime object is derived from the ECC production version (without iPPE, that is), and variants and change management are taken into account. This alternative to using PPMs is available with some restrictions as of SAP APO 3.1, and with no restrictions as of SAP APO 4.0.

Runtime objects were originally referred to as iPPE-RTOs, and later became known as PPDS-RTOs or simply RTOs. With SAP APO 4.1, the RTO was finally given a name all its own: production data structure (PDS).

PDS

> **Note**
>
> An essential property of a PDS or RTO is that it cannot be changed in APO. The only transactions available are display transactions. If you need to make specific changes to data, you must use the corresponding customer exit or BAdI during the transfer from ECC.

4.5.2 Release-Dependent Notes for RTO or PDS

The following properties and restrictions apply to using a PPM, RTO or PDS:

▸ **For phantom BOMs**
Phantom BOMs can only be mapped completely and at multiple levels (if required) using an RTO or PDS. With a PPM, the components of a phantom BOM are simply exploded and assigned to the PPM directly.

▸ **For SNP**
Up to SAP APO 4.0, an SNP-PPM cannot be derived from an RTO. An SNP-RTO does not exist.

▸ **For operation splits**
As of SAP APO 4.0, mandatory splitting can be mapped with a PPM, whereby a shorter operation duration is transferred to APO and the capacity requirements are merged.

▸ **For overlapping**
As of SAP APO 4.0, required overlapping can be mapped with a PPM.[8] As of SAP APO 5.0, overlapping operations in the routing can be mapped with a PDS.

---

8 See SAP Note 604878, also for flow manufacturing.

As of SAP APO 4.1, a PDS can also be used in the following areas:

- ▸ PP/DS subcontracting
- ▸ SNP (including subcontracting, but excluding variants and change management)
- ▸ CTM (including subcontracting)
- ▸ Block planning and CDP
- ▸ DP

Additional ECC data for PDS

With SAP APO 5.0, it is also possible to define APO-specific settings in ECC to extend the data for the PDS transfer. This means that, as with resources, all master data can be maintained in ECC in an ideal scenario (see Figure 4.10).

> **Note**
>
> The most important point to consider when deciding whether to use a PPM or an RTO/PDS is that the PDS is the most up-to-date master data structure and that further development is only expected for the PDS. Therefore, you should use a PDS unless one of the restrictions listed above necessitates the use of a PPM instead.

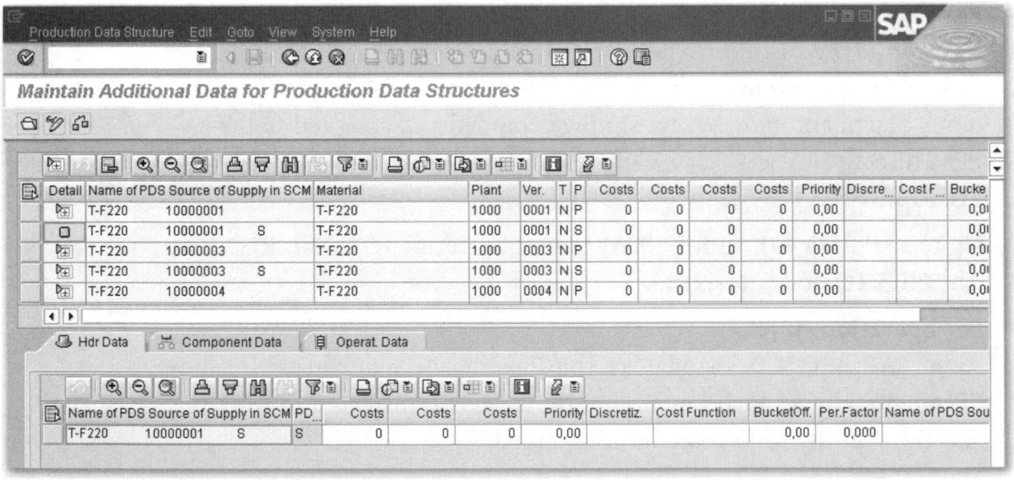

Figure 4.10 "Additional Data for Production Data Structures" Transaction in ECC, Transaction Code PDS_MAINT

The lack of an RTO for SNP is perhaps the most serious restriction up to and including SAP APO 4.0. As of SAP APO 4.1, it is preferable to use a PDS for most applications.

4.5.3 PPM and PDS Structures

A PPM has the same basic structure as a PDS (RTO) in APO. An ECC production version with a routing and BOM is transferred as a PPM or a PDS. The validities of these plans in terms of both period and lot size are based on the validities of the production versions. Different conventions are used for routing numbers in a PPM and a PDS. The routing number is an essential component of the PPM number (see Figure 4.11), while a PDS is identified by the product number (see Figure 4.12).

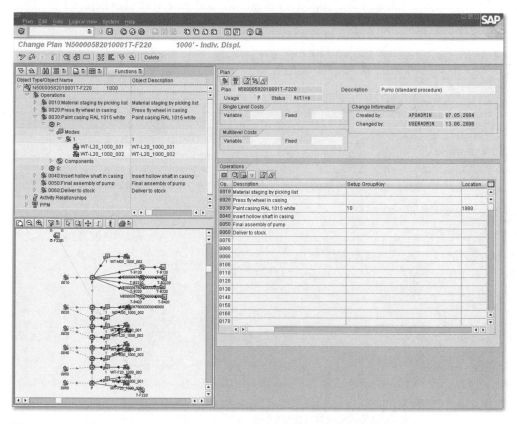

Figure 4.11 "Production Process Model" Transaction in APO, Transaction Code /SAPAPO/SCC03

In APO, a plan contains different operations. One operation contains up to three activities: a setup activity, a processing activity, and a teardown activity. These activities are linked by activity relationships, which define their logical sequence. Sequential processing can be defined by end-start relationships, for example.

Operations and activities

In addition, the activities are assigned components that are consumed (input components) or produced (output components, for the finished product or co-products).

Mode   Modes are used to assign resources to activities. A mode represents an option for executing an activity. A mode contains a primary resource and may also contain secondary resources, for example, a machine as a scheduling-relevant primary resource, and machine operators as a secondary resource (see Figures 4.11 and 4.12). If several modes are assigned to the same activity, the activity can be executed in any one of these modes, and therefore also using alternative resources.

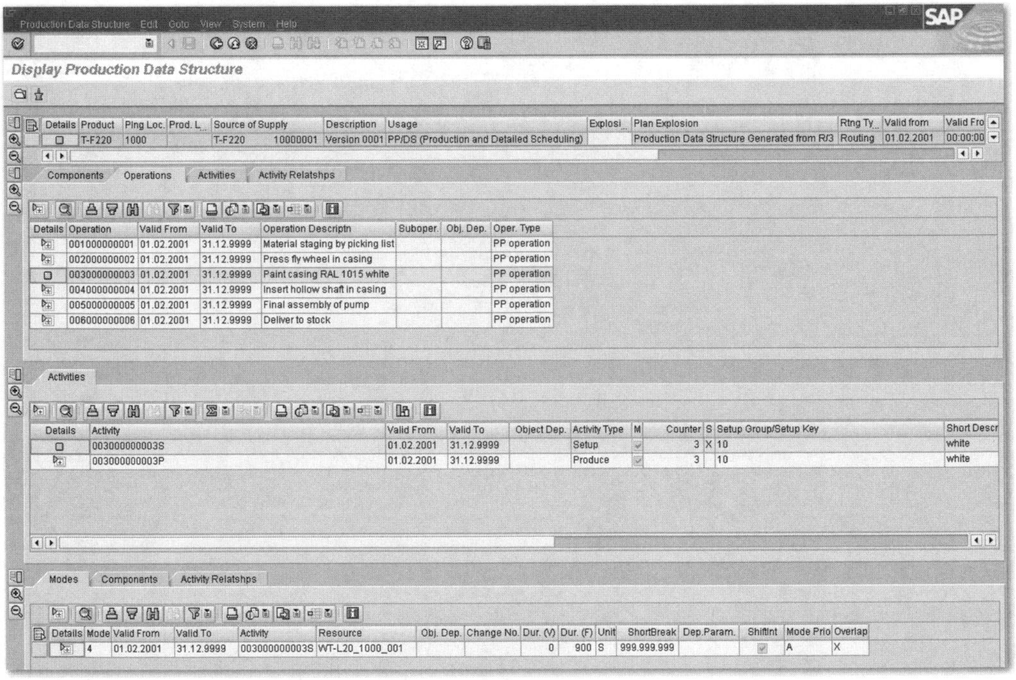

Figure 4.12 "Display Production Data Structures" Transaction in APO, Transaction Code /SAPAPO/CURTO_SIMU

4.5.4 Transfer from ECC

During the CIF transfer, the APO structures are derived from similar structures in ECC. Table 4.5 provides details of the exact relationships between these structures:

ECC	APO
Operation from routing: Operations are only transferred if they are scheduling-relevant, their operation durations are not equal to zero, and the corresponding work centers are active.	Operation
Operation segments, which are defined at the work center using scheduling formulas.	Activity
Standard sequence of operations (operations are ordered by number and, within an operation, setup is followed by processing, which is followed by teardown).	End-start activity relationships
Work centers in operations: These may contain several capacities, of which only one is scheduling-relevant. The scheduling-relevant capacity is based on the primary resource, while any additional capacities appear as secondary resources.	Mode with a primary resource and possibly also secondary resources
Parallel sequence of operations.	Start-start activity relationships
Alternative sequence[9] (requires a customer exit or BAdI to be activated for the transfer).	Alternative mode[10]

Table 4.5 Structure Elements of an ECC Routing and an APO PPM or PDS

Activity durations are calculated using scheduling formulas in the ECC work center (the formulas for the capacity requirement are irrelevant in this case). In ECC, these scheduling formulas, together with the default values in the routing, define the duration of the individual operation segments. In APO, the result of this scheduling is defined as a variable duration, and a fixed duration is also defined. Note that primary and secondary resources always have the same duration. The variable durations are based on the "base quantity" of the PPM or PDS, that is, on the output quantity of the finished product.

Activity durations

The following points should also be noted in relation to the transfer of production versions to APO:

Additional points to note

▶ **Output quantity**
The output quantity of the finished product, which is used, for example, as a basis for scheduling formulas, is derived from the base quantity of the BOM.

---

9 See SAP Note 217210.
10 Alternative modes can also result from a work center classification in ECC.

▶ **Direct procurement items**
Direct procurement items are transferred as stock items.

▶ **Setup keys and setup groups**
Setup keys and setup groups can be transferred to APO from the operation details screen of the ECC routing. For this purpose, the setup matrixes and setup keys, which cannot be transferred from ECC, must exist. Moreover, the setup matrix must be entered in the relevant resource in APO.

▶ **Component indicator**
The component indicator indicates the category of the component assigned to an activity, as shown below:

   ▶ M: Master output, header product of BOM

   ▶ I: Input, "normal" BOM component

   ▶ P: Phantom assembly

   ▶ O: Output (quantity produced), co-product or by-product—in other words, a component with a negative quantity (the only difference between co-products and by-products in ECC is the settlement rule, in that co-products are included in the settlement of the manufacturing order)

   ▶ N: Configurable master output, variant configuration

▶ **Phantom assemblies**
If phantom assemblies are used in the PDS, they must be explicitly selected as BOMs in the integration model (in this case, there must be no production version for the header material in the phantom BOM). If the phantom assembly is also planned as normal, it can also be transferred as a complete PDS.

Transferring a master recipe

Master recipes (PP-PI) are transferred the same way as routings. However, there are some differences at a granular level. In a master recipe, the operations represent logical groupings of phases, which are used to define the process steps to be executed. Therefore, operations, phases, and also secondary resources are all transferred to APO as operations. The phases and secondary resources each contain an activity of the same name. The formula for in-house production in the assigned ECC resource is relevant for scheduling a phase. In addition, the relationships between the phases in a planning recipe are transferred as activity relationships.

4.6 Mass Changes to APO Master Data

In the previous sections, we demonstrated how APO master data should ideally be maintained in ECC. The main points in relation to the most important types of master data are summarized below:

▸ **Product masters**
Product masters contain settings that are maintained from ECC and others that are specific to APO. Append structures for master data tables and customer exits for the CIF transfer provide simple options for maintaining also the APO specific settings in ECC. The change transfer can be executed in online mode.

▸ **Resources**
As of APO 4.0, resources can be completely maintained in ECC. If "external capacity" is used, no settings in APO are required. The change transfer can be executed in online mode.

▸ **Production data structures**
These can be maintained in ECC as of SAP APO 4.1, and as RTOs as of SAP APO 4.0. They cannot be changed later in APO. APO-specific settings are transferred using a BAdI (SAP APO 4.1) or by entering values in additional fields in ECC (as of SAP APO 5.0). The change transfer is executed periodically.

▸ **Production process models**
These contain fields that can be maintained in ECC, as well as other APO-specific fields. The change transfer is executed periodically for the ECC fields.

As you can see, data for product masters, resources, and production data structures does not have to be maintained in APO in many cases. However, other types of master data, such as transportation lanes or quota arrangements, can only be transferred in part from ECC or, in some cases, not at all.

As of SAP APO 3.1, a mass maintenance transaction is provided to simplify the maintenance of APO master data (in transaction MASS or MASSD, as with mass maintenance in ECC). This allows you to change:

Mass maintenance transaction for APO master data

▸ External procurement relationships

▸ Locations

▸ Production process models

▶ Products

▶ Quota arrangements

▶ Resources

▶ Transportation lanes

You select the master data type to be maintained according to its object type. You then select the documents to be changed by specifying values for the individual attributes of a component (for example, product masters can be selected by product name or procurement type). Finally, you define the attributes to be maintained (see Figure 4.13).

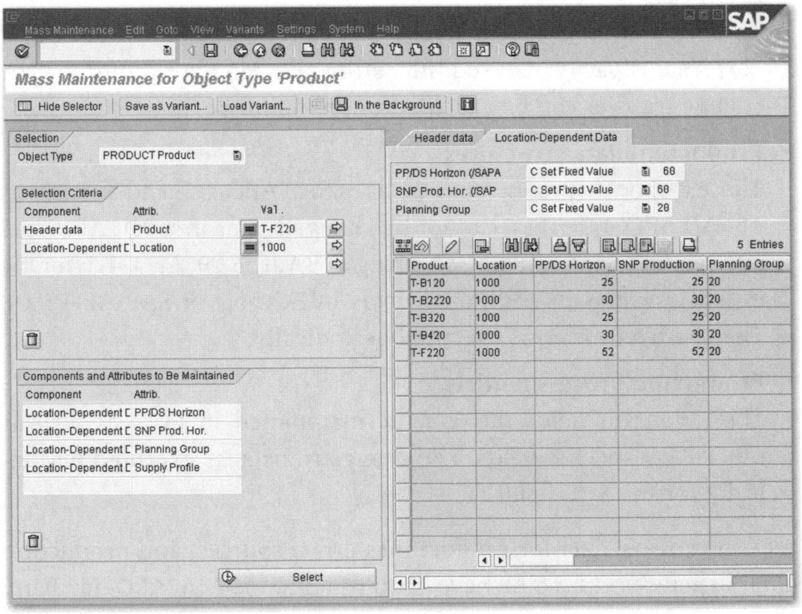

Figure 4.13 "Mass Maintenance" Transaction in APO, Transaction Code MASSD

After you have selected the master data and attributes to be changed, you can set values for the individual attributes. These values are copied to the individual master data documents, where they can be changed manually at any stage. New values can be specified for several different attributes in a single step (see Figure 4.13).

The field changes are updated when you save your changes. The changes can also be saved in the background to avoid long runtimes with large volumes of data.

Production planning with APO-PP/DS involves various functions and concepts. Understanding these functions and concepts is the key to consistent and meaningful use of production planning in APO-PP/DS.

5 Basic Functions of Production Planning

The initial approach to production planning in APO-PP/DS can be analogous to planning in ECC. Make sure that you completely understand the regular functions of ECC that are also part of PP/DS before you attempt to enhance planning with the additional options of PP/DS.

However, note that even the mapping of ECC functions in APO requires you to grasp a variety of new terms and concepts. The goal of this chapter is to explain these concepts and enable you to successfully use APO-PP/DS.

5.1 Basic Settings

The following preconditions refer to the entire system landscape. Some basic settings must also be made in customizing for APO.

5.1.1 CIF Integration

As noted in previous chapters, integration with an operational ECC system is a precondition for a useful planning process in APO-PP/DS.

The master data for planning in APO is to be transferred from an ECC system. In addition, the related transaction data should be recorded in active integration models and settings made for the transfer of results data back to ECC. The data is then available in active planning version 000.

You should also make sure that the relevant customizing settings (factory calendar, units of measure, and so on) have been transferred from ECC to APO with a transport request.

5.1.2 Global Settings

Some central settings for PP/DS are made within global settings in PP/DS customizing. In the customizing screen **Change Global Parameters and Default Values**, you must select the following settings (see Figure 5.1):

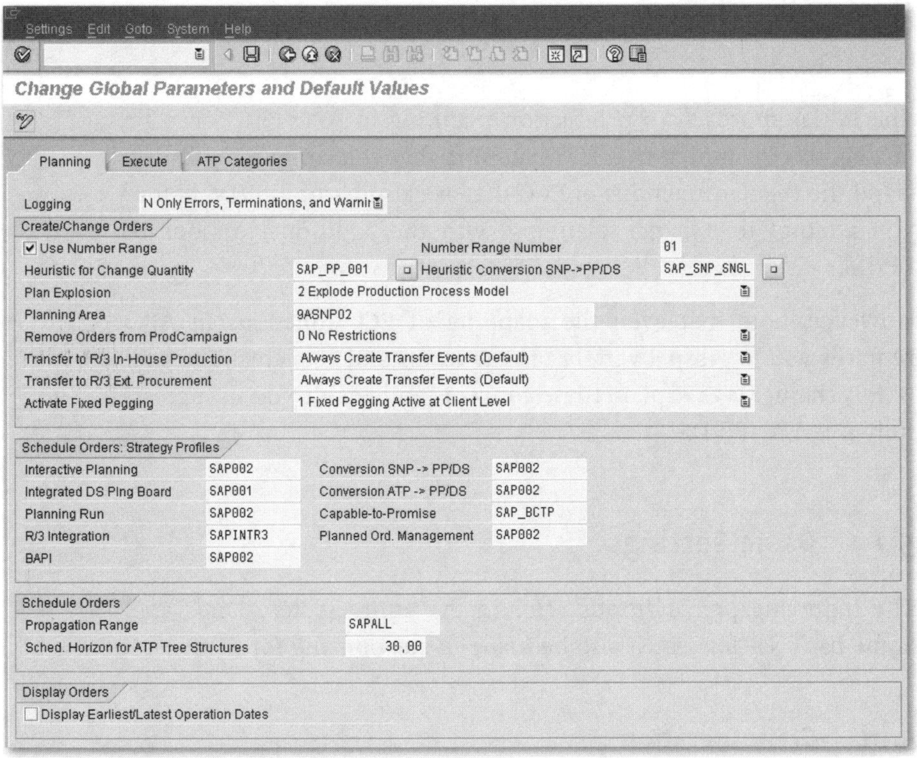

Figure 5.1 APO Customizing Screen "Change Global Parameters and Default Values" in PP/DS Customizing

▶ **Number ranges for APO orders**

This setting is optional. This setting determines if orders created in APO contain a number that corresponds to the APO number range. As soon as an order is transmitted to ECC via the CIF, it receives an order number in ECC that is based on the ECC number range. The order number is also transferred to APO.

▶ **Global heuristics and strategy profiles**
The settings made here are relevant if no other explicit settings are made within specific applications (see Sections 5.4 and 5.9.3).

▶ **Transfer of planning results to ECC**
You can define if planned orders or purchase requisitions are transferred to ECC or if the transfer occurs only after conversion in production orders or purchase orders.

You should also be aware of the ATP categories for PP/DS. They are used to define the receipt and requirement elements of production and detailed planning. They are already present in the delivery system, so you must specify a category yourself only if the executing system is not an ECC system.

Some additional basic settings that are specific to a planning version are made with Transaction **Model/Planning Version Management** (PP/DS horizon, determining the priority, and so on; see Figure 5.2).

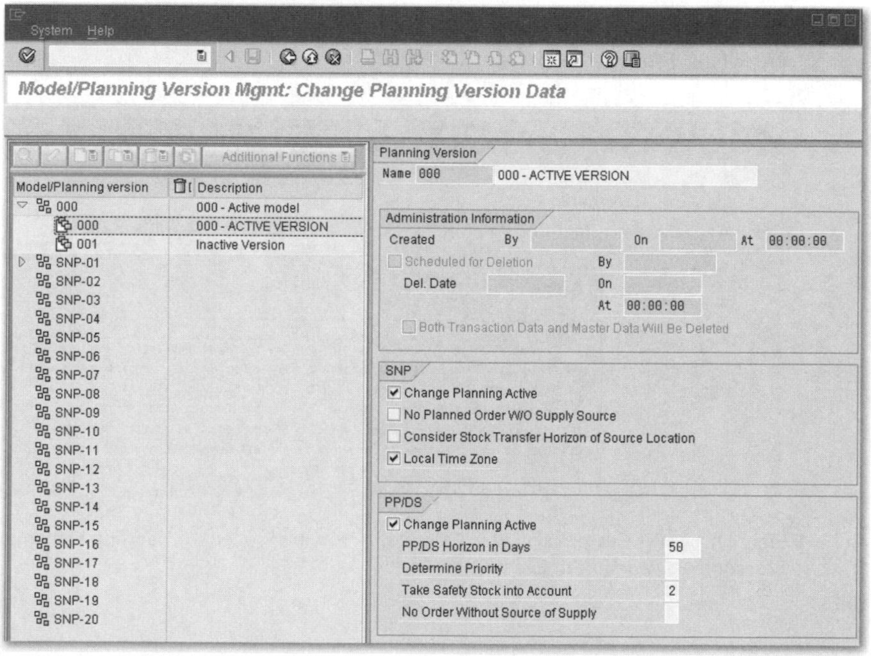

Parameters specific to a planning version

Figure 5.2 APO Transaction "Model/Planning Version Management," Transaction Code /SAPAPO/MVM, Parameters Specific to a Planning Version

Material requirements planning (MRP) distinguishes between regular MRP and consumption-based MRP. But, unlike the case with ECC,

MRP procedure

127

the APO product master does not contain a corresponding setting. Planning in APO is according to regular MRP. In any case, you can control or change the planning mechanism in APO with heuristics. Such a heuristic can be assigned to the product master and has the effect that planning occurs according to the logic defined in the heuristic (see Section 5.4.1).

In APO, you can map the reorder point method of consumption-based MRP with an appropriate heuristic. No heuristics analogous to the stochastic and rhythmical MRP familiar from ECC are present in APO, but these procedures can easily be mapped with anonymous make-to-stock production.

5.1.3   Planning Procedure

As of APO 3.1, the planning procedure determines how a product is to be planned.[1] You maintain the planning procedure in customizing (customizing screen **Maintain planning procedure** in PP/DS customizing, see Figure 5.3) and assign it to the product master in the PP/DS view (see Figure 5.4).

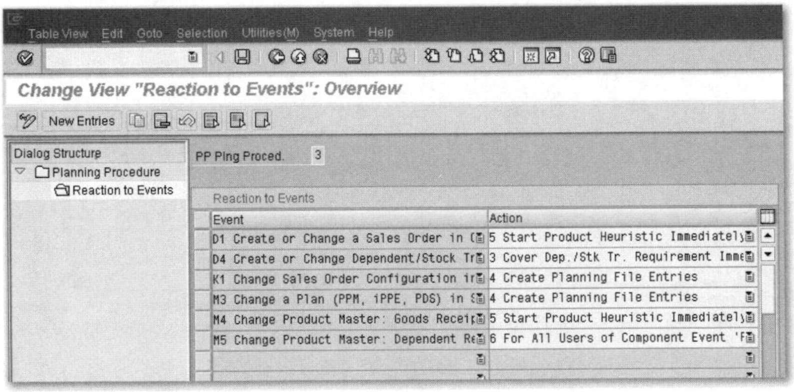

Figure 5.3 APO Customizing Step "Maintain Planning Procedure," Setting Planning Procedure 3, Reaction to Events

---

1 Up to APO 3.0, the corresponding setting is made via a selection button in the PP/DS view of the product master. The following options are available here: automatic planning in the planning run (corresponds to procedure 4), automatic planning immediately (corresponds to 3), and manual planning with/without check (1 or 2 respectively). Other settings, particularly a more exact control of the planning procedures, are not available.

When you define the planning procedure, you determine the action that should follow a specific event. Events can include **Create or change a sales order**, **New dependent requirement**, and **Change product master**. Actions can include **Generate Planning file entry**, **Start product heuristic immediately**, and so on. You can use these settings to make a very precise determination of the actions that should be executed for a product. This feature is particularly important for immediate planning. Because immediate planning requires a great deal of computer resources, it should be limited to events that are absolutely necessary so that performance is not adversely affected.

Event and reaction

The standard version contains the following four standard procedures:

Standard procedures

▶ **Planning in planning run** (procedure 4)
The product is planned in the planning run. Planning File entries are written for changes relevant to planning. This approach corresponds to the "normal" setting that defines the same behavior in ECC. It is receommended as the basic setting for all products (see Figure 5.4).

▶ **Cover dependent requirements immediately** (procedure 3)
The product is automatically planned as soon as data relevant to planning is changed (such as a new sales order or new dependent requirements). Because of its possible demand on computer resources, this procedure makes the most sense only for the Capable-to-promise (CTP) scenario and for selected products. This procedure should never be used as a standard setting for products.

▶ **Manual planning with/without check** (procedures 1 and 2)
This planning procedure makes sense only for components. In manual planning with a check, the system searches for an appropriate receipt element for the component in case of a shortage. If no timely receipt element is available, the superordinate order is created only when a receipt covers the dependent requirement. You might have to create a receipt element for the component to be able to create the superordinate order on the required date. In manual planning without a check, the component is always considered available.

> **Note**
>
> **Planning in planning run** (planning procedure 4) should always be the standard procedure for planning products in APO. It corresponds to the procedure used in ECC. When a planning-relevant change occurs, a planning file entry is written that is processed in the planning run with the planning of the product.

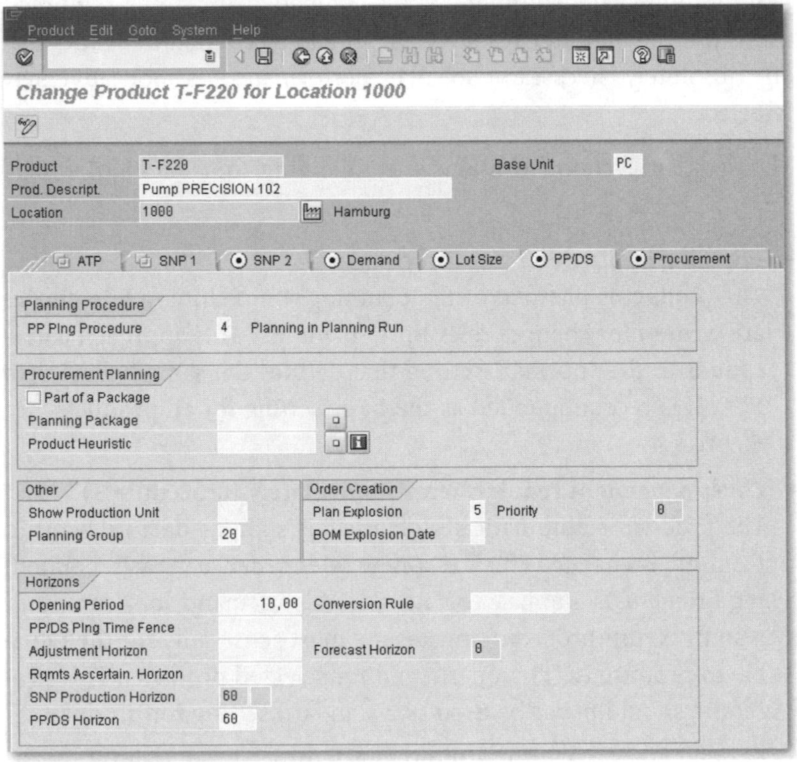

Figure 5.4 APO Transaction "Product," Transaction Code /SAPAPO/MAT1, PP/DS Tab with Planning Procedure 4

Heuristic in the planning procedure

In addition to the settings noted so far, planning procedures are also assigned a heuristic that should be used during planning of the product (see Figure 5.5). It takes effect when no other heuristic is explicitly specified in the product master (see Section 5.4.1).

Planning procedure **4** contains heuristic **SAP_PP_002**, **Planning Standard Lots**. This heuristic corresponds to the net requirements and lot-size calculation familiar from ECC.

Planning procedure **3** contains the heuristic **SAP_PP_003** (or **SAP_PP_CTP**), **Planning of Shortage Quantities**. The goal of this heuristic is to cover additional requirements in such a way that previously covered requirements remain covered. This planning flow is much more complex than the normal calculation of requirements. It is important to note that this step is executed for each individual requirement; therefore planning with this procedure can involve an enormous drain on computing resources (see Section 5.4.1).

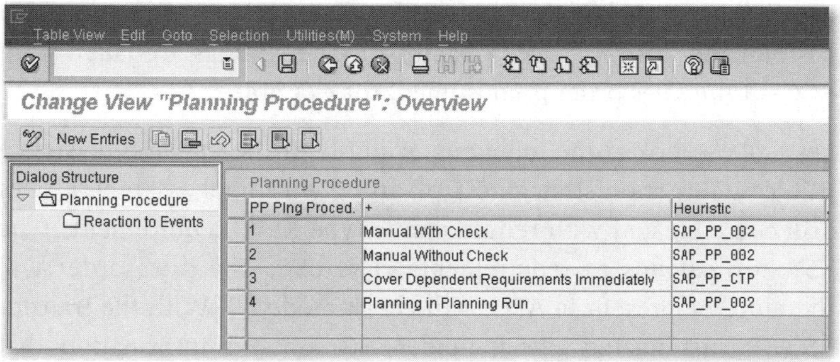

Figure 5.5 APO Customizing Screen "Maintain Planning Procedure," Heuristics of the Planning Procedures

5.2   Independent Requirements

Production planning in APO is based on independent requirements: sales orders and planned independent requirements. Typically, sales orders are transferred from ECC to APO. However, independent requirements can be transferred from ECC or created in APO. In ECC, behavior of the independent requirements is set by their requirements type, which is usually derived from the strategy group (MRP 3 view of the ECC material master) and the main strategy contained in it. APO uses a similar requirements strategy in the product master, but it affects only the planned independent requirements.

The following sections examine the operation of independent requirements in APO in more detail.

5.2.1   Sales Orders

Sales orders can be created and changed in ECC and then transferred to APO via CIF. It is impossible to maintain these documents in APO.

Check Mode

When an active integration model contains sales orders for specific materials and plants, they are transferred to APO along with the posting in ECC. The requirements type is crucial for the behavior of sales orders. In ECC, the requirements type directly corresponds to a requirements class, and the requirements class in APO corresponds to the check mode (see Figure 5.6).

ATP customizing   The appropriate check mode must be present in APO. Its presence is usually guaranteed by the CIF transfer of Available-to-Promise (ATP) customizing from ECC (see Chapter 4). The settings are taken from ECC—if the sales order is consumed, for example.

Example of planning with final assembly   Let's take a look at the following example: If the material master in ECC contains main strategy 40 (planning with final assembly), sales orders are created with requirements type KSV. Requirements type KSV corresponds to requirements class 050. The sales order will therefore be present in APO with check mode 50. With the transfer of ATP customizing, check mode 050 contains information that states that the sales order should be consumed with assignment mode 1 (with final assembly); see Section 5.2.3.

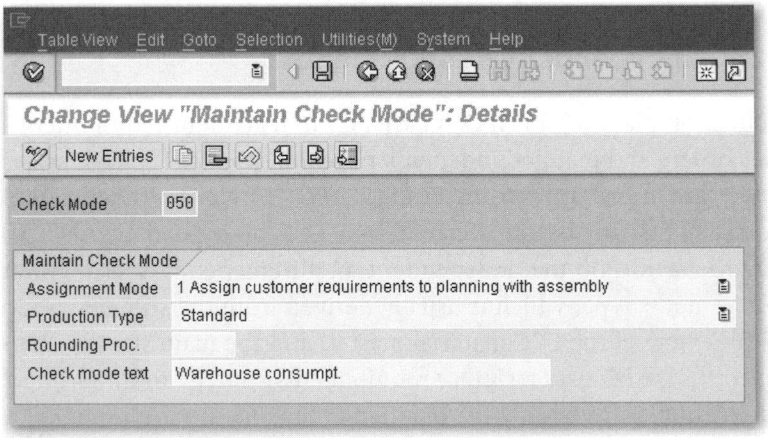

Figure 5.6 APO Customizing Screen "Maintain Check Mode" in Customizing of the Global ATP Check, Check Mode 050

Sales orders can have priorities for planning. These priorities are transferred from ECC to APO. Priorities can also be set in the product master in APO. You can set up the use of priorities in planning with model and version management.

Sales Orders as of APO 4.0 and up to APO 3.1

There are important differences between the behavior of sales orders in APO 3.1 and APO 4.0.

The behavior of sales orders as of APO 4.0 is very easy to describe: They behave just as they do in ECC. In terms of individual items, that means:

Sales orders as of APO 4.0

▸ Requested quantity and requested delivery date affect availability, irrespective of an ATP confirmation (see Figure 5.7).

▸ If a confirmed quantity and delivery date are to be used as the result of an ATP check in planning, set the sales orders with a flag for **Fixed date and quantity**.

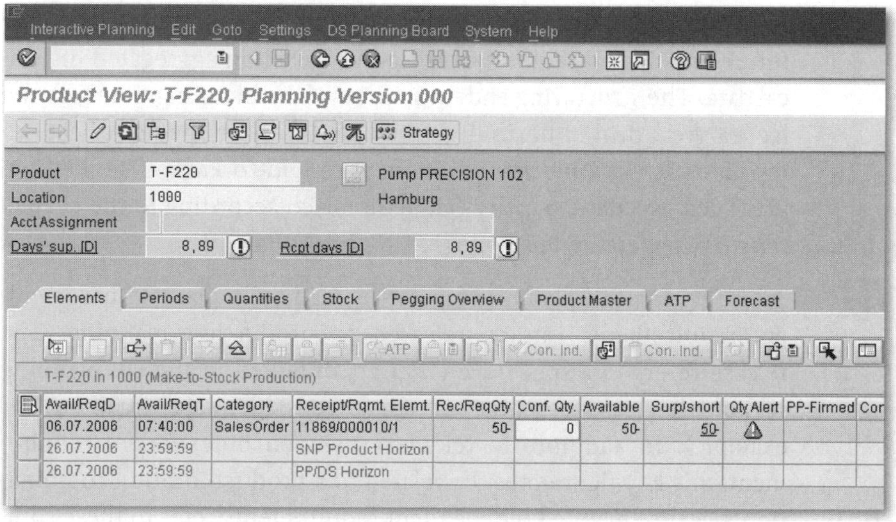

Figure 5.7 APO Transaction "Product View," Transaction Code /SAPAPO/RRP3, Sales Order in APO with a Confirmed Quantity of Zero

Up to and including APO 3.1, only the confirmed quantity of a sales order can have an effect on the available quantity in planning. Therefore, when a sales order cannot be confirmed, the confirmed quantity of zero plays no role in planning. However, you can select a setting in the APO product view to display such orders. This behavior contradicts that of ECC, where the preferred quantity has an effect on requirements.

Sales orders up to APO 3.1

When the **Fixed date and quantity** flag is set, the confirmed quantities are planned on the confirmed date, as usual.

If the preferred quantity is to be planned in APO, you can use a heuristic with an appropriate setting to do so. That's the purpose of the setting for **Use Preferred Quantity** in standard heuristic **SAP_PP_002 (Planning of Standard Lots)**.

5.2.2 Planned Independent Requirements in APO

There are many ways to obtain the planned independent requirements in APO-PP/DS. They can be released from a forecast in APO-DP, they can be transferred from ECC, and they can also be entered manually in PP/DS.

Releasing Planned Independent Requirements from APO-DP

In demand planning in APO-DP, a forecast is usually performed for future anticipated requirements figures based on aggregated historical data. The structuring and formatting of the planning numbers can have a great deal of flexibility—they are based on the use of characteristics such as **Product, Location**, and **Sold-to Party**. The key figures such as **Sales Quantity** can be itemized according to the characteristics (see Figure 5.8).

After the demand planning forecast is made, the planned independent requirements can be released to production planning. The release refers to a specific key figure contained in the DP planning session that can be set as per your needs (the sales quantity, for example). In addition, to release a planned independent requirement, this key figure must be related to a product-location combination, because planned independent requirements refer to these combinations. The planning sessions therefore normally contain the characteristics of **Product** and **Location** to create forecasts for production planning so that these relationships can be created.

The release is activated from the demand planning menu (Transaction **Release Sales Planning to SNP**). (The name of the transaction is confusing—the released requirements are also relevant for PP/DS; see Figure 5.9.) Of course, the release can also be scheduled in batch processing in the background. Maintenance of the planned independent requirements therefore occurs completely in APO; no planned independent requirements are present in ECC.

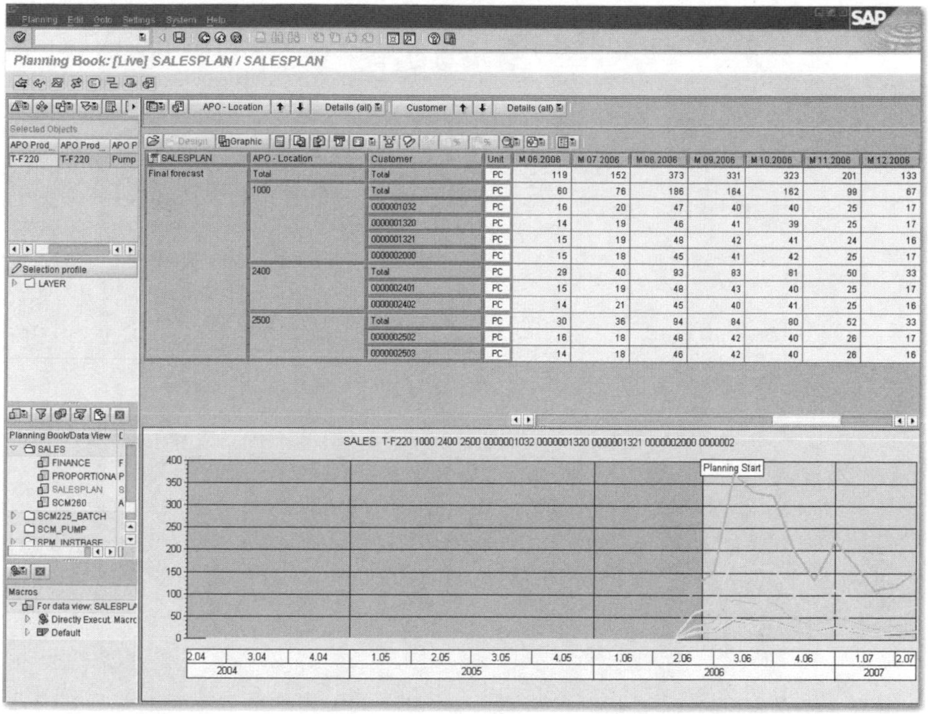

Figure 5.8 APO Transaction "Interactive Sales Planning," Transaction Code /SAPAPO/SDP94, Planning Figures with a Breakdown of the Data for a Product According to Location and Sold-To Party

Finally, note that planned independent requirements in APO-PP/DS are also generated by the entry of negative quantities, such as those in the product view. This type of procedure is mainly seen in testing, because mass maintenance of operative planned independent requirements is inappropriate in actual practice.

Negative quantities in the product view

Transfer of Planned Independent Requirements from ECC

When maintenance of the planned independent requirements for planning in APO is done in ECC, you can create the planned independent requirements as usual in ECC and transfer them to APO over the CIF. You must include the planned independent requirements for each material and plant in an active integration model. All the affected planned independent requirements are then transferred to APO. All the active planned independent requirements versions are transferred; inactive planned independent requirements are not transferred.

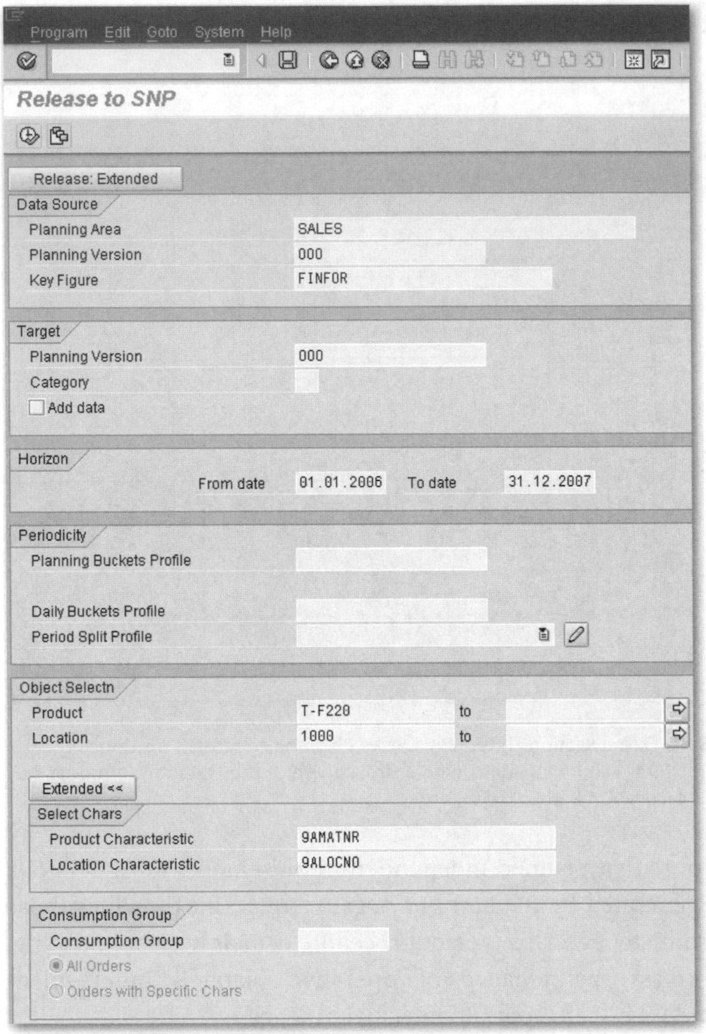

Figure 5.9 APO Transaction "Release Sales Planning to Supply Network Planning," Transaction Code /SAPAPO/MC90

Transfer from APO-DP to ECC

You can also transfer planned independent requirements from APO-DP to ECC. This kind of transfer occurs directly from APO-DP itself (Transaction **Define activities for mass processing**) rather than through the CIF. This approach makes sense when sales planning occurs in APO-DP but production planning is executed later on in ECC. Please note that planned independent requirements that were created in ECC in this manner *cannot* be transferred to APO via the

CIF. The CIF transfer is not executed for reasons of data consistency in both systems regarding the planned independent requirements— even if an active integration model contains the requirements. If the planned independent requirements created in ECC in this manner are to be transferred from ECC to APO, you must copy the requirements in ECC to another version of the active planned independent requirements. The CIF transfer then occurs as usual.

5.2.3   Requirements Strategies

The requirements strategy stored in the product master determines the behavior of the planned independent requirements in APO. The effects of a strategy result from the settings in the requirements strategy itself and from the sales order. The check mode of the sales order must be set accordingly.

The requirements strategies are defined in customizing of the APO product master. Planned independent requirements correspond to category **FA**. The logic of make-to-stock and make-to-order is defined via the planned independent requirements section. Possible consumption with or without final assembly is defined via the assignment mode. The consumption documents are set with the corresponding category group (see Figure 5.10). The category group therefore contains the list of documents against which you can consume. The standard strategies are already preset in the system as delivered.

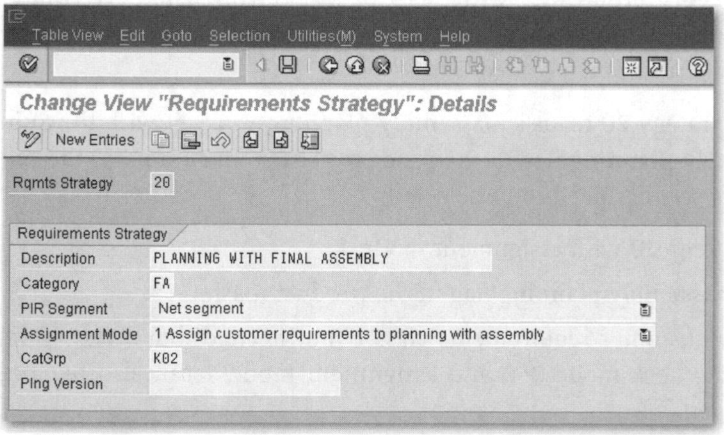

Requirements strategies in customizing

Figure 5.10 APO Customizing Screen "Set Requirements Strategy" in Customizing of a Product's Master Data, Requirements Strategy 20

Finally, the check modes of sales orders are set in ATP customizing in APO. They normally result from a transfer of ATP customizing from ECC.

Strategy 10

Anonymous make-to-stock

Strategy 10 corresponds to **anonymous make-to-stock**. Planning occurs exclusively on the basis of planned independent requirements; sales orders do not affect requirements. Planning results from the following settings:

- Strategy 10 without assignment mode
- Customer requirements class or check mode 030 without assignment mode

Strategy 20

Planning with final assembly

APO strategy 20 maps the **Planning with final assembly**. Planning occurs on the basis of planned independent requirements; sales orders affect requirements and are consumed with the planned independent requirements. Consumption occurs according to the consumption mode and consumption intervals, as set in the product master. It results from the following settings:

- Strategy 20 with assignment mode 1
- Customer requirements class or check mode 050 with assignment mode 1
- Category group K02 with sales orders (BM), customer requirements (BS), and so on. All types of sales orders that should be consumed must be included.

Subassembly planning

APO strategy 20 maps subassembly planning. It is set with the **Subassembly planning** flag in the product master. In summary, the following settings need to be selected:

- Strategy 20 with assignment mode 1
- **Subassembly planning** flag in the product master
- The customer requirements class is not needed, but sales orders with check mode 050 and assignment mode 1 can also be consumed.
- Category group K02 with independent requirements (AY) and order reservations (AZ)

Also note that the subassembly must be planned as collective requirements.

Strategy 30

Strategy 30 corresponds to **Planning without final assembly**. The planning therefore occurs without final assembly and is based on planned independent requirements. Final assembly is executed for sales orders in the individual customer section. Note that you can use the APO conversion rule concept to map the **Planning without final assembly** in various ways, some of which are better than the approach noted above.

Planning without final assembly

Forecasting without final assembly uses the following settings:

▸ Strategy 30 with assignment mode 2

▸ Customer requirements class or check mode 045 with assignment mode 2

▸ Category group K01 with sales orders (BM), customer requirements (BS), and so on. All types of sales orders that should be consumed must be included.

Conversion Rule

You can use a conversion rule to define which planned orders should be converted into manufacturing orders. During a collective conversion of planned orders using Transaction **Conversion of Orders and Purchase Requisitions**, the conversion rule lets you convert only specific orders into production orders.

Conversion rules are defined in APO customizing. For example, you can specify that only planned orders that have undergone an ATP check (confirmed orders) or that only planned orders linked to a sales order should be converted into planned orders (requirements check). In addition, you can use a BAdI for special requirements (see Figure 5.11).

If a conversion rule for a specific product is used, it is entered in the product master. You can also store a rule that applies to all products in the global parameters. Conversion rules are considered during interactive and collective conversion (see Figure 5.12). You can also override the rules manually.

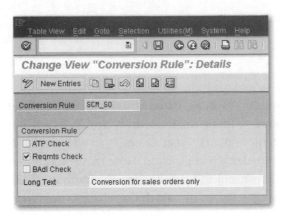

Figure 5.11 APO Customizing Screen "Maintain Conversion Rules" in PP/DS Customizing with Transfer to Execution

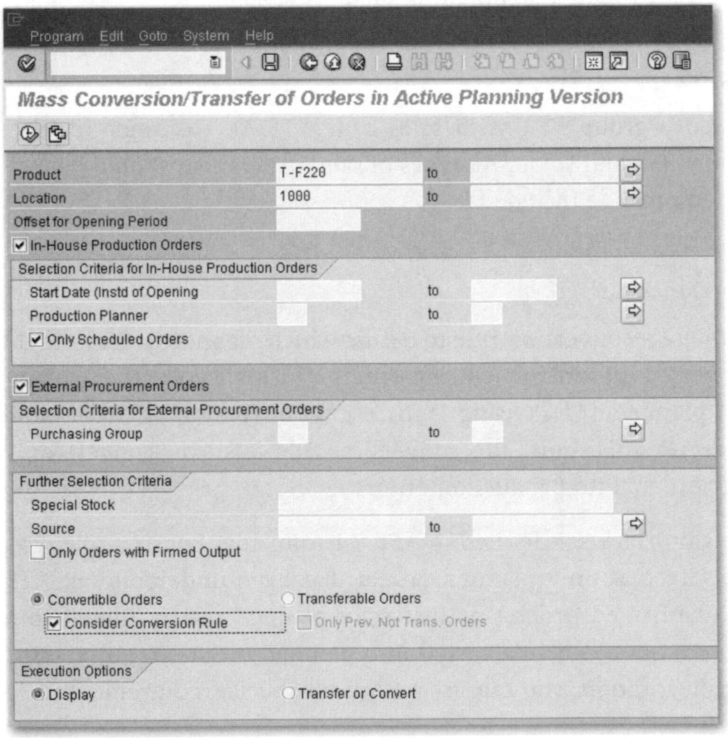

Figure 5.12 APO Transaction "Conversion of Orders/Purchase Requisitions," Transaction Code /SAPAPO/RRP7, Collective Conversion with Conversion Rule

Use for "planning without final assembly"

Conversion rules can be used in end products and in subassemblies. If you enter a conversion rule for an end product that you want to subject to a requirements check, only the planned orders linked to a sales order with pegging are converted (see Section 5.10). You can work with the subassembly and use the multi-step pegging network. The effect of working with requirements strategy 20, **Planning with final assembly**, would then correspond to **Planning without final assembly** without the individual customer section; the stocking level is set flexibly.

Strategy 40

Strategy 40 maps **Planning with planning product**. This type of planning is appropriate when various end products result from subassemblies that are virtually identical. A planning product is defined here that contains the common subassemblies. The forecast therefore occurs for the planning product and triggers the production and procurement of components for the planning product. The sales order for a final product that refers to the planning product is consumed with the forecast of the planning product and triggers procurement of the end product. The sales order for this APO strategy is contained in an individual customer planning section.

Planning with planning product

Select the following settings:

► Strategy 40 with assignment mode 3

► Customer requirements class or check mode 060 with assignment mode 3

► Category group K01 with sales orders (BM), customer requirements (BS), and so on. All types of sales orders that should be consumed must be included.

► You must select planning products separately in the integration model. A planning product is created in the product hierarchy in APO as the uppermost node to assign the material of the planning product to the end products. An entry is made in the ECC material master of the end product.

Make-to-Order Production without Forecast

No requirements strategy for make-to-order production without forecast is needed in APO. The sales orders with the corresponding check mode are simply transferred to APO.

The logic of make-to-order production is inherited by the structure of the bill of materials (BOM) to the point that the **Poss. individual customer requirement** is present in the product masters of the subassemblies and components. The **Always collective requirements** flag works the opposite way. Collective procurement in make-to-stock is switched on for a subassembly and its entire procurement branch.

5.2.4 Reducing Planned Independent Requirements

Generally, planned independent requirements are reduced by goods-issue postings in ECC inventory management. During anonymous make-to-stock production, the planned independent requirements are consumed according to the first-in, first-out (FIFO) rule. With the remaining strategies, the planned independent requirements are consumed analogously to consumption by issuing goods to the sales order or, for subassemblies, to the manufacturing order.

In addition to such normal reductions of planned independent requirements, you must also explicitly delete or reorganize the remaining requirements.

▶ **Planned independent requirements from ECC**
You must reorganize requirements in ECC (Transactions MD74, MD75, and MD76) for planned independent requirements that were created in ECC and transferred to APO. The planned independent requirements are deleted in ECC via these three reorganization steps.

▶ **Planned independent requirements from APO**
Planned independent requirements that were created in APO (by releasing requirements from APO-DP, for example) are to be adjusted in APO. You can use the APO Transaction **Planning adjustment** (Transaction Code /SAPAPO/MD74, see Figure 5.13). It is similar to ECC. Adjustment means deleting the planned independent requirements.[2]

---

2 In APO, the actual adjustment function can be executed via heuristic **SAP_PP_ 015, Adjusting Orders and Pl. Ind. Requirements**.

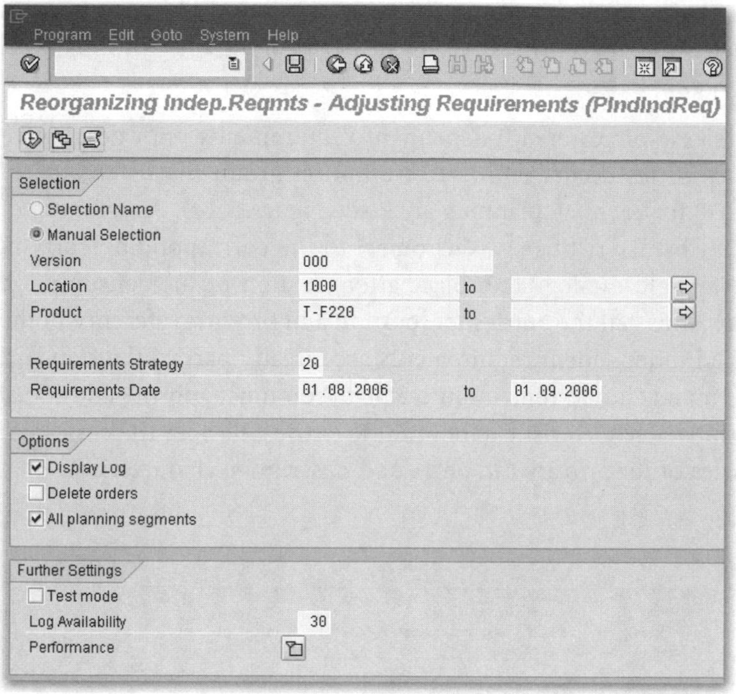

Figure 5.13 APO Transaction "Planning Adjustment," Transaction Code /SAPAPO/MD74, Reorganizing the Forecast

5.2.5 Descriptive Characteristics

Planned independent requirements refer to combinations of products and locations. The same applies when the forecast in APO-DP contains the sold-to party as a characteristic in the planning session. During the forecast with final assembly (requirements strategy 20), for example, the forecast contains the sum of the expected sales order quantities for all sold-to parties per period.

With the use of descriptive characteristics during the release of planned independent requirements from APO-DP, you can release planned independent requirements to individual customers. Instead of an overall quantity for a period in one location product, several subsets are generated for the same date. Each subset can then be consumed only with sales orders of the respective customer. You can therefore use descriptive characteristics to ensure that specific contingents (allocations) remain for individual customers—even when unexpectedly high levels of sales orders come in from other sold-to parties.

Descriptive characteristic: Customer

The descriptive characteristics are not passed on to the procurement elements (planned orders). You can perform an analysis only with the pegging links.

Consumption group The release of planned independent requirements with descriptive characteristics occurs with a consumption group that is created in APO-DP for each DP planning area (see Figure 5.14). Assignment of the DP characteristic (e.g., **Customer**) to the corresponding entry in the ATP field catalog takes place after creation of the consumption group. Note that the entries for location and product reference of the planned independent requirements are already part of the standard version and should remain untouched. You must add the additional descriptive characteristic to both these entries. Besides the customer, the sales order priority can be a good descriptive characteristic.

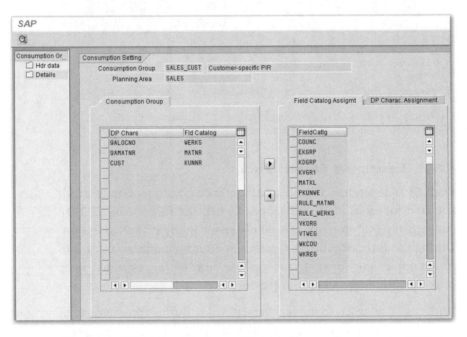

Figure 5.14 APO Customizing Screen "Maintain Consumption Group" in DP Customizing, Transaction Code /SAPAPO/CSP1

You must enter the consumption group in the affected product master. Release with the use of descriptive characteristics occurs with the additional specification of the consumption group when executing the transaction (**Extended data** for object selection, see Figure 5.15). Only the products with a consumption group in the product master are released when using descriptive characteristics.

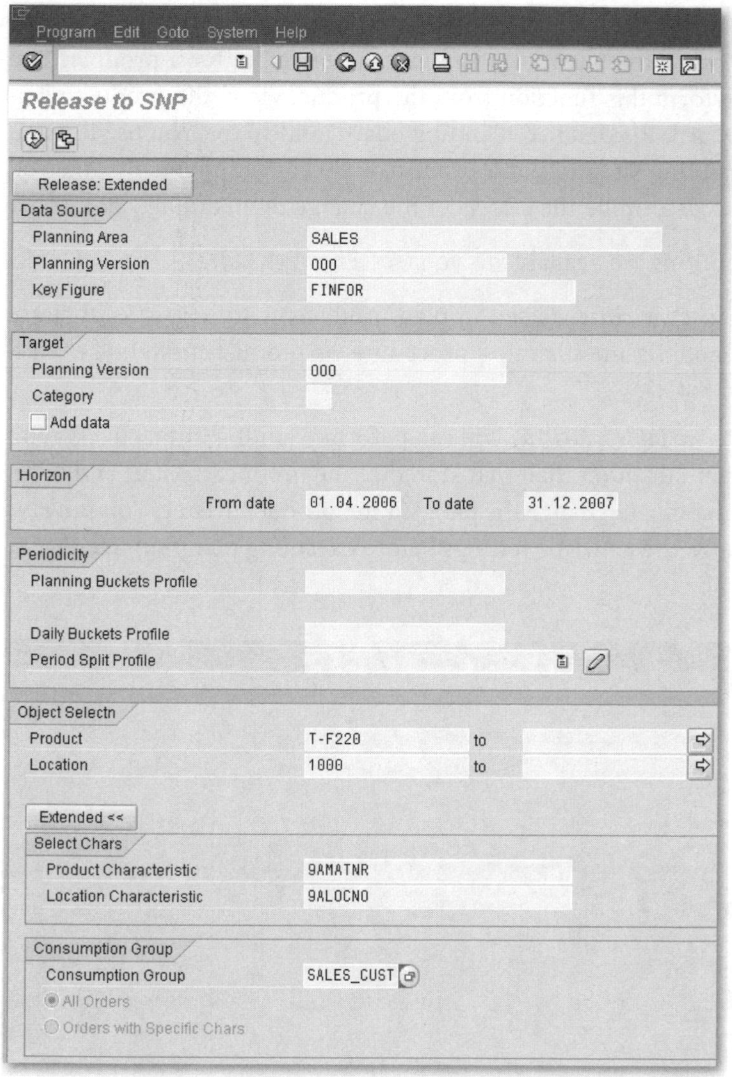

Figure 5.15 APO Transaction "Release Sales Planning to Supply Network Planning," Transaction Code /SAPAPO/MC90, Release with Consumption Group

5.3 The Planning Procedure

Product planning in APO-PP/DS can occur in two ways: first, as interactive individual planning for a product; second, as total planning for a group of products that can be freely defined (such as all products from a given plant). Total planning can occur online or in background processing.

5.3.1 Interactive Planning

With interactive planning, you execute planning for a product. You can perform this function from the product view, the product planning board, the detailed planning board, and so on. You use it when the planning situation of a product was changed manually and you want to determine the effects of the change on planning right away.

Product heuristic and variable heuristic

Two options are available to you (see Figure 5.16):

▶ *Product heuristic* is used to plan products with heuristics that are defined via the planning procedure or product masters (see Section 5.4.1).

▶ *With variable heuristic*, you can peform planning interactively with a heuristic other than that stored in the product master, and without having to change the entry in the product master. You can also change the heuristic settings before executing planning (see Figure 5.17).

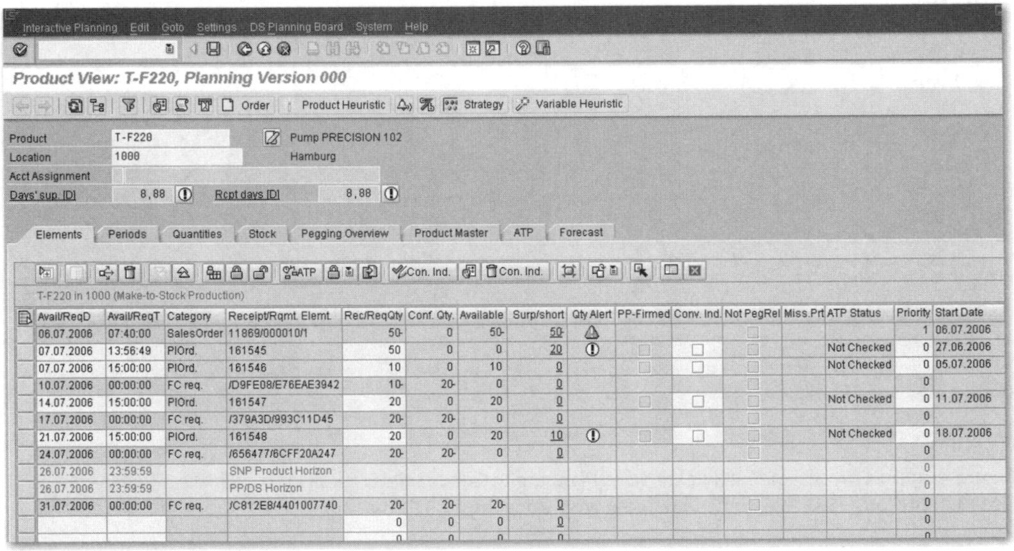

Figure 5.16 APO Transaction "Product View," Transaction Code /SAPAPO/RRP3, Product View with Buttons for Interactive Planning

In any case, note that execution of the heuristic first treats data only in a transactional simulation. The data is written to the database only when you save the planning results.

You use the heuristic profile (customizing of production and detailed planning) to define which variable heuristics can be selected. Three standard heuristic profiles are available: profile **SAP001** for the detailed planning board, **SAP002** for the product view, and **SAPREM** for the product-planning table. Each profile contains the typical heuristics for each context. If you want to make an additional heuristic available for interactive planning, you must expand the assigned heuristic profiles in the related transactions or use a different profile that contains the heuristic.

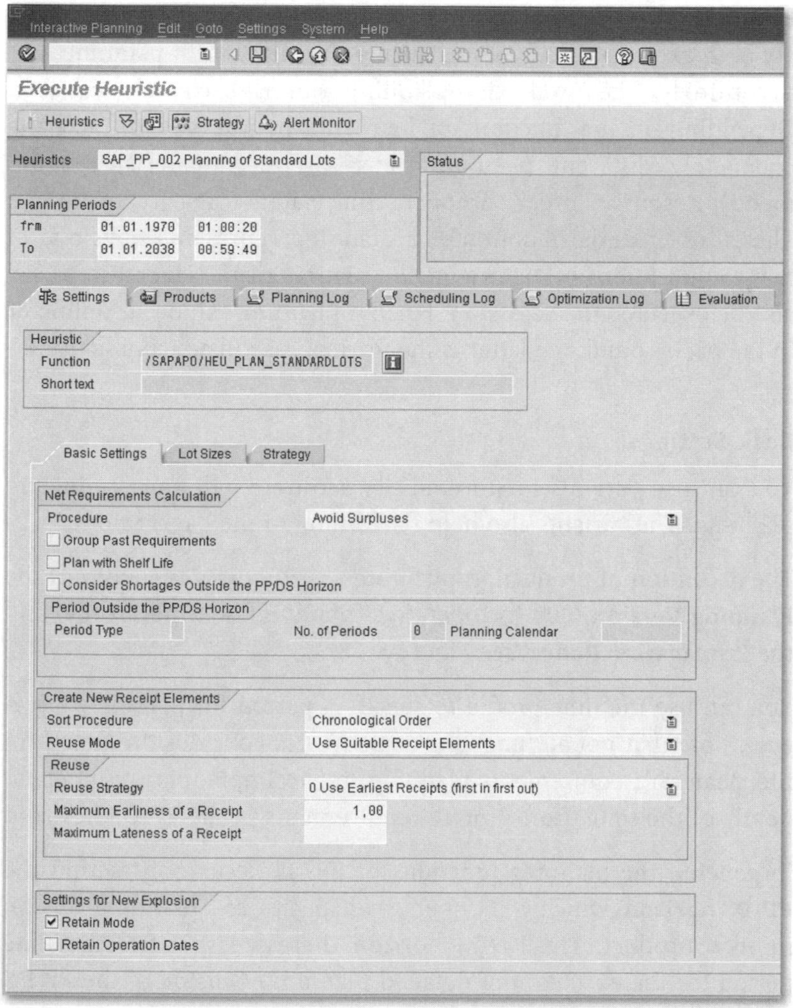

Heuristic profile

Figure 5.17 APO Transaction "Product View," Transaction Code /SAPAPO/RRP3, Calling the Variable Heuristic

Based on the potential complexity of a given planning situation, it is not always easy to estimate the effects of various heuristics or heuristics settings on planning. As a general rule, therefore, it makes more sense to work with a small selection of the available heuristics than it does to work with a selection that is too large. It can also make sense to avoid the use of variable heuristics completely in the product view.

5.3.2 Production Planning Run

Planning for groups of products and total planning for entire plants are both executed in APO-PP/DS using the production-planning run. Accordingly, the production-planning run is extremely variable. Depending on the functions or heuristics in use, you can execute completely different planning steps: product (material requirements), resource, order, or operation-related (capacity) planning. Therefore, material requirements planning represents only one of many applications of the production planning run. Several steps can also be executed in succession. Finally, planning can occur online or in the background; the latter is the normal case in actual practice.

Basic Settings

You can use variants to store all the settings to define production planning. The variants also help scheduling in the background.[3]

The definition of production planning first requires the entry of the **Planning Version** (**000** for operative planning), a **Time Profile**, and the **Propagation Range** (see Figure 5.18).

Time profile
You can use the time profile to specify a period for planning. However, note that not all functions or heuristics consider the time profile. Material requirements planning, for example, occurs independently of the time profile for all requirements in the PP/DS horizon.

PP/DS horizon
In general, the planning functions of PP/DS occur only within the **PP/DS horizon**, which you can enter as specific to a planning version or to a product. The PP/DS horizon therefore specifies the time period for the execution of detailed planning. Outside of the PP/DS

---

3 The layout of the production-planning run was completely revised in APO 5.0.

planning period, you can perform aggregated planning in the context of APO-SNP.[4]

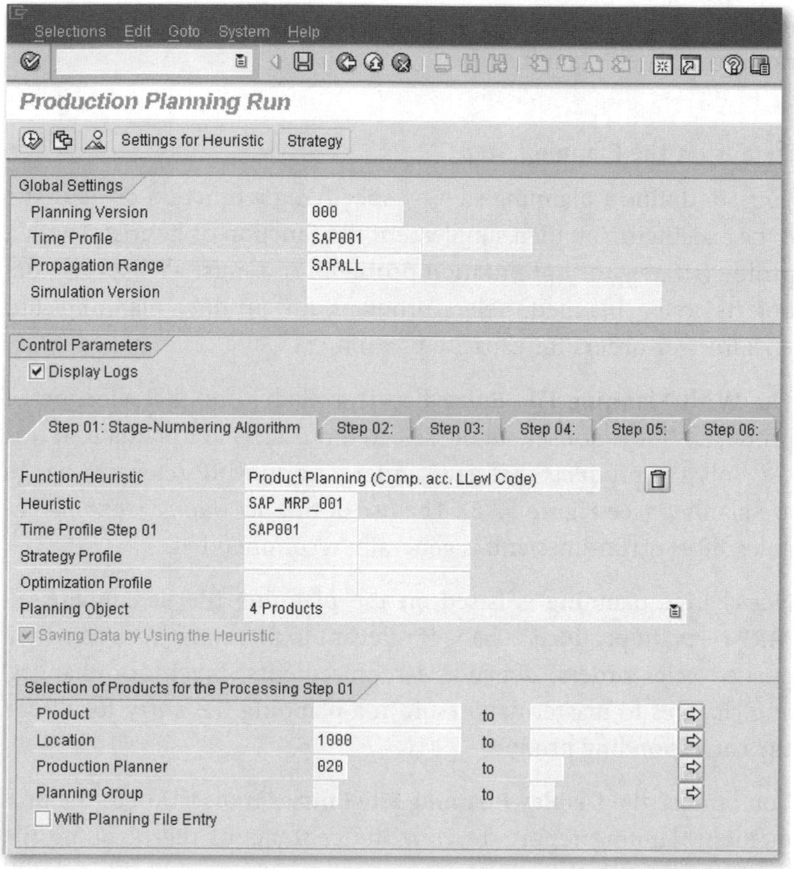

Figure 5.18 APO Transaction "Production Planning Run," Transaction Code /SAPAPO/CDPSB0

The propagation range defines the resources and products that can be planned in production and detailed planning. Propagation range **SAPALL** permits the planning of all resources and products. Propagation ranges are defined in the customizing screen **Maintain Propagation Range**.

Propagation range

---

4 The SNP planning horizon indicates from which point in time SNP planning is carried out. The PP/DS horizon and SNP planning horizon can be set so that they overlap.

The products of the propagation range are relevant to product-related planning. Planning can be changed only for products of the propagation range. For example, orders can be created only for these products. The resources of the propagation range are relevant to resource-related planning.

Details on the Planning Steps

You can define a planning step by specifying a function or heuristic to be executed. You then supplement the function or heuristic with a profile (strategy or optimization profile).[5] You must also specify the objects to be planned. Select products for product planning and resources or orders for capacity planning.

Selecting products   The **With Planning File Entry** flag is available for the selection of products. If it is not set, all the selected products are planned. If it is set, only the products that have undergone an MRP-relevant change are planned (see Figure 5.18). The use of this *net change planning* enables shorter runtimes and is generally recommended.

Planning file   Net change planning is based on the planning file; it contains all MRP-relevant products. Changes relevant to planning, such as newly created sales orders, dependent requirements, inventory changes, and changes to master data result in a planning file entry for PP for the corresponding product.

You can use the **Display Planning File Entries** transaction in the production planning reports to view the contents of the planning file (see Figure 5.19). You can also set planning entries manually in individual cases.[6]

Low-level code   The planning file also contains the low-level code of the product. The low-level code is the deepest level at which a product appears in any PPM/PDS. Low-level codes are assigned across all locations.

The low-level code is used to control the sequence of planning. During product planning, products with low-level code 0 are planned

---

5   In contrast to a function, a heuristic can be influenced using control parameters.
6   If you set the **Generate Pegging Areas** flag, you can cause the pegging areas to be generated without planning the respective location products. The pegging areas are usually generated when an order is created for the first time (in this context, stocks, planned independent requirements, and so on, are considered as orders); therefore this step is only necessary in exceptional cases.

first, followed by low-level code 1, and so on. One run therefore plans all products in the correct sequence.[7]

PlFlEnPPDS	Product	Location	S	AcAssgtObj	PlngSegTyp	Prod.Plnnr	PP/DSLwLvC	SNPLLvlC	PlFlEntSNP	PlFlEntBOP
3	T-B120	1000				020	1	2	X	X
3	T-B2220	1000				020	1	0	X	X
3	T-B2320	1000				020	1	0	X	X
3	T-B2420	1000				020	1	0	X	X
3	T-B320	1000				020	1	2	X	X
3	T-B420	1000				020	1	0	X	X
1	T-F220	1000				020	0	1	X	X
3	T-F320	1000				020	0	1	X	X
3	T-F420	1000				020	0	1	X	X
1	T-T020	1000				020	1	0	X	X
1	T-T120	1000				020	2	3	X	X
1	T-T220	1000				020	2	0	X	X
1	T-T420	1000				020	2	3	X	X
1	T-T520	1000				020	2	0	X	X

Planning File Entry for PP/DS (1)   5 Entries Found

Planning File Entry for PP/...	Short text
	No Planning File Entry
1	Use Suitable Receipt Elements
2	Delete Unfixed Receipts
3	Reexplode Plan
4	Delete Unfixed Receipts, Explode Fixed Receipts Again

5 Entries Found

Figure 5.19 APO Transaction "Display Planning File," Transaction Code /SAPAPO/RRP_NETCH, Planning Reservations for PP/DS

Note

Note the following differences between APO and ECC regarding the low-level codes: Low-level codes in APO are *not* recalculated automatically for changes to master data. Instead, you must perform a recalculation explicitly with heuristic **SAP_PP_020** (stage-numbering algorithm). Accordingly, we recommend that you begin the first step with heuristic **SAP_PP_020** or execute it regularly (weekly, for example; see Section 5.5).

---

7 The case of recursive BOMs is taken into account here.

Planning groups
(as of APO 4.0)

Available as of APO 4.0, the planning group is another grouping and selection criterion for products. You define a planning group in customizing of PP/DS; you assign a product to a planning group in the product master.

5.3.3 Capable-to-Match (CTM)

The capable-to-match (CTM) procedure is an alternate form of planning that is not based on the production planning run or heuristics. It is a planning procedure in APO-SNP that can also be used in PP/DS in appropriate cases.

Principle of
CTM planning

The CTM procedure supports simultaneous quantity and capacity planning with which previously prioritized requirements are compared to permitted stocks and receipt elements. The requirements can be prioritized according to any criteria you wish: customer, product, due date, and so on. Requirements coverage then occurs with a rules-based search process that can include the definition of multiple levels and plants. For example, if your own plant cannot cover the requirements for a component, you can check to see if the product is available in another location and then perform a stock transfer in a timely manner. Planning then generally occurs in consideration of production capacities and component availability. You must also decide ahead of time if manufacturing receipt elements may be created in the context of CTM planning.

Flow of
CTM planning

CTM planning occurs according to the following schema: The requirements with the highest priority are covered first; the previously defined, rules-based search process is run for these requirements. If the requirements can be covered, the first solution found is used. Otherwise, a check is run to see if delayed coverage is possible. If the check is unsuccessful, a check is run to see if a partial delivery is permitted and possible. If no solution is found, the requirement remains uncovered and the next requirement is checked, and so on.

Note that CTM planning does consider planning parameters like priorities and quotations, but considers them as soft, marginal conditions. They are kept only *if possible*. Also, the CTM procedure does not have an optimizing character because it generally uses the first workable solution that it finds.

5.4 Heuristics

A *heuristic* is a planning function that can be parameterized and that can be used to execute planning or a planning step for selected objects. The planning objects of heuristics can be products, resources, orders, or operations.

The concept of heuristics is a central concept in planning with APO-PP/DS. A number of planning steps are executed by heuristics. Accordingly, the planning steps can be easily designed variably—by selecting the appropriate heuristic. In ECC, however, the planning run is usually fixed. Changes to the run require a modification. In APO-PP/DS, you simply have to select a different heuristic or create a new heuristic that then simply becomes part of the overall process.

> **Note**
>
> The heuristics solve different tasks. Note that not all heuristics can be substituted for each other. Instead, heuristics fall into various groups. The heuristics of a given group can be used for the same task or issue—they therefore represent different alternatives.

The standard version of APO includes numerous heuristics for various tasks related to production planning and detailed scheduling. The heuristics are stored in PP/DS customizing (see Figure 5.20). A heuristic is defined by an algorithm that can be influenced by control parameters specific to it. You can therefore create a new heuristic by copying an existing heuristic and then modifying the control parameters as you wish. You can also create completely new algorithms that you program yourself and incorporate them to the SCM system (see Appendix).

Definition in customizing

> **Note**
>
> Customizing contains comprehensive documentation on individual heuristics. Please see the documentation to learn about the functions provided by a specific heuristic.

Heuristic	Short Description	Algorithm	
SAP001	Schedule Sequence	/SAPAPO/HEUR_PLAN_SEQUENCE	
SAP002	Remove Backlog	/SAPAPO/HEUR_RESOLVE_BACKLOG	
SAP003	Schedule Sequence Manually	/SAPAPO/HEUR_PLAN_SEQUENCE_MAN	
SAP004	Minimize Runtime	/SAPAPO/HEUR_REDUCE_LEADTIME	
SAP005	Schedule Operations	/SAPAPO/HEUR_DISPATCH	
SAP_CDPBP_01	Reschedule Blocks	/SAPAPO/MC01_HEU_BLOCKS_SCHED	
SAP_CDPBP_02	Adjust and Reschedule Block Limits	/SAPAPO/MC01_HEU_BLOCK_ADJUST	
SAP_CDPBP_03	Enhanced Block Maintenance	/SAPAPO/BLRG_HEUR_BLK_MAINT	
SAP_CDPBP_04	Block Maintenance, Called Interactively	/SAPAPO/MC01_R05_RES_EDIT_HEUR	
SAP_CDS_A01	Admissibility OK Without Check	/SAPAPO/HEU_CDS_ADMI_OK_WO_CHK	
SAP_CDS_A02	Tolerance Check	/SAPAPO/HEU_CDS_TOLCHK_LCDDS	
SAP_CDS_F01	Confirm Compliance Without Check	/SAPAPO/HEU_CDS_MATCHING_CONF	
SAP_CDS_F02	Days' Supply Check	/SAPAPO/HEU_CDS_DSUP_CHK	
SAP_CDS_F03	Product Heuristic w. Days' Supply Check	/SAPAPO/HEU_CDS_PHEU_DSUP_CHK	
SAP_CHECK_01	Check PDS	/SAPAPO/CULL_PDS_CHECK_HEUR	
SAP_DS_01	Stable Forward Scheduling	/SAPAPO/SFW_HEUR_FW_STABLE	
SAP_DS_02	Enhanced Backward Scheduling	/SAPAPO/SFW_HEUR_BW_EXT	
SAP_DS_03	Change Fixing/Planning Intervals	/SAPAPO/HEUR_REL_FIXINT_MAINT	
SAP_DS_04	Activate Seq.-Dependent Setup Activities	/SAPAPO/HEUR_ACTIVATE_SETUPACT	
SAP_LEN_001	Length-Based Heuristic	/SAPAPO/EOGL_LENGTH_01	
SAP_LEN_002	Manual Creation of LOP Order	/SAPAPO/EOGLM_HEUR	
SAP_MLO_BU	Multi-Level, Order-Related - Bottum-Up	/SAPAPO/HEU_MLO_PLANNING	
SAP_MLO_TD	Multi-Level, Order-Related - Top-down	/SAPAPO/HEU_MLO_PLANNING	
SAP_MMP_HFW1	Model Mix Planning Run 1	/SAPAPO/SEQ_MODELMIX_RUN_01	
SAP_MOP_001	Multiple Output Planning Heuristic	/SAPAPO/EOG_HEU_PLAN_MOP	
SAP_MOP_002	Manual Creation of MOP Order	/SAPAPO/EOGM_HEUR	
SAP_MRP_001	Product Planning (Comp. acc. LLevl Code)	/SAPAPO/HEU_MRP_PLANNING	
SAP_MRP_002	Product Planning (Plan Comp. Immdiately)	/SAPAPO/HEU_MRP_PLANNING	
SAP_PCM_CRT	Create Production Campaigns	/SAPAPO/HEUR_PCM_CREATE	
SAP_PCM_DIS	Dissolve Production Campaigns	/SAPAPO/HEUR_PCM_DISSOLVE	
SAP_PCM_ODEL	Delete Setup/Clean-Out Orders	/SAPAPO/HEUR_PCM_ORDERS_DELETE	
SAP_PCM_SRVA	Create Setup/Clean-Out Orders	/SAPAPO/HEUR_PCM_SERVICE_ADAPT	
SAP_PI_001	Merge Orders (Container Resources)	/SAPAPO/HEUR_MERGE_ORDERS	
SAP_PMAN_001	Critical Path	/SAPAPO/PMAN_HEUR_CRIT_PATH	
SAP_PMAN_002	Infinite Forward Scheduling	/SAPAPO/PMAN_HEUR_FW_COMPACT	
SAP_PMAN_003	Infinite Backward Scheduling	/SAPAPO/PMAN_HEUR_BW	
SAP_PP_001	Change Order Manually	/SAPAPO/HEU_ORDER_CHANGE	

Figure 5.20 APO Customizing Screen "Maintain Heuristics" in PP/DS Customizing, Transaction Code /SAPAPO/CDPSC11, Complete List of Heuristics

5.4.1 Product Heuristics

Product heuristics define the planning of a product. They can be entered explicitly in the **PP/DS** tab in the product master. If no entry is present in the product master, the standard heuristic of the planning procedure is used.

Typical Product Heuristics

Table 5.1 lists some typical product heuristics.

Heuristic	Short description
SAP_PP_002	**Planning of Standard Lots**: "Normal" planning of the product based on the lot size stored in the product master
SAP_PP_003	**Planning of Shortage Quantities**: Planning only of shortage quantities; exisiting orders remain as is. Relevant for CTP.
SAP_PP_004	**Planning of Standard Lots in Three Horizons**: Planning with various lot sizes in three time horizons
SAP_PP_005	**Part-Period Balancing**: Optimizing lot-sizing procedure
SAP_PP_013	**Groff Procedure**: Optimizing lot-sizing procedure
SAP_PP_007	**Reorder Point Planning**: Reorder point planning with a reorder point from the product master
SAP_PP_C001	**Planning of Standard Lots for Conti-I/O**: Planning that considers continuous input/output in PDS/PPM

Table 5.1 Typical Product Heuristics

Heuristic **SAP_PP_002, Planning of Standard Lots**, is particularly important. It corresponds to the normal planning of a product with use of the lot size defined in the product master. It is the standard heuristic in planning procedure 4, **Planning in the Planning Run**, and therefore represents the normal case for product planning.

Planning standard lots

In heuristic **SAP_PP_002**, you can set a reuse mode (for new planning or change planning, for example). If nothing is specified, the reuse mode from the planning file is used.

With heuristic **SAP_PP_003, Planning of Shortage Quantities**, only new shortage quantities with new procurement proposals are filled. The entire product is not replanned. Planning procedure 3, **Cover Dependent Requirements Immediately**, contains this procedure; it is relevant only for CTP. The goal of this heuristic is to cover additional requirements in such a way that previously covered requirements remain covered. Therefore, it runs according to the following schema:

Planning of shortage quantities

1. The shortage is calculated with the new requirement.

2. A procurement element for the calculated deficit is created.

3. The surplus (because of the new procurement element) is calculated, and the new requirement is created on the surplus.

4. If needed, a last step reduces the surplus.

This flow is quite different from the normal, one-level, and individual planning of a product according to **Planning of Standard Lots**.

Lot-sizing procedures and reorder point planning

Appropriate heuristics can be created for special lot-sizing procedures that go beyond the options for the lot-size setting in the product master. The approach of creating appropriate heuristics also includes various optimizing lot-sizing procedures for which cost optimization for storage and ordering costs is executed. You must store the related cost functions in the product master. Finally, you can also map reorder point planning in APO-PP/DS with an appropriate heuristic.

To some extent, special planning functions are also addressed with product heuristics. For example, if you want to plan using the function of continuous input and output on PPM/PDS, you can do so with the corresponding heuristic in the product master.

> **Note**
>
> Product heuristics help plan a product. They are assigned to a product via the planning procedure or specified explicitly in the product master. Normal planning of a product with the lot sizes defined in the product master occurs with heuristic **SAP_PP_002**. Special lot-sizing procedures or special planning procedures can be realized via alternate product heuristics.

Lot Sizes and Strategy Settings

As of APO 4.0, you can set the lot size in the relevant product heuristics either in the product master or in the heuristic itself. By default, the related flag is not set; therefore the lot size from the product master is used (see Figure 5.21).

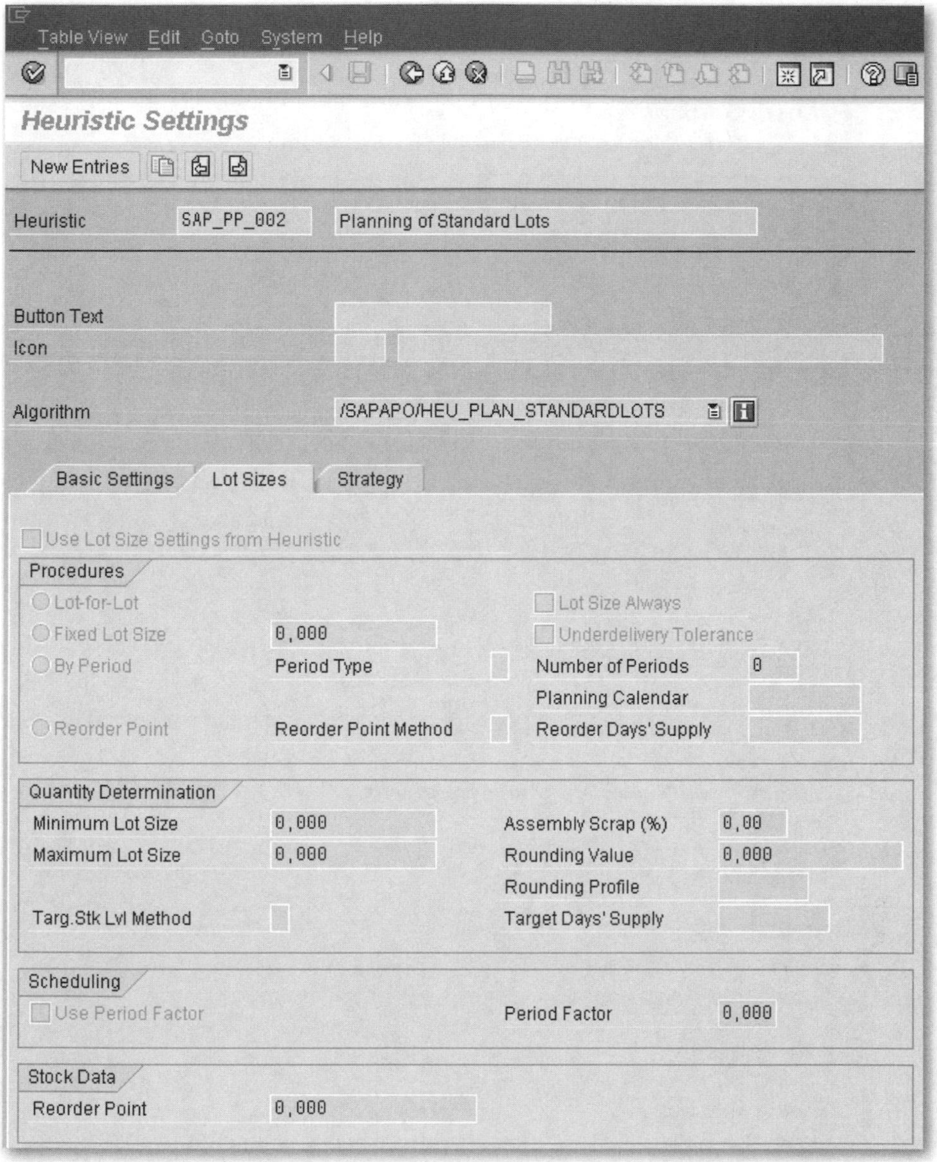

Figure 5.21 APO Customizing Screen "Maintain Heuristics," Transaction Code /SAPAPO/CDPSC11, Heuristic SAP_PP_002 with "Lot Sizes" Tab

As of APO 4.0, PP heuristics also contain all strategy parameters needed for planning in the **Strategy** tab (see Figure 5.22). In a production-planning run, products are planned with the heuristics assigned to them—that is, with the strategy settings given here (see Section 5.9.3).

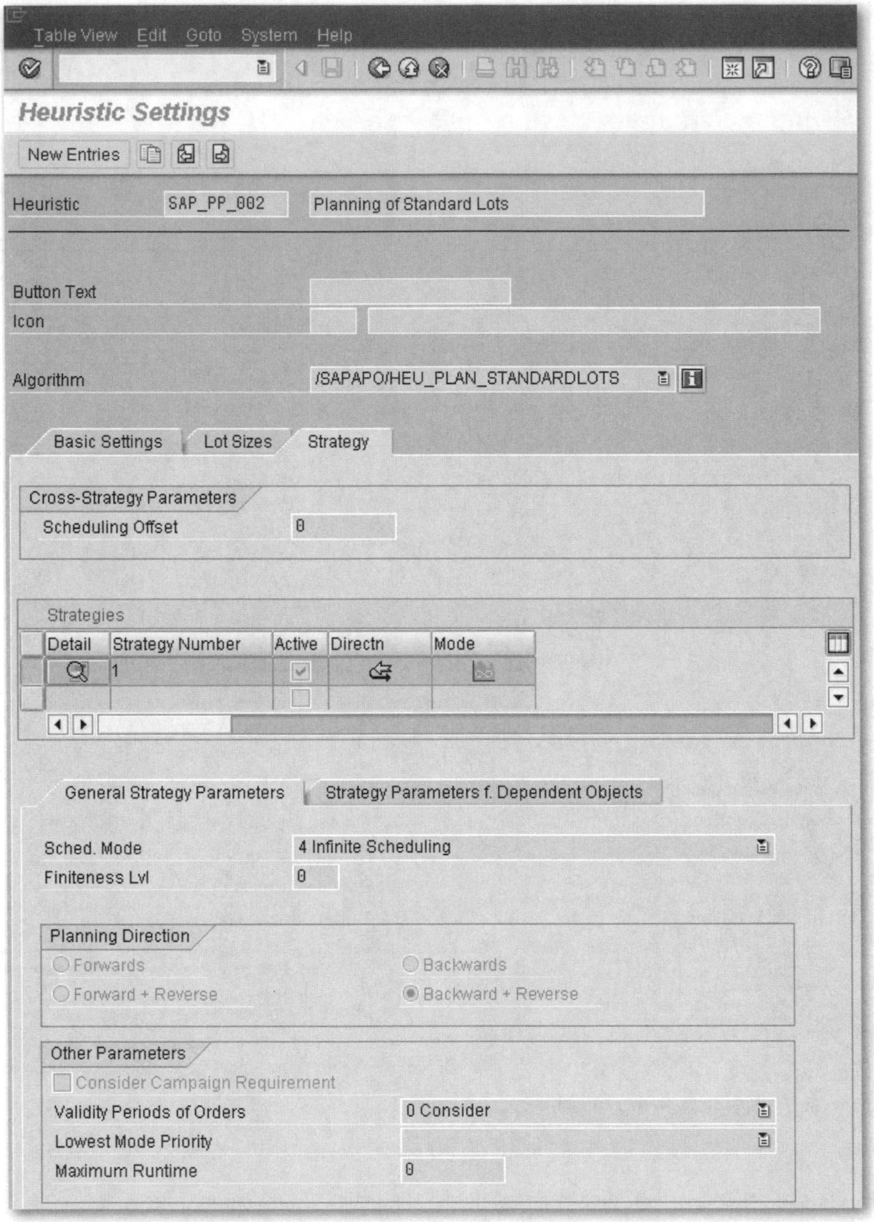

Figure 5.22 APO Customizing Screen "Maintain Heuristics," Transaction Code /SAPAPO/CDPSC11, Heuristic SAP_PP_002 with "Strategy" Tab

Up to and including APO 3.1, the heuristics do not have strategy settings. Instead, the strategy is given in each application (like the production planning run) with an appropriate strategy profile, independently of the heuristic. If no default is set here, the strategy profile in the global parameters of PP/DS for the application is used—for example, via the **Planning Run** field for production planning. The behavior is analogous for interactive planning with the **Interactive Planning** field.

Behavior up to APO 3.1

> **Note**
>
> Up to APO 3.1, the strategy is specified independetly of the PP heuristic. The procedure is significantly different in APO 4.0. There the strategy for product planning is set with the PP heuristic. In the PP heuristic, you are restricted to strategy settings that make sense in the context of product planning.

If you upgrade from APO 3.1 to APO 4.0, the PP heuristics have a flag for **Use strategy settings from heuristics**. If the flag is not set, the system behavior for this heuristic will mimic that of APO 3.1.[8] However, we recommend that you use the new logic.

Strategies for upgrading from APO 3.1

Heuristics Packages

With a heuristics package that is maintained in the product master in the PP/DS view, you can group various products that should be equally planned with the same heuristic (see Figure 5.23). The packages can be created manually or automatically by the system—for example, with product substitution (see Section 5.12).

The effect of such a package is that all products of the package are planned together. For example, planning a package for heuristic **SAP_PP_002** plans all the requirements of the products in the package according to their temporal sequence.

In manual heuristics packages, you can group products that should be manufactured on the same assembly line, products that are manufactured in one production process (main product and by-product), and so on. Manually created heuristics packages are primarily used in finite planning.

---

8 See SAP Note 768293; it is possible to obtain the **Use Strategy Settings from Heuristic** button in newly installed systems as well.

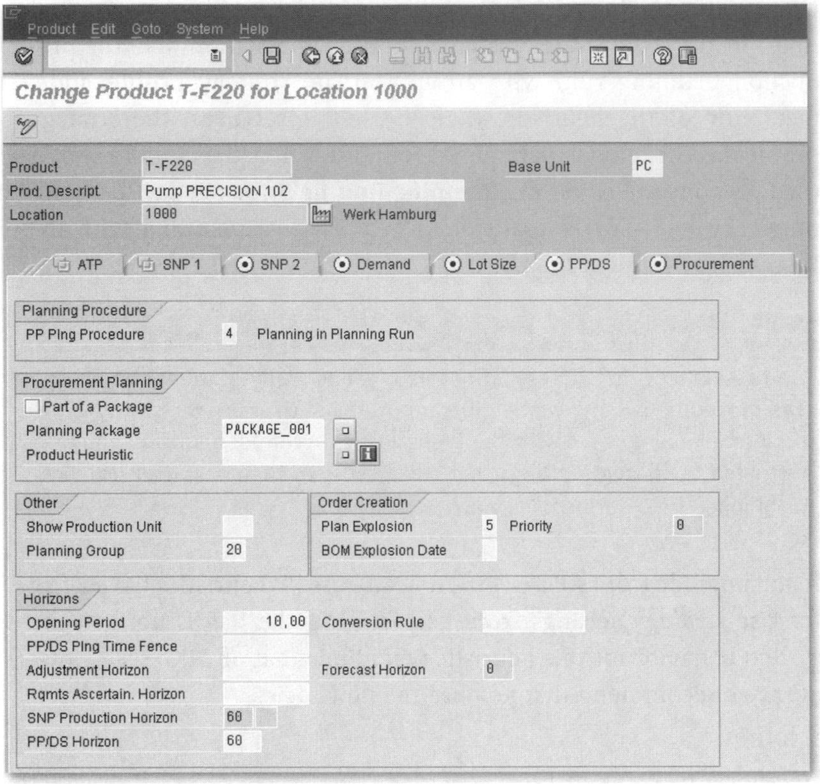

Figure 5.23 APO Transaction "Product," Transaction Code /SAPAPO/MAT1, Product Master with Heuristics Package

5.4.2 Heuristics for Flow Control

Product heuristics define planning for individual products, but a heuristic for flow control defines the overall flow of MRP and therefore the sequence of planning for selected products. You can certainly use these heuristics across plants. In other words, you can select products from several plants for this step. Two different methods are available for flow control:

Planning Components According to Low-Level Code (Heuristic SAP_MRP_001)

The flow with heuristic **Product planning (Comp. acc. LLevl Code) (SAP_MRP_001)** corresponds in function to the material requirements planning run in ECC-MRP (see Figure 5.18). Basically, the selected products are then planned in the order of their low-level codes.

> **Note**
>
> The **SAP_MRP_001** method is very fast and recommended for all product planning.

Plan Components Immediately (Heuristic SAP_MRP_002)

The heuristic **Product Planning (Plan Comp. Immediately)** (SAP_MRP_002) offers the second option for controlling the flow of product planning. Here too, the selected products are first planned in the order of their low-level codes. A deviation from this sequence (which represents the difference between this heuristic and heuristic **SAP_MRP_001**) arises only for components with **Automatic Planning** set for the planning method (with planning method 3, for example; see Section 5.1.3). These components are planned immediately when a dependent requirement appears. If the dependent requirements can be covered later, the delay is redirected as indicated above. The planned order for the end product lags accordingly, and schedule alerts appear directly at the level of the end product.

This method involves much more effort than normal planning according to low-level codes. You can reach a similar result when a planning according to low-level codes is combined with multilevel bottom-up planning. Accordingly, heuristic **SAP_MRP_002** is rarely used in real life.[9]

5.4.3 Service Heuristics

In addition to the traditional planning steps in a production planning process, you can use a variety of additional heuristics for somewhat special tasks.

The following list provides examples of some special service heuristics:

▸ You can use heuristic **SAP_PP_009**, **Rescheduling: Bottom-Up** (shifting requirements to receipt elements): You can reschedule the dependent requirements of components so that they are cov-

---

9 The flow control, **SAP_MRP_002**, should be used with a heuristics package (so that you can plan the end products equally) and with rescheduling instead of net change planning.

ered by receipt elements. The shift of dependent elements means a shift of the related planned orders at the level of the end product.

▶ You can use heuristic **SAP_PP_010**, **Rescheduling: Top-Down** (shifting receipt elements to requirements): You can reschedule receipt elements so that they fulfill later requirements. The shift of dependent requirements for components means that the related planned orders at the subassembly level are also shifted.

▶ You can use heuristics **SAP_PP_019** and **SAP_PP_011** to collectively create or remove fixed pegging relationships (see Section 5.10.2).

▶ If you use a sales order with priorities, the assigned sales order inherits the priorities. This can be a problem when a planned order and its priority is later linked to a different sales order (with a different priority) because of a new situation, because the restructuring of the pegging links does not change the priority. But you can use service heuristic **SAP_PP_012** to adjust the priorities in the planned orders to the linked sales orders.

▶ You can use heuristic **SAP_PP_014**, **Ascertaining Pl. Ind. Requirements** to analyze the still-open planned independent requirements. You can then use the results of the analysis to request that the customer issue sales orders. The analysis is therefore particularly helpful with the use of descriptive characteristics.

▶ The adjustment function enables you to bring planned independent requirements in line with sales order quantities. This approach is particularly useful if you used strategy 20, especially if you want to avoid producing partial quantities for which no sales orders have arrived by a specific date. You can make the adjustment with heuristic **SAP_PP_015**. You can also adjust or delete existing procurement proposals. You can specify both the period of adjustment and the requirements ascertainment horizon in the product master or in the heuristic.

5.5 Example of a Complete Planning Run

Usually a production-planning run to create a consistent procurement plan consists of several steps—often as many as ten. The various options that exist to combine individual steps into an efficient complete run vary a great deal and, of course, depend on the case at hand. To address the interplay of individual heuristics, the present section describes a conceivable method based on a simple example. See Chapter 7 for more complex examples.

Planning occurs across three low-level codes: end product, subassembly, and component. The capacity bottleneck occurs in the production of the subassembly. The goal of the production-planning run is to create a capacity-balanced plan for the production of the subassembly.

In this situation, the following steps would be conceivable for a complete run:

Steps of the production planning run

1. **Stage-Numbering Algorithm**
   The stage-numbering algorithm (**SAP_PP_020**) for determining the low-level codes should normally be executed to guarantee consistent planning. You can begin by scheduling planning it for all products.

2. **Material requirements planning**
   Normal MRP occurs with heuristic SAP_MRP_001. You must select all the relevant products (end product, subassembly, and components) for the heuristic. With this planning, the individual products are planned according to the product heuristic from the product master or from the planning method.

3. **Propagation or delays from the component level**
   MRP occurs top-down and infinitely, therefore some delays might occur because of the lead times. The delays typically appear in date and time violations in the components. You can use heuristic **SAP_ PP_009** to resolve the backlogs—they can be propagated to the end product from the component level.

4. **Capacity planning for the subassembly**
   The step of (finite) capacity planning can occur with the function for detailed scheduling, **SAP001, Schedule Sequence**. This step typically refers to bottleneck resources. In this example, it refers to the resources of subassembly manufacturing for which an exact scheduling sequence can be required based on the strategy profile.

5. **Adjustment to the date shifts of the subassembly**
   Capacity planning for the subassembly generally leads to a shift in subassembly orders. These shifts can affect the end product and the components. You can use heuristics **SAP_PP_99** and **SAP_PP_ 010** with bottom-up (for the end product) or top-down (for the components) to propagate the data shifts in the BOM structure.

But the plan is not yet consistent—even after these planning steps. When adjusting the dates for subassembly planning, problems can also occur when procuring the components. These problems can then force delays in the subassemblies and in other areas. Additional planning steps might be necessary, meaning that the planning complexity will quickly increase with the number of low-level codes and the resources to be planned finitely. When you consider these potential problems, you realize the importance of avoiding all unnecessary complication ahead of time and, in particular, to limiting finite planning to as few resources as possible.

Using the Optimizer

The Optimizer offers an alternative method of performing capacity planning and the subsequent adjustment of dates (see Chapter 6). You can use the Optimizer to review all constraints on the production plan simultaneously and to create a consistent plan in which capacity overloads no longer appear and procurement dates are not missed. Basically, you can solve the whole problem in one step (see Chapter 7).

Of course, you can also use the Optimizer in a targeted manner—to optimize setup time for the production of a subassembly, for example (see Section 5.11).

The problem of manual intervention

APO-PP/DS is generally used in runs similar to the one described above. When addressing the question of to what extent individual steps should be linked and run automatically, note that increasing complexity makes it more and more difficult for the planner to understand the results of planning and, if necessary, be able to intervene manually. You must consider this issue thoroughly when you are trying to determine your optimal planning flow. You should strive for a good compromise between automation and transparency.[10]

5.6   Firming

Firming a planned order (or a purchase requisition) helps to protect the order from machine-based changes. Manual changes, however,

---

10 To better understand the results of a production plan that consists of several steps, it can make sense to copy intermediate results (for example, the status after top-down requirements planning or before capacity planning) into nonactive planning versions.

can be made at any time. Various types of firming are possible in the APO order.

5.6.1   Manual Firming

You can firm individual orders manually. When you change orders manually, the associated firming flags are set automatically. You can cancel firming at any time.

Manual change of an order quantity or an order date sets the **Output Firmed** flag. The quantities of the order cannot be changed during automatic planning. The status corresponds to freezing the order header of an ECC planned order (see Figure 5.24).

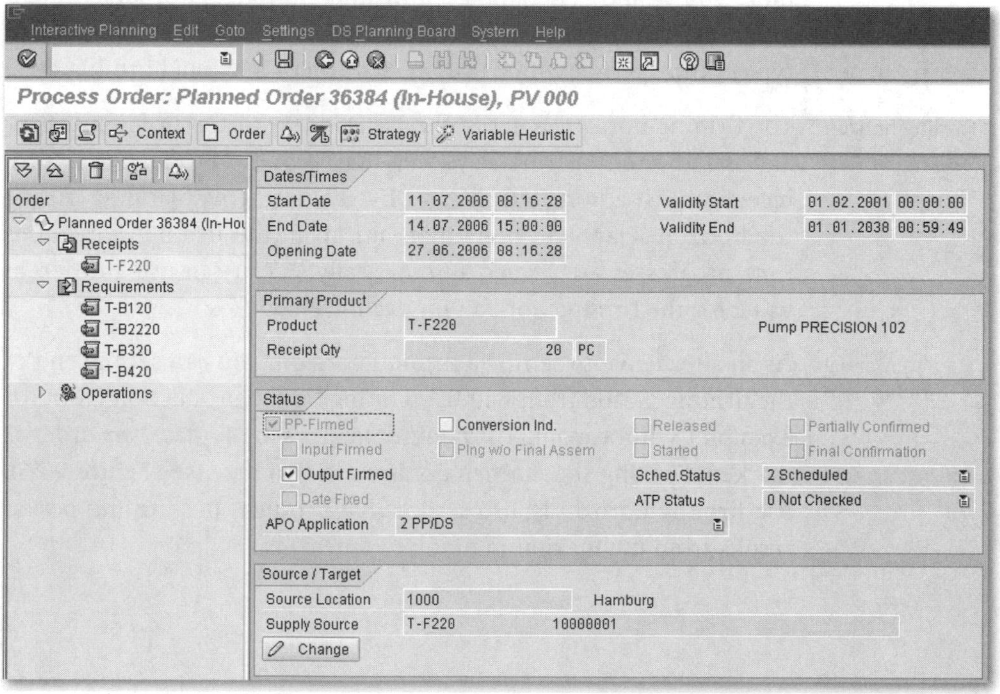

Output firmed

Figure 5.24 APO Transaction "Product View," Transaction Code /SAPAPO/RRP3, Detailed Display of a Planned Order with Firming Flags

If you change the component quantity of an order manually, the **Output Firmed** and the **Input Firmed** flags are both set. Firming the input freezes the dependent requirements of an order. The PPM/PDS can no longer be changed for this order. The status corresponds to the component freeze flag in the ECC planned order.

Input firmed

Date fixed   You can fix an operation of an order in the detailed scheduling planning board. A fixed operation cannot be shifted during optimization. Orders with a fixed operation are marked with the **Date Fixed** flag.

PP-firmed

> **Note**
>
> If the **Output Firmed**, **Input Firmed**, or **Date Fixed** flags are set, the **PP-Firmed** flag is set consequently. Firmed (or fixed) orders cannot be changed by automatic requirements planning.

5.6.2   Firming Based on a Firming Period

Manual firming helps protect individual, manual changes to orders. If you want to firm orders globally to stabilize the production planning, you would generally use a firming period. All orders with an order end date in this period are then PP-firmed. You can define this type of time period with a firming horizon or a manual firming date.

Firming horizon   The firming horizon is set in the PP/DS view of the product master and is indicated in work days (see Figure 5.25). Production is protected against automated changes by requirements planning during the horizon. Planned orders that end up in the firming horizon as time progresses are firmed automatically.[11] You can use a different value for the firming horizon for each product.

Manual firming date   As an alternative to setting a firming horizon, you can set the end of the firming period from within planning (in the production view, for example) with a manual firming date. To set the date, an order is marked. Firming should then occur up to that date (see Figure 5.26). If a firming horizon is also set for that product, the firming period results from the maximum of the two periods.

---

11 The firming horizon is transferred from the ECC material master. However, contrary to in ECC, in APO there are no different firming types available to choose from. In APO-PP/DS, firming via the firming period is similar to ECC firming type 1.

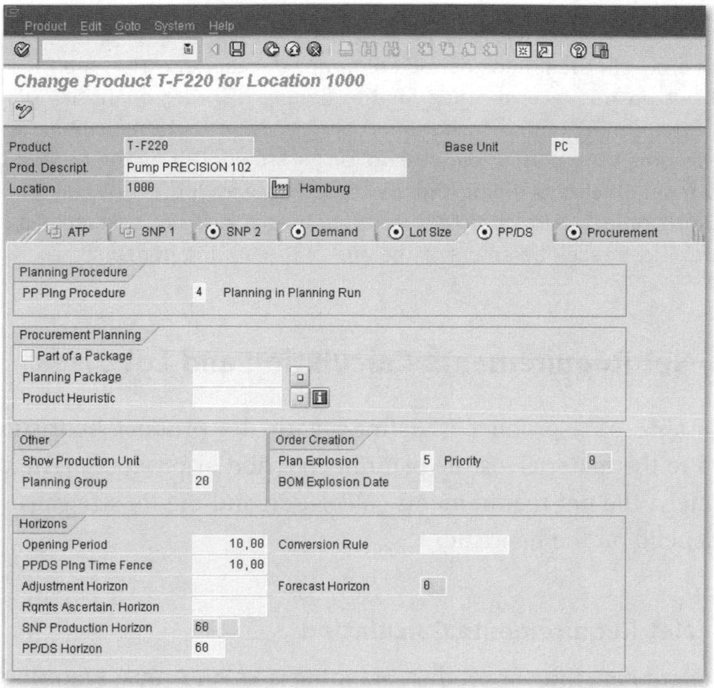

Figure 5.25 APO Transaction "Product," Transaction Code /SAPAPO/MAT1, Product with PP/DS Firming Horizon

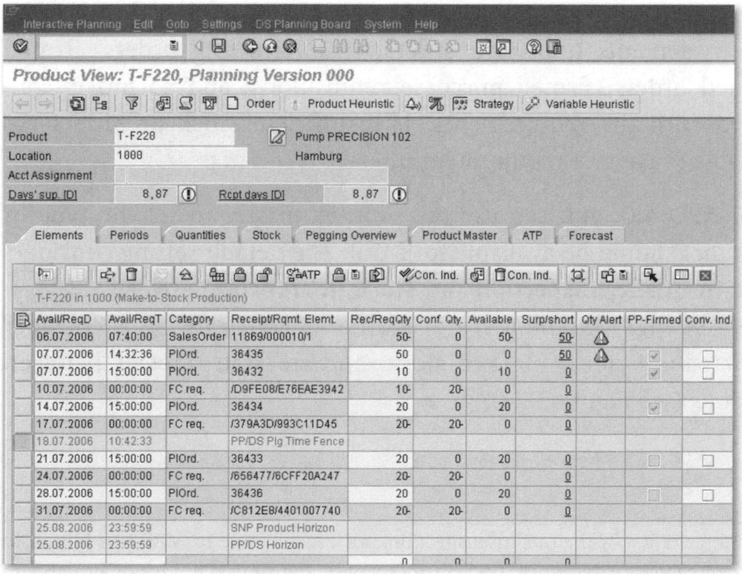

Figure 5.26 APO Transaction "Product View," Transaction Code /SAPAPO/RRP3, Manual Firming Date (PP/DS Firming Horizon)

> **Note**
>
> Planned orders in the firing period are firmed *dynamically*. They are **PP-firmed** but do not receive a flag for the firming of order quantities or dates. If the firming period is shortened or deleted so that the orders no longer lie within this period, they are no longer firmed. During the firming period, requirements planning cannot create any new orders or change any existing orders. New shortages in the firming period are covered—at the latest—by a receipt element at the end of the firming horizon.

5.7 Net Requirements Calculation and Lot Sizes

The planning of a product is defined with the product heuristic assigned to the material via the planning method or product master. Accordingly, the net requirements calculation and the lot size calculation depend on the heuristic.

5.7.1 Net Requirements Calculation

Planning standard lots

The standard heuristic for product planning is **SAP_PP_002**, **Planning of Standard Lots**. It represents the normal case of product planning as part of material requirements planning. With this heuristic, planning first performs a net requirements calculation in a manner similar to ECC-MRP. The total of stock available for MRP and confirmed receipt elements (purchase orders, manufacturing orders, firmed planned orders, firmed purchase requisitions, and so on) is contrasted with the requirements. If insufficient stock or orders are available to cover a requirement, there is a *shortage*.

Stock available for MRP

As of APO 4.0, you can use the product master to set the type of stock that should be available for MRP. The default setting considers **Stock in Quality Inspection** and **Stock in Transfer Between Sublocations** (storage locations). In addition, you can also consider restricted-use stock, blocked stock, and stock in transfer between locations (see Figure 5.27).[12]

---

12 Up to APO 3.1, the quality inspection stock is available to MRP in addition to the freely available stock. Locked stock can be transferred but is not available to MRP. This standard logic can be manipulated via a customer exit (see SAP Note 487166).

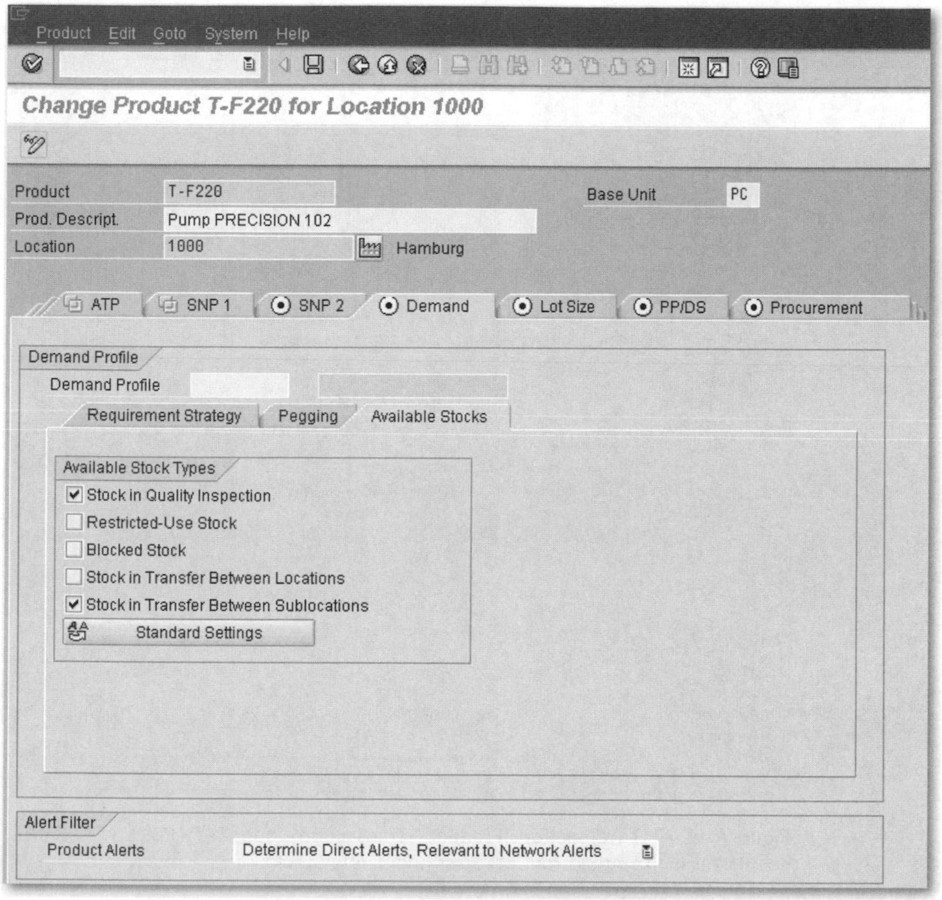

Figure 5.27 APO Transaction "Product," Transaction Code /SAPAPO/MAT1, Product Master with Types of Available Stock

You can also consider safety stock in planning (see Figure 5.28). The safety stock is not available for MRP; it is subtracted from the stock available for MRP. It is transferred from the ECC material master. Similarly, you can consider a safety days' supply so that the receipt elements to satisfy the shortage are created earlier by the corresponding period. It corresponds to the **Safety Time** in the ECC material master; this field is transferred to the APO product master as appropriate.

Safety stock and safety time

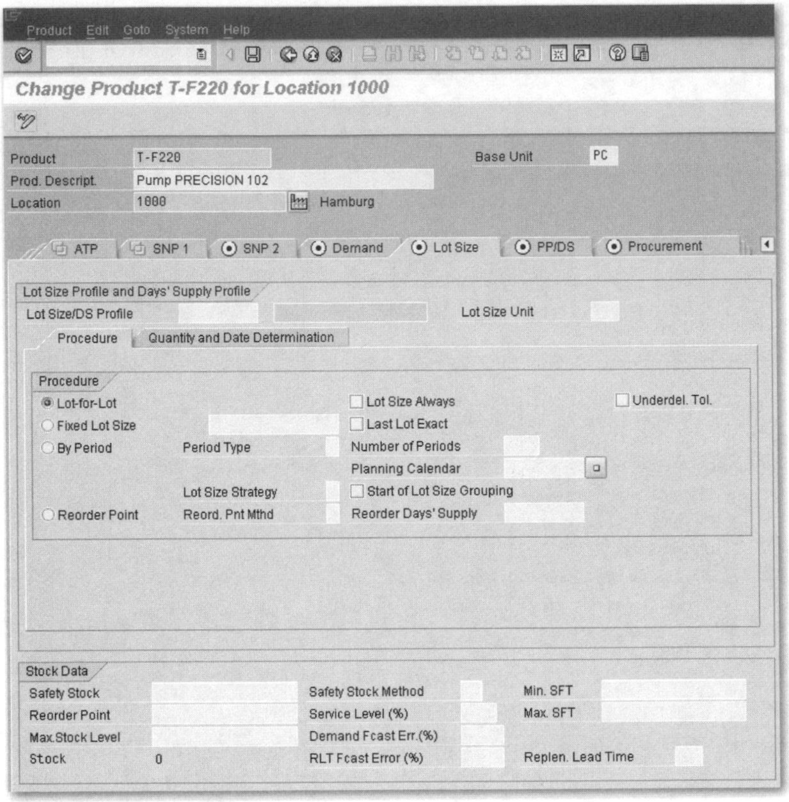

Figure 5.28 APO Transaction "Product," Transaction Code /SAPAPO/MAT1, Product Master with Settings for Lots Sizes and Safety Stock

5.7.2 Lot Size Calculation

The shortage quantity and shortage date are the starting point for lot size calculation. The lot size calculation is dependent on the heuristic.

Lots size when planning standard lots

For planning standard lots, the lot size is generally defined via the product master, but as of APO 4.0, it can be defined directly with the heuristic, using the **Use Lot Size Settings from Heuristic** flag.

Lot size settings in the product master

The lot size settings in the product master result from the corresponding ECC settings and are transferred to APO through the CIF. You can use the following methods (see Figure 5.28):

► **Lot-for-Lot**
With lot-for-lot, an order proposal is created at an exact time. It is the same size as the shortage. A separate order is created for each

requirement. If a procurement proposal for the entire quantity of the shortage of a day is to be created (similar to ECC), you can use the daily lot size.

▶ **Fixed Lot Size**
The fixed lot size uses the fixed lot size defined in the product master. If the quantity of a fixed lot size is insufficient to eliminate the shortage, several lots are scheduled in the amount of the fixed lot size for the same date until there is no more shortage.

▶ **By Period**
The by-period method combines the procurement of the requirements quantities within a period into one lot size. The periods can be **hours**, **days**, **weeks**, **months**, or any period you define according to the **planning calendar**. You can set the number of periods in which the procurement quantity should be summarized in the **Number of Periods** field. The resulting receipt element can be placed on the date of the first requirement, at the beginning of the period, at the end of the period, or during the period via the **Period Factor**.[13]

You can define the lot sizes more exactly with rounding and with minimum and maximum lot sizes — to adjust planning the product requirements to production, delivery, or transport quantity units, for example. The following options are available: **Minimum lot size** (minimum procurement quantity per lot under which the quantity may not fall), **maximum lot size** (maximum procurement quantity per lot that cannot be surpassed), **rounding value** (value used as the basis for rounding), and **rounding profile** (staggered rounding). These settings in the product are also transferred from ECC to APO, but you must create the rounding profile in APO.

Rounding

If these options for the lot size calculation are inadequate, you still have access to additional lot size heuristics (see Section 5.4.1).

---

13 By default, the period length of an **Hour** and a period factor unequal to 0 (period start) or 1 (period end) cannot be transferred from ECC. For these settings, you must use a customer exit for CIF transfer.

5.8   Determining the Supply Source

In the event of a shortage, an order for procurement in the amount of the lot size is created. The supply sources that may pertain to this order depend on the quantity, date, and the procurement type entered in the product master.[14]

5.8.1   Procurement Types

In-house production

In-house production can occur in the planning location or, as of APO 4.0, in another, separate location.[15] To create a corresponding planned order, a PPM or PDS is to be selected as the supply source. The **Plan explosion** field in the product master must be used first to determine whether a PPM or a PDS will be used by the system to create the order.[16]

Production in a different location (as of APO 4.0)

If production takes place in a different location, this information is stored in the ECC material master of the planning location via a corresponding special procurement key for in-house production (see Figure 5.29). In-house production is set in the material master of the production plant; a production version with routing and BOM (master recipe) is also maintained. If this data is selected in an integration model for transfer to APO, a corresponding PPM or PDS is created in addition to the products.

Flow of production in a different location

Planning of the product then occurs in the planning location, but production and planning of the components occurs in the production location. The PPM/PDS for in-house production is present in the production location, and the planning location is entered in the PPM/PDS (see Figure 5.30). If planning is performed in the planning location, the PPM/PDS is exploded in the production location. A planned order with a receipt element is created in the planning location; capacity planning and planning of the components occurs in

---

14 For individual planning versions, you can also set it so the creation of an order can be done without a supply source with regard to in-house production or external procurement. However, during the execution of the planning at the very latest (production order or purchase order), a supply source is necessary.

15 In APO 5.0, you can also perform withdrawals from a different location.

16 If the planned order is created as the actual requirement at a later stage and the PPM/PDS is no longer valid at that point in time, you can use the **Order Validity Periods** flag in the strategy to define the behavior of the system.

the production location. The goods receipt of the end product is created directly in the planning location so that you don't have to perform a follow-up stock transfer from the production location to the planning location.

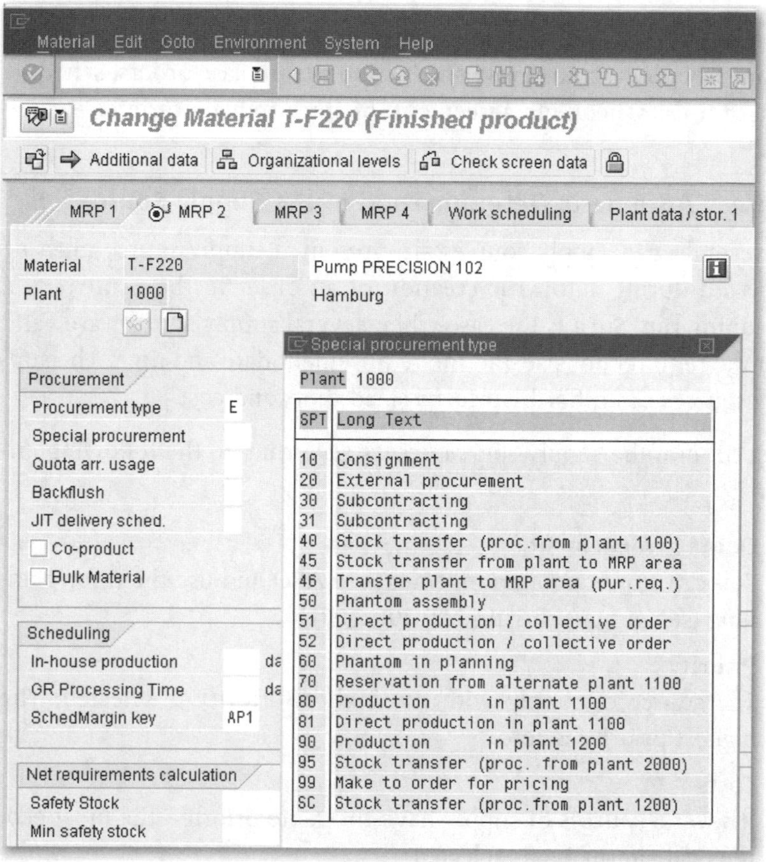

Figure 5.29 ECC Transaction "Change Material Master," Transaction Code MM02, MRP 2 View with Special Procurement Key

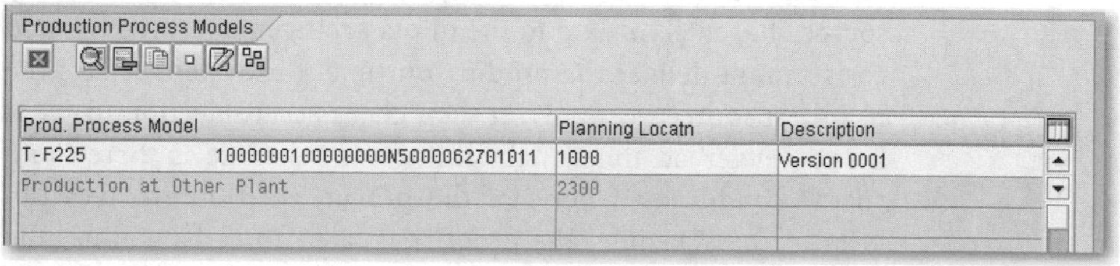

Figure 5.30 APO Transaction "Production Process Model," Transaction Code /SAPAPO/SCC03, PPM for Production in a Different Plant

External
procurement

External procurement can involve both procurement from external vendors and a stock transfer from another location. Planning occurs with purchase orders or schedule lines for the APO scheduling agreement. A stock transfer from another plant with a stock transfer order is also part of external procurement.

If both types of procurement are permitted, the system can create planned orders for in-house production or purchase orders, schedule lines for the scheduling agreement, or stock transfer orders.

5.8.2 Automatic Determination of the Supply Source

If several valid supply sources are present, a supply source must be selected during automatic creation of an order in the context of a planning run. Such is the case when several supply sources are valid for the required lot size and the requirement date and time. The supply sources can differ by priority, lead time, and cost.

Selection of the supply source occurs according to the following criteria:

1. **Quota arrangement**
   You can store quota arrangements in APO and use them for planning (see quota heuristic **SAP_PP_Q001**).

2. **Priority**
   The source of supply with the highest priority is selected. The highest priority is zero.

3. **Costs**
   If several sources of supply have the same priority, the most economical alternative is selected.

4. **Keeping the schedule**
   The production planning run always chooses the supply source that can deliver the required quantity on time. If the supply source chosen according to the quota arrangement, priority, and costs cannot deliver the product on time, the system selects the next-best source of supply. It then checks that selection to see if it can deliver on time. Maintaining the schedule is therefore a "hard" condition. If none of the procurement alternatives can keep to the schedule, the order is created for a later time; the alternative with the shortest delay is selected.

You maintain the **Priority** of the PPM in the product–plan assignment. Similarly, you maintain **Costs** in the PPM. You can specify costs for the actual procurement process (single level costs) and for the complete procurement process (multilevel costs)—see Figure 5.31. **Single Level Costs** are relevant only for SNP optimization; **Multilevel Costs** are relevant for PP/DS.

Priority and costs in PPM

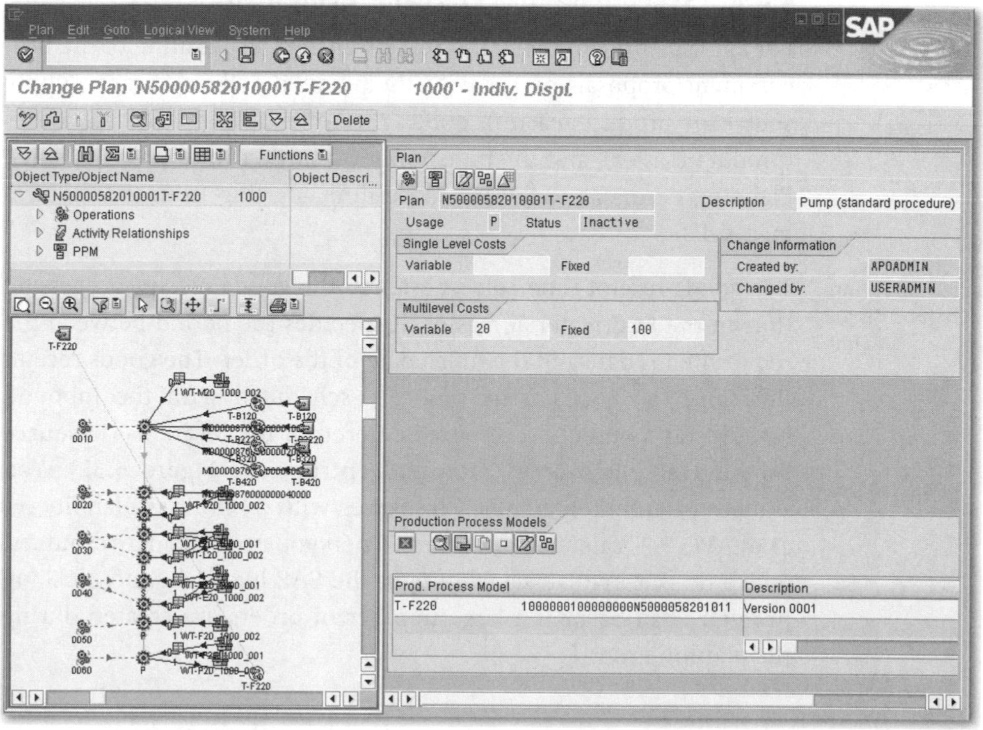

Figure 5.31 APO Transaction "Production Process Model," Transaction Code /SAPAPO/SCC03, PPM with Costs

For the PDS, you maintain the parameters from the ECC (see Chapter 4).

Priority and costs in PDS

For external procurement and stock transfers, you maintain costs in the transportation lane. For purchasing info records, scheduling agreements, and contracts, you can transfer the costs from the ECC.

Priority and costs with external procurement

Note

The result of the automatic determination of the supply source is, in the ideal case, the best supply source in terms of priority, costs, and ability to maintain the schedule.

5.9   Scheduling

Procurement elements are scheduled after the requirements calculation, the calculation of lot sizes, and the determination of the supply
source.

5.9.1   Scheduling for External Procurement

For external procurement and stock transfers, scheduling of the procurement proposals occurs with the planned delivery times (supply
source or product master), goods receipt times, goods issue times
(product master), and the transportation times (transportation lane).
Planning occurs as backward scheduling, starting from the requirements date.

Goods receipt time and goods issue time

The goods receipt time corresponds to the goods receipt processing
time in the ECC material master. It specifies the period between the
requirements date and the finish date of the order. The goods receipt
time and the goods issue time are scheduled with the inbound
resource and outbound resource entered in the location **(Resource
Inbound** and **Resource Outbound** entries, see Figure 5.32). You
should use infinitely planned resources with 24-hour availability or,
as of APO 3.1, calendar resources. When you use calendar resources,
which do not involve scheduling in the SAP liveCache, no blocking
problems can occur if a large number of orders are created during
the planning run.[17]

5.9.2   Scheduling for In-House Production

Scheduling of a planned order for in-house production occurs on the
basis of the lead times in PPM and PDS along with the goods receipt
time. Therefore, an APO planned order is always scheduled in detail.
In other words, the order contains all the operation and activity
dates (see Figure 5.33). The dates of the dependent requirements are
placed on the start dates of the assigned activities. You can also use
an offset in the input component to change the instant in time of the
dependent requirements.

---

17 Basically, you can also plan goods receipt and goods issue times finitely. However, it is advisable to map such a process through an operation in PPM/PDS.

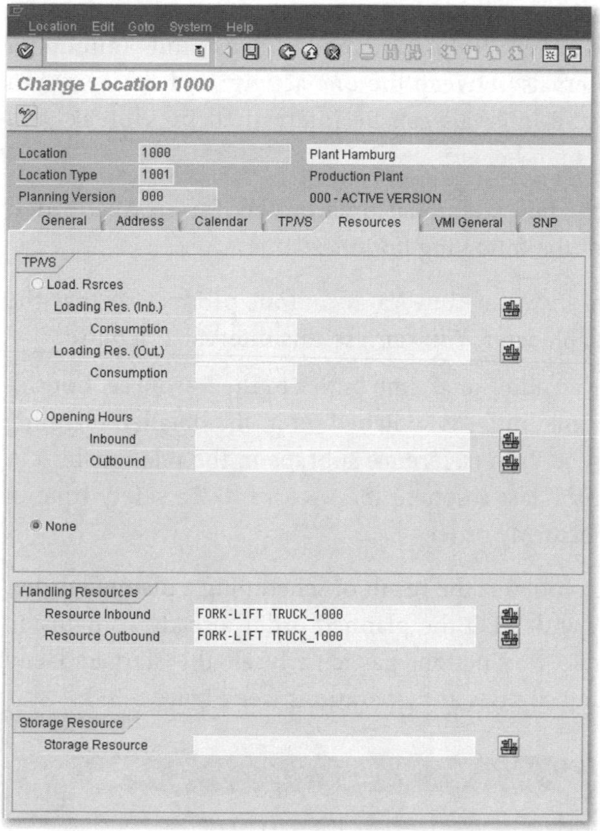

Figure 5.32 APO Transaction "Location," Transaction Code /SAPAPO/LOC3, Location with Inbound and Outbound Resources

During scheduling of a planned order, the start and finish dates of individual activities are determined based on the times in PPM/PDS and the available capacity of the resources involved.[18] The exact length of an activity depends, in particular, on the *time factor*, which results from the utilization rate or the general breaks from the available capacity of the resources.

Scheduling the activities

If, for example, an activity that lasts an hour is performed on a resource with a utilization rate of 90%, and if the available capacity of eight hours includes a break of one hour, the activity is stretched to a length of 1 hour * (100/90) * (8/7) = 1.27 hours. The *time factor* here is therefore 100/90 * 8/7 = 1.27.

Time factor from the resource

---

18 The production calendar doesn't play a role here. It only becomes important if you must determine horizons that don't have any relationship with a resource.

Time interval between activities Additional marginal conditions can result from the settings in PPM/PDS. For example, additional temporal constraints (minimum and maximum intervals between the one activity and the next) can exist. Sometimes the intervals can be interrupted by a break, and sometimes they cannot be, etc.

Buffer in an APO order If you want to schedule additional time buffers for an APO order, you can use one of the following options:

▶ You can assign an offset time to an output product so that the product is available later. You can use this interval as a buffer.

▶ You can specify an additional time buffer in the **Resource**. Consideration of this time buffer is switched on in the detailed planning strategy and in the PPM (reference subtype in the relationship). A time buffer on the last resource then works like a safety time in the ECC manufacturing order.

Scheduling in the APO planned order The planned order contains the result of scheduling a planned order. Unlike with ECC, with APO the planned order already contains all the data relevant to production, particularly all the start and end times of individual activities and operations (see Figure 5.33).

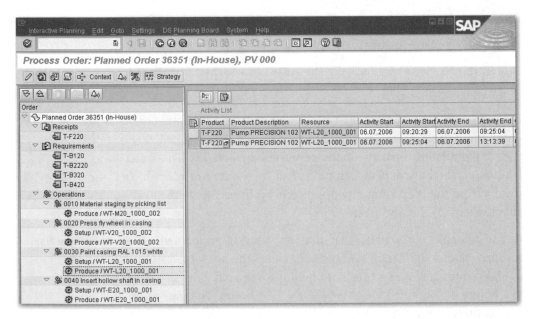

Figure 5.33 APO Transaction "Product View," Transaction Code /SAPAPO/RRP3, Details of the Planned Order

5.9.3 Planning Strategy

With the detailed planning strategy, you define how the system performs the scheduling and rescheduling of orders. There are two different scenarios here.

In product planning (in the production planning run or in interactive planning from the product view), the strategy is generally (as of APO 4.0) defined directly by the heuristic. Here only *infinite* planning makes sense. Bucket finite planning can make sense in the context of CTP.

With *rescheduling in the context of capacity planning* or during manual creation of an order, etc., the strategy is defined with the strategy profile directly in the application (in the product view or the detailed planning board, for example) or with the basic setting in the global PP/DS parameters. In this case, finite planning can also make sense. You can make use of the complete functional scope of the strategy profile here.

Strategy Settings of the Product Heuristic

In the strategy settings of the product heuristic, you can use only the settings that play a role in infinite planning or in bucket finite planning for CTP (see Figure 5.22).

Note
In general, you use the planning mode of **Infinite Planning Backwards with Revese Direction**, which corresponds to normal backward scheduling without consideration of the capacity loads. Product planning therefore produces planned orders with infinite planning.

Planning mode "Backward Infinite Planning"

Up to and including APO 3.1, the system performs requirements planning finitely without any difficulty. It checks the capacity load and searches for open places for the orders as early as the creation of an order. That sounds good—at first. It only takes one step to a finite production plan. But please note that this finite plan isn't necessarily a good plan. Just consider a few problems.

Problems of finite requirements planning

In requirements planning, the products are planned according to low-level codes; the requirements are planned alphabetically within a product in a temporal sequence. If end products and components demand the same resources, the logical sequence is reversed. Products that appear later in the alphabet in a low-level code are at a disadvantage, i.e., they become loser products. The priority of orders can be considered only occasionally. Resources are filled in sequence. In the event of overloads, no balanced delays occur and the problems increase exponentially with the load on the resources, the number of finitely planned resources, and the restrictions and requirements of the master data.

To summarize, such a plan—even when ameliorated somewhat by heuristics packages—requires at least some reworking. And you would have to have started from an almost random and difficult-to-grasp situation. We simply acknowledge what has happened in dozens of cases in the real world.

> **Note**
>
> Finite requirements planning makes sense only under certain conditions. Such planning does not offer a solid foundation for reworking the plan. Intelligent production planning generally begins with infinite requirements planning. The result of such planning is then used for controlled and targeted capacity planning.

General Strategy Settings via the Strategy Profile

Strategy profile

The entries in a strategy profile explicitly define a strategy, such as that used for manual creation of an order or in capacity planning. A strategy profile can contain several active strategies so that the system tries to schedule the order according to the defined sequence. If the first strategy fails because it is too restrictive, the system tries to schedule the order using the second strategy, and so on (see Figure 5.34). In this context, many more options make sense than in the case of product planning. In particular, you can use a finite planning mode.

Strategy views

Various views are available as of APO 4.0 to display or edit strategies: the PP view for settings typical to PP (from the product view, for example), the DS view (from the detailed scheduling planning board, for example) for settings typical to DS, and the expert view for all the settings of a strategy (see Figures 5.35 and 5.36). These views make it easier to gain an overview of the relevant settings.

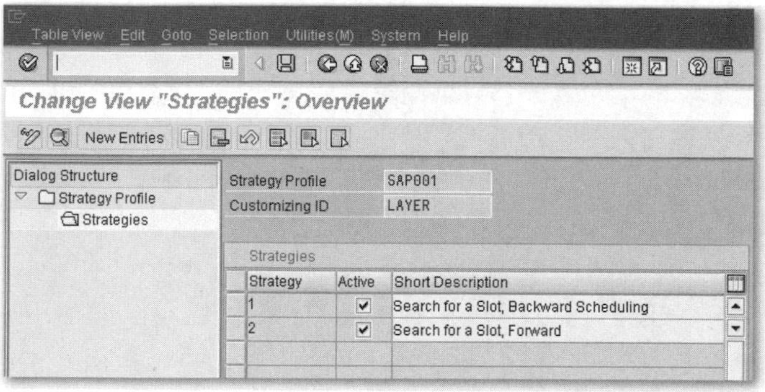

Figure 5.34 APO Customizing Screen "Maintain Strategy Profile" in Customizing of Master Data, Strategy Profile with Several Strategies

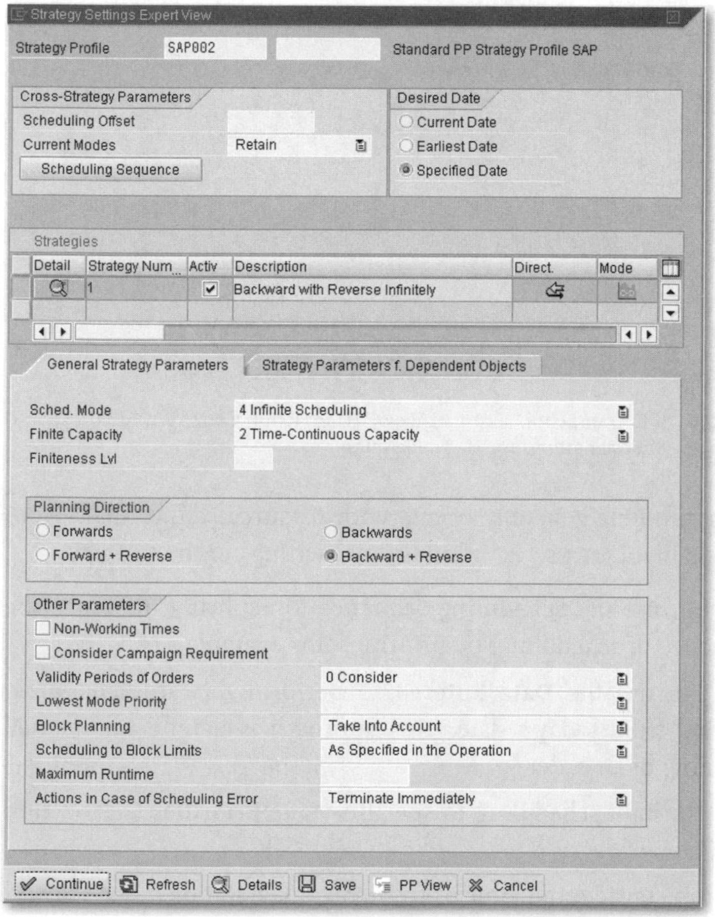

Figure 5.35 APO Transaction "Product View," Transaction Code /SAPAPO/RRP3, Calling the Strategy Profile from the Product View

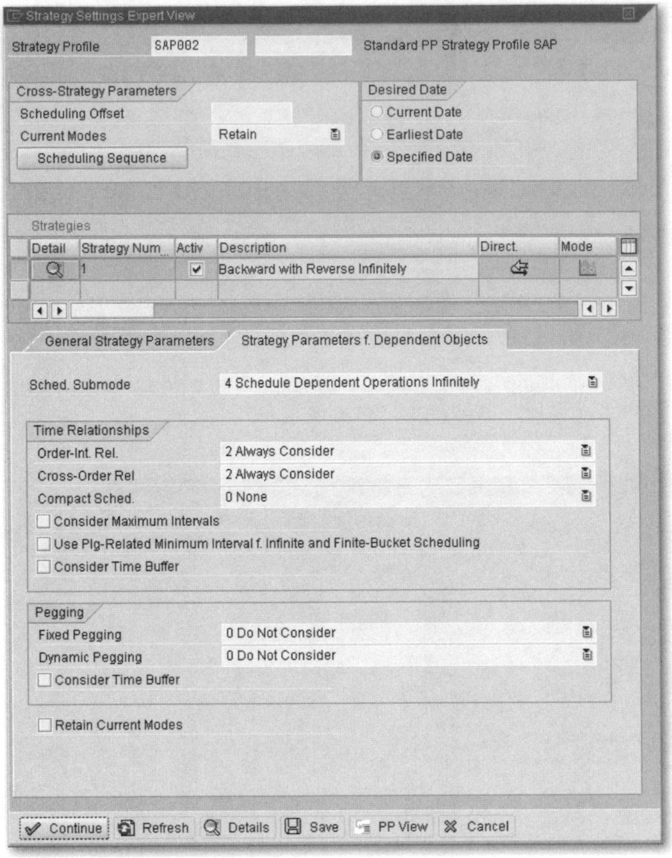

Figure 5.36 APO Transaction "Product View," Transaction Code /SAPAPO/RRP3, Strategy with Special Settings for Finite Planning

Finite scheduling

Finite scheduling generally occurs with resources rather than products. This involves a series of additional settings in the strategy:

▸ You can use the **Scheduling Sequence** to explicitly influence the sequence of scheduling, by priorities, for example.

▸ You can use the **Date Entered** to perform forward scheduling starting from today's date. This approach is helpful for manual planning of an order.

▸ You can limit scheduling to specific **Mode Priorities** (see Section 5.9.5).

▸ You can consider dynamic or fixed **Pegging Relationships** (see Section 5.10).

▸ You can consider **Order-Internal Relationships** and so on.

The **Backward search for gaps with reverse** mode is an example of a finite planning mode. With this mode, the scheduling of an order searches backwards for free capacity gaps in all the resources to be planned finitely to schedule the activities. If you consider the example of an order with several operations on various finite resources and maximum times between the operations when the production resources have already been partially used, it soon becomes clear that, in many cases, you cannot plan without some additional steps. If a reversal of the planning direction is permitted, a solution will be found—in the forward direction at the latest.

Planning mode "Search for Gaps"

Basically, finite planning occurs only for resources that are planned finitely (see Figure 5.37). The following statement briefly describes the exact context.

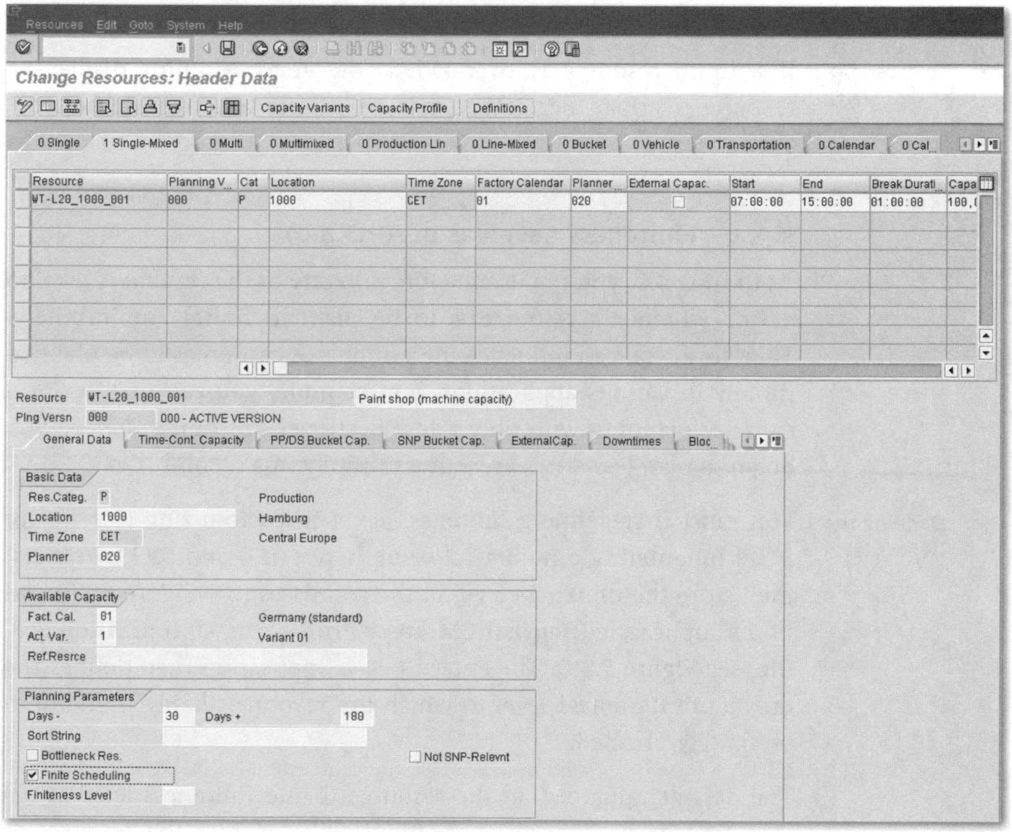

Finite resources

Figure 5.37 APO Transaction "Resource," Transaction Code /SAPAPO/RES01, Resource with Finite Scheduling Flag

Summary

A finite strategy plans only finite resources finitely. An infinite strategy performs infinite planning of all resources, both finite and infinite. Therefore, infinite resources are always planned infinitely.

Please note that as a general rule *not* all resources are to be considered as finite in planning. Theoretically, of course, a resource cannot be used at more than 100% of capacity and is therefore, in fact, finite. However, in the real world, one or a few resources will prove to be bottlenecks. If the plan works for the bottlenecks, it will also work for the rest of the resources.

Note

You should only consider bottlenecks as finite in planning.

Resource overload alerts

If a finite resource is overloaded, the Alert Monitor displays a resource overload alert. Overloads on infinite resources do not trigger an alert.

5.9.4 Finiteness Level (as of APO 4.0)

As of APO 4.0, you can use the functionality of the finiteness level to define whether a resource is to be planned finitely or infinitely. Therefore, you can influence the number of resources to be planned finitely in various applications. For example, you can first perform capacity planning with only a few bottleneck resources before you begin to plan less-critical resources finitely in a second step.

Defining the finiteness level

You must first define a finiteness level in customizing (see Figure 5.38) by entering a numerical value between 0 and 9999. You can then store the finiteness level in the resources (see Figure 5.40) and in the application (**Heuristic**, **Strategy Profile**, and **Optimization Profile**, see Figure 5.39). The entry in each application then defines the maximum finiteness level to which the resources being used are to be finitely planned.

The default value of 0 in the resource (or no finiteness level at all) therefore means that all applications will consider the resource as finite. That's why the system initially sets a finiteness level of 0 for all resources that have the flag set for **Finite Planning**.

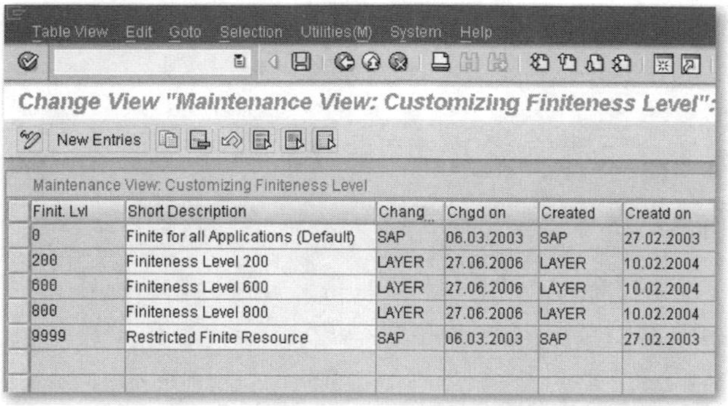

Figure 5.38 APO Customizing Screen "Define Finiteness Level for Resources" in PP/DS Customizing

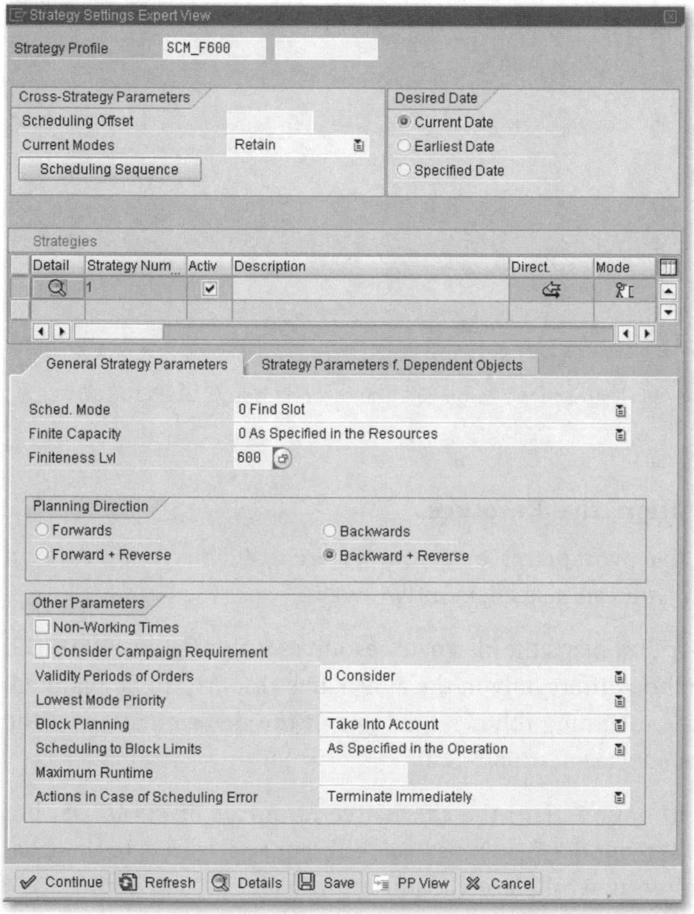

Figure 5.39 APO Transaction "Product View," Transaction Code /SAPAPO/RRP3, Calling a Strategy Profile with Finiteness Level

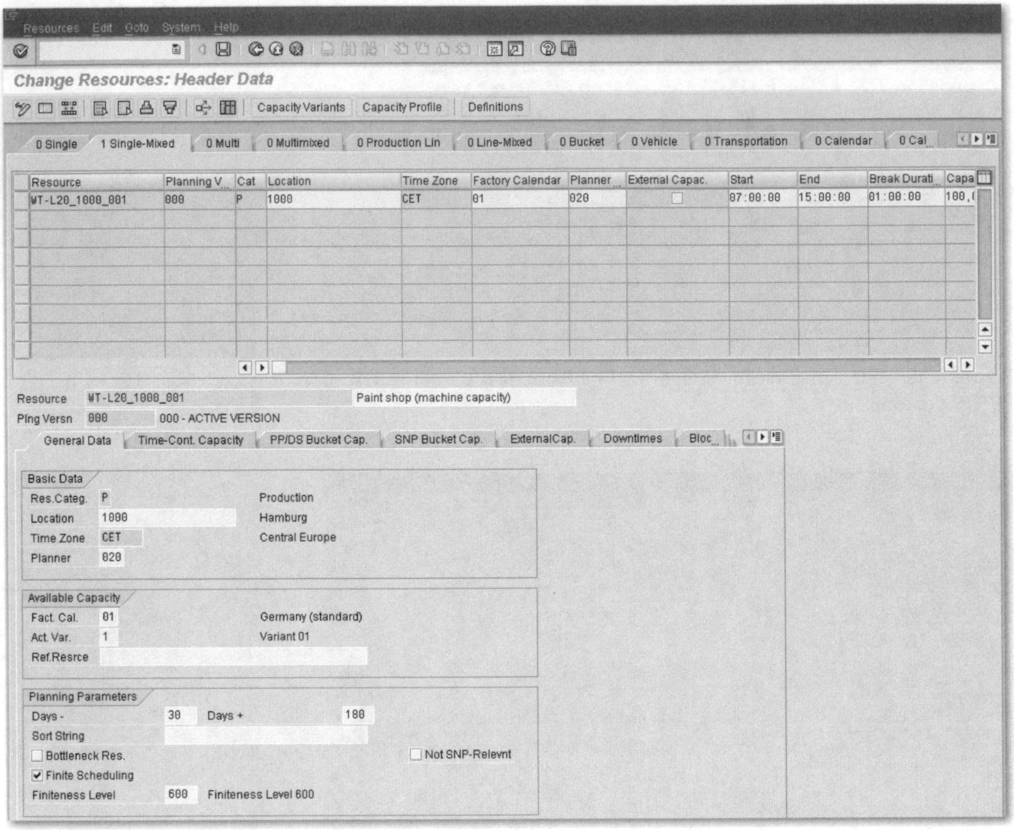

Figure 5.40 APO Transaction "Resource," Transaction Code /SAPAPO/RES01, Resource with Finiteness Level

5.9.5 Alternative Resources

If alternative workplaces or resources are available to execute an operation, you can plan them in two ways.

PPM/PDS alternative — The first option maps the alternate resources via different PPM/PDS. Each one then differs only in the alternative resource to be planned. In this case, planning follows the logic of the determination of the supply source (see Section 5.8.2).

Alternative modes — The second option plans the alternative resources in PPM/PDS, but with alternate modes. You must use different approaches to the standard routing or, workplace classification in ECC; these settings are mapped with alternative modes for an activity in PPM/PDS (see Chapter 4).

Note

If several modes are present for an activity, you must select a mode for scheduling. When modes with equal standing are present in backward scheduling, the system selects the mode with the latest start for the activity.

Selecting a mode

Mode priorities

You can target planning of individual modes using the mode priority. You can assign a mode a priority from A to O for automatic mode selection (A is the highest priority) and a priority of Z for purely manual planning. The priorities affect planning when you use a strategy to define the priority at which scheduling may occur (see Figure 5.41). Consider the following example: You use a finite strategy profile in which the first active strategy may use only mode priority A, the second may use priorities up to B, and the third may use priorities up to O. Scheduling will then first use the preferred machine with A. When it no longer has any capacity, use of machine B is also permitted. When no more scheduling can occur there, all mode priorities are allowed.

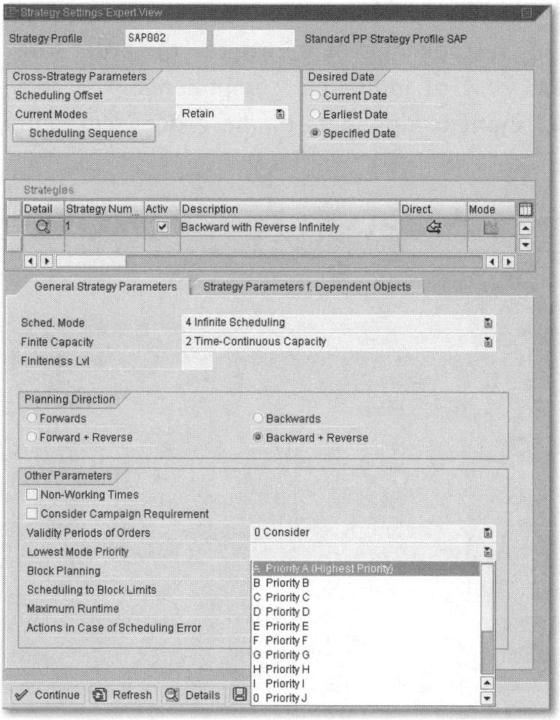

Figure 5.41 APO Transaction "Product View," Transaction Code /SAPAPO/RRP3, Calling a Strategy Profile with Settings for Mode Priority

5.9.6 Scheduled Planned Orders

In APO-PP/DS, planned orders are generally created as *scheduled* orders, whether their planning occurs finitely or infinitely. Capacity planning in PP/DS therefore occurs as a rescheduling of orders.

If you want to deviate from this basic behavior, you can set the planning method as of APO 4.0. Up to APO 3.1, you can only do this with a customer exit.

5.10 Pegging

Pegging involves a link that creates a logical relationship between the receipt elements and requirements elements of a product within a location. The system uses these pegging relationships to assign requirements to receipt elements. The links always result from availability and requirements dates within a pegging area, in which product, location, and account assignment (make-to-stock or make-to-order, etc.) correspond to each other.

You can see the pegging relationships of an order in the order's display: Call the detailed view of individual components. The same applies to output and input components of the order (see Figure 5.42).

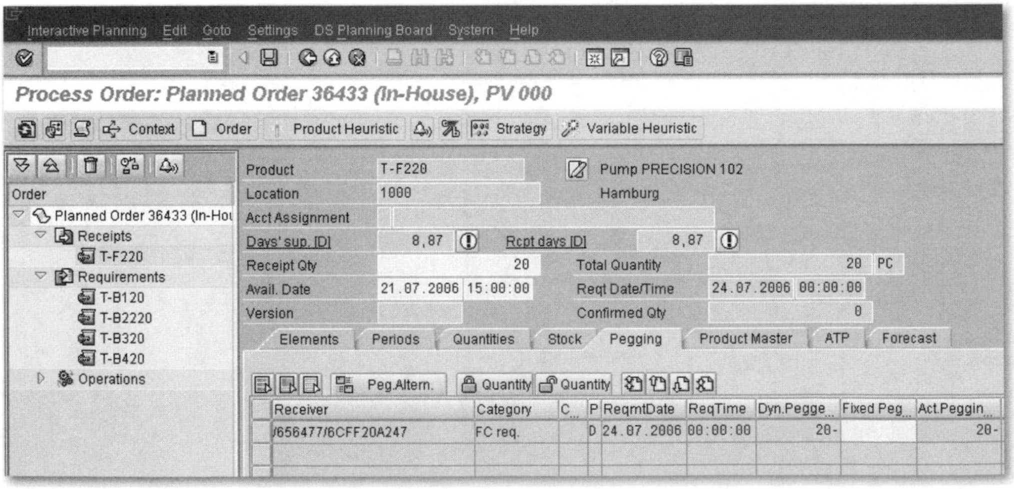

Figure 5.42 APO Transaction "Product View," Transaction Code /SAPAPO/RRP3, Planned Order with Pegging Display

Pegging relationships can stretch from independent requirements to the assigned planned orders and their dependent requirements, and even to the entire BOM structure. The total of the relationships is called a (multilevel) pegging network. You can display the pegging network of an order using the **Context** report of the order from the product view (see Figure 5.43). However, please note that alerts are visible in the product view only when a corresponding alert profile has been stored (see Chapter 6).

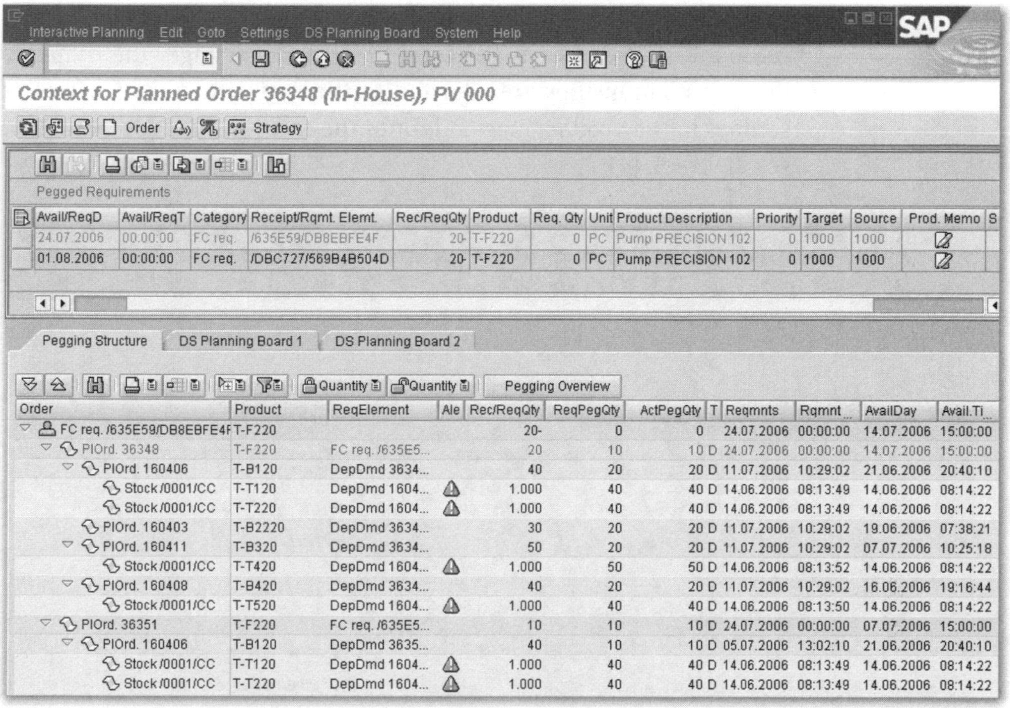

Pegging network

Figure 5.43 APO Transaction "Product View," Transaction Code /SAPAPO/RRP3, Details of the Planned Order, Context of an Order with Alerts

---

Caution

Pegging involves an analysis that refers to existing orders and requirements. It occurs independently of requirements planning. The primary applications of pegging include the analysis of production planning, capacity planning, and optimization.

The core of pegging in APO-PP/DS corresponds to the dynamic assignment of requirements elements and procurement elements as

Comparison with ECC

listed in ECC in the context of current requirements/stock lists and in the evaluation with the order report or the pegged requirements. The essential difference between the two is that the APO pegging structure is stored in the database and is therefore available for a variety of other applications. A variety of settings can also influence the setup of the pegging structure in APO.

5.10.1 Dynamic Pegging

Unless you switch it off, *dynamic pegging* is executed automatically. As soon as requirements or receipt elements change, the dynamic pegging relationships are adjusted to the new situation. A series of settings in the product master defines the relationships (**Demand** tab, see Figure 5.44).

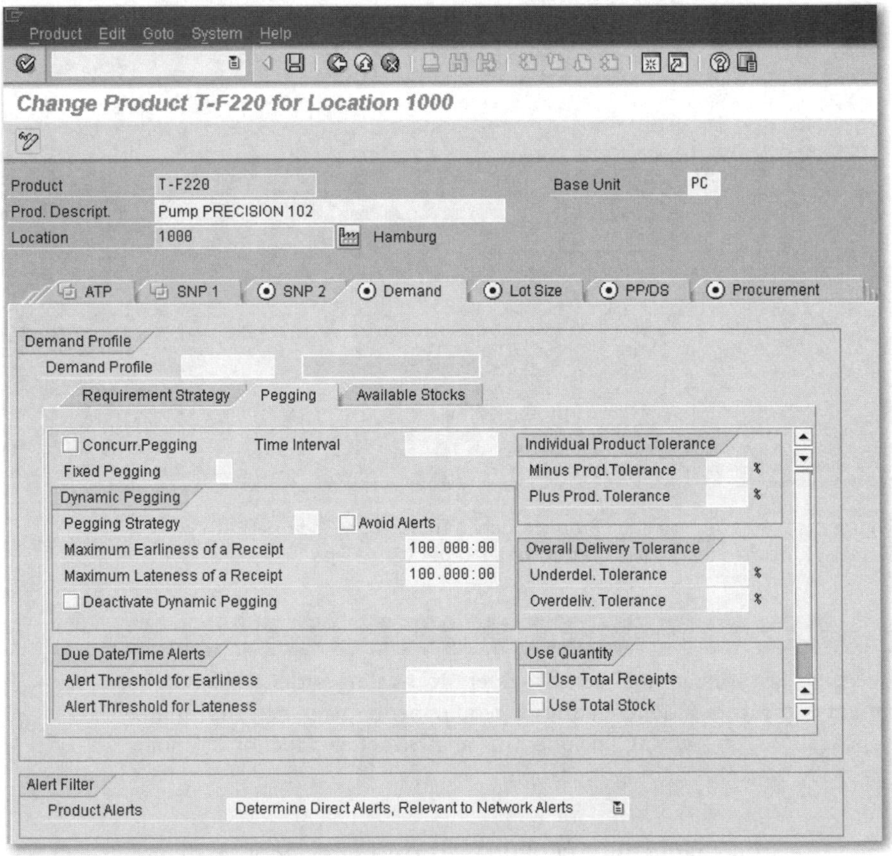

Figure 5.44 APO Transaction "Product," Transaction Code /SAPAPO/MAT1, "Demand" Tab with Pegging Settings

You use the pegging strategy to define how demand is covered by the assignment of receipt elements. You use the **Maximum Earliness (Lateness) of a Receipt** to specify the length of time that a receipt element can lie before or after a requirements element so that the system sets a pegging relationship regardless of the distance in time. No pegging links are generated for larger intervals of time. You can also set the degree of earliness (lateness) for which a date alert is issued.[19]

Note	Pegging and alerts

> Date alerts are generally based on pegging relationships. If a pegging relationship between a requirements and a receipt element cannot be set up, the system generates a quantity alert.

To receive date alerts, it might help if you enable pegging with long or practically infinite maximum periods of lateness or earliness.[20]

As of APO 4.0, you can also switch off pegging in the product master. Please note that when you select this option, it affects all applications that work with dynamic pegging. Detailed planning, PP/DS optimization, certain PP/DS heuristics, and more are affected, and date alerts can no longer be generated.

When an alert occurs in the component level of a multilevel pegging network, you can make the alert visible in the entire network and particularly for the related end product by selecting the network alert in the product view, the alert monitor, and so on (see Figure 5.45). You can use the **Product Alert** flag in the product master to filter the output of alerts (as of APO 4.0). For less-critical products, you can switch off all alerts or only network alerts.

Network alerts

---

19 The time intervals are determined on the basis of a continuous time bar, that is, factory calendars or shift models are not taken into account.

20 Note that up to APO 4.0, the days' supply analysis is based on the pegging relationships, which means that this setting usually doesn't provide any useful information regarding the days' supply. As of APO 4.1, the days' supply logic works in such a way that the first shortage quantity or the first date alert determines the days' supply.

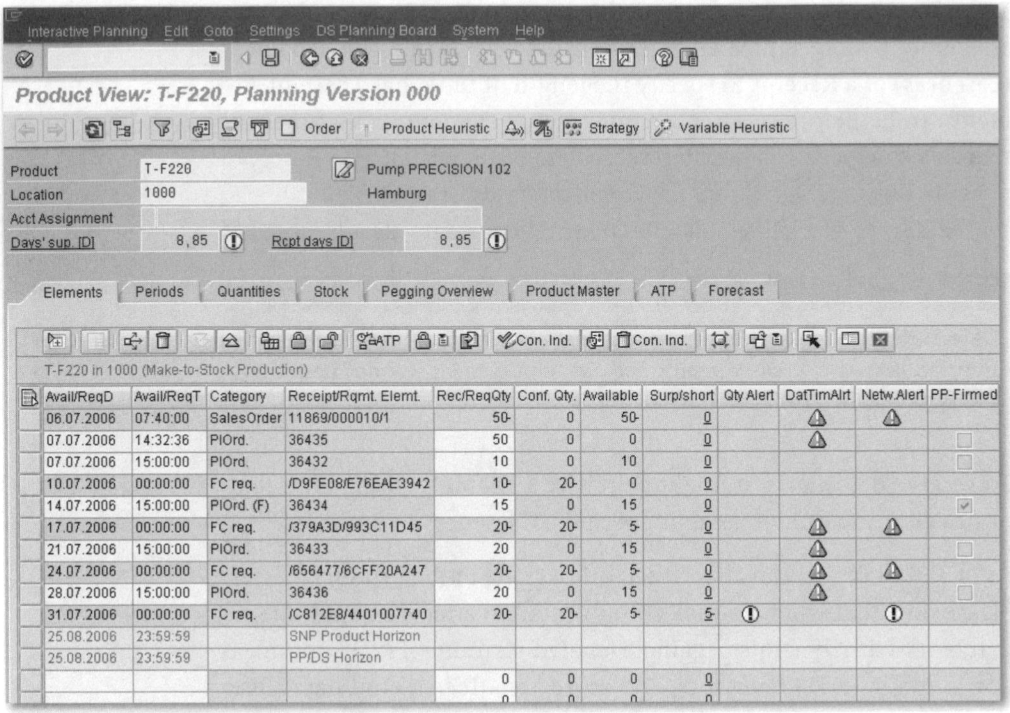

Figure 5.45 APO Transaction "Product View," Transaction Code /SAPAPO/RRP3, Product View with Columns for Quantity, Date and Time, and Network Alerts

5.10.2 Fixed Pegging

Dynamic pegging relationships can be fixed so that the system no longer automatically changes the pegging relationships, even if planning changes. Fixed pegging assigns a specific quantity of a product receipt to a specific requirement.

Manual fixing

You can set fixing manually for individual orders, and you can also fix the links to partial quantities or alternate orders (an alternative to the proposal from dynamic pegging).

Mass fixing

You can perform mass fixing of pegging relationships with heuristic **SAP_PP_019**, **Fix Pegging Relationships** (see Figure 5.46). You can execute this heuristic individually so that you generate one-level fixed pegging for the selected products. Or you can combine it with planning to generate a multilevel pegging network.

You can use heuristic **SAP_PP_011**, **Delete Fixed Pegging Relationships**, to delete pegging relationships. You can determine whether

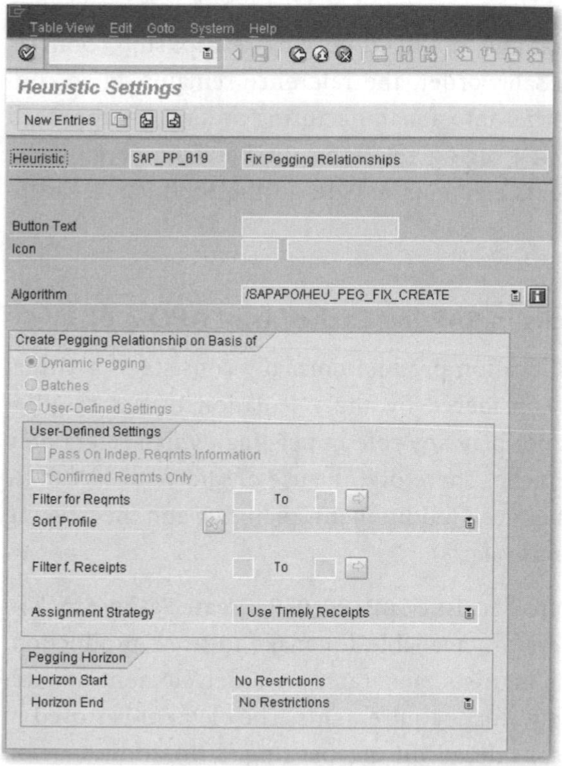

Figure 5.46 APO Customizing Screen "Maintain Heuristics," Transaction Code /SAPAPO/CDPSC11, Heuristic SAP_PP_019 to Fix Pegging Relationships

you want to delete manually or automatically fixed pegging relationships.

Fixed pegging is primarily used in automated capacity planning, when the pegging links should be considered during a particular period for specific orders and components. Consider the following procedures: The first step of the procedure fixes the pegging relationships with the appropriate heuristic, followed by execution of capacity planning with a strategy that considers the fixed pegging relationships. The last step then deletes the pegging relationships (see Chapter 7).

Using fixed pegging

Please note that up to and including APO 4.0, fixed pegging disappears with the change of documents, for instance, when an order is converted.

As of APO 4.1, the fixed pegging relationships remain after a change of documents. For example, if a fixed pegging relationship connects a planned order to a sales order, the reference remains when converting the planned order into a manufacturing order. This approach ensures that the fixed pegging relationships between receipt elements and requirements elements remain during production execution.[21]

Inheriting fixed pegging as of APO 4.1

5.10.3 Safety Stocks in SAP liveCache (as of APO 4.0)

The safety stock of a location product normally consists of a virtual requirement that is considered by the calculation of net requirements, but that does not play any role in pegging, which refers only to orders in SAP liveCache. Therefore, the use of safety stocks can be inherently different between requirements planning and the pegging structure (along with the alerts).

As of APO 4.0, standard heuristic **SAP_PP_018, Create Safety Stock in SAP liveCache**, is therefore available for make-to-stock production. The execution of this heuristic generates an order element of category SR for static safety stock requirements. The element is stored in SAP liveCache and considered during pegging.[22] (In addition, you must also activate safety stocks depending on the planning versions by using the setting **Consider safety stock requirements in SAP liveCache**.)

5.11 Setup Times in Planning

There are two different ways that you can schedule a setup activity in APO-PP/DS:

► **Sequence-independent**
A general setup time that does not depend on the actual conditions is scheduled with the normal activity durations of the setup

---

21 See SAP Notes 698427 and 704583. To transfer a pegging relationship from a production order to inventory stock, you must activate this function in ECC customizing.
22 Apart from PP/DS, the global ATP check can also consider the safety stock requirements.

activity in PPM/PDS. Lot-size-independent durations are typical for setup activities.

▶ **Sequence-dependent**
Setup times that depend on the state of the resource (as defined by the setup key or a setup group) can be scheduled via the **Setup Matrix** that specifies the length of the setup time from a previous setup state to a follow-up setup state. Sequence-dependent setup times can be used only for single activity resources.

The setup matrix is defined in the master data of product planning and cannot be transferred from ECC. The setup matrix is a transition matrix that contains the setup length of every possible setup transition. The setup length is needed to take the resource from one setup state to another. It can also contain setup costs that might be relevant to optimization (see Figure 5.47).

Setup matrix

Display Setup Transitions

| Location | 1000 | |
| Setup Matrix | PAINT SHOP | Paint Shop |

Setup Transitions

S	Predecssr	Successor	Setup Time	Unit	Setup Costs
		*	15	MIN	0
	*	1	100	MIN	0
E	10	10	4	MIN	0
E	10	20	40	MIN	0
E	10	30	60	MIN	0
E	10	40	80	MIN	0
E	10	50	100	MIN	0
E	10	60	20	MIN	0
E	20	10	120	MIN	0
E	20	20	4	MIN	0
E	20	30	40	MIN	0
E	20	40	60	MIN	0
E	20	50	80	MIN	0
E	20	60	20	MIN	0
E	30	10	120	MIN	0
E	30	20	100	MIN	0
E	30	30	4	MIN	0
E	30	40	40	MIN	0
E	30	50	60	MIN	0

Figure 5.47 APO Transaction "Setup Matrix," Transaction Code /SAPAPO/CDPSC7, Display of a Setup Matrix

Sequence-depen-
dent setup times

To use sequence-dependent setup times, you must enter the **Setup Matrix** in the independent resource (see Figure 5.48). You must also enter the **Setup Key** in PPM/PDS for the relevant operations or enter the **Setup Group**, which you can transfer from the ECC routing. In addition, you must also set the **Setup Activity** flag in the setup activity so that the setup time is read from the setup matrix.

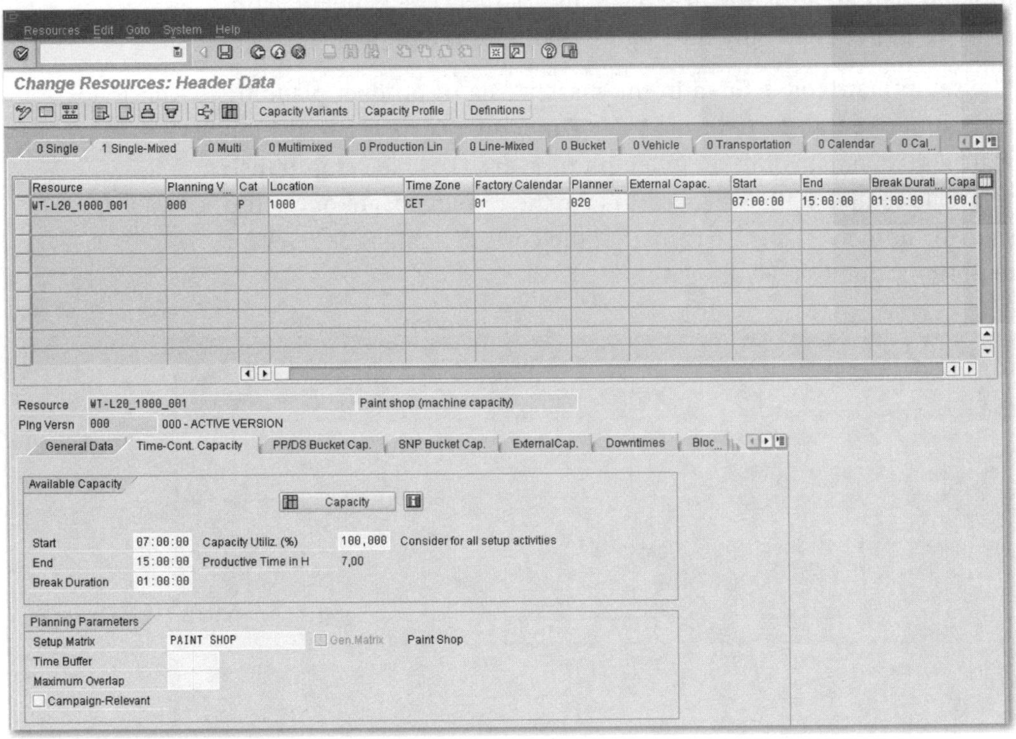

Figure 5.48 APO Transaction "Resource," Transaction Code /SAPAPO/RES01, Resource with Setup Matrix

With these settings, the setup activity is automatically scheduled according to the setup matrix during scheduling.

Setup optimization

Sequence-dependent setup times and setup costs are especially important with setup optimization using the PP/DS Optimizer. You can optimize the production plan in light of the total of the setup times or the total of the setup costs (see Chapters 6 and 7).

5.12 Product Interchangeability (as of APO 4.0)

APO-PP/DS uses the functionality of product interchangeability for the functionality of phase-out control, which replaces one product with another. It is available as of APO 4.0.

Product interchangeability is defined in the master data via **product interchangeability groups**. For planning in PP/DS, you must create an interchangeability group of the **supersession chain group**. In the interchangeability group type, you store substitution chains that specify a follow-up product for a product and a validity date (see Figure 5.49). With the direction of interchangeability and the use-up strategy of the supersession chain, you define whether and how any leftovers of the previous product can be used up before the follow-up product is procured.[23]

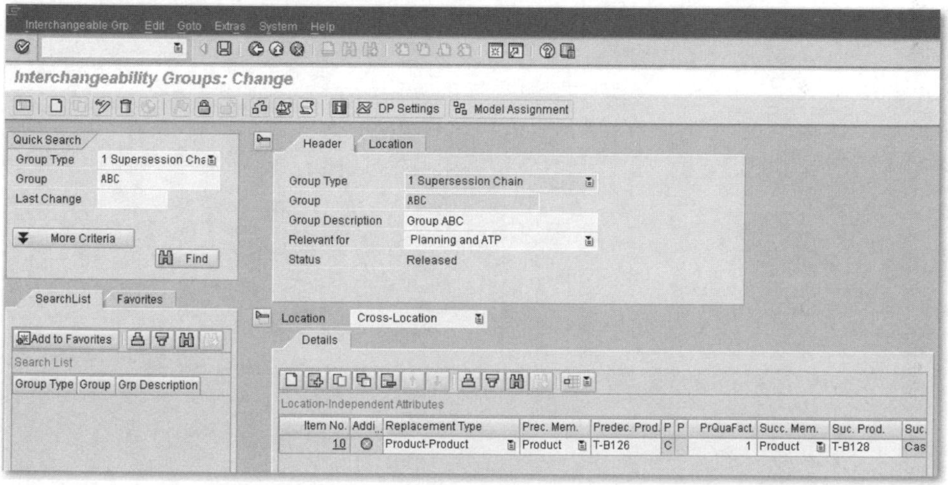

Interchangeability group

Figure 5.49 APO Transaction "Maintain Interchangeability Group," Transaction Code /INCMD/UI, Maintenance of a Supersession Chain

When you maintain the supersession chain, an appropriate planning package is automatically created for the affected location products (planning package type 001: planning package for supersession chains). The planning package contains heuristic **SAP_PP_I001**, which is used to plan the products of the supersession chain in the correct sequence.

Planning package

---

23 For information on the transfer of ECC data for phase-out control to APO, see SAP Notes 617281 (as of Release 4.6C) and 617283 (prior to Release 4.6C).

Planning with supersession chains

When you plan with supersession chains, the requirements of the preceding and follow-up products are transferred as substitution orders that appear in the preceding product as a receipt element and in the follow-up product as a requirement. This requirement leads to procurement of the follow-up product (see Figure 5.50).

Product View: T-B126, Planning Version 000

Product: T-B126 — Casing
Location: 1000 — Hamburg
Acct Assignment:
Days' sup. [D]: 8,10   Rcpt days [D]: 9.999,99

Tabs: Elements | Periods | Quantities | Stock | Pegging O...

T-B126 in 1000 (Make-to-Stock Production)

Avail/ReqD	Avail/ReqT	Category	Rec/RqtEle	Rec/R...	Conf.	Avail...
27.06.2006	12:21:47	Stock	/0001/CC	10	10	10
28.06.2006	13:02:10	DepDmd	36503/0001	10-	0	0
05.07.2006	14:51:53	PlOrd.	36489	10	0	10
05.07.2006	14:51:53	DepDmd	36499/0001	10-	0	0
12.07.2006	14:51:53	PlOrd.	36488	10	0	10
12.07.2006	14:51:53	DepDmd	36497/0001	10-	0	0
19.07.2006	14:51:53	PlOrd.	36490	10	0	10
19.07.2006	14:51:53	DepDmd	36501/0001	10-	0	0
26.07.2006	14:51:53	PlOrd.	36520	10	0	10
26.07.2006	14:51:53	DepDmd	36504/0001	10-	0	0
02.08.2006	14:51:53	Subst.ord.	161685/1/1	10	0	10
02.08.2006	14:51:53	DepDmd	36500/0001	10-	0	0
09.08.2006	14:51:53	Subst.ord.	161686/1/1	10	0	10
09.08.2006	14:51:53	DepDmd	36506/0001	10-	0	0
16.08.2006	14:51:53	Subst.ord.	161687/1/1	10	0	10
16.08.2006	14:51:53	DepDmd	36502/0001	10-	0	0
23.08.2006	14:51:53	Subst.ord.	161688/1/1	10	0	10
23.08.2006	14:51:53	DepDmd	36505/0001	10-	0	0
30.08.2006	14:51:53	Subst.ord.	161689/1/1	10	0	10
30.08.2006	14:51:53	DepDmd	36507/0001	10-	0	0
06.09.2006	14:51:53	Subst.ord.	161690/1/1	10	0	10
06.09.2006	14:51:53	DepDmd	36498/0001	10-	0	0
13.09.2006	14:51:53	Subst.ord.	161691/1/1	10	0	10
13.09.2006	14:51:53	DepDmd	36496/0001	10-	0	0
14.09.2006	23:59:59		SNP Product H			
14.09.2006	23:59:59		PP/DS Horizor			

Product View: T-B128, Planning Version 000

Product: T-B128 — Casing
Location: 1000 — Hamburg
Acct Assignment:
Days' sup. [D]: 9.999,99   Rcpt days [D]: 9.999,99

Tabs: Elements | Periods | Quantities | Stock | Pegging Ov...

T-B128 in 1000 (Make-to-Stock Production)

Avail/ReqD	Avail/ReqT	Category	Rec/RqtEle	Rec/R...	Conf.	Avail...
27.06.2006	12:24:25	Stock	/0001/CC	10	10	10
02.08.2006	14:51:53	Subst.req.	161685/1/1	10-	0	0
09.08.2006	14:51:53	PlOrd.	36516	10	0	10
09.08.2006	14:51:53	Subst.req.	161686/1/1	10-	0	0
16.08.2006	14:51:53	PlOrd.	36519	10	0	10
16.08.2006	14:51:53	Subst.req.	161687/1/1	10-	0	0
23.08.2006	14:51:53	PlOrd.	36515	10	0	10
23.08.2006	14:51:53	Subst.req.	161688/1/1	10-	0	0
30.08.2006	14:51:53	PlOrd.	36518	10	0	10
30.08.2006	14:51:53	Subst.req.	161689/1/1	10-	0	0
06.09.2006	14:51:53	PlOrd.	36517	10	0	10
06.09.2006	14:51:53	Subst.req.	161690/1/1	10-	0	0
13.09.2006	14:51:53	PlOrd.	36521	10	0	10
13.09.2006	14:51:53	Subst.req.	161691/1/1	10-	0	0
14.09.2006	23:59:59		SNP Product H(			
14.09.2006	23:59:59		PP/DS Horizon			

Figure 5.50 SAP APO Transaction "Product View" (Two Models), Transaction Code/SAPAPO/RRP3, Product Views with Substitution Orders as Receipt Element for the Preceding Product and Requirement for the Follow-Up Product

Components in planned orders

If the product to be substituted involves the components of a planned order, the substitution order therefore covers the dependent requirement, which appears as a requirement for the follow-up component. If the planned order is ultimately converted into a manufacturing order, the old components are then replaced by the new components *in the order itself*.

Similarly, the replacement takes place when executing an ATP check with the use of substitution chains.

5.13   Executing Planning in ECC

Note the basic rule for planning in APO-PP/DS: Planning occurs in APO-PP/DS; planning is executed in ECC. The planned order (or the purchase requisition) is converted into a manufacturing order (or purchase order, respectively) in APO to execute planning.

Unlike in ECC, in APO planned orders already contain all the production dates. If a planned order is transferred to ECC, the ECC planned order contains only the basic dates and all dependent requirements. The production start and end dates are transferred as basic dates. Integration at the level of detailed scheduling is therefore not realized for the planned orders. For this reason, the conversion of planned orders must occur in APO.

The conversion of an APO planned order corresponds only to setting the conversion flag (manually for one order or via mass conversion for orders and purchase requisitions, see Figure 5.12). If an APO planned order with the conversion flag is transferred to ECC through the CIF, a corresponding manufacturing order is created in ECC. The order assumes the production dates determined in APO.

The integration of the orders is maintained. Specific status information or production confirmations that are created in ECC and are relevant to planning are transferred from ECC to the APO order. All data relevant to planning must be and remain consistent (see Figure 5.51). In addition, the ECC production order also contains a variety of functions to execute production—functions that do not require integration with the APO order, such as printing of the order papers and consumption.

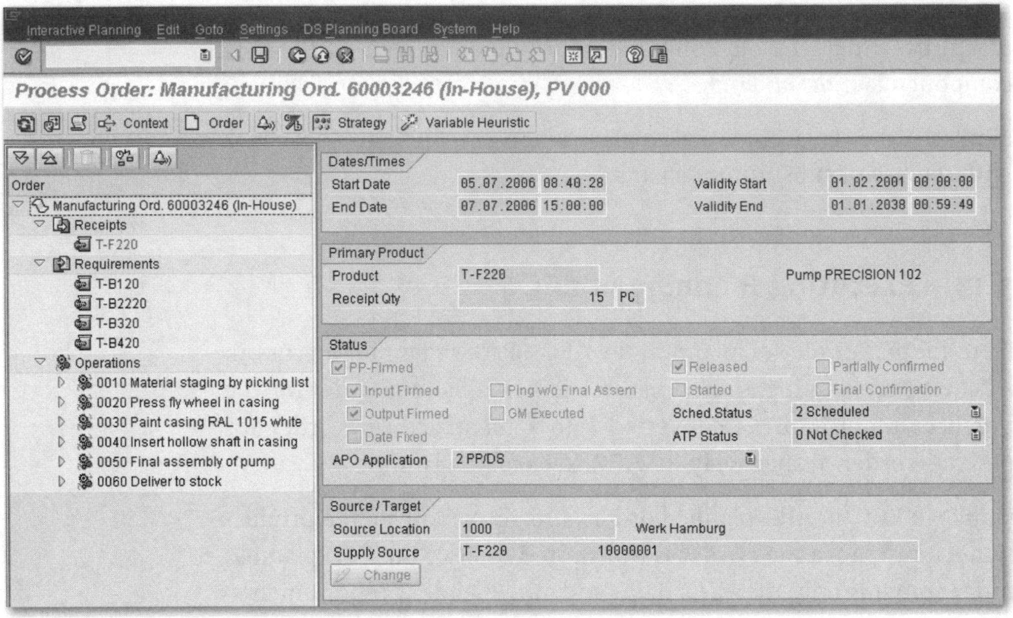

Figure 5.51 APO Transaction "Product View," Transaction Code /SAPAPO/RRP3, Details of a Production Order

The evaluation tools of APO-PP/DS are vitally important for an efficient assessment of planning results. These tools enable focused and interactive processing of the planning situation.

6 Tools to Evaluate and Process Planning

You can use graphical and table-based evaluation tools for interactive planning and to evaluate the planning results. The orientation and goals of your planning determine the selection of tools. You must make a fundamental differentiation between the evaluation and processing of an individual location product—which refers to a product within a plant—and the mass selection of several products that are then simultaneously or sequentially processed and evaluated. You must also distinguish between PP and DS planning activities, or, in simpler terms, between requirements and capacity planning.

The following sections describe the most important tools of production planning and detailed scheduling in terms of these properties and characterize them according to their business background.

6.1 Order Views

The tools summarized as *order views* enable you to view and process MRP elements based on products and locations. Depending on the goals of processing, various individual transactions come into play: receipts view, requirements view (in which you can call several products), order processing, pegging overview, and the product view (which can refer to an order or a product).

The product view is the central tool for requirements planning. It provides you with a complete and informative overview of the requirements and stock situation for a location product and is therefore the APO equivalent to the **Stock requirements list** in ECC. The following sections focus on the product view of a product, because it contains most of the functionality of the receipts view, the requirements view, order processing, and the pegging overview.

6.1.1 Entering the Product View

As shown in Figure 6.1, you enter the planning situation of a location product with the planning version, product, and location. As another option, you can also use a selection rule or directly access special stock.

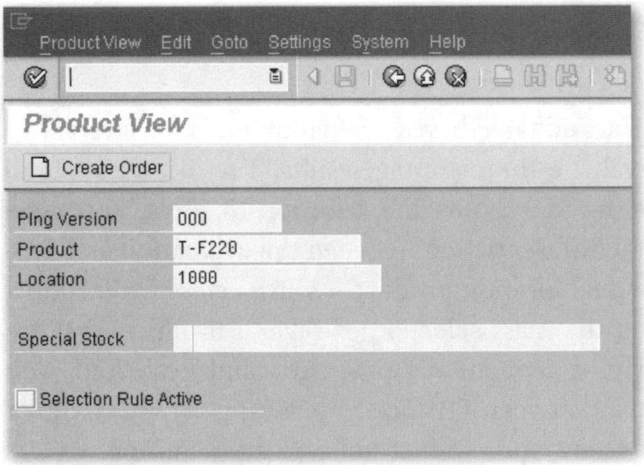

Figure 6.1 "Product View" Transaction in APO, Transaction Code /SAPAPO/RRP3, Initial Screen of the Product View

6.1.2 Structure of the Product View

The product view (see Figure 6.2) shows the MRP elements of a location product in a table. The temporal sequence goes from top (older elements) to bottom (future elements).

"Account statement" for a product

The product view provides traditional evaluation functions for a location product. Here you can read the entries for the quantity and date situation like an account statement. Goods receipts and issues are identified by date, and you can see the expected stock quantity for every date. You also have the option to change the planning situation of a location product in a targeted manner with individual MRP elements or to plan the relevant product interactively as a whole.

Tabs in the product view

Supplemented background information on the current situation of the product is displayed directly (such as **Days' supply**) or on separate tabs: **Product Master** in display mode, **Pegging Overview**, and— if available—the **Forecast** or the **Consumption** Situation.

You can find more detailed information on each MRP element directly in the table row (such as exception messages) or in the detail view after you call the MRP element.

Avail/ReqD	Avail/ReqT	Category	Receipt/Rqmt. Elemt.	Rec/ReqQty	Conf. Qty	Available	Surp/short	Qty Alert	PP-Firmed	Conv. Ind	Not PegRel M	ATP Status	Priority	Start Date	Start Time	Req. Qty	BUn	Categ
27.06.2006	12:34:21	Stock	/0002/CC	20	20	20	0						0			0	PC	Valua
07.07.2006	15:00:00	PrdOrd (R)	80003245	20	0	40	0		✓			Not Checked	0	04.07.2006	08:16:28	0	PC	Produ
10.07.2006	00:00:00	FC req.	/4D358D/56536BCA48	40-	40-	0	0						0			0	PC	Plann
14.07.2006	15:00:00	PlOrd. (F)	38624	20	0	20	0		✓	☐		Not Checked	0	11.07.2006	08:16:28	0	PC	Plann
17.07.2006	00:00:00	FC req.	/882320/1B5D19BF4E	20-	20-	0	0						0			0	PC	Plann
21.07.2006	15:00:00	PlOrd.	36527	20	0	20	0		☐	☐		Not Checked	0	18.07.2006	10:29:02	0	PC	Plann
24.07.2006	00:00:00	FC req.	/0556E8/1B4C25864E	20-	20-	0	0						0			0	PC	Plann
28.07.2006	15:00:00	PlOrd.	36523	20	0	20	0		☐	☐		Not Checked	0	25.07.2006	10:29:02	0	PC	Plann
31.07.2006	00:00:00	FC req.	/0C3AD0/43E44AA140	20-	20-	0	0						0			0	PC	Plann
04.08.2006	15:00:00	PlOrd.	36522	20	0	20	0		☐	☐		Not Checked	0	01.08.2006	10:29:02	0	PC	Plann
07.08.2006	00:00:00	FC req.	/4E5B21/79430D045	20-	20-	0	0						0			0	PC	Plann
11.08.2006	15:00:00	PlOrd.	38526	20	0	20	0		☐	☐		Not Checked	0	08.08.2006	10:29:02	0	PC	Plann
14.08.2006	00:00:00	FC req.	/787312/CAFF401646	20-	20-	0	0						0			0	PC	Plann
18.08.2006	15:00:00	PlOrd.	36525	20	0	20	0		☐	☐		Not Checked	0	15.08.2006	10:29:02	0	PC	Plann
21.08.2006	00:00:00	FC req.	/31022C/D8F7DC5149	20-	20-	0	0						0			0	PC	Plann
25.08.2006	23:59:59		SNP Product Horizon										0					End c
25.08.2006	23:59:59		PP/DS Horizon										0					End c
28.08.2006	00:00:00	FC req.	/FEAD3F/F3F8D61046	20-	20-	20-	20-	⚠					0			0	PC	Plann
				0	0	0	0						0			0	PC	
				0	0	0	0						0			0	PC	
				0	0	0	0						0			0	PC	

Product View: T-F220, Planning Version 000

Product: T-F220 — Pump PRECISION 102
Location: 1000 — Hamburg
Acct Assignment:
Days' sup. ID: 12,48 — Rcpt days ID: 61,48

Elements | Periods | Quantities | Stock | Pegging Overview | Product Master | ATP | Forecast

T-F220 in 1000 (Make-to-Stock Production)

Figure 6.2 "Product View" Transaction in APO, Transaction Code /SAPAPO/RRP3, Product View in Change Mode

Planning segments

Depending on the business background, the product view can refer to various planning segments (forecast segment and make-to-order segments, for example) that are usually required because of a special inventory management.

Please note that in this case, horizons like the SNP production horizon or the PP/DS horizon are displayed only in the make-to-stock segment, because that is the only place where they are effective.

6.1.3 Application of the Product View

Interactive planning

Along with the purely evaluative functionality for the current planning situation of a product in a specific location, interactive processing of the planning results with the product view is extremely important. Once you have activated the change mode, you can edit changeable MRP elements—individually and manually, for example. Double-click to drill down to the details on the MRP element.

Using heuristics

In the real world, a typical planning process for interactive planning of the entire situation of a product also includes various useful tools like heuristics, dynamic exception messages (use an appropriate alert profile here), or the overview tree. You can access heuristics in change mode with the product heuristic as described in Chapter 5 (default) or with the variable heuristic (exceptional case). In general, planning occurs only for the product itself, not for its subassemblies or for other products. The planning result is binding only after it is saved to the database, therefore after you perform interactive planning, you can evaluate the result and cancel it if it does not meet your needs.

Converting MRP elements

In the product view, planning is completed with the conversion of the planned orders or purchase requisitions into production orders and purchase orders. You can also perform this step manually from the product view for each planned order. For mass application, you can use a separate mass conversion (see Chapter 5).

> **Note**
>
> Conversion must always occur in APO so that ECC can also access the procurement dates that are calculated in APO.

Capacity situation

The planned orders created under PP/DS are always lead-time scheduled and can therefore generate capacity requirements on the resources involved. This allows you to go to the capacity requirements situation of a planned order from its detailed view.

6.1.4 Customizing the Product View

Settings in the product view

To configure the product view to your personal requirements, it's best to take a look at the user settings first: You can make comprehensive default settings (with several profiles) specific to a user.

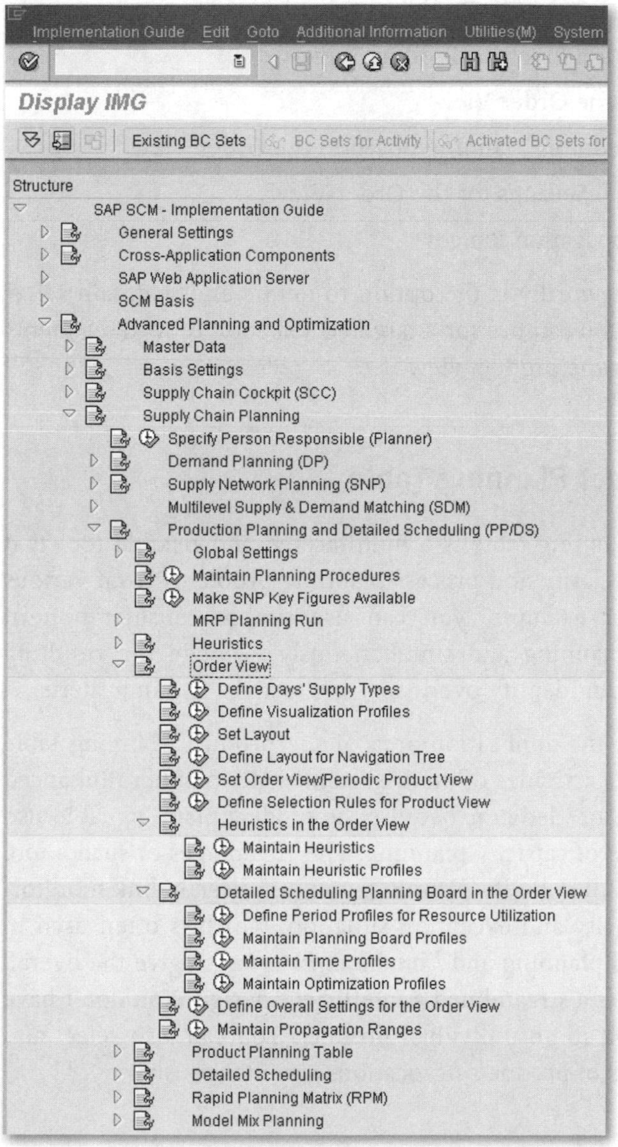

Figure 6.3 APO Customizing of PP/DS, Submenu for Order View

Actual customizing (see Figure 6.3) refers to the following settings:

▶ Define Days' Supply Types
▶ Define Visualization Profiles
▶ Set Layout
▶ Define Layout for Navigation Tree

- ▶ Set Order View/Periodic Product View
- ▶ Define Selection Rules for Product View
- ▶ Heuristics in the Order View
- ▶ Detailed Scheduling Planning Board in the Order View
- ▶ Define Overall Settings for the Order View
- ▶ Maintain Propagation Ranges

Particularly noteworthy is the option to define and maintain selection rules that you can use for a targeted selection of MRP elements when you enter the product view.

6.2   Product Planning Table

Quantity and capacity planning

The product planning table is a multifaceted and flexible tool that you can use to clarify and process planning problems from various viewpoints. For example, you can use simple consideration of requirements planning and simultaneously evaluate the resulting capacity situation, identify overloads, and analyze dynamic alerts.

In many cases, the application area of the product planning table goes beyond the activities of the traditional MRP planner. Enhanced responsibility is needed here because the product planning table also includes aspects of capacity planning. The advantages of such a tool are obvious. With quantity planning, you can directly link monitoring of the capacity and exception situation, which is often used in period-oriented planning and *lean manufacturing* to give the overall planning process a streamlined and efficient design. You don't have to limit yourself to an individual product. You can also select and consider groups of products or locations simultaneously.

6.2.1   Entering the Product Planning Table

You should select objects with the aspect of performance in mind: Use appropriate constraints to limit the selection.

Criteria for getting started

In addition to limiting the selection to a particular planning period, you might also limit the selection of products to be planned. In these cases, the system will offer you all the resources for planning that are used in the context of the related production data structures or production process models. Conversely, you can also use the selection for a resource in the **Resource** tab for a simple way to select all the products that can be produced on the respective resource. Similarly, you can select the **Production planner** to find the objects for which the planner is responsible. As shown in Figure 6.4, tabs are available to organize the various startup options.

You can also use **Extended selection** to limit the selection to specific MRP elements, such as products with requirements or receipt elements.

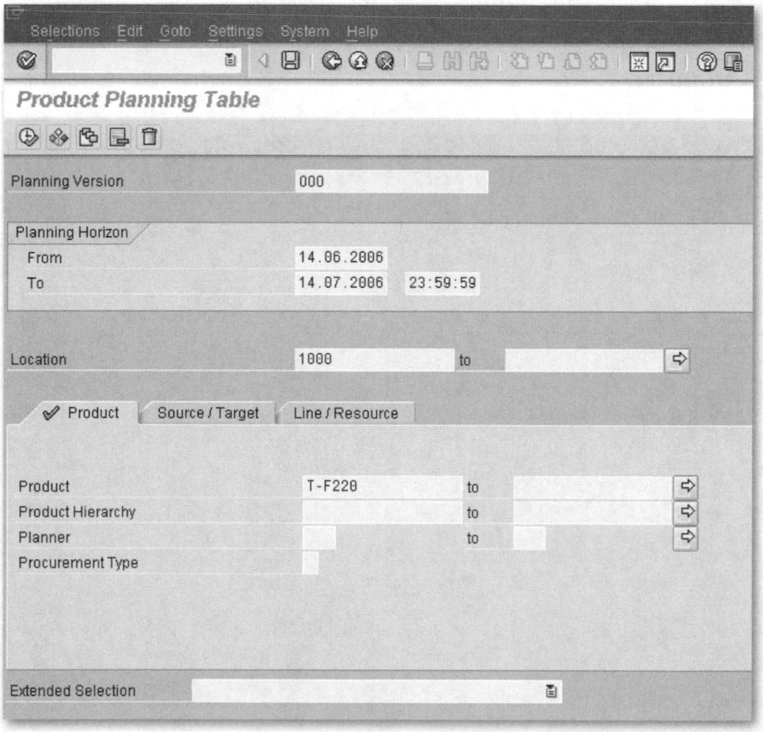

Figure 6.4 "Product Planning Table" Transaction in APO, Transaction Code /SAPAPO/PPT1, Startup Screen of the Product Planning Table

6.2.2   Structure of the Product Planning Table

The product planning table is primarily responsible for the APO mapping of the planning table of repetitive manufacturing from ECC, which traces the line and period-oriented planning of lean manufacturing. That's why the basic structure here is similar. However, the application area of the product planning table is significantly more extensive.

Navigation
structure; chart
selection
In general, the left side of the screen displays the navigation structure currently in use (top) and the charts selection (bottom); see Figure 6.5. The right-hand side of the screen contains the activated charts. You can display up to three charts simultaneously, along with the detailed view of an MRP element. You can manage the settings for chart selection by specific users and store the settings in variants. In addition to the traditional, period-oriented view, you have other options for views. The additional views extend the application area of the product planning table far beyond that of pure period-oriented planning. The additional views include an alert monitor, a product view (individual elements), a detailed scheduling board, and the Optimizer.

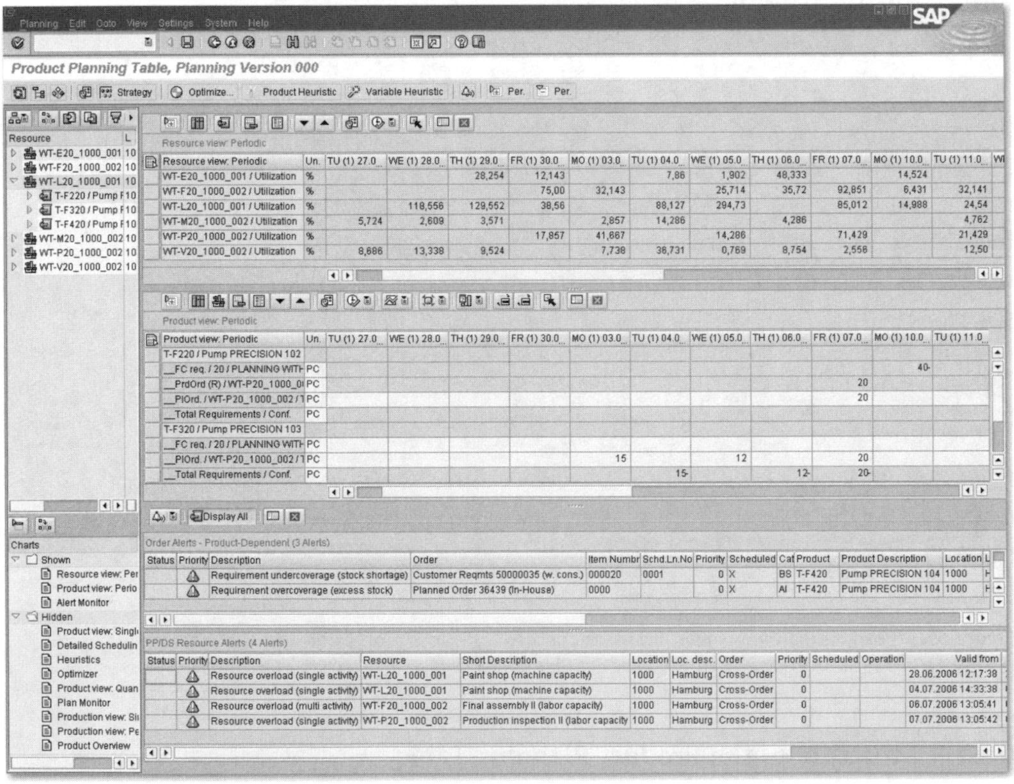

Figure 6.5 "Product Planning Table" Transaction in APO, Transaction Code /SAPAPO/PPT1, the Product Planning Table with Three Charts During Quantity and Capacity Planning

6.2.3 Application of the Product Planning Table

In Figure 6.5, **Resource view: Periodic**, **Product view: Periodic**, and the **Alert Monitor** have been selected in the chart selection. In terms of configuration, these selections represent a typical application in the area of period-oriented planning. By using these tools, you can interpret the requirements and procurement situation for a specific product (**Product view: Periodic**) or change it in the white-colored lower fields that are ready for input. The resulting dynamic exception messages (like shortages or resource overloads) are displayed in the chart of the Alert Monitor. You can use the PP/DS alert profile to select what exception messages to display and at what level (as errors, warnings, or information). You can manage the PP/DS alert profile from the product planning table or in the Alert Monitor (see Section 6.7).

An application is therefore an interactive, exception-based or alert-based planning to create or improve the production program, which is based on the *dynamic exception messages* that occur. At the same time, you can use **Resource view: Periodic** to interpret and monitor the overall load situation on the resources in the period under consideration. Particularly for line-loading planning, this approach represents an elegant combination to monitor the date and capacity situation in the period under consideration. And it does so in the context of manual or partially automated requirements planning that is executed in the chart of the product view.

Alert-based planning

In the event of overloads, you can determine the pegged requirement by double-clicking on the related capacity requirement to find the reason for the overload, such as an existing load from another product. The planner can then reschedule to an alternative resource or solve the problem situation in a different period.

Pegged requirement

In many practical applications, the information that requirements planning produces a 100 % load on the resources in use is sufficient. It means that a feasible plan was created and that it can be used to trigger production. But if several orders appear in each period in this type of scenario, and if a mandatory sequence of orders and operations are set to be performed within one day or even within one shift, you must also perform sequencing. In simple cases (as part of repetitive manufacturing), you can perform the sequencing with the help of the chart of the detailed scheduling board.

Sequence planning

Automated
planning

In addition to purely interactive, manual planning, the product planning table also enables you to use heuristics or the PP/DS Optimizer to trigger automatic planning. But that ability does not by any means exclude follow-up, interactive changes to the results of planning. Chapter 7 describes such processes, including the use of the product planning table.

Production list

After the close of planning, you can use **Resource view: Periodic** to create a printout of the resource load or the production program (production list) that is redirected to shop floor control.

6.2.4 Customizing the Product Planning Table

Settings of the
product planning
table

Numerous user settings are available for the product planning table. They affect the profile, appearance, the contents of columns and rows, and so on.

Customizing of the product planning table (see Figure 6.6) allows you to make numerous basic settings:

► Define Days' Supply Types
► Maintain Extended Selection
► Define Visualization Profiles
► Set Layout
► Define Layout for Navigation Tree
► Create Periodic Planning
► Maintain Optimization Profiles
► Heuristics in the Product Planning Table
► Detailed Scheduling Planning Board in the Product Planning Table
► Define Overall Settings for the Product Planning Table
► Maintain Propagation Ranges

The entry for overall settings is particularly noteworthy: You use it to maintain the overall profile. You manage the heuristics that you can call from the product planning table with the corresponding entry. You can configure the planning table and the navigation tree in a variety of ways.

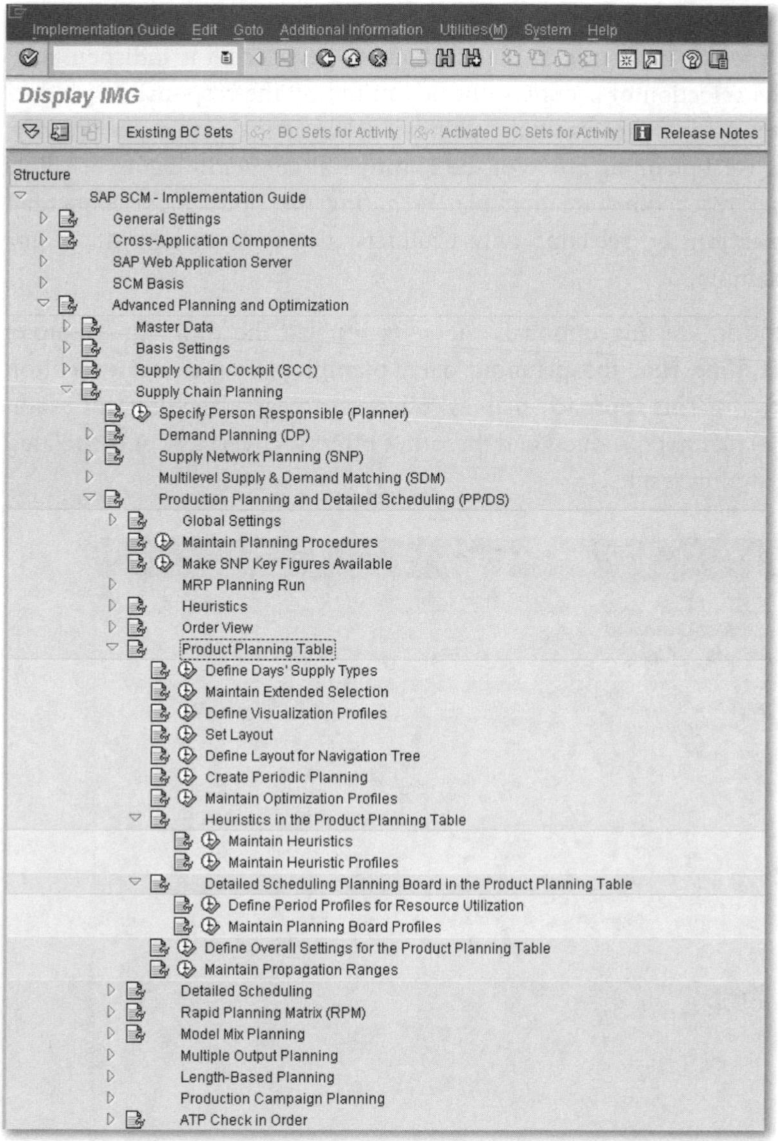

Figure 6.6 APO Customizing of PP/DS, Submenu for Product Planning Table

6.3   Product Overview

The product overview is a useful tool for daily work with mass data.   **Mass selection**
As of SAP SCM 4.0, you can implement collective access in a prese-
lected group of products, which is similar to the collective display of
the MRP lists in ECC.

6.3.1 Entering the Product Overview

Criteria for getting started

A specific limitation of the products to be selected is indispensable. The selection of products can be limited by the responsible production planner; for example, you can select specific products directly, or use a planning group or the **Planner**, as shown in Figure 6.7. Further restrictions are possible, including the options for **Expanded selection**, by selecting only products that show requirements, for example.

One interesting option is the selection via the (last, for example) planning run, the planning date, planning groups, and exception groups. This approach enables collective access to the (last, for example) planned products and therefore offers an overview of the related planning results.

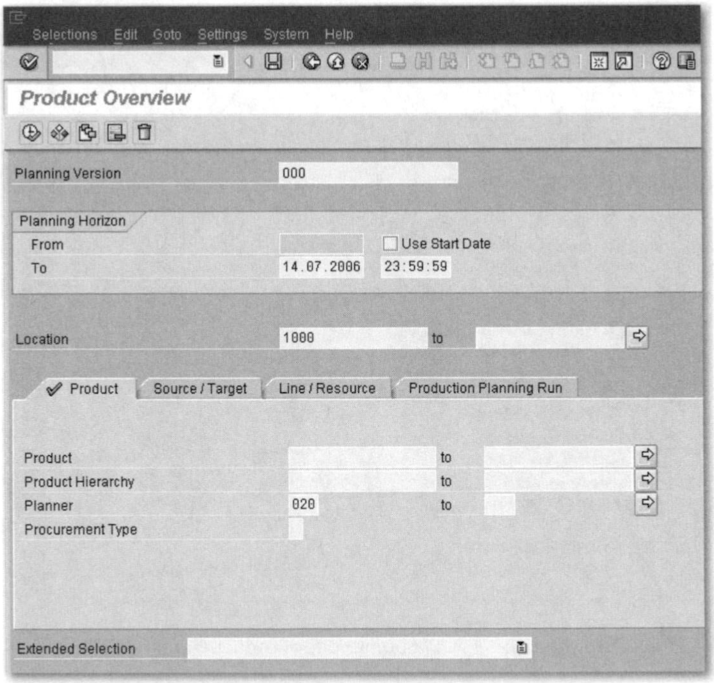

Figure 6.7 "Product Overview" Transaction in APO, Transaction Code /SAPAPO/POV1, Initial Screen of the Product Overview

6.3.2 Structure of the Product Overview

The product overview is designed like a table and provides a compact and informative overview and an insight into the situation of each of the products selected. Each product and the most important related information are displayed in an individual row. Such information includes any exception messages, information on stocks and days' supply, the largest shortages and surpluses, and the availability situation. Figure 6.8 shows a product overview. You can change and prepopulate the selection and sequence of the visible columns and make other layout settings for specific users.

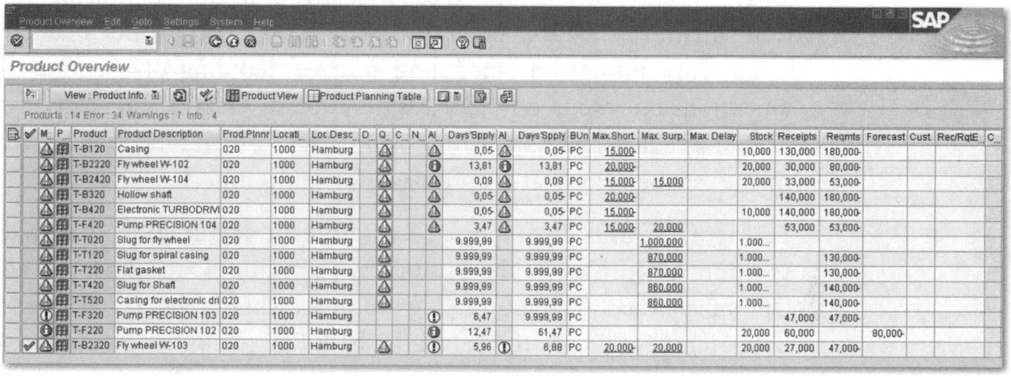

Figure 6.8 "Product Overview" Transaction in APO, Transaction Code /SAPAPO/POV1, Product Overview for Mass Selection of Products

6.3.3 Application of the Product Overview

Daily work with the product overview might consist of planners creating an overview of MRP for their own products. This can be done early in the morning, after a planning run has been performed successfully the previous night. Planners can create such an overview with the appropriate access criteria and by sorting the products displayed according to the sequence defined by the criteria. Targeted processing — product by product — usually occurs next.

Overview of the overall situation

In this context, the most critical products are usually considered first. You can obtain additional help by navigating to the product view and by using the product planning table and the Alert Monitor to clarify and handle planning problems from various viewpoints.

Systematic handling of problem cases

You use the processing indicator to distinguish between products that have already undergone processing and those that have not yet been considered. As of SAP SCM 5.0, you can have the indicator reset automatically at a logon or at midnight, or you can reset it manually.

Processing indicator

6.4   Detailed Scheduling Planning Board

Whereas the previous sections covered the product overview tool that can primarily be assigned to requirements planning, the following sections cover a tool related to detailed scheduling.

Graphical planning tool

The detailed scheduling planning board provides you with graphical planning functionality that is almost exclusively used in application areas entrusted with dedicated capacity planning and monitoring the load situation. The tasks associated with this context include manual or partially automated scheduling and rescheduling of orders and operations on resources with consideration of the available capacity load, the requirement dates/times, and other constraints, such as setting up sequencing that is optimized for setup times.

This work is usually supported by automatic features like detailed scheduling heuristics or the Optimizer. The planning results from the Optimizer usually undergo follow-up processing or are at least verified interactively with the detailed scheduling planning board.

Because of the effort involved and the numerous related constraints, in many real-world cases capacity planning is performed in a binding manner and in detail only for the bottleneck resources contained in the production process.

6.4.1   Entering the Detailed Scheduling Planning Board

Options for getting started

You have various options for accessing the detailed scheduling planning board. Views 1–3 offer the option to enter the transaction with an overall profile predefined by SAP. However, the user can also modify the overall profile with the variable view before access (see Figure 6.9). For example, you can choose appropriate subprofiles or change the **Work Area**. But you can also achieve faster, direct access without maintaining profiles with a direct selection via resources or the planner. You can then expand the selection later in the detailed scheduling planning board.

Work area and propagation range

You can change the work area from the initial screen. The work area defines the objects displayed in the detailed scheduling planning board. The selection of resources occurs directly with explicit selection or indirectly with selected orders or their operations. The products and resources that can be planned are defined in the propagation range. Accordingly, all the elements required for planning must be contained in the propagation range. Objects not contained in this area are considered frozen during planning. In customizing of the propagation range, you also have the option to design the propagation range and the work area with equal coverage.

You can define a new work area and change an existing work area from the initial screen. **Sets** enable the grouping of selection criteria within a view in this context. Logical AND links apply to selection criteria. For better performance, you should implement an efficient and restrictive limitation of the objects.

Selection using sets

You can define additional limitations by specifying the display and planning periods (use the **Time profile**).

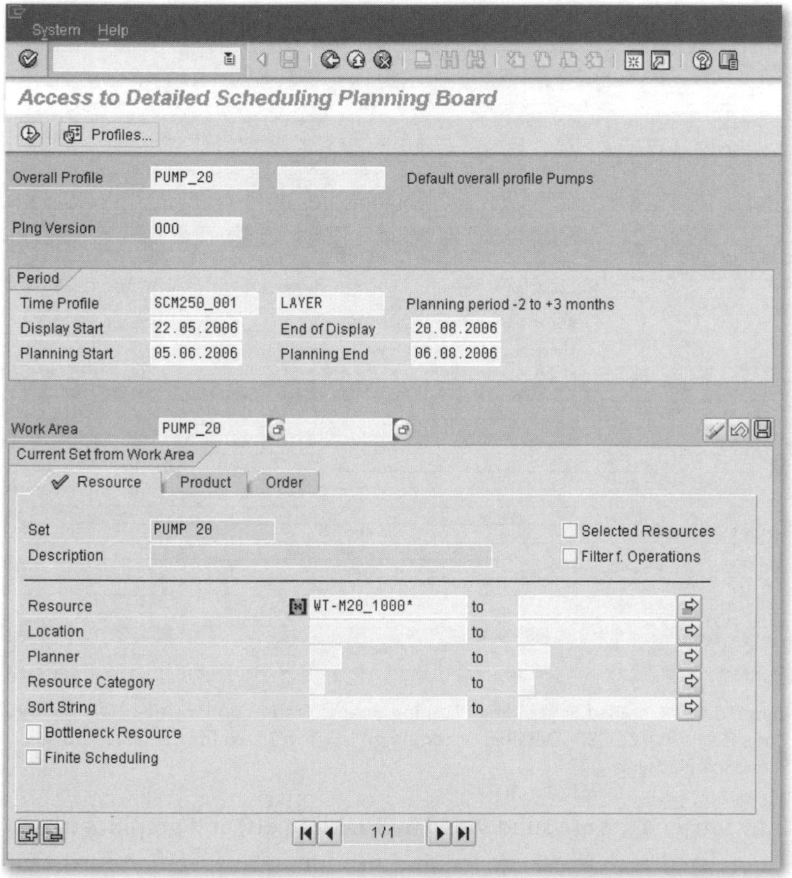

Figure 6.9 "Detailed Scheduling Planning Board" Transaction in APO, Transaction Code /SAPAPO/CDPS0, Initial Screen of the Detailed Scheduling Planning Board (Variable View)

6.4.2 Structure of the Detailed Scheduling Planning Board

Charts   The display of the resource schedule plan and the related inventory management is implemented in various charts within the detailed scheduling planning board (see Figure 6.10). You have options for charts on the resource situation, the product inventory, the orders, the operations, activities, and network displays of orders and operations. As of SAP SCM 5.0, selection help is also available for products and resources: a navigation area, or *shuffler*, which you can display on the left-hand side of the screen.

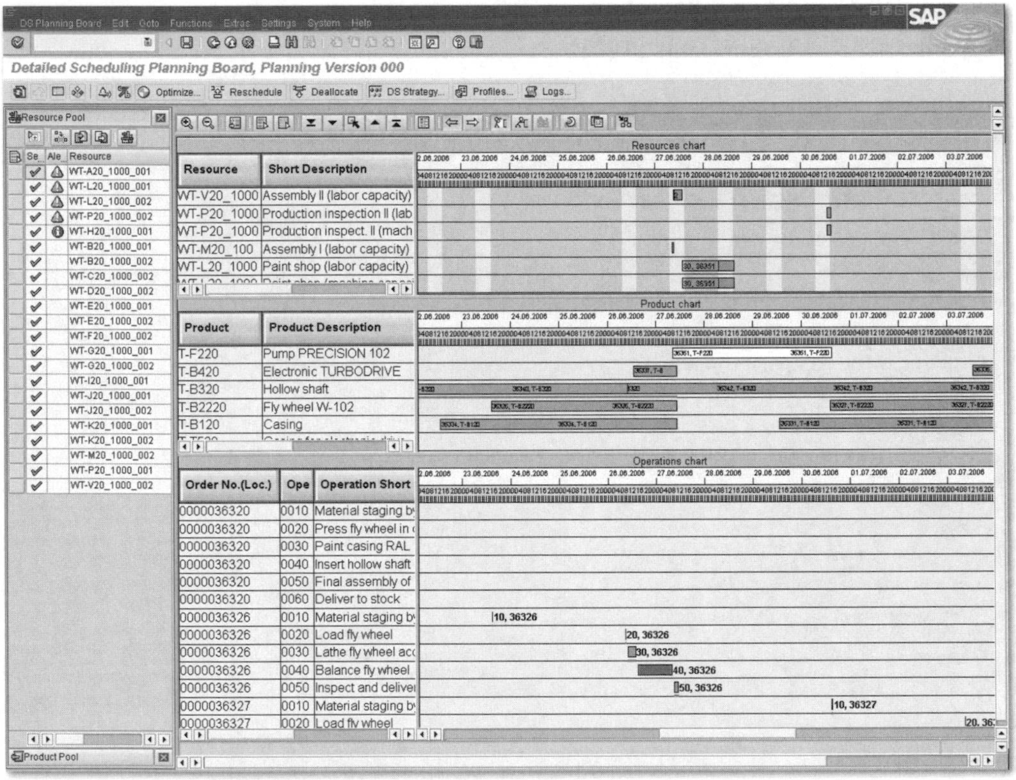

Figure 6.10 "Detailed Scheduling Planning Board" Transaction in APO, Transaction Code /SAPAPO/CDPS0, Detailed Scheduling Planning Board for Capacity and Sequence Planning

Individual charts are subdivided into tables (left) and graphics (right). The related resources, orders, and products are specified further in the table area. The diagram area displays the objects in graphical form according to their period of time and prolongation. You can store additional and general status information with symbols and colors in the layout of the planning board profile.

Comprehensive menus contain several utilities for the detailed scheduling planning board and round out the appearance of this tool.

6.4.3 Application of the Detailed Scheduling Planning Board

When using the detailed scheduling planning board, you have access to a comprehensive range of functions.

Important constraints for manual planning are available in the *detailed scheduling strategy* (DS strategy) for interactive planning. That's where you store entries, some of which apply only in combination with finite resources:

Detailed scheduling strategy

▸ Finite or infinite planning: During an attempt to schedule an operation on an occupied resource, the system reacts by rescheduling or by scheduling the operation and an exception message

▸ Finite planning (i.e., in case of finite planning, which way it is carried out: find slot in planning direction insert operation or squeeze-in operation)

▸ The planning direction (starting from the requirement date/time in a negative or positive direction)

▸ Manual planning in non-working times: permitted or not

▸ The scheduling sequence (based on the defined sort criteria)

▸ The inclusion or exclusion of internal order relationships: affects the relationships and the related time constraints

▸ The inclusion or exclusion of pegging relationships

These items are the basis of the central planning steps for regenerative planning, deallocation, and rescheduling operations on the resources in the detailed scheduling planning board with the goal of creating a feasible production program. You can perform some of these tasks with the respective buttons and perform others with drag-and-drop functionality or by entering a date and time during scheduling.

Scheduling Scheduling in the sense of regenerative planning loads the related operation onto the resource by using the currently valid strategy settings and generating the related capacity requirements. Scheduling is therefore also possible for already planned operations. This is useful when the overall situation or the strategy settings have changed.

Rescheduling Rescheduling might be required in an existing planning situation with several scheduled operations to create a new sequence if order prioritization changes or to shorten the related setup times and therefore possibly create room for additional operations. The related operation is shifted to a later time or assigned to an alternate resource.

Deallocation The deallocation status is primarily used when the date and time and the reference to a resource for an operation already exist based on earlier scheduling, but when the binding line loading must be cancelled because of orders with a higher priority. Otherwise, the resource would have already been blocked for the higher-priority order. The initial scheduling state is usually generated during requirements planning with the customizing setting of the planning procedure.

Undo function In your daily work, you will find the undo functionality particularly useful. It enables the cancellation of steps or a series of steps executed during manual planning. It applies to the functionalities of reallocation, deallocation, and drag and drop.

The following options and functionalities are especially noteworthy for interactive detailed scheduling:

▶ Interactive use of detailed scheduling heuristics

▶ Calling the PP/DS Optimizer

▶ Options to reload resources, interrupt operations, or store fixing intervals

▶ Highlighting objects for visual identification or logical summary

▶ Drilling down into multiple loadings

▶ Creating or changing orders

▶ Going to numerous other transactions

You can also use the following options:

▶ The operations or order lists—a summary of the objects planned to date (see Figures 6.11 and 6.12)

Chc	Order Number	Category	Priority	FullySched	PrtySched	Fixed	OutputFir	Input Fir	Ca	Ext	PeggedRqmt	PegReqOrNo	Loc	Product	Product Description	Reqmt Qty	Total Qty	Rec/ReqQty	BUn	Reqmt
	0000036320	PlOrd. (F)	0	☑	☐	☐	☑	☐			1000		1000	T-F220	Pump PRECISION 102	10	10	10	PC	
	0000036348	PlOrd.	0	☑	☐	☐	☐	☐			1000		1000		Pump PRECISION 102	5	5	5	PC	
	0000036349	PlOrd.	0	☑	☐	☐	☐	☐			1000		1000		Pump PRECISION 102	10	10	10	PC	
	0000036350	PlOrd.	0	☑	☐	☐	☐	☐			1000		1000		Pump PRECISION 102	20	20	20	PC	
	0000036351	PlOrd.	0	☑	☐	☐	☐	☐			1000		1000		Pump PRECISION 102	20	20	20	PC	
	0000036352	PlOrd.	0	☑	☐	☐	☐	☐			1000		1000		Pump PRECISION 102	20	20	20	PC	
	000060003246	PrdOrd (R)	0	☑	☐	☐	☑	☑			1000		1000		Pump PRECISION 102	15	15	15	PC	
	0000036330	PlOrd.	0	☑	☐	☐	☐	☐			1000	0000036348	1000	T-B420	Electronic TURBODRIVE	5	20	20	PC	
	0000036330	PlOrd.	0	☑	☐	☐	☐	☐			1000	000060003246	1000		Electronic TURBODRIVE	15	20	20	PC	
	0000036333	PlOrd.	0	☑	☐	☐	☐	☐			1000	0000036320	1000		Electronic TURBODRIVE	10	20	20	PC	
	0000036333	PlOrd.	0	☑	☐	☐	☐	☐			1000	0000036349	1000		Electronic TURBODRIVE	10	20	20	PC	
	0000036335	PlOrd.	0	☑	☐	☐	☐	☐			1000	0000036352	1000		Electronic TURBODRIVE	20	20	20	PC	
	0000036337	PlOrd.	0	☑	☐	☐	☐	☐			1000	0000036350	1000		Electronic TURBODRIVE	20	20	20	PC	
	0000036338	PlOrd.	0	☑	☐	☐	☐	☐			1000	0000036351	1000		Electronic TURBODRIVE	10	10	10	PC	
	0000036339	PlOrd.	0	☑	☐	☐	☐	☐			1000	0000036350	1000	T-B320	Hollow shaft	20	20	20	PC	
	0000036340	PlOrd.	0	☑	☐	☐	☐	☐			1000	0000036351	1000		Hollow shaft	20	20	20	PC	

Figure 6.11 "Detailed Scheduling Planning Board" Transaction in APO, Transaction Code /SAPAPO/CDPS0, Operations List Chart

Detailed Scheduling Planning Board, Planning Version 000

Order	Operati	SuboperNo	Resource	Product	Product Short Description	Total Qty	Rec/ReqQty	BUn	T	R	AUn	Oper.	BUn	O	A	Start Date	Start Time	End Date	End Time	Op.Duratn
0000036330	0010		WT-C20_1000_002	T-T520	Casing for electronic drive	20	20	PC				20	PC			19.06.2006	10:56:24	19.06.2006	11:07:50	0/00:11:26
0000036333	0010		WT-C20_1000_002		Casing for electronic drive	20	20	PC				20	PC			10.07.2006	12:46:07	10.07.2006	12:57:33	0/00:11:26
0000036335	0010		WT-C20_1000_002		Casing for electronic drive	20	20	PC				20	PC			03.07.2006	12:46:07	03.07.2006	12:57:33	0/00:11:26
0000036337	0010		WT-C20_1000_002		Casing for electronic drive	20	20	PC				20	PC			26.06.2006	12:46:07	26.06.2006	12:57:33	0/00:11:26
0000036338	0010		WT-C20_1000_002		Casing for electronic drive	10	10	PC				10	PC			14.06.2006	09:46:29	14.06.2006	09:57:55	0/00:11:26
0000036339	0010		WT-G20_1000_001	T-T420	Slug for Shaft	20	20	PC				20	PC			16.06.2006	10:34:46	16.06.2006	14:34:47	0/04:00:01
0000036339	0010		WT-G20_1000_001		Slug for Shaft	20	20	PC				20	PC			16.06.2006	10:34:46	16.06.2006	14:34:47	0/04:00:01
0000036340	0010		WT-G20_1000_001		Slug for Shaft	20	20	PC				20	PC			09.46.30	09:46:30	14.06.2006	13:46:31	0/04:00:01
0000036340	0010		WT-G20_1000_001		Slug for Shaft	20	20	PC				20	PC			14.06.2006	09:46:30	14.06.2006	13:46:31	0/04:00:01
0000036341	0010		WT-G20_1000_001		Slug for Shaft	20	20	PC				20	PC			14.06.2006	09:46:30	14.06.2006	13:46:31	0/04:00:01
0000036341	0010		WT-G20_1000_001		Slug for Shaft	20	20	PC				20	PC			14.06.2006	09:46:30	14.06.2006	13:46:31	0/04:00:01
0000036342	0010		WT-G20_1000_001		Slug for Shaft	20	20	PC				20	PC			23.06.2006	10:34:46	23.06.2006	14:34:47	0/04:00:01
0000036342	0010		WT-G20_1000_001		Slug for Shaft	20	20	PC				20	PC			23.06.2006	10:34:46	23.06.2006	14:34:47	0/04:00:01
0000036331	0010		9999_1000_002	T-T220	Flat gasket	20	20	PC				20	PC			29.06.2006	13:13:40	03.07.2006	08:50:49	3/19:37:09
0000036331	0010		WT-A20_1000_001		Flat gasket	20	20	PC				20	PC			29.06.2006	13:13:40	03.07.2006	08:50:49	3/19:37:09
0000036332	0010		9999_1000_002		Flat gasket	10	10	PC				10	PC			14.06.2006	09:46:29	16.06.2006	07:40:47	1/21:54:18
0000036332	0010		WT-A20_1000_001		Flat gasket	10	10	PC				10	PC			14.06.2006	09:46:29	16.06.2006	07:40:47	1/21:54:18
0000036334	0010		9999_1000_002		Flat gasket	20	20	PC				20	PC			22.06.2006	13:13:40	26.06.2006	08:50:49	3/19:37:09
0000036334	0010		WT-A20_1000_001		Flat gasket	20	20	PC				20	PC			22.06.2006	13:13:40	26.06.2006	08:50:49	3/19:37:09

Figure 6.12 "Detailed Scheduling Planning Board" Transaction in APO, Transaction Code /SAPAPO/CDPS0, Order List Chart

▶ The WIP list (the *work in progress* that has not yet been confirmed)

▶ The production overview—here you can view the status of individual production quantities

▶ The Alert Monitor—to monitor date/time violations and overloads

> ▶ Charts on the resource load, network display for orders and operations, and product inventory (not only is it always displayed, but you also can view it as a separate, dynamic chart)

> ▶ Reports and logs

Measures for detailed scheduling

The measures to correct overloads are not limited to regenerative planning or rescheduling of operations. You can also use alternate modes (if available) or increase the available capacity (with access to master data: generally or temporally limited). If necessary, you can also change the production quantities, also in the detailed scheduling planning board. The latter context involves quantity planning (like a manual change of the quantity of planned orders) that is not subject to the strategy settings of the DS strategy profile but is performed according to the settings stored in the PP strategy profile of the overall profile of the detailed scheduling planning board.

Overview

Options to correct overloads:

▶ Regenerative planning

▶ Rescheduling: changing the sequence, for example

▶ Rescheduling to an alternate resource

▶ Increasing the available capacity

▶ Reducing the production quantity

The right mouse button plays an important role in planning activities, because the related menu contains many of these functions (depending on the context) for efficient processing of the plan. The functions include navigating to other views, the display and changing of MRP elements, modifications, and marking.

6.4.4 Settings for Detailed Scheduling Strategies

In both interactive and automatic planning, the settings in the detailed scheduling strategy define how the system should behave during scheduling or rescheduling activities. Therefore, the strategy settings play an important role in detailed scheduling. They can influence the planning properties in many ways.[1]

---

1 The following sections describe the most important settings up to and including SAP APO 5.0.

In your daily work, the planning mode stored in the strategy makes an important and basic statement about the behavior of the system during planning. In the context of detailed scheduling, the following planning modes are available and helpful: Planning mode

Find Slot (Finite Planning: Backward with Possible Reverse)

During planning, the system searches for the next available slot after the requirements date/time for the operation to be scheduled, and does so with backward planning. It first searches backward in time. Because this approach does not necessarily result in successful scheduling, you can also use the supplemental approach, **with reverse**. If the search backward through time does not find an appropriate slot before today's date, the system is permitted to "reverse,"—in this case, to look for slots forward in time. This approach corresponds to *finite forward planning*. You can use the offset time to shift the reverse time from today's date. With the find-slot procedure, scheduling therefore generally occurs only in free areas on the finite resource under consideration.

Insert Operation

This mode affects only finite, single resources. If no slot is available on such a resource or if the available slot is too small for scheduling, you can use the **Insert operation** mode first to create a large-enough slot in the area of the requirements date/time by temporally shifting the existing objects in the planning direction. With this approach, the existing sequence remains in place. That applies to the entire order structure and therefore works only when no relationship is violated during the creation of the slot. Otherwise, the operation is not inserted.

Squeeze-In Operation

This procedure, also jokingly called "Parisian parking," enables scheduling on the required date by shifting the existing load in both temporal directions (starting from the required date) so that a sufficiently large slot exists at the required location for the operation to be planned. If doing so violates time constraints, the entire sequence is automatically shifted into the direction of the future. This procedure is only available for finite, single resources.

Append Operation

The system attempts to schedule the operation after the last operation on the resource under consideration. The desired date and the planning direction play no role here.

Insert Operation and Close Gaps Until End

This mode first inserts an operation according to the **Insert operation** procedure. In the next step, any slots in the planning direction are closed by means of rescheduling. This procedure is cancelled as soon as a fixed operation is present or a relationship would be violated. The original planning sequence remains intact when closing the slot.

Searching for a Bucket with Free Capacity

When using a finite PP/DS bucket capacity in the resource (as of SAP SCM 4.1), you can use this mode in the context of a bucket-oriented capacity check (see *CTP scenario*) and with block planning.[2] Here, the system checks only to see if the time window determined by scheduling has enough free capacity for the operation to be scheduled or for the order. Scheduling in the corresponding bucket occurs infinitely, and the capacity can be aligned in a follow-up step with sequence planning.

Infinite Scheduling (Backward with Possible Reverse)

This planning mode is generally used with requirements planning (scheduling occurs without consideration of the resource load on the required date) and does not involve automatic rescheduling in the event of an overload. Instead, a problem that arises because of an overload with finite resources is indicated only by an exception message (resource overload) and must be resolved in a subsequent step. With this method, a possible reversal is involved if the starting date of production ends up in the past with backward scheduling.

---

2 Block planning enables you to use a previously stored, structured reservation of resources for specific products in order to achieve an efficient block-based utilization with optimized setup. Block planning is primarily used in certain industry solutions (wood, metal, paper, and textile processing industries).

Infinite Sequencing

As of SAP SCM 5.0, you can use this infinite planning mode to reschedule the selected operation with the dependent operations without creating slots in this structure or changing the existing capacity situation. Infinite planning depends on the required date. In time intervals of already existing resource loads, overloads may occur that can be handled after infinite sequencing has taken place.

With this procedure, dependent operations are always planned infinitely, regardless of the detailed settings. You can plan both single resources and multiple resources with this mode. If operations with sequence-dependent setup times exist, this mode is not recommended.

In addition to the planning mode, the following strategy settings play an important role in detailed scheduling:[3]

Additional strategy settings

Scheduling Offset

The scheduling offset shifts the current planning time by a positive (into the future) or negative time value (into the past). The value can be used to define the earliest possible starting date of an operation. An order that is created to be scheduled forward from the current time is already late just a few seconds after planning. If you use a positive offset time, you can avoid this problem.

Current Modes

This entry contains a setting to determine if the mode currently in use during planning must be kept or if the system can automatically select from the available alternatives.

Scheduling Sequence

You can use a field selection with several criteria to create a logic for the sorting sequence when scheduling objects. This setting is vitally important in the context of automated capacity planning.

---

3 The settings described here refer to the overall view of the strategy settings.

Desired Date

With regenerative planning, scheduling begins with the current situation of the operation (**Current Date**), as early as possible (**Earliest Date**), or at a date entered interactively (**Specified Date**).

Finite Capacity

This setting defines the capacity to be used in the context of finite planning if PP/DS bucket capacity also exists as an alternative to time-continuous capacity. The preconditions here are a finite resource and an appropriate strategy. With bucket-oriented planning, you can perform a capacity check at the level of the time interval (bucket) with the following statement: The operation can still find the required free capacity in the desired period with consideration of the existing overall load. In this case, scheduling is infinite and, if necessary, must still undergo detailed scheduling with downstream sequencing. Planning that uses time-continuous capacity directly states the dates and times of the orders. Application areas of PP/DS bucket capacity include bucket-oriented capacity checking: CTP check and block planning.

Finiteness Level

This setting represents the maximum finiteness level of a resource for which finite planning occurs on this resource. If the entry for this value in the resource is greater than the finiteness level given here, the resource is planned infinitely (see Chapter 5).

Planning Direction

The search for a scheduling date occurs in the temporal direction selected here. If the search is unsuccessful, a reversal enables a change in the direction of the search.

Non-Working Times

When you create or reschedule orders, you can permit scheduling of operations in non-working time, independently of the planning mode. No change to the resource is required for this.

Scheduling non-working times (breaks, holidays, and weekends) is recommended when scheduling problems occur in individual cases.

For example: An (non-interruptible) operation must still be completed, regardless of the work time defined for the resource. The prerequisite is that no other constraints are violated in the process. Such operations are planned under the assumption that the available resources in non-working times behave exactly as they do in the working time immediately preceding the non-working time and they are firmed with planning.

Consider Campaign Requirement

Setting the appropriate flag means that operations unrelated to a campaign may not interrupt an existing campaign[4] (industry-specific process).

Validity Periods for Orders

The flag determines if the validity period of the corresponding order should be considered when scheduling or rescheduling. In particular, you can limit the consideration to dependent orders.

Background: The validity period of an order results from the validity of its source of supply (PPM/PDS). When an order is shifted during planning and therefore ends up in an area in which the previously selected PPM/PDS is no longer valid, you can use this setting to determine how to proceed.

Lowest Mode Priority

This is the lowest priority of a mode that is considered during automatic mode selection (see Chapter 5).

Comply with Block Planning

You should set this flag by default unless you use *external* optimization that should not consider block limits or firmed blocks.

---

4 In contrast to block planning, a campaign is not planned deductively but is generated dynamically by the Optimizer. The objective of a campaign is the setup-optimized bundling of an execution. In production, for example, you can run several approaches for a production process and manage them using batches, whereas in planning, the approaches are considered as bundled. Therefore a campaign occurs at the order and batch levels, but not at the operations level. Campaigns are predominantly used in the chemical and pharmaceutical industries.

Scheduling at Block Limits

This entry indicates which operations are scheduled at block limits for block planning (default setting: **As specified in the operation**).

Maximum Runtime

The entry enables the specification of a maximum runtime that the system may use during scheduling of complex problems before the process is terminated.

Action at Scheduling Error

As of SAP SCM 4.1, you have another "outlet" for planning: *error-tolerant scheduling*. The system reacts as indicated here if a problem that cannot be resolved appears during scheduling of an order. Such can be the case, for example, when manual planning finds slots for all but one operation, and the last operation cannot be rescheduled. It avoids rescheduling of the entire order. The outlet function allows you to reschedule the order against the constraint. The situation with the problematic operation must be resolved subsequently, if possible.

Planning Submode

To schedule dependent operations on dependent resources, you can use various submodes (e.g., infinite, deallocate, and find slots). Depending on the planning mode on the selected resources, only certain settings make sense here.

Order-Internal Relationships

Order-internal relationships involve the transition between the activities of operations and can be not considered, considered in propagation range, or always considered. With consideration, the constraints included are the maximum interval and the process-related minimum interval between the individual activities of an operation. You can activate separate observance of maximum intervals by setting the **Consider Maximum Intervals** flag.

Non-consideration can lead to a breaking up of the related order, which should generally be avoided in the real world.

Cross-Order Relationships

Cross-order relationships involve the transition between various orders. They can be not considered, considered in propagation range, or always considered. The precondition for considering the cross-order relationships is that order-internal relationships are also considered.

Compact Scheduling

The goal of compact scheduling is to create scheduling for deallocated operations or complete orders with the shortest possible intervals between individual operations—a reduction of lead times. Compact planning uses order-internal relationships.

Without compact planning, shifting the last operation of an order shifts only that operation. The remaining operations stay as is, provided the other constraints allow it. When you use compact planning, the complete order is shifted, if possible, to keep the lead time of the order as short as possible.

Using the Planning-Related Minimum Interval with Infinite and Bucket-Finite Planning

When you activate this setting, the system uses the planning-related minimum interval instead of the process-related minimum interval (to be transferred from the routing to PDS or maintained in PPM) between operations. This switch should not be activated during the planning process (consequence: loss of the existing "good" planning and poor performance).

Consider Time Buffer (Relationships)

The time buffers of resources are involved when you consider time-based relationships in scheduling and rescheduling. The related minimum intervals are increased correspondingly.

Fixed Pegging

With this setting, you determine if the fixed pegging relationships to other objects should be considered during scheduling and rescheduling of an activity, an operation, or an order. If fixed pegging is not considered, rescheduling occurs without time limitation. The original structure can be lost. If fixed pegging (at least within the propagation range) is considered, the scheduling and rescheduling must occur for the requirements in good time, possibly by rescheduling dependent objects that are linked by fixed-pegging relationships. If that approach is impossible, scheduling and rescheduling does not occur. Order-internal relationships are the precondition for consideration.

Note that with high loads on resources in the real world, manual rescheduling with the use of pegging, in particular, can quickly become futile if the system must look for slots for orders and operations of the complete, multilevel pegging structure.

Dynamic Pegging

With this setting, you determine if the dynamic pegging relationships to other objects should be considered during scheduling and rescheduling of an activity, an operation, or an order. Non-consideration can mean the loss of an originally dynamic pegging relationship: Previously covered requirements can suddenly become uncovered because of a new planning situation and the newly created pegging network. If dynamic pegging is considered, the objects located within a propagation range must be scheduled or rescheduled so that they can recreate a dynamic pegging relationship to a dependent object. Firmed and fixed elements such as sales orders and firmed planned orders are considered as firmed and therefore limit planning.

Consider Time Buffer (Pegging)

Resource time buffers are included in the consideration of pegging (and additional order-internal relationships) in scheduling and rescheduling. The availability date lies ahead of the requirements date by the length of the time buffer.

Keep Current Modes (Dependent Objects)

When this flag is set, the system retains the mode when rescheduling a dependent operation. Alternate resources are not used automatically. Otherwise, the use of alternate modes selects the mode automatically according to priority or starting date (see Chapter 5).

Depending on the planning mode and the goals and scope of the planning process, you might have to consciously set specific constraints somewhat less restrictively than the planning process actually intends. This is also referred to as "softening the constraints" in order to come up with feasible plans for complex planning problems. From the aforementioned, this includes the following settings:

Outlets for planning

▶ Error-tolerant scheduling: With mass rescheduling, in particular, it prevents an order that is to be rescheduled from being blocked by an individual, non-schedulable operation. You can also set some actions here in the event of a scheduling error.

▶ Non-consideration of the validity areas of orders

▶ Permissibility of reversing the planning direction

▶ Permissibility of lower mode priorities in conjunction with the option of automatic mode selection

▶ Appropriate selection of the planning submode (for the dependent objects)

▶ Use of an appropriate finiteness level (to plan only the actual bottlenecks finitely as a first step)

▶ Non-consideration of relationships: For example, during rescheduling relationships between operations that should remain in force can lead to a necessity of rescheduling dependent operations automatically. Follow-up rescheduling of other orders can then result.

▶ Non-consideration of dynamic and fixed pegging. However, if pegging is not to be considered during detailed scheduling, if you reschedule a requirement, the related receipt element is not rescheduled. This might cause a delay, which you can determine with an alert.

▶ If needed, a termination criterion for scheduling—for highly complex scheduling problems.

Support of Interactive Planning with Detailed Scheduling Heuristics

Detailed scheduling heuristics support interactive capacity planning. You can store the heuristics in the heuristics profile and execute them interactively from the detailed scheduling planning board. Basically, the heuristics include the following:

▶ **Schedule Sequence (SAP001)**: Schedule selected operations according to a previously defined scheduling sequence, such as priorities or requirement times.

▶ **Remove Backlog (SAP002)**: Reschedule operations from the past to the future—possibly by using the offset time.

▶ **Schedule Sequence Manually (SAP003)**: The selected operations are scheduled manually in a graphical sequence.

▶ **Minimize Runtime (SAP004)**: First, selected resources—and therefore all the operations planned on them—are firmed. Starting from here, the remaining operations of each order are rescheduled so that minimum intervals exist between them.

▶ **Schedule Operations (SAP005)**: The selected operations with the **deallocated** status are scheduled.

▶ **Stable Forward Scheduling (SAP_DS_01)**: For multilevel removal of backlogs or to remove overloads. The scheduling sequence and the resource assignment remain in place. The required dates can be violated here.

▶ **Enhanced Backward Scheduling (SAP_DS_02)**: For multilevel finite planning oriented toward the customer's requested dates and scheduled backward from that point.

▶ **Change Fixing/Planning Intervals (SAP_DS_03)**: Fixing intervals and planning intervals can be recreated here, replaced, or deleted. You can also deactivate specific sequence-dependent setup activities.

▶ **Activate Sequence-Dependent Setup Activities (SAP_DS_04)**: Here you can reactivate the setup activities deactivated with SAP_DS_03.

See the Appendix for the availability of individual heuristics based on the release status.

6.4.5 Customizing the Detailed Scheduling Planning Board

Settings for the
detailed schedul-
ing planning board

You can configure the detailed scheduling planning board in many ways. Customizing of detailed scheduling (see Figure 6.13) supports comprehensive options for settings:

- ▶ Maintain strategy profiles
- ▶ Heuristics in detailed scheduling
- ▶ Maintain work areas
- ▶ Maintain optimization profiles
- ▶ Maintain propagation ranges
- ▶ Maintain overall profiles
- ▶ Maintain time profiles
- ▶ Settings for the detailed scheduling planning board
- ▶ Settings for the resource planning table

Profile maintenance is vitally important for the detailed scheduling planning board, because profiles organize the most important settings and options for making a difference.

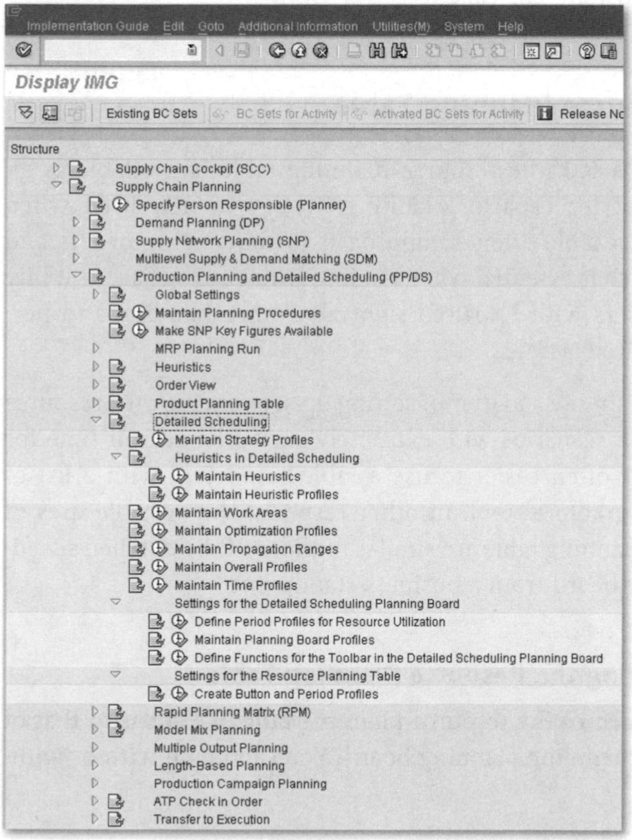

Figure 6.13 APO Customizing of PP/DS, Submenu for Detailed Scheduling

You can define the layout of the planning board using the planning board profile. This ability affects several elements:

▶ Chart selection

▶ Field selection and sorting the columns

▶ The format of rows in the table section of each chart

▶ The objects in the diagram section (such as the temporal flow of product stocks, the network displays, and the temporal situation of operations and orders)

▶ The row formats and graphic objects to be used

▶ Graphical display of activities, operations, and orders — depending on their properties

▶ The content of the context menus

▶ The selection of functions or buttons for the toolbar (possibly with a separate customizing call)

6.5   Resource Planning Table

As of SAP SCM 5.0, the resource planning table is available as an interactive tool for capacity planning. It is primarily used when working with a table-oriented approach to sequencing orders and operations. Such is essential when dealing with issues of accessibility that enable users with impaired sight and other handicaps to perform the required actions.

Also when it's simply a matter of setting up sequencing on a resource or dealing with scenarios with extremely varied lengths of time for the orders, it's often easier to use a table-based tool with a list of orders than a graphical tool. In other respects, the possible uses of the resource planning table are similar to those of the detailed scheduling planning board from a business standpoint.

6.5.1   Entering the Resource Planning Table

The initial screen of the resource planning table is similar to that of the detailed scheduling planning board. You can begin with or without a profile.

When getting started, you can select several resources. However, unlike the situation with the detailed scheduling planning board, here you can access the worklist when planning only element by element, you can examine and plan resource for resource.

6.5.2 Structure of the Resource Planning Table

As shown in Figure 6.14, the resource planning table consists of several charts. A navigation structure is found on the left-hand side and serves several purposes. In addition to the management of the resource pool that corresponds to the selection criteria at startup, the navigation structure opens the *shuffler*, which provides access to various heuristics that are relevant in the context of detailed scheduling. You can also use the clipboard that is part of the Pick and Drop functionality. Pick and Drop differs from the design of Drag and Drop— it first copies the object to be moved into an intermediate storage, similar to the Microsoft Windows Clipboard. During planning, you can also view changed objects and display them via the entry in the context menu **Display operation in work area** in the work area to the right of the navigation structure with a checkmark.

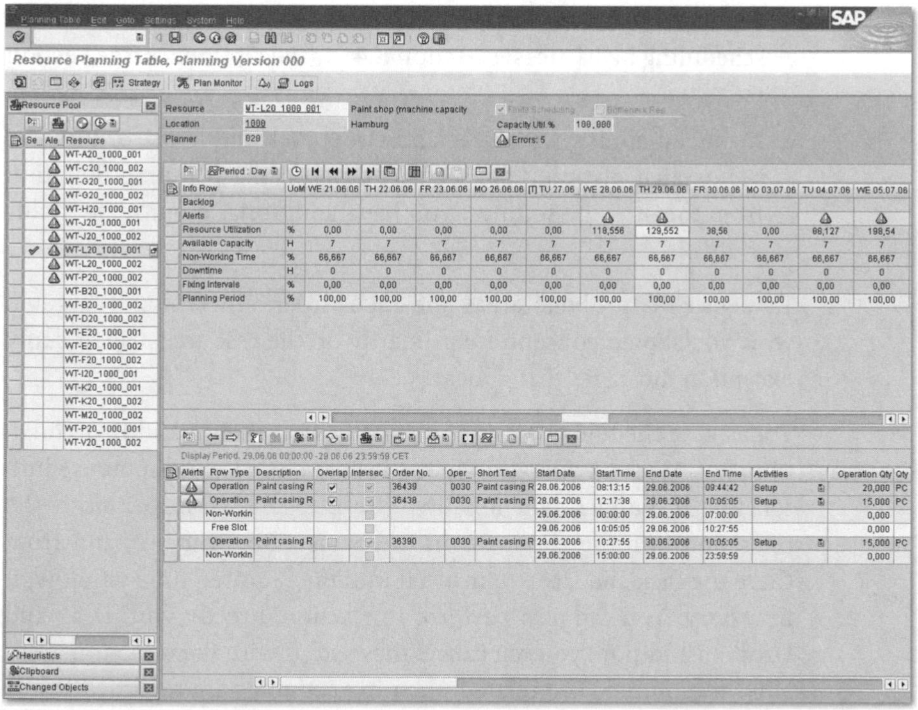

Figure 6.14 "Resource Planning Table" Transaction in APO, Transaction Code /SAPAPO/RPT, Tabular Capacity Planning

Work area:
periodic view, list
of operations

The work area consists of two charts: a *periodic view* and a *list of operations*. The data displayed here always refers to a (selected) resource. For the selected period split, the periodic view displays the relevant information on backlogs, alerts, resource utilization (in percent), available capacity, non-working time, downtime, fixing intervals, and the relationship of the planning period and the display period. This display is period-oriented with a time axis that runs from left to right.

The list of operations contains a chronological list of all the time elements in the display period: non-working times, free time windows, operations, and so on. Each operation is displayed in a separate row that also contains related information on the different activities and on the times, lengths, and properties of operations. The **Overlap** flag indicates an operation overlapped by at least one other operation. You can identify the overlapping operation by clicking on the flag.

6.5.3 Application of the Resource Planning Table

Partially auto-
mated planning
or Pick and Drop

In general, two types of planning are supported:

▶ Sequence planning in the usual form with the use of a detailed scheduling heuristic (see Section 6.4) or the Optimizer (see Section 6.6).

▶ Manual planning with Drag and Drop, Pick and Drop, or input of the explicit planning date. Depending on the planning direction from the strategy settings, you have additional input-ready fields available.

To detect the problem areas and focus in an efficient and targeted way, you should concentrate primarily on the resource load and any exception messages that appear.

You can reschedule operations manually or with Pick and Drop functionality. Mark an operation in the list area, use the right mouse button to call the pick functionality with the context menu, insert the operation into the clipboard in the navigation structure, and from there use Pick and Drop to insert it into the required time window, if necessary. You can also perform this action directly with Drag and Drop. In addition, you can cancel these steps with the undo functionality, if required. The related planning activities are recorded in the planning log.

The scenarios planned in this manner primarily include pure sequence planning of one resource, rescheduling backlogs, and in simple capacity leveling. It is used less with bucket-oriented planning or when a specific pegging or relationships should be included.

6.5.4 Customizing the Resource Planning Table

The user-specific settings of the resource planning table primarily relate to the display and to general settings.

Settings for the resource planning table

The settings for the resource planning table in customizing relate to the period profiles and the button profiles; both are found in customizing of detailed scheduling (see Section 6.4).

6.6 PP/DS Optimizer

The PP/DS Optimizer is a high-performance tool for the creation and improvement of a production plan. Various constraints can affect the results of optimization.

6.6.1 Basics of PP/DS Optimization

The PP/DS Optimizer has specific properties that distinguish it significantly from the calculation procedure of heuristics and from the SNP Optimizer. Generally, the SNP Optimizer handles aggregated, period-oriented plans that are created and improved based on lean master data. Linear and analytical problem-solving procedures can usually meet such goals. But the situation looks different when it involves the solution of complex problems from PP/DS, problems that require consideration of several constraints. The effort needed to find an exact solution to the problem increases with the number of possible permutations. To put it more exactly, the effort needed increases by the factorial of the orders to be planned. In this case, even a small, two-digit number of orders to be planned would require thousands of years of computer time to find an exact analytical solution. Therefore, the PP/DS Optimizer offers selective procedures that lead to realistic computing times (in minutes or hours)—but without a guarantee that the absolutely optimum solution for the problem has been found. From the set of possible solutions, it's very likely that some solutions are found by the PP/DS Optimizer, but not all of them. In

Optimization concepts in SAP APO

comparison, a heuristic leads to exactly one solution. Using the same constraints, several optimization runs can produce different results. Based on these properties, it's clear that the computing time entered by the user as a termination criterion for the optimization run is extremely important. In general, the higher the amount of computing time, the higher the quality of the solution. However, the reverse is not always true: More computing time is not a guarantee for the improvement of a solution that has already been found.

6.6.2 Entering the Optimizer

The PP/DS Optimizer is not called as an independent transaction, but from within corresponding applications. It can be called interactively in the detailed scheduling planning board or product planning table. The following statements throughout this section apply to the latter. The Optimizer can also be run with specification of an optimization profile in the production planning run (see Chapter 7).

Initial dialog (interactive optimization)

To limit optimization to an interval, you can use the settings available in the initial screen of interactive planning (see Figure 6.15). The optimization horizon is the period in which planning is optimized. The elements to be optimized must lie completely within the time window considered during optimization (**Start of Horizon** and **End of Horizon**). Objects completely or partially outside the time window are regarded as firmed and are not changed.[5] The earliest scheduling of these elements occurs on the date of the **Start of Optimized Schedule**.

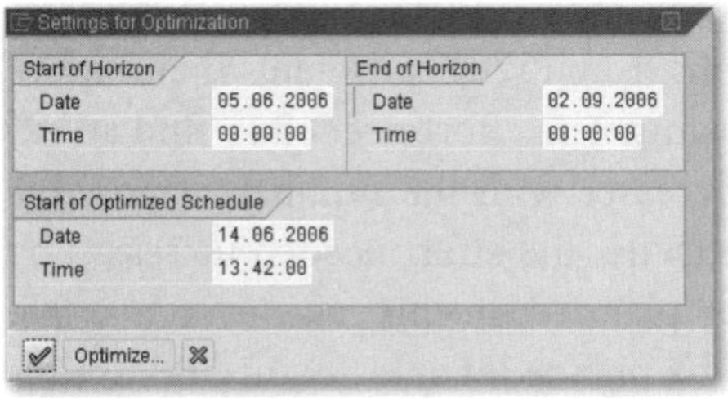

Figure 6.15 SAP APO Transactions "Detailed Scheduling Planning Board," Transaction Code /SAPAPO/CDPS0 or "Product Planning Table," Transaction Code /SAPAPO/PPT1, Initial Screen of the PP/DS Optimizer

---

5 Note that in the context of the Optimizer you should not mistake firming with firming related to the PP/DS planning time fence. This horizon is generally not considered by the Optimizer (see SAP Note 517426).

Note that a very short-term optimization makes sense only in the area of *automated production control*, because manual production always requires reaction times (to print shop floor papers, and so on).

6.6.3 Structure of the Evaluation View of the Optimizer

After the initial screen, the next screen provides information on the quality of the solution that has been found both during and after successful optimization.

The four charts shown here display information on the status of the optimization, messages, the values of the related optimization parameters (including deallocation costs), and the solution process over time in a graphic (see Figure 6.16).

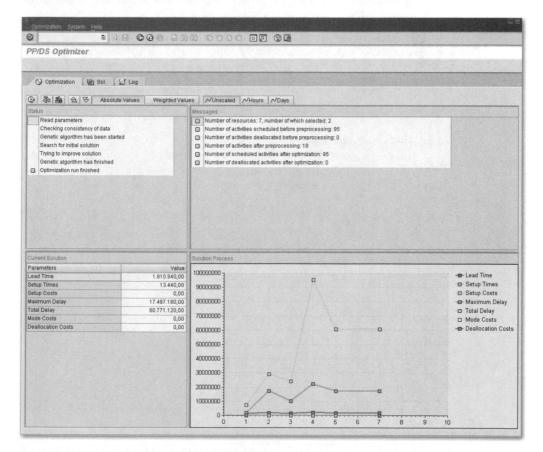

Figure 6.16 SAP APO Functionality "PP/DS Optimizer," Evaluation Screen of the Optimizer

From this evaluation view, you can use a button to view the parameters of the optimization, to change the parameters set by the optimization profile to some extent, and to start optimization (or restart it) interactively.

6.6.4 Parameterization of the Optimizer

You can select basic settings for the Optimizer through the optimization profile, customizing of the detailed scheduling planning board or of the product planning table, or using Transaction /SAPAPO/CDPSC5 (see Figure 6.17). When you start the Optimizer, you might have to adjust or change some of these basic settings because of the current planning situation. The exact settings of the optimization parameters to achieve an optimal result depend, of course, on the actual planning problem.

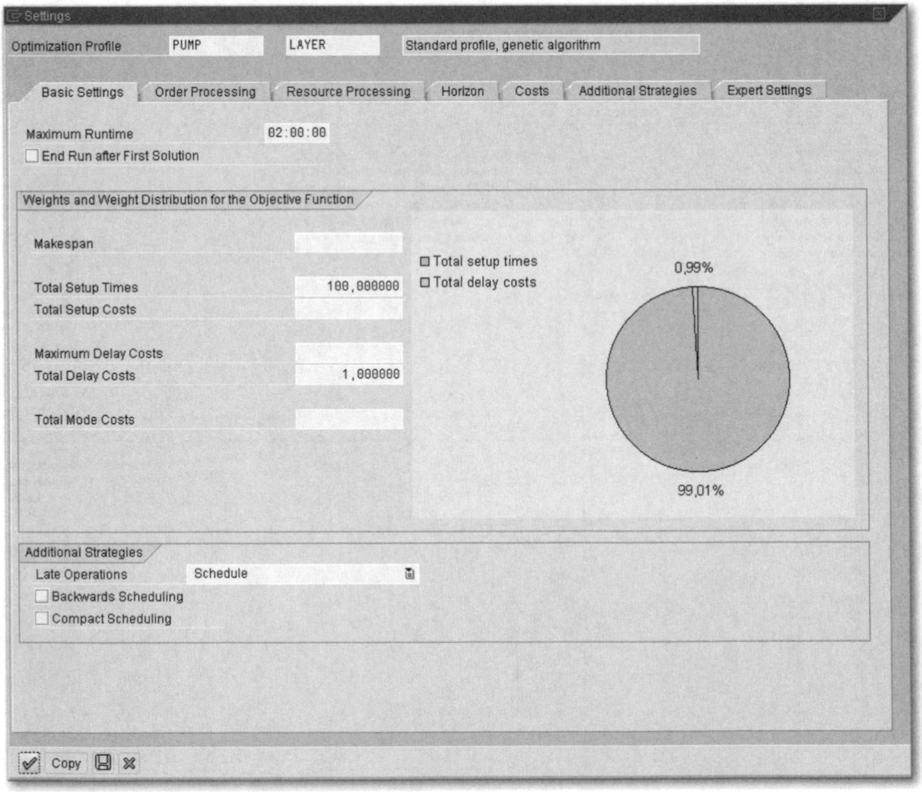

Figure 6.17 SAP APO Customizing Screen "Maintain Optimization Profile," Transaction Code /SAPAPO/CDPSC5, Optimization Profile for Parameterization of the Optimizer

Basic Settings

The Optimizer works based on costs. This means that the objective of optimization is to minimize the overall production costs. This cost reduction is achieved with an *objective function* made up of individually weighted key figures. You can use the following weighting factors W_i (i = 1...5) to influence the orientation of optimization:

Objective function

$$
\begin{aligned}
\textit{Production costs} = \quad & W_1 * \textit{makespan} + \\
& W_2 * \textit{total of the setup times} + \\
& W_3 * \textit{total of the setup costs} + \\
& W_4 * \textit{maximum delay costs} + \\
& W_5 * \textit{total of the delay costs} + \\
& W_6 * \textit{total of the mode costs}
\end{aligned}
$$

The following notes simplify the interpretation of these influencing factors:

Minimizing the *makespan* or the overall lead time aims at a maximum load on the optimized bottleneck resources in the short term. The system attempts to minimize the overall time needed to process orders and operations with consideration of the existing constraints.

Makespan

Minimizing the total of the setup times is possible if the time needed to set up from one setup status to the next is dependent on exactly that sequence (setup-status-dependent setup time with *dynamic setup*). In a paint shop, for example, the time required to set up from a dark color to a light one is likely longer than it is in the opposite direction. In such cases and in similar cases, an optimization objective can be to create an optimal sequence from the standpoint of the total of the required setup times. The result would be that the system summarizes the operations of similar setup statuses into blocks. Long setup times would then appear only when changing between two different setup statuses.

Setup times

Minimizing the total of the *setup costs* is necessary only when the system needs to have the costs and setup times described independently of each other. This can be the case when identical setup times differ on various resources in terms of cost-related evaluation and must therefore be decoupled from the setup time. Otherwise, the setup time criterion is sufficient.

Setup costs

Delays
The Optimizer can penalize *delays* that occur in terms of the defined requirements date/time that lie within the optimization horizon with delay costs. Two approaches are available:

▸ You can permit short delays in similar forms, which will help you avoid individual, significant delays: a minimization of the maximum delay costs.

▸ You can formulate the total of the delays as a target value and can calculate a minimum value across the overall delay for all orders. This approach does not exclude individual, obvious delays.

In general, you can define delay *costs* as dependent on the order priority; you would use higher costs for sales orders with a higher priority. This approach should help you avoid delays for high-priority orders.

Mode costs
Mode costs penalize the frequent (via fixed costs) and long-lasting (as defined with variable costs) use of alternate work centers. The alternate work centers must already be available in the system in master data and contained in the propagation range. You can link them to optimization via *alternative modes*. You can use high mode costs to avoid having the system repeatedly schedule an emergency work center that is normally used in the training center, for example. Such a resource would then be used only if no other solution can be found.

Trade-offs
It should be obvious that optimization always works between somewhat contradictory constraints and different interests, such as sales interests and production interests. This is referred to as a *trade-off*.

It's also clear that the influencing factors have somewhat different natures (costs and times) and therefore possess different physical units. To enable a comparison of the individual totals within the formula for calculating the production costs, costs are converted into times. The following applies here:

Costs vs. times

Note
A standardized cost of 30 corresponds to 30 seconds.

Example: The makespan and the setup costs should be considered as weighting criteria when using the Optimizer. When both times behave in a ratio of 500:1, the weighting must behave like 1:500 to create comparability.

Additional Settings

You can define the orders and types of orders available to the Optimizer and that are therefore to be planned and scheduled. Certain objects (like partially confirmed operations) are considered firmed during optimization. Some others can be set as firmed so that the Optimizer does not shift them. You can also make settings concerning the selected and non-selected resources, for example, you can include resource buffers, and plan resources finitely only from a distinct finiteness level on.

This approach employs the so-called window technique to solve a complex and time-consuming planning problem. After successful optimization, the time window in which optimization has been completed is shifted in temporally overlapping steps. The solution of the overall problem involves a combination of the individual solutions that have been calculated. This process is set by default in terms of the parameters, but you can change the parameterization in the optimization profile.

Time decomposition

If you use the Optimizer in the context of background processing, you store the optimization horizon that you otherwise enter interactively on the **Horizon** tab.

Special settings

Other special settings can apply to *campaign optimization*, which is useful in industry-specific processes, such as those in the chemicals and pharmaceuticals industries. In this case and as part of setup optimization, the Optimizer bundles similar orders or batches that can be dynamically shifted during planning.

Another interesting option creates operations (and their successors) with a certain time delay as **deallocated** rather than as **scheduled**. The planner can therefore react by displaying scheduled and deallocated operations in different charts in the detailed scheduling planning board and easily create a worklist.

The **Explain result** option enables you to add additional important information to the log so that you can better interpret and understand the planning result.

The **Maximum runtime** is a vitally important termination criterion. In the past, a rule of thumb has been to allow about 10 minutes of optimization for about 5,000 activities. This number of activities is, of course, proportional to the performance of the processor in use. That's why it makes sense to select the option **End run at the first solution** initially in a test phase and then use it as an orientation value for the runtime.

Optimization Procedures

Two quite different optimization concepts exist. You should use the one that proves appropriate based on requirements and constraints.

> **Note**
>
> When it's a matter of basic feasibility of complex optimization problems, the use of constraint programming is preferred. If feasibility is not the issue, but an improvement of an existing solution is, optimization is based on the genetic algorithm.

Constraint-based programming

Constraint propagation programming uses knowledge about the effects of a partial solution that has been found and creates constraints from it so that you can considerably limit the search area based on solutions that can be excluded. During an additional search, the criterion that produces a better solution than previously found is considered. In fact, the method works heuristically, so that you really can't tell if the absolute optimum will be found. This algorithm is interesting for complex constraints that make it difficult to find a feasible solution.

Genetic algorithm

The genetic algorithm is a stochastic search procedure that runs like evolutionary processes in nature. Initial solutions are generated and used to successively reproduce solutions with a survival-of-the-fittest principle. The termination criterion is generally the runtime that has been set. The stochastic characteristic explains why the algorithm can lead to different results in different runs for the same problem. Accordingly, the absolute optimum is not guaranteed here. Generally good solutions are found. You can use this procedure to execute efficient sequences as long as not too many constraints exist.

Hard and soft constraints

The standard version of SAP APO includes several *standard optimization profiles* that are already parameterized. You can select and modify them as needed for a given scenario. SAP recommends that you use the standard parameterization initially. The settings of the constraints (calendar, dates, time relationships, material and capacity availabilities, and interruptibility of activities) are very important in this context. They decide on the degree of freedom regarding optimization. This is particularly critical because most constraints are to be interpreted as "hard:" They must be accepted as immovable. Also important are the few constraints that you can define as "soft:" They can and must function as an outlet during optimization. Examples include required dates or maximum time intervals for shelf life, for example.

See Chapter 7 for the typical use of the Optimizer as part of a concrete business scenario.

6.7 Alert Monitor

The Alert Monitor is a cross-application tool that you can use during planning to manage and evaluate exception messages centrally. Therefore, it can consider not only the exceptions that occur in the context of PP/DS planning, but also alerts from other areas such as ATP, SNP, and DP. Messages about problems are transferred automatically from the application to the Alert Monitor. Each exception message relates to a specific problem situation.

The primary task of the Alert Monitor is to list exception messages in a structured manner. The messages correspond to the defined selection criteria. The Alert Monitor provides information on situations that require adjustments in planning. Note the distinction between the reason for the exception and its properties. Using exception messages, the Alert Monitor can provide general information on the problem situation itself, but not necessarily on why the exception occurred.

6.7.1 Entering the Alert Monitor

After you call the transaction, you can first maintain an overall profile, unless a profile was created previously and was possibly set up as a default setting (see Figure 6.18).

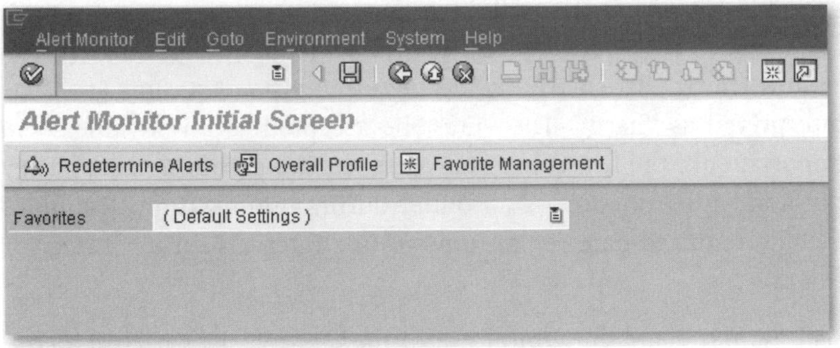

Figure 6.18 "Alert Monitor" Transaction in APO, Transaction Code /SAPAPO/AMON1, Initial Screen of the Alert Monitor

6.7.2 Structure of the Alert Monitor

Overall profile

The overall profile of the Alert Monitor is the central point for settings (see Figure 6.19). The overall profile works as a filter for the alerts to be displayed. Selection variants enable selection of specific products, a selection via the production planner, resources, and so on.

The exception messages themselves are managed in application-related alert profiles that are assigned to the overall profile. These profiles include a PP/DS alert profile, an SNP and DP alert profile, and an ATP alert profile. You can access each one with a tab within the overall profile. Individual exception messages are summarized by content and managed in folders in each application-related view.

Error, warning, and information

Depending on the type of alert, you can define nuances that you can in many cases set with three priority categories. You can store threshold values to display problem situations by importance as an error, warning, information, or not even as an alert. For example, you might want to tolerate a delay of a product in terms of the related requirement of up to an hour (no alert). But if the delay lasts from one to three hours, an information message is displayed on the related MRP element. If the delay lasts from 3–24 hours, a warning appears. A delay over 24 hours would display an error. In the cases described above, you would store the values of 1, 3, and 24 for the exception messages of product delay in the PP/DS alert profile.

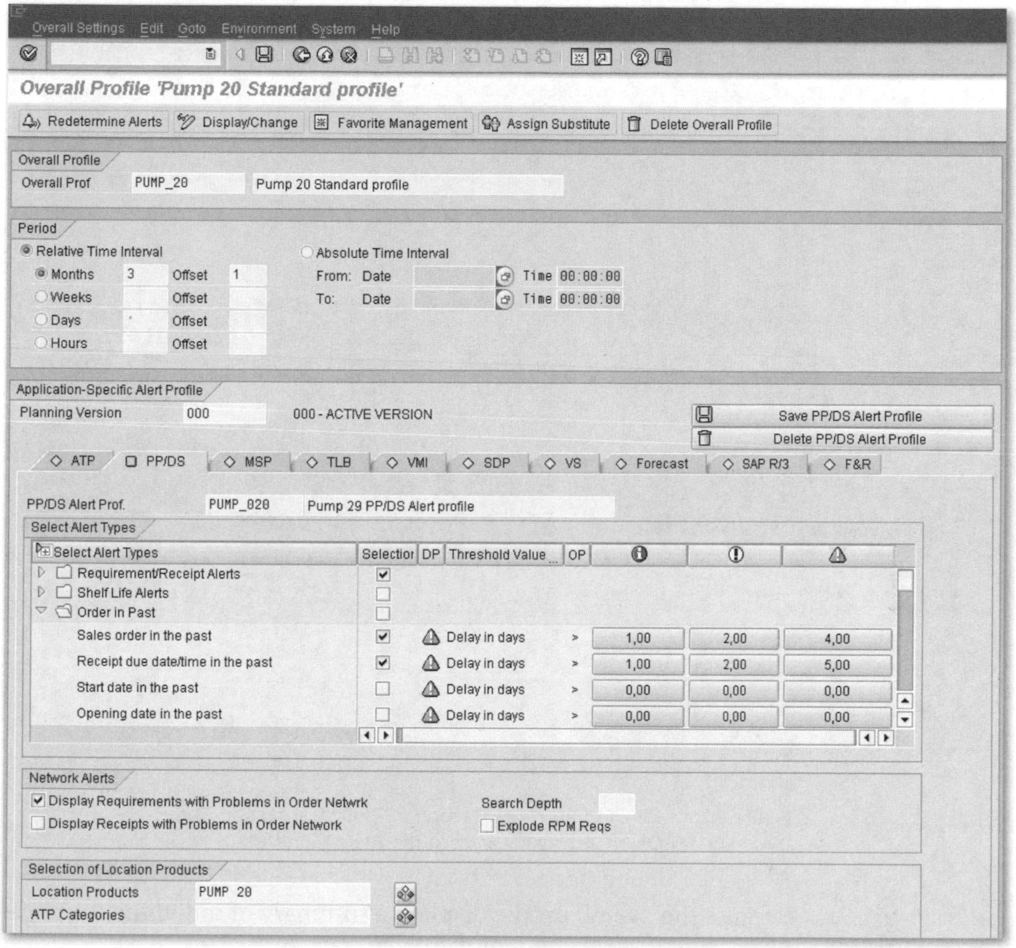

Figure 6.19 "Alert Monitor" Transaction in APO, Transaction Code /SAPAPO/AMON1, Overall Profile of the Alert Monitor

6.7.3 Application of the Alert Monitor

To use the Alert Monitor, all you have to do is call the transaction and select the previously defined overall profile. **Redefine alerts** makes a new selection based on the criteria stored in the overall profile.

After redefinition of the messages that appear, the Alert Monitor displays them systematically (see Figure 6.20). You can then drill down for detailed evaluation.

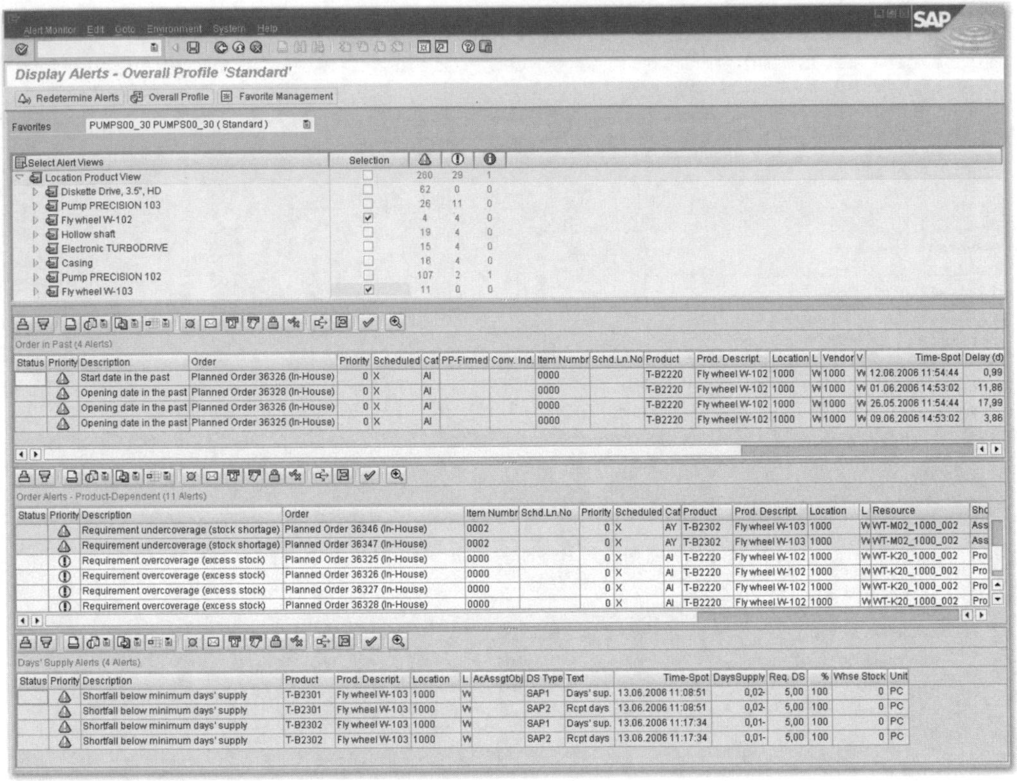

Figure 6.20 "Alert Monitor" Transaction in APO, Transaction Code /SAPAPO/AMON1, Display of Alerts in the Alert Monitor

Because the overall profile displays a summary of individual, application-specific profiles for PP/DS, ATP, DP, and so on, it plays a predominant role in the cross-application Alert Monitor. But if you are in an application (the product view in PP/DS, the detailed scheduling planning board, or the product planning table), you can select the application-related PP/DS profile to filter PP/DS alerts in the application in a user-specific way.

In real life, often additional options for alert management come into play. They include options to display a colleague's alerts when filling in for the colleague, analyze them, transfer (redirect) exception messages, and hide messages you do not want.

6.7.4 Customizing the Alert Monitor

You can choose additional basic settings for the Alert Monitor, settings that go beyond those for exception messages, in customizing of the Alert Monitor (see Figure 6.21):

Settings of the
Alert Monitor

Figure 6.21 APO Customizing of SAP SCM Basis, Submenu of the Alert Monitor

- ▶ Define number ranges for alerts
- ▶ Activate/deactivate applications in Alert Monitor
- ▶ Maintain prioritization of alert types
- ▶ Define additional statuses in Alert Monitor
- ▶ Limit additionally defined statuses to specific alert object types

- ▸ Maintain database alert types for demand planning and SNP
- ▸ Maintain dynamic alert types for demand planning and SNP
- ▸ Business Add-Ins (BAdIs) for the Alert Monitor
- ▸ Alert Notification Engine

Note that you have the option to deactivate applications (SNP/DP, ATP, etc.) in the Alert Monitor. If you select this option, the related tabs are then hidden in the overall profile.

The knowledge that you gained from the previous chapters should now serve as a foundation for a number of typical scenarios based on real-life examples, all of which are predicated on finite planning.

7   Advanced Processes in APO-PP/DS

PP/DS offers you many different tools, enabling you to determine a feasible production plan for a specific requirements situation. Depending on the applicable business scenario, various approaches may be appropriate here. You might also find it useful to strategically combine several concepts. Ultimately, this all depends on many underlying conditions, such as:

- Will order priorities be included?
- Will alternative procurement sources or resources be available, and if so, how will they be modeled?
- Is setup-configuration-dependent setup used (setup matrix)?
- Is single-level or multilevel planning employed?
- Are the *bottlenecks* known, or do they only arise from the planning situation?

Modeling criteria

During the modeling, you must not only focus on the process itself, but also consider what consequences may arise from a particular procedure. For example, in many areas it is often essential that the planning result is clear and transparent. In this case, manual planning that is performed step by step would be more suitable than fully automated planning. With other scenarios, the automation can play a major role. Here, the goal is to generate as little manual involvement as possible, which is why the system is given the utmost freedom during the planning. What could prove to be a disadvantage here is that the empirical possibilities of an experienced planner might not be considered, and therefore a planning result would be created by the system, more or less, without any comment.

With our objective being to achieve a feasible, and preferably even beneficial, resource utilization, we will present several basic scenarios below. These scenarios are developed from a given planning situation and are designed to violate the minimum number of basic conditions.

7.1 Finite Planning with the Planning Run

The production planning run is a versatile and flexible platform for performing requirements and capacity planning functions. In particular, it can be fully automated using previously created, parameterized variants. However, this may not always be the silver bullet you're looking for; it really depends on the requirements and the basic conditions inherent in the planning.

7.1.1 Finite Requirements Planning

"Finite MRP run" When creating a feasible production program, one method that comes to mind is a finite requirements planning. Here, the low-level code method of the requirements planning would need to undergo a simultaneous finite planning of the operations on the affected resources (see Chapter 5). This option of a *simultaneous quantity and capacity planning* (or of a "finite MRP," i.e., the materials requirements planning heuristic **SAP_MRP_001** in conjunction with a finite planning strategy) was supported by previous release versions (up to and including APO 3.1). Nevertheless, experience has shown that this method can generally lead to serious disadvantages with large data volumes, both in terms of the performance and the quality of the solution. Consequently, SAP has been officially advising against using this "finite MRP run" since Release 4.0 of SAP SCM and now only allows this procedure to be used following consultation with SAP or in very special scenarios (e.g., Capable-to-Promise (CTP)).

7.1.2 Finite Planning as Multi-Step Procedure

MRP II concept The sequential execution of a materials requirements planning and a capacity planning (e.g., during a production planning run) is both possible and recommended. In this case, the low-level code method of the requirements planning is used to cover the requirements, and without taking into account the resource situation (infinite). Only in a subsequent step are the resulting capacity requirements reconciled with the available capacity of the resources involved. We have learned that this concept produces transparent and high-quality results in practical scenarios.

Modeling the Automated Planning

There is no "standard method" when it comes to the order of the individual steps in a production planning run. With a production planning run, you will always encounter the requirement of characterizing the operational business process in detail and mapping this into the individual steps of the planning run. Invariably, a requirements planning will always precede a capacity planning. Nevertheless, given the high degree of flexibility of the production planning run, based on the scenario to be mapped and its complexity, you can for example decide yourself as to the following:

Flexible use of the planning run

▶ The specifications of the requirements planning: single-level, multilevel by low-level code or by including the "immediate planning" in the event of potential deadline delays

▶ The specifications of the capacity planning: detailed planning heuristic, function or PP/DS Optimizer

▶ Whether the overall planning for each low-level code can be executed, or whether cascading or iterations are necessary here

▶ Whether a classical top-down planning will accomplish your goals, or whether, due to the bottleneck situation, a bottom-up planning or a middle-out planning is also necessary

A useful fundamental procedure is to build a typical planning scenario and initially run it through step by step and then analyze it based on the effects of the individual heuristics and functions. During a second phase, you can combine the tested functions in a variant of the production-planning run and verify it using additional cases as part of your overall planning.

From the test phase to the planning run

By using the PP/DS Optimizer, you can create a feasible production plan automatically. A simple procedure might look as follows:

1. Calculation of the low-level codes

2. Multilevel requirements planning, infinite

3. Optimization of all resources

In many application cases, there is often a need to utilize additional knowledge about bottlenecks in order to strategically parameterize such a planning run. Alternative or additional steps may be required for this, particularly in the area of capacity planning. We would like to reproduce this in the following section using a specific example. We will also explicitly illustrate the provisional results during the overall planning so that we can better interpret the individual steps and their effects.

Sample Process

Requirements situation
We have three sales orders (in this case, over 20 units each) for a finished product that show the same desired delivery date (see system example in Figure 7.1).

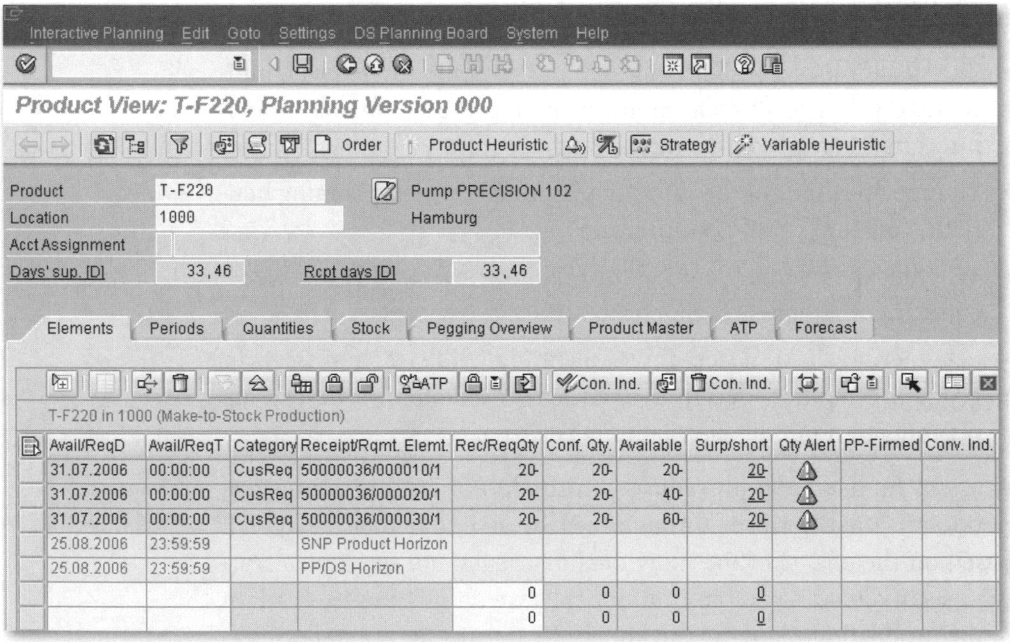

Figure 7.1 APO Transaction "Product View," Transaction Code /SAPAPO/RRP3, Requirements Situation for the Sample Process

The bottleneck within the production in this example is a paint shop (single resource) that is accessed in an operation in manufacturing the finished product. This resource should therefore be in the foreground during finite planning. The resulting dependent requirements are subsequently taken into account.

We can conceivably use various approaches to tackle this problem. We will describe a representative process that uses several planning concepts collectively by merging them.

The planning procedure that we selected in this example involves the following steps:

1. Determining the low-level codes of the materials involved from the underlying master data using the service heuristic **Stage Numbering (SAP_PP_020)**

2. Multilevel infinite requirements planning of the materials involved according to the low-level code method (process heuristic **SAP_MRP_001**)

3. Rescheduling of operations on the bottleneck resource **Paint shop** (finite scheduling) with the detailed planning function **Reschedule (SAP001)**

4. Optimization run for the remaining resources

The mode of operation of the individual steps will be described and explained in more detail below.

Step 1: Stage Numbering

The low-level codes in APO are newly determined using the service heuristic **SAP_PP_020** (see Figure 7.2). A step like this will be required if changes have arisen since the last time this heuristic was scheduled to the master data (PPM, PDS) of a product linked with the BOM, where these changes mean that the low-level code is no longer correctly stored in the system.

Calculation of the low-level codes

In APO, this heuristic therefore fulfills the function of the automatic low-level code alignment known from ECC and, in times of uncertainty, should always be started before the multilevel requirements planning that accesses these low-level codes. This stage numbering heuristic changes nothing in the planning situation.

This first step in the production planning run is parameterized via the planning object **Products** and, if appropriate, suitable restrictions to the products.

Step 2: Infinite Requirements Planning, Multilevel

Based on the low-level codes from Step 1, the products to be planned are selected and planned infinitely according to the low-level code

Infinite MRP run

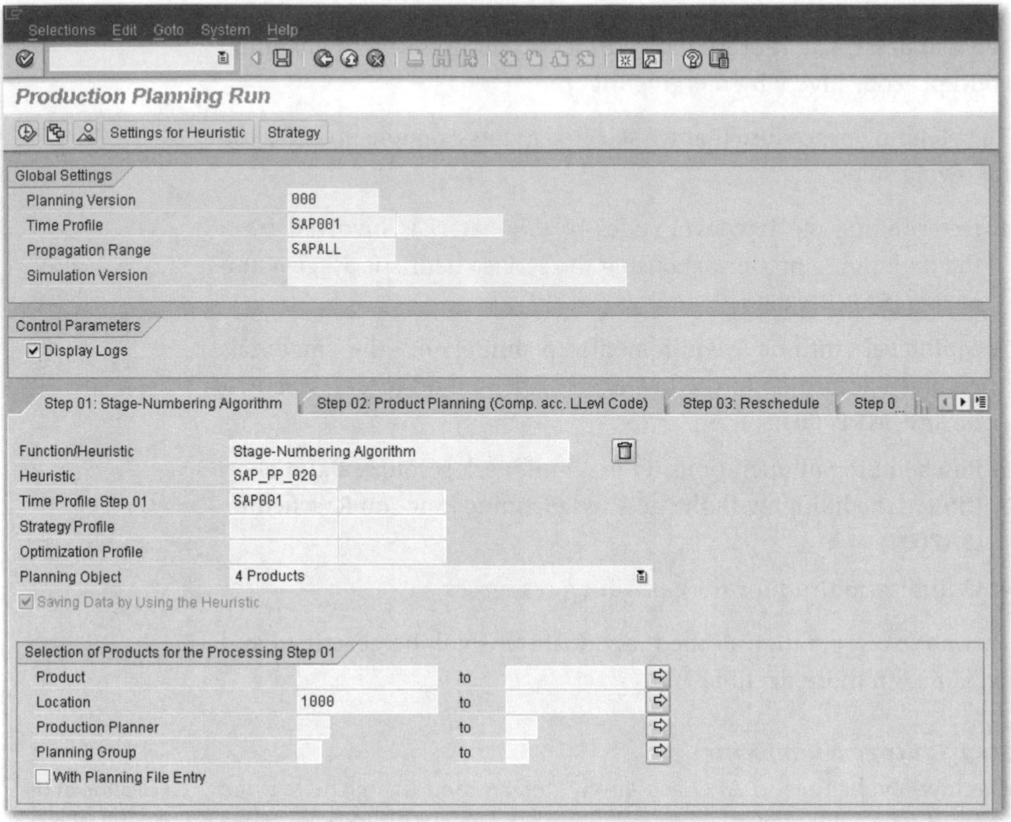

Figure 7.2 APO Transaction "Production Planning Run," Transaction Code /SAPAPO/CDPSP0, Stage-Numbering Algorithm for Calculating the Low-Level Codes

method. The technical process here corresponds to the multilevel requirements planning known from ECC, which only orients itself to the time schedule and also disregards the existing workload situation of the resources.

You can select this via the planning object **Products** and the corresponding selection criteria (see Figure 7.3).

Because there are simultaneous customer requirements in this example, the requirements planning initially delivers receipts in the form of planned orders that are produced at the appropriate time (see Figure 7.4) and therefore are parallel to each other in terms of time.

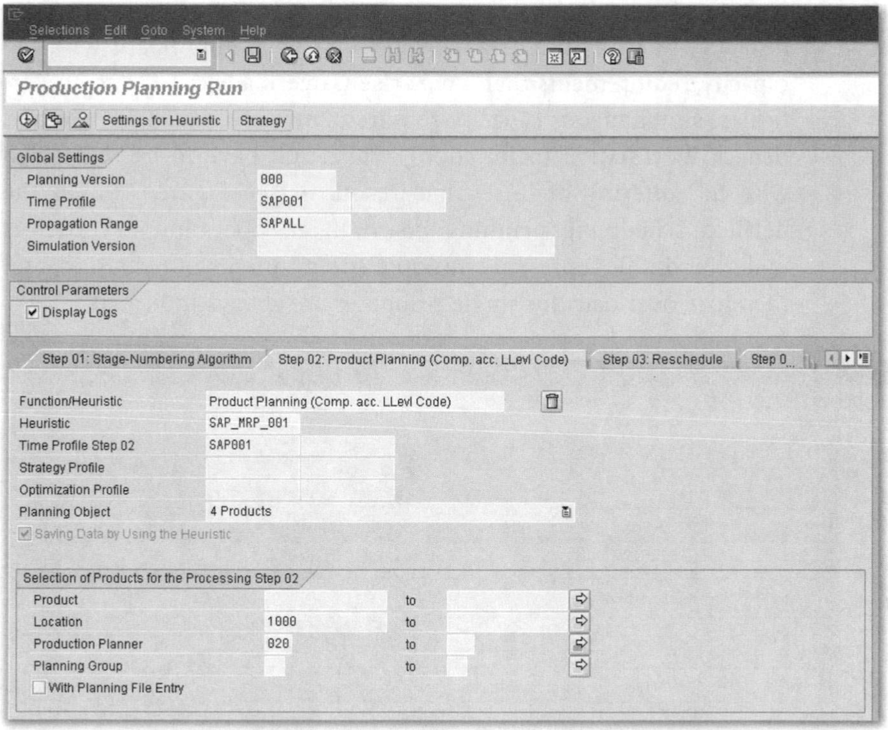

Figure 7.3 APO Transaction "Production Planning Run," Transaction Code /SAPAPO/CDPSP0, Process Heuristic for the Requirements Planning According to the Low-Level Code Method

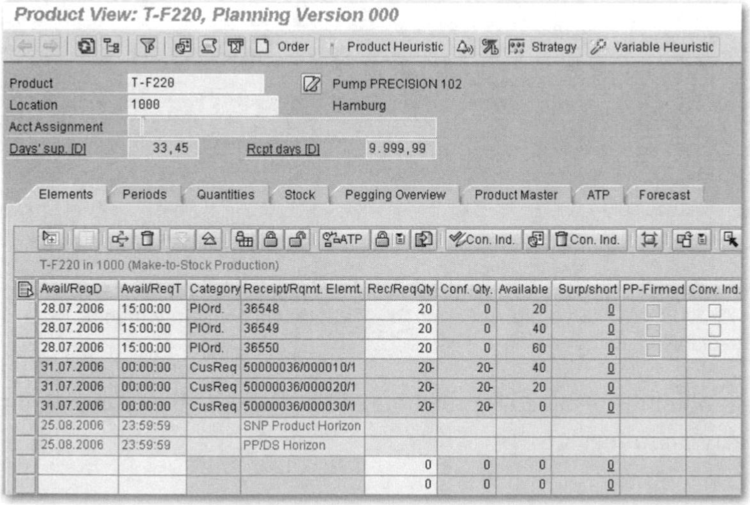

Figure 7.4 APO Transaction "Product View," Transaction Code /SAPAPO/RRP3, Receipts Following Completed Requirements Planning

255

If the available capacity of the resources involved is compared, for instance, by using the detailed scheduling planning board with the capacity requirements that have arisen, overloads can occur. In particular, simultaneous capacity requirements are created for the bottleneck workstation (paint shop), which still have to be reconciled with the offering of this single resource (see Figure 7.5). In the detailed scheduling planning board, if an operation or order is underlined, this represents multiple commitments of resources, and therefore overloads for single resources are always indicated.

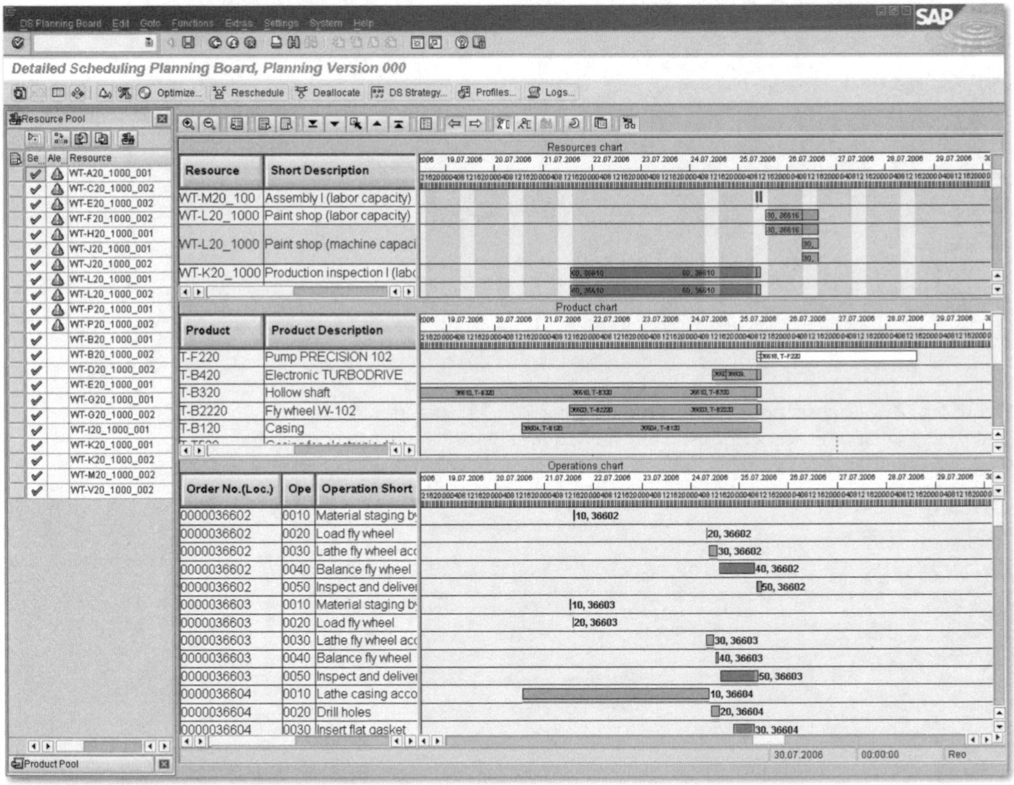

Figure 7.5 APO Transaction "Detailed Scheduling Planning Board," Transaction Code /SAPAPO/CDPS0, Multiple Resource Allocation Following the Infinite Requirements Planning

This problem is resolved for the bottleneck resource by a subsequent capacity planning.

Step 3: Reschedule Function

The purpose of function **Reschedule (SAP001)** is to allow you to plan the bottleneck resource in terms of its capacity. Since it is a single resource, only one activity can be executed at any one time. As a result of the requirements planning, the parallel operations of the paint shop are arranged sequentially according to the strategy settings stored in function **SAP001** when the function is executed. Since we want to avoid schedule slippage, a backward planning is stored in the strategy of the selected strategy profile (see Figure 7.6) in this case.

Capacity planning for the bottleneck resource

Unlike the requirements planning, this planning step explicitly relates to the operations of the bottleneck resource, which is why the planning object **Resources** is specified by the selection of the paint shop.

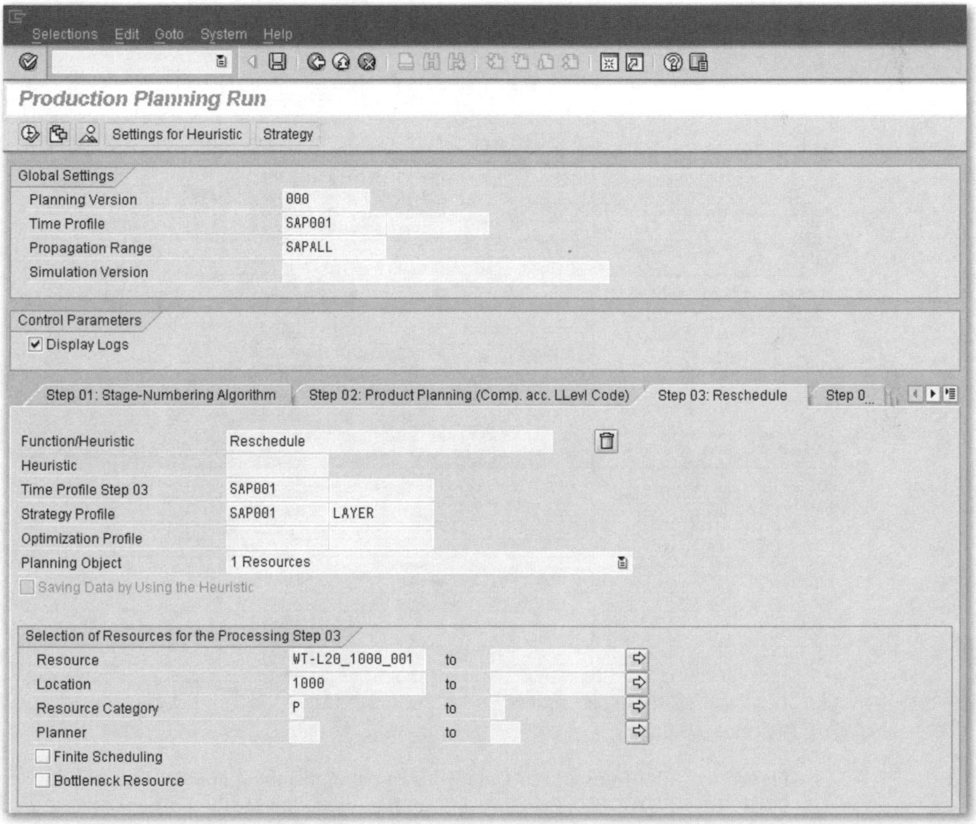

Figure 7.6 APO Transaction "Production Planning Run," Transaction Code /SAPAPO/CDPSP0, Function "Reschedule" for the Capacity Planning of the Bottleneck Resource

This causes a rescheduling of the bottleneck resource so that the operations that were originally created at the same time are now arranged sequentially, in other words, directly one after the other, through the planning mode **Find Slot** (see Figure 7.7).

The operations that depend on this rescheduling are also planned according to the stored strategy settings for dependent objects. After this planning step, an assessment of the resource situation produces a feasible allocation on the bottleneck resource. However, in this step all additional resources are not explicitly included in the capacity leveling, which is why overloads may occur again (see Figure 7.8). These overloads should be eliminated as much as possible in a subsequent step using the PP/DS Optimizer.

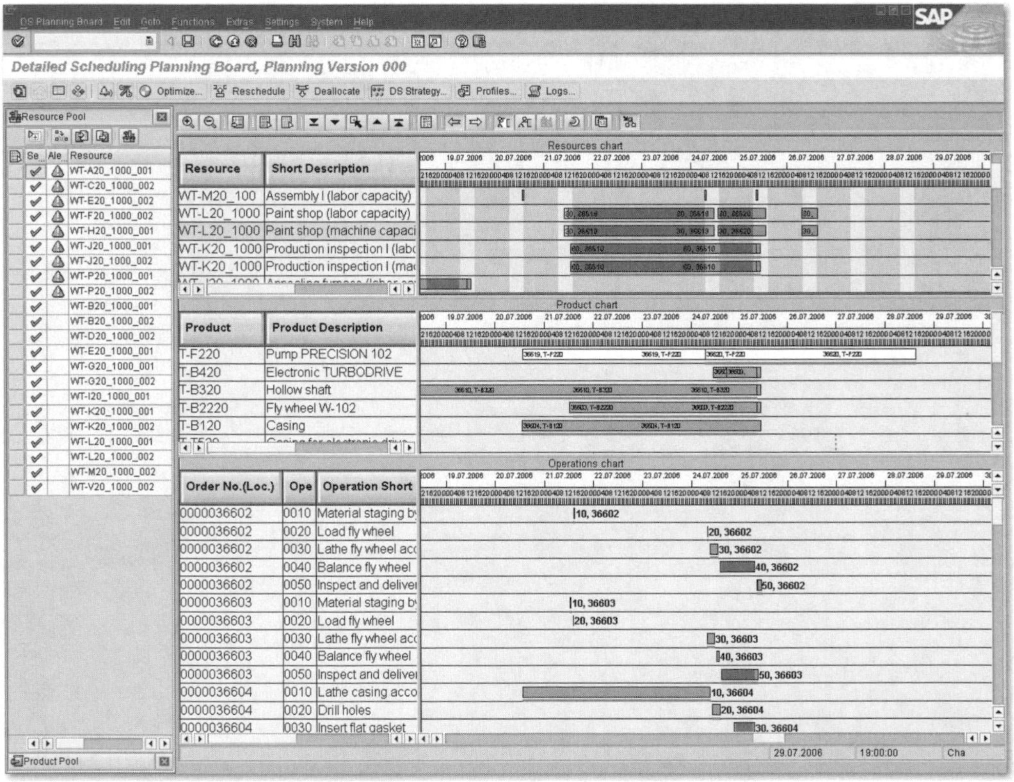

Figure 7.7 APO Transaction "Detailed Scheduling Planning Board," Transaction Code /SAPAPO/CDPS0, Sequential Resource Allocation for the Bottleneck Resource

Step 4: Optimization of Additional Resources

In the previous step, we adjusted the planning situation to the bottle-neck resource. All other resources should now also be reconciled in terms of their capacities. The PP/DS Optimizer accomplishes this using the assigned weighting of optimization parameters (e.g., over-all lead time, setup effort, delays), which you store in the optimiza-tion profile. In order not to endanger the already achieved, desired planning situation on the bottleneck resource for the optimization operation involved, the production planner uses the planning object **Resources** to exclude the bottleneck resource during the optimiza-tion (see Figure 7.9).

Optimization of all other resources

Figure 7.8 APO Transaction "Detailed Scheduling Planning Board," Transaction Code /SAPAPO/CDPS0, "Resource Utilization" Chart, Bottleneck Resource Is No Longer Overloaded

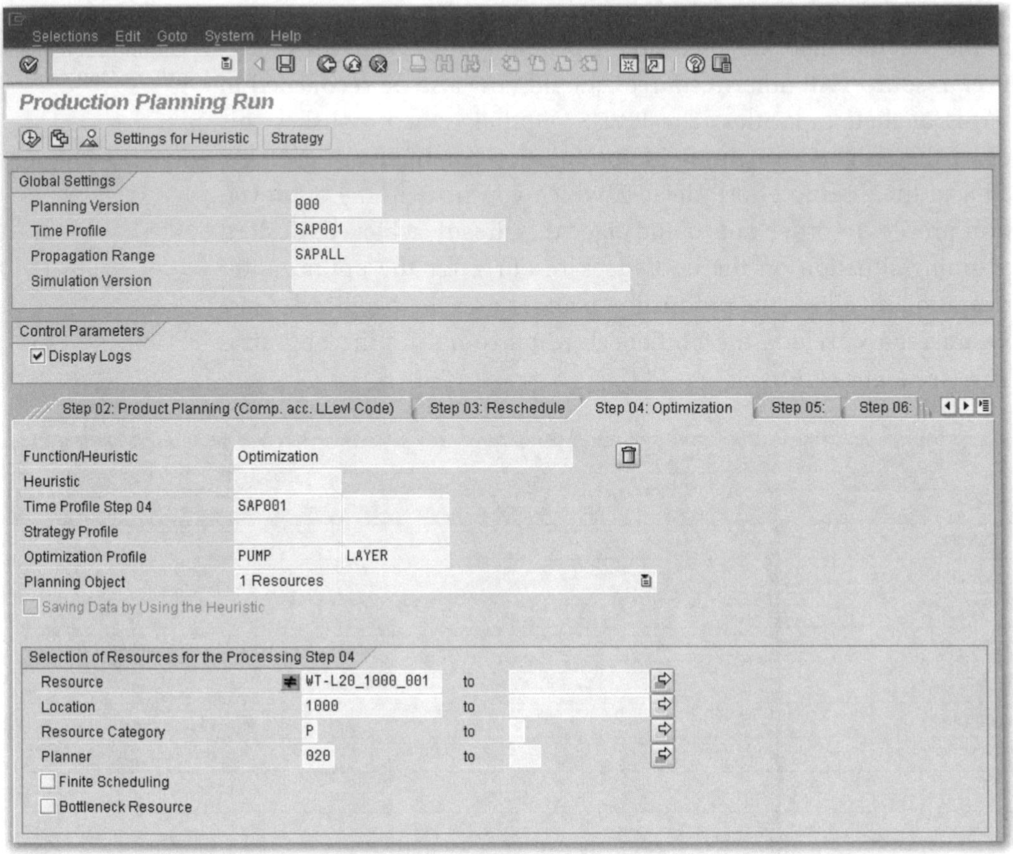

Figure 7.9 APO Transaction "Production Planning Run," Transaction Code /SAPAPO/CDPSP0, Optimization of All Remaining Resources

The bottleneck resource that is not included counts as being fixed for the PP/DS Optimizer so that the corresponding operations are not shifted during the optimization. Depending on the parameterization of the optimization, the overall planning situation may look completely different, but resource overloads in this final step are nevertheless eliminated in the optimization interval considered—if at all possible (see the result in Figure 7.10).

The PP/DS Optimizer brings unfixed operations forward in time, taking the basic conditions into account, to close gaps in the short-term period. For the current scenario, this allows for a timely requirements coverage by a "feasible" production program. According to this, the product view (see Figure 7.11) now assigns different availability data and times for the different planned orders.

Figure 7.10 APO Transaction "Detailed Scheduling Planning Board," Transaction Code /SAPAPO/CDPS0, "Resource Utilization" Chart Overloads No Longer Occur in the Optimization Period

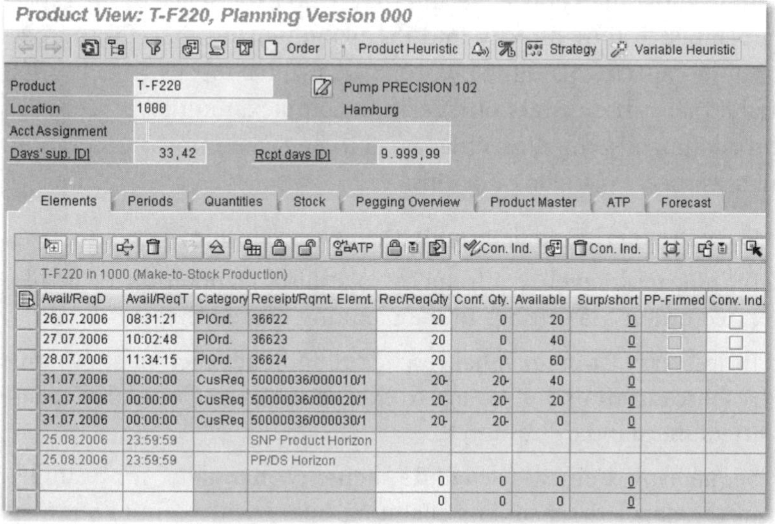

Figure 7.11 APO Transaction "Product View," Transaction Code /SAPAPO/RRP3, Resources Following Completed Capacity Planning and Optimization

261

Nonetheless, in such cases it is possible that overloads may occur as before, for example, if there are problems that cannot be fully resolved (lower total capacity available than capacity requirements), or if the elements affected are located outside or partially outside the optimization horizon. These operations are generally considered as fixed for the optimization.

When considering these and other similar examples, you will notice that in some cases the results of the optimization are regarded as "suboptimal." You should keep in mind here, considering the comments in Chapter 6, that each optimization run is designed to create *one* feasible solution—even with longer optimization durations, this does not necessarily have to be the best solution possible under all conceivable viewpoints.

Manual post-processing

You can therefore optionally allow an interactive step to follow the planning run. During this step, the planner first verifies the situation that has arisen, by using the detailed scheduling planning board, for example, and the tools and resources available there. After this analysis, a strategic interactive postprocessing can be done using the appropriate strategy settings (see Chapter 6), if necessary.

Partially Automated Variant

Manual sequencing

As an alternative to the procedure just described above, you may want to allow the knowledge and first-hand experience of the capacity planner to flow directly into the planning, and therefore to perform the capacity planning by primarily manual means. This is often vital if there are several bottlenecks in complex, multilevel scenarios and additional setup difficulties need to be taken into consideration. Such a process may look like this:

1. Stage numbering to determine the low-level codes

2. Infinite multilevel requirements planning, generation of deallocated orders via settings in the planning procedure

3. If necessary, some manual rescheduling in advance to alternative resources (infinite), so as not to exceed the overall available capacity of the standard resource.

4. Sequencing, heuristic **Schedule sequence manually**, for example, in the detailed scheduling planning board with a finite strategy, mode **Insert operation**, dependent operations initially planned infinitely and compactly, relationships taken into account

5. Scheduling of additional operations (including assemblies) according to the top-down principle, sort sequence according to the strategy settings

Since there is no optimization, the partially automated variant offers you the advantage of a better understanding of the planning result and how it has been obtained. Due to the interaction that is required, this procedure is not suitable for a fully automated planning run.

7.2 Setup-Optimal Sequencing with the PP/DS Optimizer

If the setup problem of the bottleneck resource is not important, or if it is of minor importance, scheduling the operations and orders is usually a straightforward process, because you can use the scheduling sequence in the planning strategy. Nevertheless, if a considerable optimization potential is attached to the setup sequence in which individual operations are to be handled, that is, if setup matrices are used and the total setup time accruing in a production program is largely dependent on the scheduling sequence due to the setup-condition-dependent changeovers, in most cases the PP/DS Optimizer is the most effective tool for the planning. You can use the PP/DS Optimizer to take several bottlenecks into account at the same time, order priorities can be included, and a multilevel optimization is possible. Since the PP/DS Optimizer does not create or delete any orders, but rather merely reschedules them, a previous requirements planning is a prerequisite for using the PP/DS Optimizer.

Setup-condition-dependent setup times

7.2.1 The PP/DS Optimizer as an Interactive Planning Tool

Using the PP/DS Optimizer you can weight individual operational business criteria to achieve a strategic optimization in relation to the basic conditions sought (see Chapter 6). In particular, it is possible not only to include the PP/DS Optimizer in the production planning run, but also to start it interactively from a planning tool (product planning table, detailed scheduling planning board). This may especially be an interesting variant in scenarios where the optimization step—based on the result of a previous requirements planning—is to be performed repeatedly, with changed parameterizations if re-

Interactive setup optimization

quired, until a satisfactory result is obtained. Following the integration in a planning run that we have already seen, the next example deals with such an interactive application of the optimization, where the emphasis is on the ability to understand both cause and effect.

7.2.2 Sample Process for Interactive Setup Optimization

We will look at three finished products produced in-house. They are differentiated by color (white, yellow, blue). In the work step "paint," a resource is used that represents a bottleneck for capacity reasons (**Paint shop**, modeled as a single resource). The changeovers between the individual setup conditions are described in the master data of production planning via a setup matrix, because the time commitment required for a setup activity depends on the relevant preceding status. The assemblies are available in this sample scenario.

Requirements Planning

Requirements situation

Let's assume that within a short-term horizon of around one month there are three requirements in this example for each of the end products (see Figure 7.12).

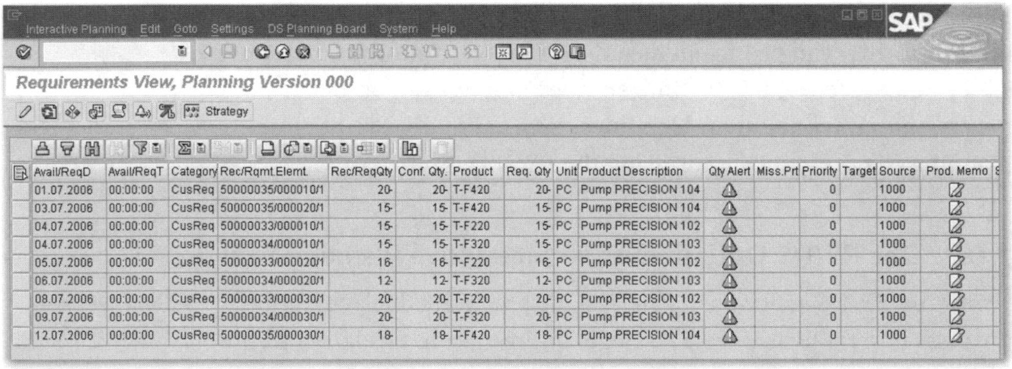

Avail/ReqD	Avail/ReqT	Category	Rec/Rqmt.Elemt.	Rec/ReqQty	Conf. Qty.	Product	Req. Qty	Unit	Product Description	Qty Alert	Miss.Prt	Priority	Target	Source	Prod. Memo
01.07.2006	00:00:00	CusReq	50000035/000010/1	20-	20-	T-F420	20-	PC	Pump PRECISION 104			0		1000	
03.07.2006	00:00:00	CusReq	50000035/000020/1	15-	15-	T-F420	15-	PC	Pump PRECISION 104			0		1000	
04.07.2006	00:00:00	CusReq	50000033/000010/1	15-	15-	T-F220	15-	PC	Pump PRECISION 102			0		1000	
04.07.2006	00:00:00	CusReq	50000034/000010/1	15-	15-	T-F320	15-	PC	Pump PRECISION 103			0		1000	
05.07.2006	00:00:00	CusReq	50000033/000020/1	16-	16-	T-F220	16-	PC	Pump PRECISION 102			0		1000	
06.07.2006	00:00:00	CusReq	50000034/000020/1	12-	12-	T-F320	12-	PC	Pump PRECISION 103			0		1000	
08.07.2006	00:00:00	CusReq	50000033/000030/1	20-	20-	T-F220	20-	PC	Pump PRECISION 102			0		1000	
09.07.2006	00:00:00	CusReq	50000034/000030/1	20-	20-	T-F320	20-	PC	Pump PRECISION 103			0		1000	
12.07.2006	00:00:00	CusReq	50000035/000030/1	18-	18-	T-F420	18-	PC	Pump PRECISION 104			0		1000	

Figure 7.12 APO Transaction "Requirements View," Transaction Code /SAPAPO/RRP1, Requirements for the Three End Products

Resource situation after the requirements planning

The requirements planning for the three products initially creates timely receipts (where possible). Nevertheless, these are not reconciled in terms of capacity with the relevant resource offering, particularly not for the bottleneck resource considered. You can deduce this, for example, from the product planning table (see Figure 7.13).

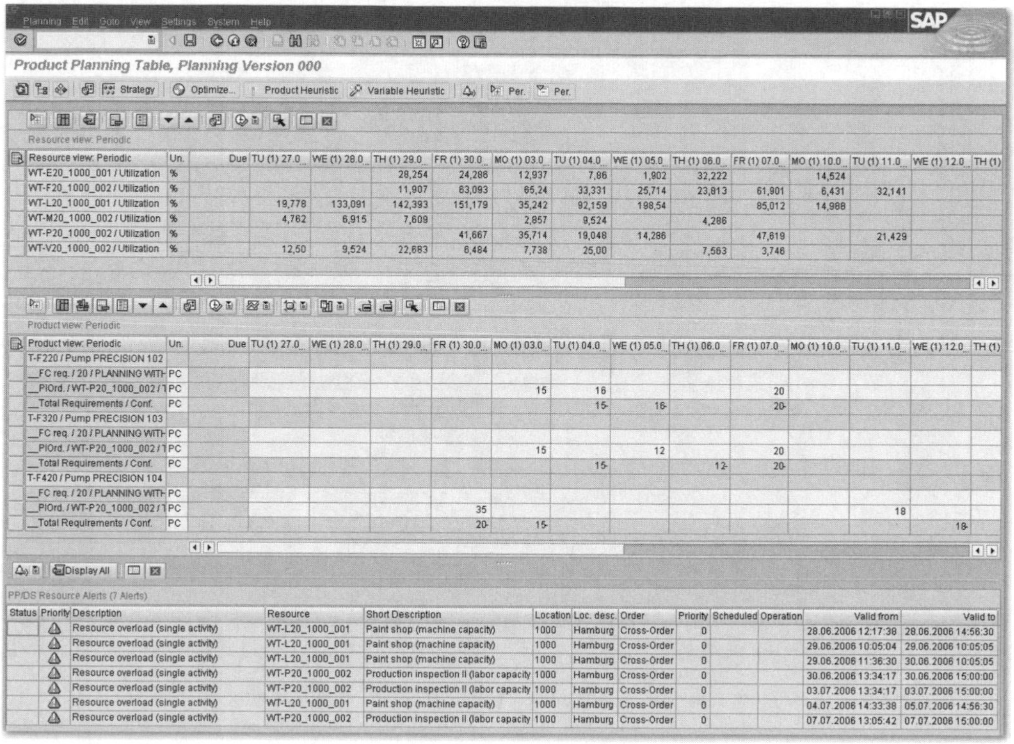

Figure 7.13 APO Transaction "Product Planning Table," Transaction Code /SAPAPO/PPT1, Resource Allocation in Periodic View Following the Requirements Planning

According to this example, the initial situation for the interactive operation of the bottleneck resource comprises receipts that have been created in a requirements-oriented way and infinitely planned, and these receipts do not have an operation sequence (operations have parallel times, see Figure 7.14) or their operation sequence is random.

If you analyze the situation of the bottleneck resource for this planning stage, as expected you can find overloads that will now to be cleaned up as part of the optimization.

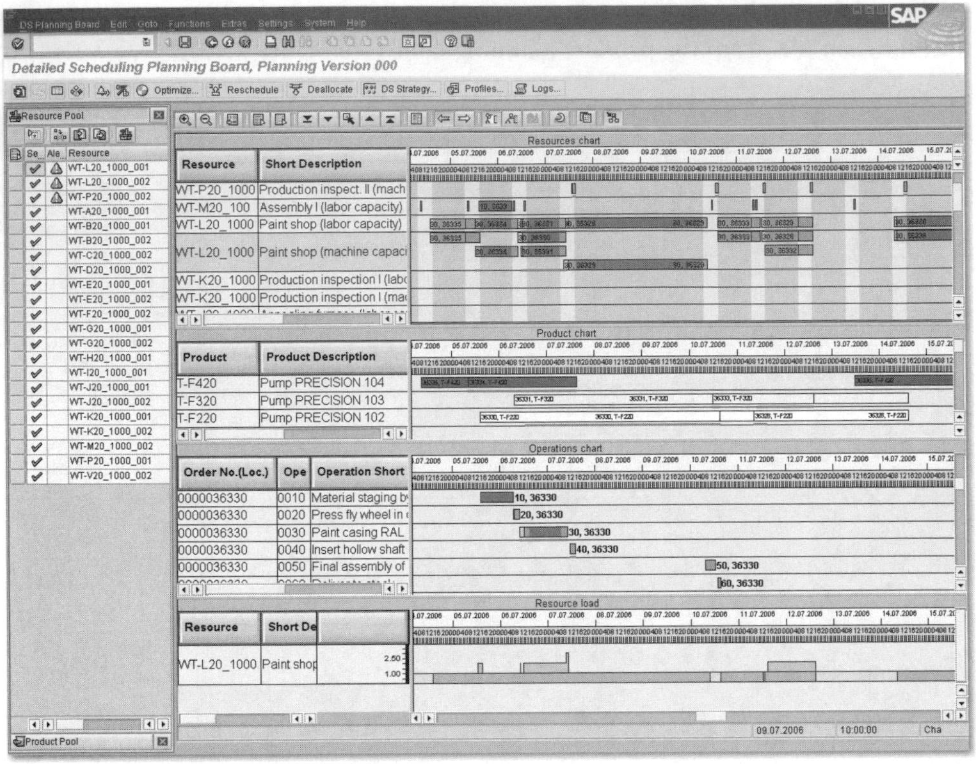

Figure 7.14 APO Transaction "Detailed Scheduling Planning Board," Transaction Code /SAPAPO/CDPS0, Randomly Arranged Operations and Overloads on the Bottleneck Resource

Optimization in Relation to Setup Times

Pure setup optimization

We first want to parameterize the PP/DS Optimizer in the optimization profile in such a way that only the setup optimization is in the foreground (here this is done by weighting the setup time total with the numerical value of 250 and all other criteria with 0). The PP/DS Optimizer is started interactively from the detailed scheduling planning board, after the **paint shop** has been selected for the optimization process. The progress in time of the quality of the result is shown during the optimization (see Figure 7.15).

Once the optimization is complete, if you look at the navigation structure and the resource chart of the detailed scheduling planning board (see Figure 7.16), you will see that the overload situation has already been mitigated, particularly in relation to the bottleneck resource.

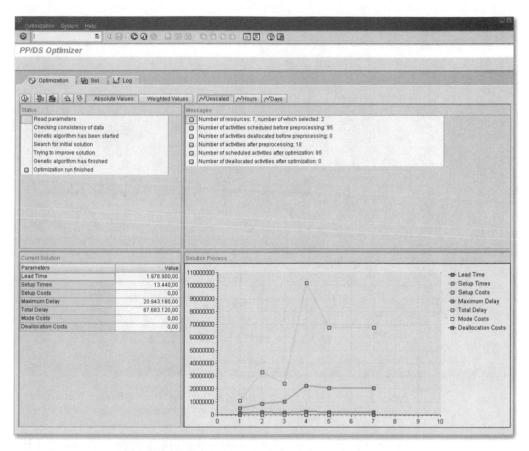

Figure 7.15 APO Transaction "Detailed Scheduling Planning Board," Transaction Code /SAPAPO/CDPS0, Functionality of the PP/DS Optimizer, Progress of the Setup Optimization

Due to the specifications in the optimization profile and the time values stored in the setup matrix (see Figure 7.17) for the different setup transfers, the following result may occur in this example: The system first schedules all of the paint operations for white pumps, then all of the paint operations for yellow pumps, and finally all of the paint operations for blue pumps. There are two reasons for this sequence: the setup effort between two identical colors is minimal, and the transitions from bright colors to dark colors can be achieved with less time input than the other way around (e.g., due to the relevant cleaning work required).[1]

---

1 In the setup matrix (see Figure 7.17), the setup key 10 stands for white, 20 stands for yellow, and 40 stands for blue.

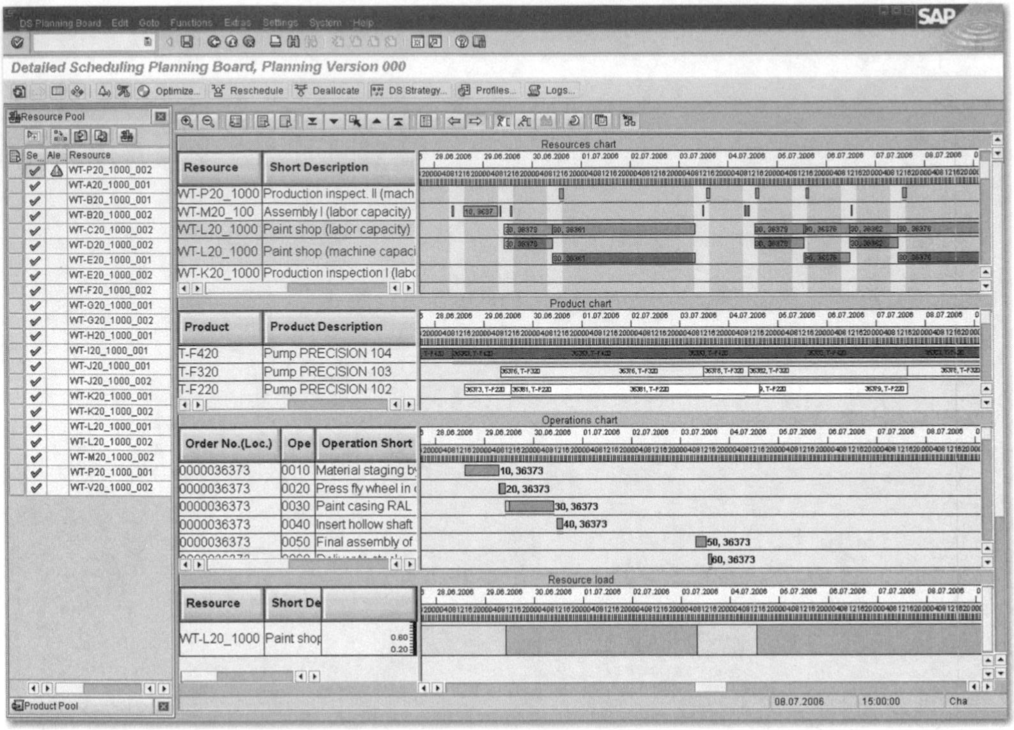

Figure 7.16 APO Transaction "Detailed Scheduling Planning Board," Transaction Code /SAPAPO/CDPS0, Result of Pure Setup Optimization

Since the specification of a *pure* setup optimization means that the system does not consider the requirement dates, obviously the requirement dates for such an optimization result may be infringed. This is shown in the **network view** of the detailed scheduling planning board (see Figure 7.18). In our system example, some of the planned orders (represented by horizontal bars) are available too late for the corresponding requirements (represented by downward-pointing triangles).

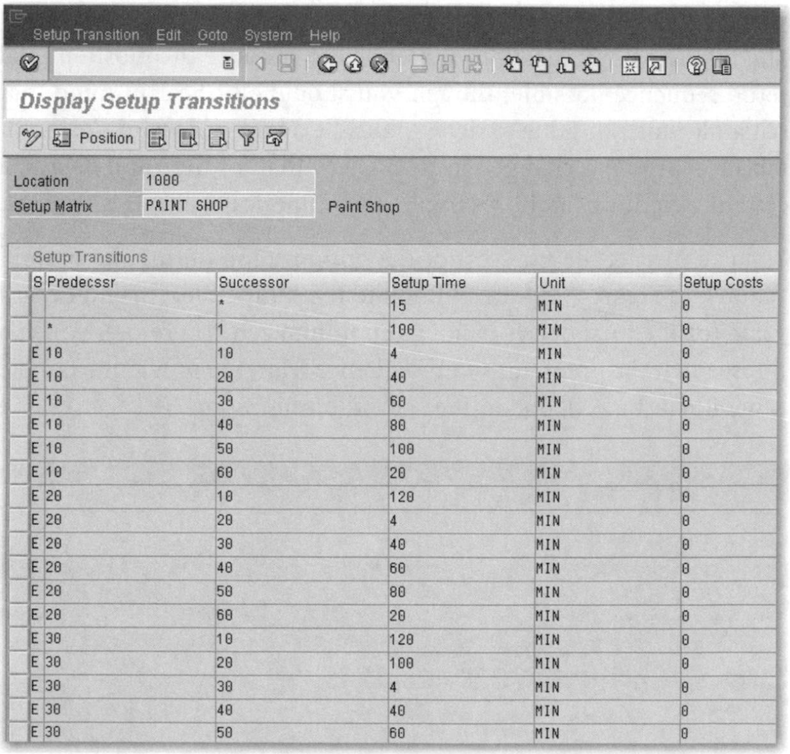

Setup Transition Edit Goto System Help

Display Setup Transitions

Position

Location 1000

Setup Matrix PAINT SHOP Paint Shop

Setup Transitions

S	Predecssr	Successor	Setup Time	Unit	Setup Costs
		*	15	MIN	0
	*	1	100	MIN	0
E	10	10	4	MIN	0
E	10	20	40	MIN	0
E	10	30	60	MIN	0
E	10	40	80	MIN	0
E	10	50	100	MIN	0
E	10	60	20	MIN	0
E	20	10	120	MIN	0
E	20	20	4	MIN	0
E	20	30	40	MIN	0
E	20	40	60	MIN	0
E	20	50	80	MIN	0
E	20	60	20	MIN	0
E	30	10	120	MIN	0
E	30	20	100	MIN	0
E	30	30	4	MIN	0
E	30	40	40	MIN	0
E	30	50	60	MIN	0

Figure 7.17 APO Transaction "Setup Matrix," Transaction Code /SAPAPO/CDPSC7, Setup Matrix of the Bottleneck Resource

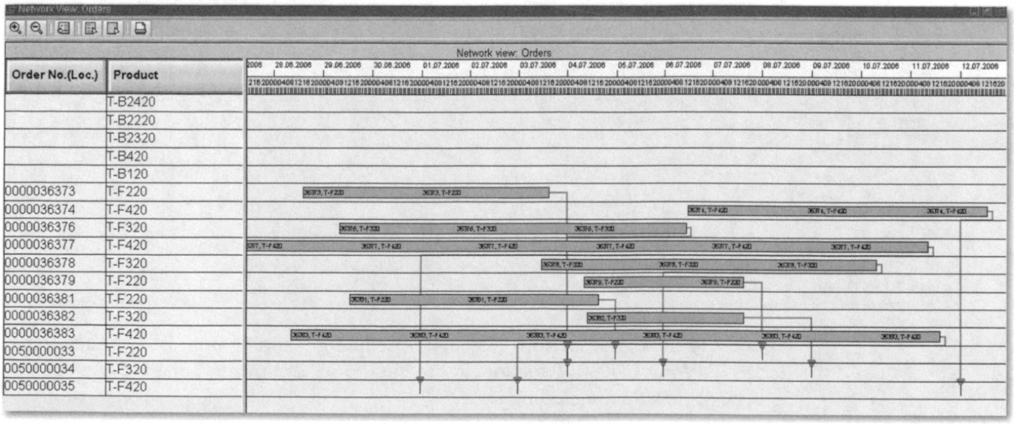

Figure 7.18 APO Transaction "Detailed Scheduling Planning Board," Transaction Code /SAPAPO/CDPS0, Network View of the Orders for the End Product Following Pure Setup Optimization

Setup Optimization Taking Delays into Account

Setup optimization with as few delays as possible

The following optimization is intended to produce the most optimal setup sequence possible, though you should also bear in mind that schedule violations due to delays must be avoided. The original optimization profile is changed in such a way that for the **Total delays**, a certain weighting (in this example, the numerical value 2) is entered.

You can inspect the progress of the optimization during the optimization (see Figure 7.19). In addition to the setup times, the numerical value for the total delays is now also minimized. Therefore, you can foresee that the optimum setup sequence from the previous example cannot be achieved, due to the second optimization criterion.

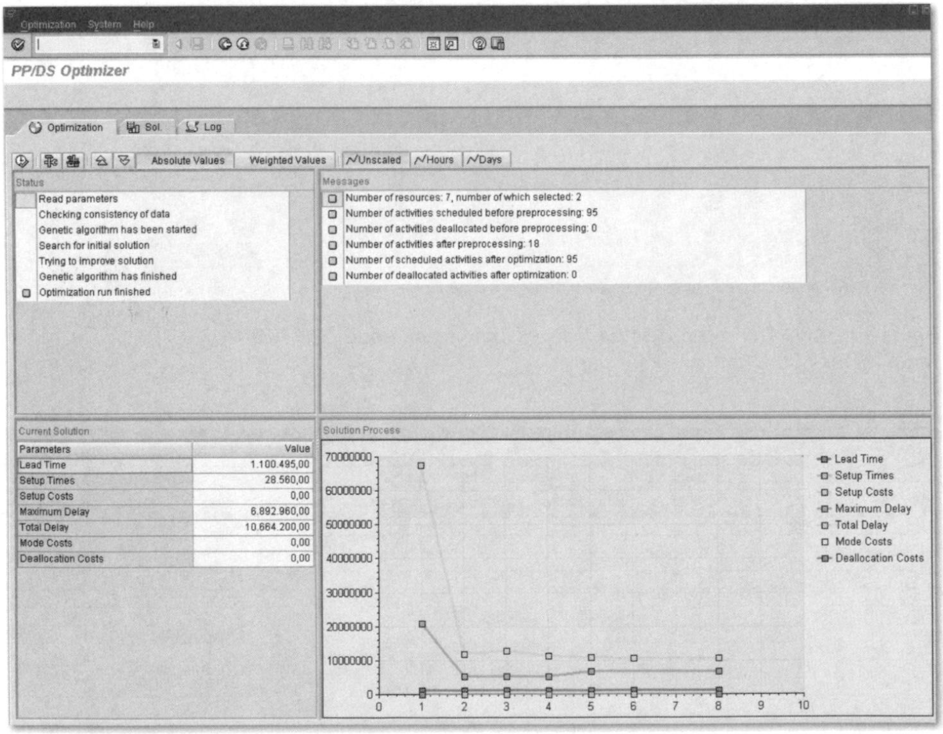

Figure 7.19 APO Transaction "Detailed Scheduling Planning Board," Transaction Code /SAPAPO/CDPS0, Functionality of the PP/DS Optimizer, Time Progress of the Setup Optimization, Including Delays

The detailed scheduling planning board allows you to see the result of the new optimization (see Figure 7.20): The operations again underwent a sequencing, so therefore, there are no overloads on the bottleneck resource.

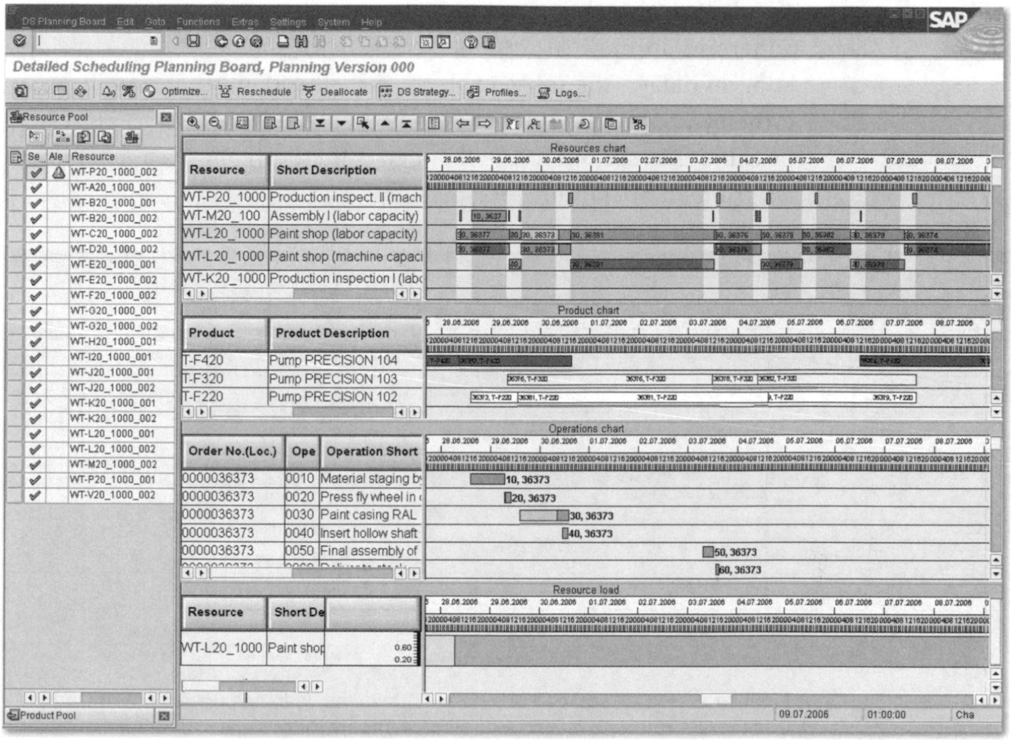

Figure 7.20 APO Transaction "Detailed Scheduling Planning Board," Transaction Code /SAPAPO/CDPS0, Result of the Setup Optimization Including Delays

If we now analyze the sequence of the operations on the bottleneck resource, we can see that a suboptimal sequence results compared with the pure setup optimization. In our example, the paint shop would work through the nine operations required as follows:

Blue – Blue – White – White – Yellow – Yellow – Yellow – White – Blue.

As before, this sequence shows a certain block construction, which is beneficial with regard to the setup input required, nevertheless, the block construction is restricted by the schedule that must be adhered to if possible. This principal characteristic of an optimization result, which satisfies the basic conditions mentioned earlier, can be verified through the **network view**, in which delays now rarely have any importance whatsoever (see Figure 7.21).

Result: We notice that while it is generally no longer possible to adhere to an optimal setup sequence with the additional consideration of delays, the setup problem is included as far as possible nevertheless, so that the assigned schedule is adhered to as closely as possible. The second result obtained is therefore more suitable, overall, from an operational perspective.

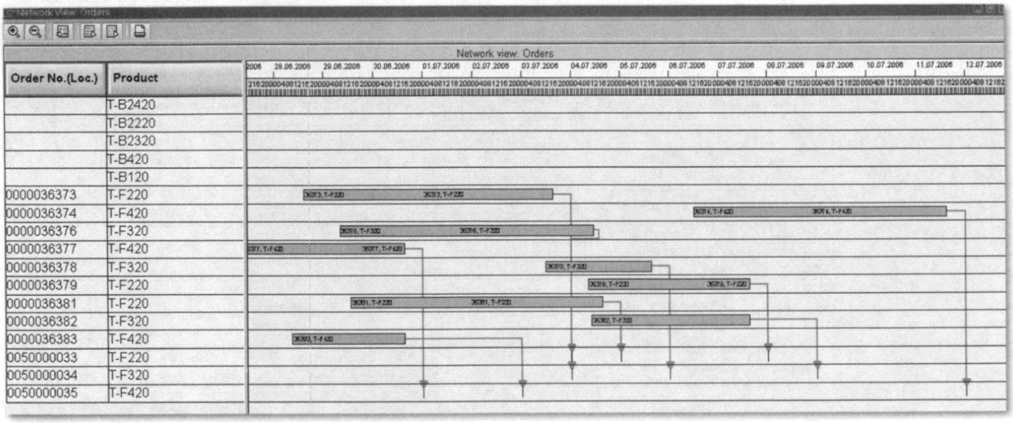

Figure 7.21 APO Transaction "Detailed Scheduling Planning Board," Transaction Code /SAPAPO/CDPS0, Network View of Orders for the End Product Following Setup Optimization Including Delays

7.3   Capable-to-Promise (CTP)

"Appropriate for a promise to be made in relation to it"

The CTP method (*Capable-to-Promise*) is an option for performing a multilevel finite requirements planning from the availability check of a sales order, and thereby for triggering production if the desired product is not available. Here it is important to note that the ATP function (*Available-to-Promise*) has been extended in such a way that if the product requested is not available, an—initially simulative— feasibility study is performed in the system. As a result, the system indicates whether—and if so, when—the relevant product will be available if the sales order triggers procurement and production of the product, taking consideration of the desired delivery date and including the currently applicable resource allocation situation in the production plant. Once the sales order is confirmed and saved, in this initially simulative situation, the corresponding procurement elements, with all of their capacity requirements, will be dispatched to the resources.

7.3.1 Prerequisites for the CTP Procedure

A CTP check is only possible if the sales order (created in ECC) undergoes its availability check in APO (see Chapter 3). The required detail settings will still be given as part of a sample process.

The following list gives an overview of the most important basic conditions for the CTP procedure:

Ancillary conditions and modeling recommendations

▶ Sales and production must either work in close harmony (*time continuous CTP*), or you must instead use the *bucket-oriented CTP procedure* for a certain decoupling of the two departments (see explanations below).

▶ The ATP customizing must be prepared accordingly, and there must be an active integration model for the ATP check in APO of the product considered .

▶ The finished product and the assemblies to be included in the procedure must be equipped with an automatic planning procedure in the product master.

Furthermore, it is recommended that you include the lowest possible number of BOM levels in the modeling, to minimize the number of conditions and so the procedure will only be applied if the current business situation allows sufficient gaps for a finite scheduling of additional orders. You will notice that if you adhere to these conditions, the quality of the solutions that you achieve using CTP will remain relatively good. However, the quality will rapidly decline as soon as a certain resource load level has been reached and there are no longer sufficient gaps available.

7.3.2 The CTP Process

In the standard process, a sales order is created in the sales of the ECC, and availability of that product for the order is checked using the Global ATP check (GATP). The ATP availability check is activated in the customer requirements class, which belongs to the customer requirements type of the sales order. To perform the check in APO, you must have created an active integration model for the ATP check.

Production in the event of non-availability

When the ATP customizing is transferred from ECC, the customer requirements classes are mapped as the so-called "check mode" in APO, and therefore in APO the basic behavior of an incoming sales

Customizing for the CTP check

order with a particular requirements class is known. Nevertheless, the central setting for the CTP check is performed in the check instructions, which belongs to this check mode and the business event. Here, the setting **Availability Check first, then Production**. It is possible to combine this with a previous rules-based availability check (for example, to only trigger production once all plants have been searched and there are no substitution products available). This would also be activated in the check instructions (Figure 7.22 shows the check instructions for our example).

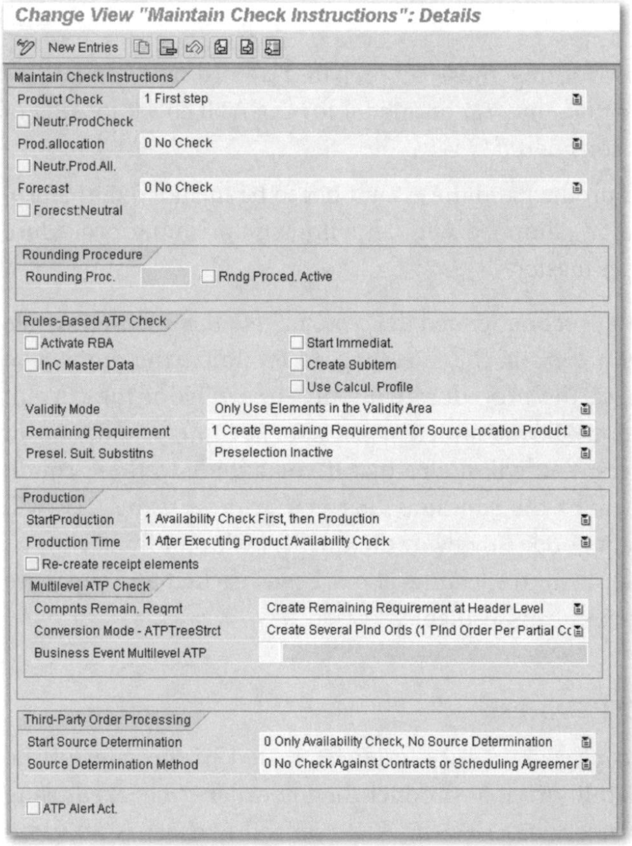

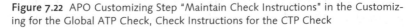

Figure 7.22 APO Customizing Step "Maintain Check Instructions" in the Customizing for the Global ATP Check, Check Instructions for the CTP Check

In the following sample process, a make-to-stock strategy (**planning with final assembly**) is used to create a sales order for a finished product. The ATP customizing allows for production to be triggered in cases where full availability in the plant is absent.

In the example, the quantity requested by the sales order is 60 units, however there should only be a plant stock of 40 units (no fixed receipts). Using this example, first we will analyze the system behavior for the time-continuous CTP concept. Then we will explain the differences that are present in a bucket-oriented check.

Sample process

Time-continuous CTP

With the time-continuous CTP method, in the case of production the required planned orders—and thus operations—are generated and are dispatched definitively and to the precise second to the corresponding resources.[2]

In this example, a sales order is created (see Figure 7.23) that is to be checked using the CTP method according to the ATP check instructions stored in the APO customizing.

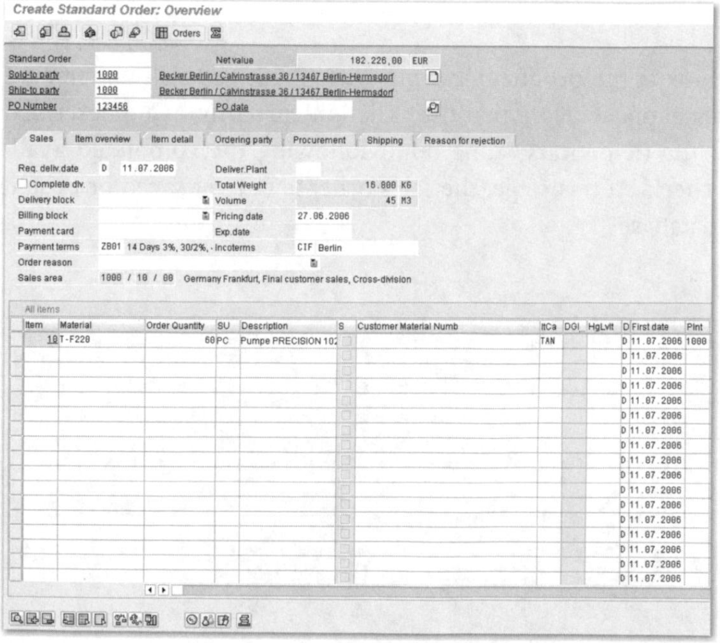

Figure 7.23 ECC Transaction "Create Sales Order," Transaction Code VA01, Sales Order with Availability Check Button (Bottom, Seventh Button from the Left)

---

2 A CTP procedure with infinite planning is conceivable and technically possible, but a confirmation created with this procedure is rather noncommittal. Therefore, it is advisable in this scenario, that you remove only non-critical resources from the finite planning.

The dialog box for the availability check (see Figure 7.24), which can be called from the sales order, may very well contain a complete confirmation of the desired quantity against the background of the CTP check, even though this required quantity is only partially in stock.

APO Availability Check: Delivery proposal (Sales order)

One-time delivery	Full Delivery	Delivery proposal	Check instructions	Scope of check	ATP		

Order Item	18		Schedule Line	1		
Product	T-F228			Pump PRECISION 102		
Production Plant	1888		Hamburg			
Requested Date	11.07.2006 08:30		Open Quantity	60		PC
Fixed date and qty			Max. Partial Delivery	9		

Sched. Line Overview

SL Date	SchLinTime	MtlAvailDt	MatAvailTm	Ti	Confirmed Quantity	ONE	FULL	Confirmed Qty	Pro
11.07.2006	08:30:00	11.07.2006	07:48:00	CET	60			60	
	00:00:00		00:00:00					0	
	00:00:00		00:00:00					0	
	00:00:00		00:00:00					0	

Figure 7.24 Dialog Box for APO-CTP Check Showing the Test Result for This System Example—Can Be Called from the ECC Sales Order or Appears Automatically in the Event of Problems

If you look at the product view in Figure 7.25, you will understand why this happens. Note that the situation currently being described reflects the (temporary) time point following the completed availability check. At this stage, the sales order is not yet saved or posted to the database!

Product View: T-F220, Planning Version 000

Strategy

Product	T-F228		Pump PRECISION 102
Location	1888		Hamburg
Acct Assignment			
Days' sup. IDI	9.999,99	Rcpt days IDI	9.999,99

Elements	Periods	Quantities	Stock	Pegging Overview	Product Master	ATP	Forecast

ATP | Con. Ind. | Con. Ind.

T-F220 in 1000 (Make-to-Stock Production)

	Avail/ReqD	Avail/ReqT	Category	Receipt/Rqmt. Elemt.	Rec/ReqQty	Conf. Qty.	Available	Surp/short	Qty Alert	PP-Firmed	Conv. Ind.
	27.06.2006	14:22:11	Stock	/0002/CC	40	40	40	40			
	10.07.2006	12:00:00	PlOrd.	161814	20	0	60	0			
	10.07.2006	12:00:00	SalesOrder	Temporary Requirement	20-	20-	40	0			
	25.08.2006	23:59:59		SNP Product Horizon							
	25.08.2006	23:59:59		PP/DS Horizon							

Figure 7.25 APO Transaction "Product View," Transaction Code /SAPAPO/RRP3, Stock/requirements Situation Following the Availability Check, but Prior to the Sales Order Being Saved

Due to the—at this point, still simulative—CTP requirement, a temporary requirements element occurs through the remaining requirements quantity that has not already been confirmed through the stock (in this example, a temporary requirement of the category **SalesOrder** of **20 units**). Due to the automatic immediate planning, this requirement immediately results in a corresponding procurement element (in this example, a timely planned order of the category **PlOrd** of **20 units**). Due to the settings in the planning procedure, this procurement element has the characteristic of having been created through an automatic, finite requirements planning. The confirmation of the remaining requirements quantity therefore relates to this receipt that has just been created by simulation.

Temporary requirement

Based on this temporary situation, we would like to note the following points:

▶ A simultaneous availability check for this product from a second sales order cannot mistakenly confirm against the stock that is already included in a check or against receipts that have been included.

▶ The operations of the procurement element that is created and the procurement element itself can already be verified at this stage in detailed scheduling (e.g., in the resource and the order view of the detailed scheduling planning board).

Therefore, two sales employees who each subject a sales order to the CTP check at the same time see different receipts (the person "simulating first" may also access existing stocks, for example). If necessary, separate receipts are created finitely for each CTP process. In particular, the employee responsible may already see the operations of the simulatively created planned orders on the resources in the detailed scheduling planning board during the detailed planning at the CTP check stage (that is, when the sales order has not yet been saved) and using, for example, the order number from the APO number range,[3] he or she may identify these as simulative elements (see Figure 7.26).

---

3 At this stage no return to ECC has yet occurred due to the pending posting so that "simulative" elements can be easily distinguished from "operative" elements.

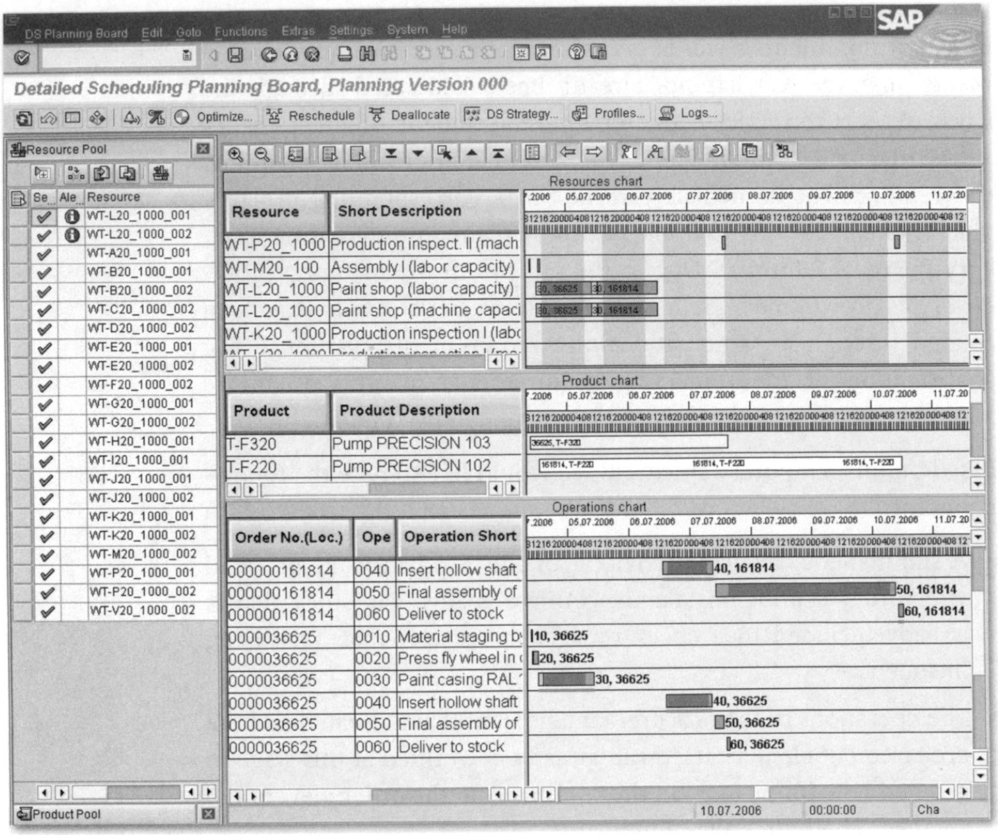

Figure 7.26 APO Transaction "Detailed Scheduling Planning Board," Transaction Code /SAPAPO/CDPS0, Existing (Here, Number Range 36xxx) Orders and Operations Simulatively Created via CTP (Here, Number Range 161xxx)

No commitment is given yet at this stage. If the customer or the sales employee performing the execution should decide against the CTP confirmation offered, he or she can reject the sales order. The simulatively dispatched elements are then also in turn rejected, and the corresponding capacity loads and any blocked stock are released again.

Multilevel concept   The CTP procedure explicitly allows a multilevel finite requirements planning. This means that you can ensure the availability of the assemblies required to manufacture the finished product: The procurement element at the finished product level terminates secondary requirements for the BOM components. If you have also included the assemblies in the check process with an automated finite planning, these requirements are immediately planned on the corresponding resources. If timely scheduling at a lower level is not possible, the entire order structure is shifted into the future until a scheduling can take place. In this case, the desired delivery date at the finished product level generally cannot be adhered to, therefore a delayed confirmation is offered.

Slim scenarios

> **Note**
>
> You should realize that with each additional assembly that is included in the check, the probability of a successful scheduling will decrease, because many additional conditions arise. For this reason, SAP recommends that such a scenario be modeled as slimly as possible, that only the assemblies that really are problematic be included, and that their critical operations be given a finite scheduling.

Furthermore, during a time-continuous CTP, depending on the process, there is the danger of a fragmentation of operations, which can be problematic, particularly for bottleneck resources. Help may be possible via a periodically triggered setup optimization.

Once the CTP-checked sales order is saved, an equalized situation directly arises from the point of view of production due to the immediate planning. The sales order appears bindingly with its complete quantity and is, in this example, timely covered via stock and an additional procurement element (a planned order) that has been immediately created (see Figure 7.27).

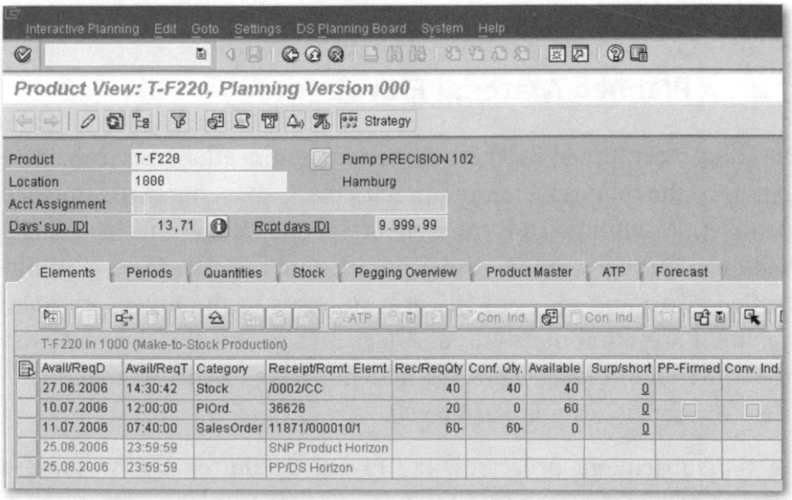

Figure 7.27 APO Transaction "Product View," Transaction Code /SAPAPO/RRP3, Stock/Requirements Situation After Saving the CTP-Confirmed Sales Order

Bucket-Oriented CTP

Put simply, during the time-continuous CTP procedure the sales department dispatches operations to the production resources right on time. This is not easy to implement in many operational business scenarios. As an aid, the bucket-oriented CTP concept pursues an uncoupling of the sales and the production view. Furthermore, this process also carries with it the positive side effect of improved overall performance.

PP/DS bucket capacity
Conceptually, the same path is followed as for the time-continuous CTP principle. The separation of the sales and the production responsibility is achieved by introducing a so-called "PP/DS bucket capacity" (see Chapter 6), which is to be stored in the relevant resource. When the sales order is entered, a CTP check against free capacity is only run on the basis of these buckets (i.e., time intervals such as days or weeks). As a result of the availability check, the sales employee therefore only gets, for example, the statement "Delivery is possible in calendar week XY," while a subsequent detailed planning based on this statement (in the area of production's responsibility) only decides how the corresponding operations are ultimately scheduled based on this confirmation. The bucket-oriented concept always requires a subsequent detailed scheduling, because the advance bucket-oriented planning is only run in a period-oriented and bucket-finite manner.

7.4   Planned Material Flow

In many operational business scenarios, you need a fixed reference between the requirements and procurement elements at the finished product, assembly, and component levels. While this is usually achieved through make-to-order production, the associated administrative effort and the consequences in terms of the inventory management are often not desired. Alternatively, you can therefore use the function of the *fixed pegging* to definitively fix the planned material flow across several BOM levels.

In the subsequent processes, the PP/DS Optimizer always plays a central role in generating a feasible production plan. Therefore, in the case of complex scenarios (many orders, multiple BOM levels, high loads, restrictive conditions), you should remember the general prerequisites of a successful optimization.

> **Note**
>
> The number and quality of successful reschedulings decreases as the complexity increases. Therefore, it is often advisable to create outlets, for example, to formulate conditions that are actually "hard" as "soft," in order to allow a sufficient degree of freedom to the PP/DS Optimizer.

The scenarios described in the following section use the fixed material flow.

7.4.1 Fixed Material Flow Using Pegging ATP

In this availability check scenario, the ATP check of the sales order can be performed via the fixed pegging links. In order to do this, you must:

"Characteristic evaluation"

▸ Work in **check mode** with the production type **Characteristic evaluation** (the description here is rather misleading—see Figure 7.28)

▸ Use the desired setting **Consider pegging** in the **check control** (see Figure 7.29)

▸ Refer to SAP Note 601813, which contains application cases, properties, and restrictions for the "characteristic evaluation."

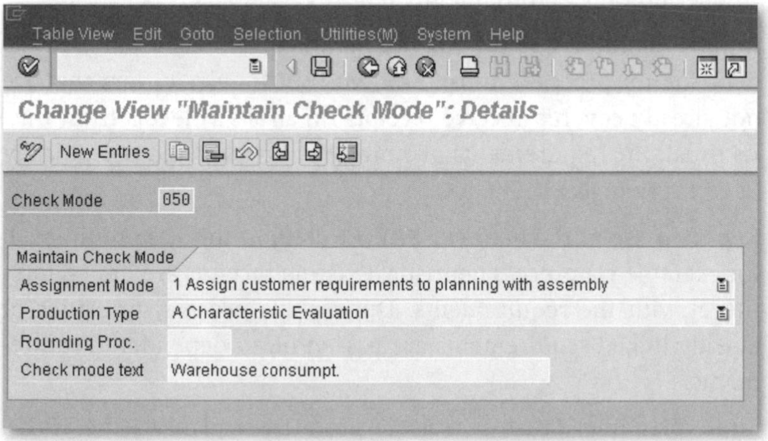

Figure 7.28 APO Customizing Step "Maintain Check Mode" in the Customizing of the Global ATP Check, Check Mode for the Pegging-Oriented Availability Check

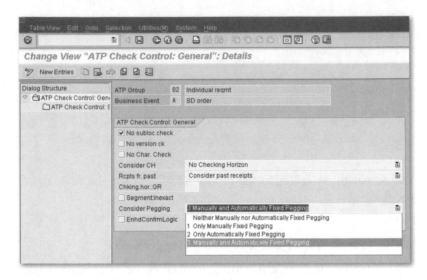

Figure 7.29 APO Customizing Step "Maintain Check Control" in the Customizing of the Global ATP Check, Check Control for the Pegging-Oriented Availability Check

The process initiates the following key steps:

1. Receipt of sales orders: Sales orders arrive continuously and are—if possible—directly confirmed in the dialog ATP.

2. Application of the heuristic **SAP_PP_019** to create fixed pegging: The heuristic is performed on a single level for the finished products and links the last confirmed allocations of the sales order, in order to maintain the generated assignments. This process should run periodically and frequently (e.g., every hour).

3. Infinite multilevel requirements planning, for example, via the heuristic for process control **SAP_MRP_001**: Sales orders that are not already covered receive receipts on all BOM levels from this. As usual, the requirements planning can be triggered periodically (e.g., every night).

4. Repeated use of the heuristic **SAP_PP_019**, in this case multilevel, for example via process heuristic: Existing receipts are linked multilevel with the requirements. During this process, priorities of already linked requirements are passed on to dependent requirements.

5. Finite planning: Create a feasible production plan via the PP/DS Optimizer.

6. Backorder processing: Due to the current planning situation, unconfirmed sales orders and new sales orders are ATP-confirmed where possible, if necessary including the checking horizon.

7.4.2 Fixed Material Flow Using the Material Requirements Planning

In many cases, there will never be material availability at the time that a sales order is created, therefore an availability check performed from a sales order will always have a negative result. A requirements planning should therefore be run first, prior to the ATP check.

Usual case of non-availability

The corresponding process may be as follows, including the fixed material flow:

1. Entry of sales orders: Sales orders arrive in all the time but are not ATP-confirmed.

2. Infinite multilevel requirements planning, for example, via the process heuristic **SAP_MRP_001**: Receipts are generated for the sales orders that are not covered. As usual, planning is run periodically in the nightly background job.

3. Application of the heuristic **SAP_PP_019** to create fixed pegging: The heuristic is included in a multilevel process (process heuristic) and bindingly links the structures that result from the multilevel requirements planning. This process can run periodically during the nightly background job.

4. Finite planning with the PP/DS Optimizer: An optimization is performed based on the existing structures.

5. Backorder processing: ATP confirmations are issued for the sales orders, if necessary including the checking horizon.

7.4.3 Fixed Material Flow to Support the Optimization

In the context of an optimization it is possible to consider the fixed pegging relationships in the form of pegging networks as binding, multilevel structures. In these cases, where possible, only complete, multilevel linked structures are rescheduled, and no new links are created. The main process involves the following steps:

Multilevel optimization

1. Entry of sales orders: A continuous process, where a confirmation is possible but not imperative.

2. Infinite multilevel requirements planning, for example, via the process heuristic **SAP_MRP_001**: Sales orders that are not covered receive the required receipts. The requirements planning must be triggered periodically (e.g., nightly).

3. Fixing the pegging using the heuristic **SAP_PP_019**, in this case multilevel—for example, using a periodically (nightly) scheduled process heuristic: Existing receipts are multilevel-linked with the requirements. Selection criteria for creating the fixed pegging links can be taken into account in the heuristic **SAP_PP_019** (see Figure 7.30).

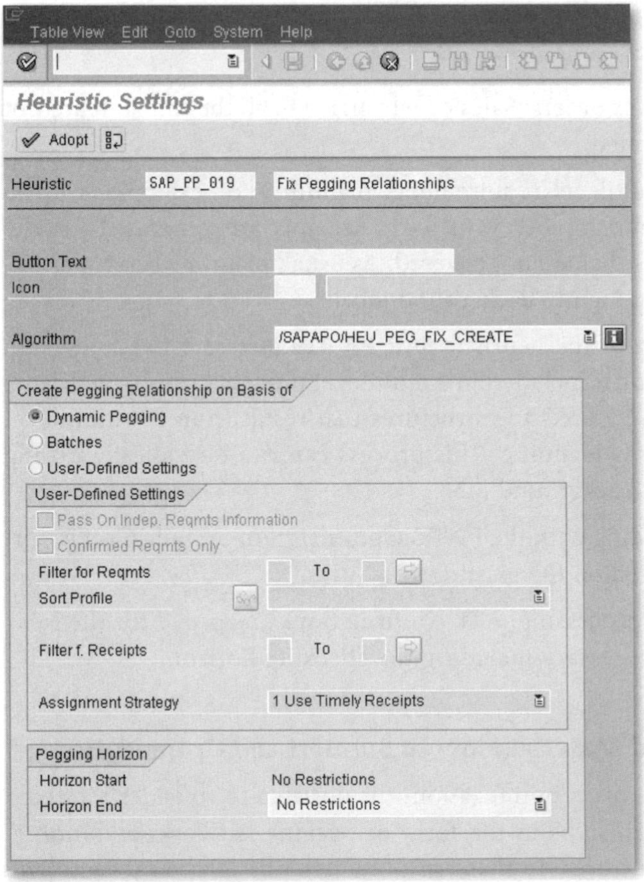

Figure 7.30 APO Customizing Step "Maintain Heuristics" in the PP/DS Customizing, Transaction Code /SAPAPO/CDPSC11, Heuristic for Fixing Pegging Relationships

4. Finite planning: The PP/DS Optimizer can be used to create a feasible production plan including the fixed pegging relationships; also to be triggered periodically (e.g., nightly).

5. Employment of the heuristic **SAP_PP_011** to delete the fixed pegging links—these have fulfilled their purpose once the optimization is complete.

6. Backorder processing in the same way as for the preceding processes.

7.4.4 Fixed Material Flow to Support the CTP Procedure

The availability check within the CTP procedure (see Section 7.3) allows the procurement to be initiated in the event of non-availability for the finished products, assemblies, and components included in this multilevel check. There is a danger here in using the time-continuous CTP procedure of a fragmentation of the individual operations on the resources (e.g., disproportionately large numbers of "coincidental" gaps between the operations). A downstream optimization is therefore often used here as an aid. So as not to separate the originally linked objects, in the following process the requirements and receipts are firmly linked across multiple levels before the PP/DS Optimizer counteracts the fragmentation across multiple levels:

Help in case of fragmentation

1. Sales orders are continually entered, while in each case the availability check is to be performed according to the CTP method. As a result, confirmations are issued against existing elements or against elements that have been specifically created for this.

2. Application of the heuristic **SAP_PP_019** to create fixed pegging: The heuristic is only performed on a single level here for the finished products and links the last confirmed allocations, in order to maintain the generated assignments. This process should run periodically and frequently (e.g., hourly).

3. Infinite multilevel requirements planning, for example, via the process heuristic **SAP_MRP_001**: Any sales orders that are not covered receive the required resources, while deeper BOM levels that may not be included in the CTP check are also scheduled. The requirements planning must be triggered periodically (e.g. nightly).

4. Repeated use of the heuristic **SAP_PP_019**, in this case multilevel, for example, via the process heuristic: Existing receipts are multilevel-linked with the requirements. In the course of this, priorities of already-linked requirements are passed on to dependent requirements.

5. Finite planning: Use of the PP/DS Optimizer to create a feasible production plan using the fixed pegging links.

6. Backorder processing: Runs the same way as for the previous processes.

7.5 Multi-Resource Planning with the Wave Algorithm

We would now like to consider a scenario where there is a bottleneck resource and in which the setup problem is of lesser significance. Furthermore, one or several alternatives should be available for the bottleneck and the planning should be run in a quantity- and period-oriented way (in other words, not order-oriented). The latter ensures that planned orders can be split as required, should this be necessary due to the resource situation. This is often the case in the area of repetitive manufacturing. In such an environment, use of the PP/DS Optimizer is often less appropriate or not required. Instead, the multi-resource planning can be performed using a special heuristic, the **wave algorithm**.

Alternative production data structure

As the only automated procedure of the PP/DS having these specific characteristics, this algorithm allows a systematic finite resource utilization planning incorporating different sources of supply (i.e., different production data structures or production process models). This is an important and fundamental distinction from switching to an alternative resource by selecting an alternative mode that is realized *within* a production data structure or a production process model.

7.5.1 Prerequisites for the Multi-Resource Planning

Besides the setup problem that can be disregarded, the scenarios to be mapped must not be too complex. Such cases are especially widespread in the area of *lean manufacturing*. Here the topic of setting up usually plays a secondary role, because planned orders are often "long-running" or many similar planned orders are scheduled in a row. In such scenarios, the bottleneck resource is rarely set up. In many cases, the mapping of a setup activity is performed, if necessary, by simply blocking the resource using an appropriately dimensioned planned order that is scheduled for a dummy material that has previously been specifically created for this.

When you use the wave algorithm (**multi-resource planning primary resource**), the operational background should also satisfy the conditions listed below.

- There are no products of different low-level codes with mutual dependencies (the procedure works on a single level, therefore each MRP level must be scheduled individually—a multilevel application is possible through the production planning run).

- No provision is made for an order or product prioritization during the scheduling.

- Costs, characteristics, or shelf lives do not need to be taken into account.

- There is only one operation for each PDS or PPM.

Prerequisites

7.5.2 Multi-Resource Planning Process

In the context of the restrictions mentioned, you can use the wave algorithm to perform a finite requirements and line utilization planning. Here, specific provision is made for scheduling several products and (through the assignment to PDS or PPM) several resources at the same time.

Finite requirements and line utilization planning

Operation and Sample Process

We will use an example to better understand the multi-resource planning concept.

There are two production lines in a production plant that are each accessed and mapped as a resource in the system for each product, and in each case through a separate production data structure. According to a given requirements situation (see Figure 7.31), we want to plan and manufacture three different localization products on these production lines.

Master data and parameterization

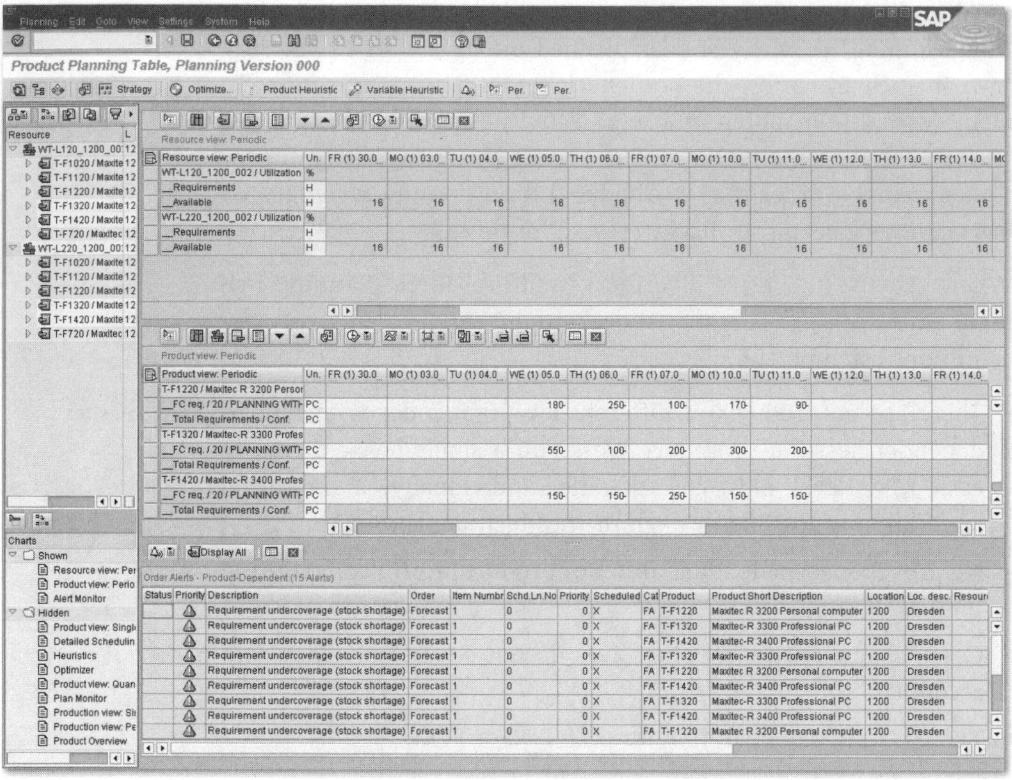

Figure 7.31 APO Transaction "Product Planning Table," Transaction Code /SAPAPO/PPT1, Available Capacity, Requirements Situation for Three Products and Exception Messages That Appear

In ECC, each material has several production versions that enable you to access the various production lines available (see Figure 7.32). In APO, a production line is mapped using a separate production data structure in each case. The multi-resource planning is able to execute a cross-line utilization planning based on this master data.

Primary resource

In a typical application scenario, a production line 1 that enables efficient production, for example, thanks to new acquisitions, is to be prioritized (e.g., through the higher production rate to be selected as a so-called *primary resource*). This means that requirements are to be preferentially covered by this production line 1. Only if overloads appear on this line—in other words, if the requirement in a time window exceeds the maximum production capacity of this preferred line—should the older production line 2 be included in the production and take over the remaining requirement.

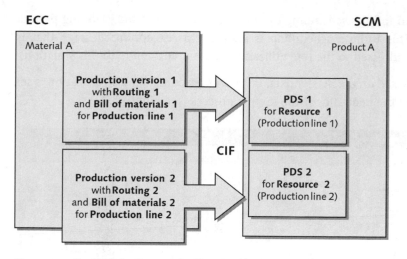

Figure 7.32 Master Data Concept for Mapping Alternative Production Lines Within the Multi-Resource Planning Using a Material A

Let's assume for our sample process that the production rates with which the products can be manufactured on the lines, according to the production data structures, are a maximum of 30 units per hour on line 1 and 20 units per hour on line 2. If needed, both lines are available in double-shift operation (16 hours deployment time per day) and should be scheduled on a daily basis.

If, in exceptional cases, the total capacity offered by the two production lines will not cover the accrued requirements quantity in a given day, the two lines are loaded up to a given threshold (in this sample process here, 80% of the maximum possible load), and the remaining requirement is satisfied in the time window immediately preceding it, again with preference given to the primary resource, if necessary also including the alternative resource. If even this available capacity is not enough, the system will continue moving backwards in time looking for free capacity—like a wave pattern moving to the left along the time axis. Since in practical scenarios searches for free capacity space generally become increasingly hopeless the closer one approaches the current date, an outlet is required for the production quantities that cannot be finitely scheduled during a "backwards wave." This is first accomplished by a "wave reflection" taking place once today's date is reached—further searches for capacity gaps therefore take place in a forward direction in time. If in the future sufficient capacity is still not found on the available production lines, an infinite scheduling can be run at the end of the planning period. This infinite scheduling is assigned an exception message that is addressed to the line utilization planner and refers to this situation.

Based on the master data, the aforementioned parameterization is set in the heuristic for the sample process (see Figure 7.33).

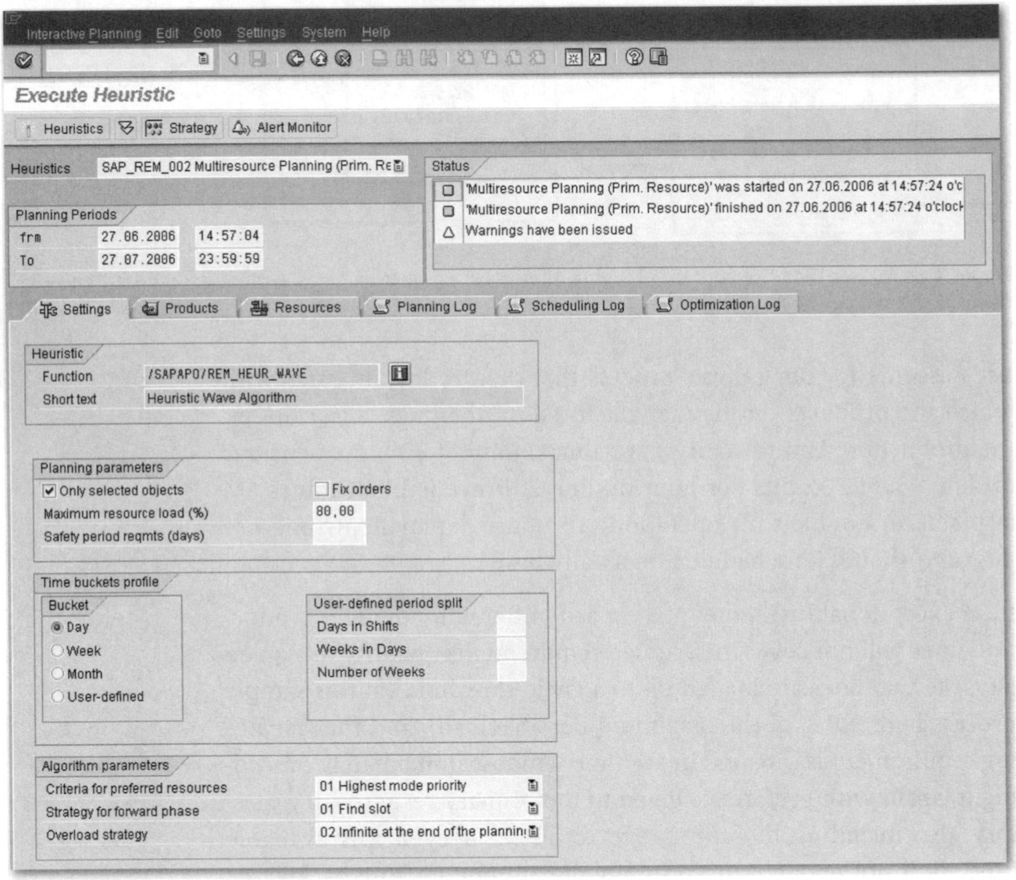

Figure 7.33 APO Transaction "Product Planning Table," Transaction Code /SAPAPO/PPT1, Variable Heuristic, Parameterization of the Wave Algorithm /SAPAPO/REM_HEUR_WAVE in the Interactive Planning

In addition to selecting the **products** to be scheduled, you must choose the two **resources**, the production lines 1 and 2, on the corresponding tabs.

The heuristic for multi-resource planning can always be included in a production planning run and therefore can be planned low-level code for low-level code. However, if this heuristic is used interactively, as is the case here, this is a single-level planning, and it is generally called from the product planning table. Once the planning is complete, the logs for an initial analysis can be understood (see Figure 7.34).

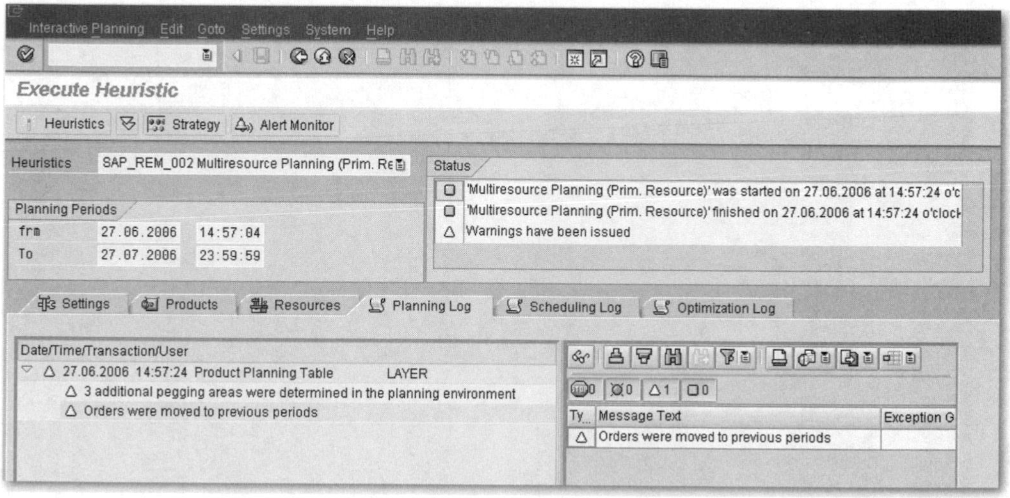

Multi-resource planning and product planning table

Figure 7.34 APO Transaction "Product Planning Table," Transaction Code /SAPAPO/PPT1, Variable Heuristic, Log Entries for the Wave Algorithm /SAPAPO/REM_HEUR_WAVE Once Interactive Planning Is Performed

The planning result is evaluated in the product planning table (see Figure 7.35).

If we first consider the resource situation in the upper chart, it is clear that, as desired, a preferred utilization of the primary resource is obtained in the corresponding period. The specified upper limit (in our example, 80% of the total utilization per time interval) is not exceeded. Any remaining quantities are scheduled on the alternative resource or are shifted to the time window that lies before it in time. The chart for the periodic product view displays the requirements and the procurement elements created for these requirements by the system that lead to the resulting resource utilization. Here you can again see that in applying the wave algorithm, a scheduling of planned order quantities onto the alternative line can only be performed if the first production line in the same time window has already reached its capacity.

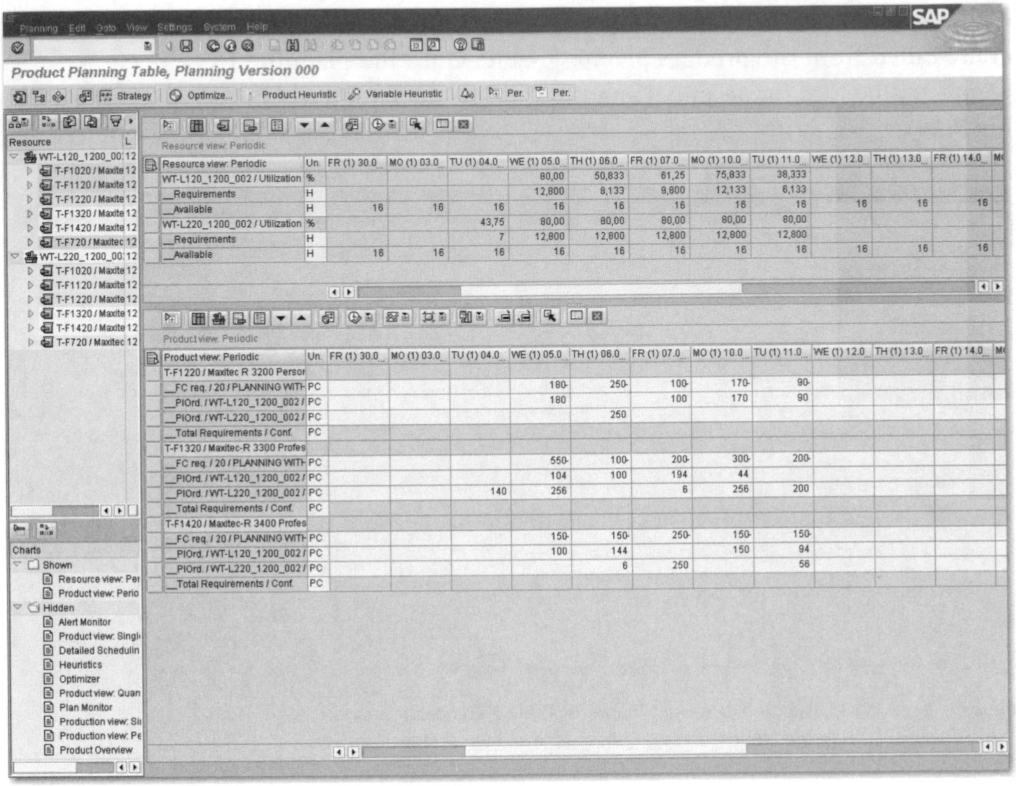

Figure 7.35 APO Transaction "Product Planning Table," Transaction Code /SAPAPO/PPT1, Result Following Planning Using the Wave Algorithm

Interactive correction If there is sufficient total capacity offered, the multi-resource planning will determine a feasible production plan, though this may not yet be "optimal" from the planner's point of view. Since the PP/DS Optimizer will generally withdraw at this point, when in doubt, you can get by with a subsequent manual correction of the calculated production program, preferably using the product planning table and the dynamic alerts that can be displayed in it. To do this, activate the alert monitor chart in the product planning table (exception-based planning, see Chapter 6).

In our example, a manual rescheduling of a planned order quantity is carried out, and the associated consequences are analyzed (see Figure 7.36). Here, the time-shifting of the quantity of 140 units for the second product considered from July 4 to July 6 (e.g., with the goal of closing a production gap) results in a schedule violation of the corresponding requirement and an overload on the corresponding resource. The planner can obtain this information from the dynamically-appearing alerts and react accordingly.

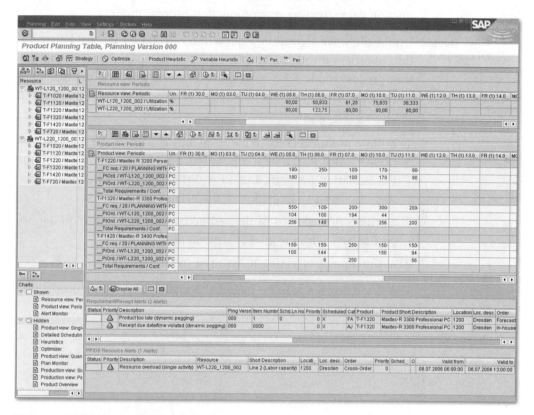

Figure 7.36 APO Transaction "Product Planning Table," Transaction Code /SAPAPO/PPT1, Manual Correction of the Planning Result Using Dynamic Exception Messages

Finally, we would like to point out that the heuristic **multi-resource planning primary resource (SAP_REM_002)** enables an automatic simultaneous quantity and capacity planning under the aforementioned conditions, which is linked at the same time to a cross-PDS (or cross-PPM) line utilization planning. As a matter of principle, this process can be extended to other products and more than two resources.

7.5.3 Alternative to Multi-Resource Planning

Multi-resource planning cannot be applied in all scenarios, due to the restrictive conditions involved. However, this method offers the only complete solution for scheduling several alternative resources that are mapped on the master data side through a respective production data structure or a production process model.

Quota Arrangement

Unlike the wave algorithm, a quotation can allow a targeted distribution of orders through several production data structures or production process models (or even more generally, several procurement sources). A corresponding alternative process may therefore contain the following steps:

1. Infinite multilevel requirements planning with the process heuristic **SAP_MRP_001**; here it is possible, but not necessary, to include the quotation heuristic **SAP_PP_Q001** as a product heuristic, once there is already a quotation in the master data

2. Optimization of each of the resources included in the quotation, particularly with the goal of sequencing

3. Manual postprocessing if required (rescheduling)

The first two steps can be included for automation in a production planning run.

This list contains basic menu paths of the application components in SAP ECC 6.0 and SAP SCM 5.0.

A   Menu Paths

A.1   ECC Core Interface

Create Integration Model [CFM1]: ECC • Logistics • Central Functions • Supply Chain Planning Interface • Core Interface Advanced Planner and Optimizer • Integration Model • Create

Activate Integration Model [CFM2]: ECC • Logistics • Central Functions • Supply Chain Planning Interface • Core Interface Advanced Planner and Optimizer • Integration Model • Activate

Display Integration Model [CFM4]: ECC • Logistics • Central Functions • Supply Chain Planning Interface • Core Interface Advanced Planner and Optimizer • Integration Model • Display

Delete Integration Model [CFM7]: ECC • Logistics • Central Functions • Supply Chain Planning Interface • Core Interface Advanced Planner and Optimizer • Integration Model • Delete

Change Transfer of Master Data [CFP1]: ECC • Logistics • Central Functions • Supply Chain Planning Interface • Core Interface Advanced Planner and Optimizer • Integration Model • Change Transfer • Master Data

Change Transfer of Production Process Model—Send Changes [CFP3]: ECC • Logistics • Central Functions • Supply Chain Planning Interface • Core Interface Advanced Planner and Optimizer • Integration Model • Change Transfer • Production Process Model • Send Changes

Change Transfer of Production Process Model—Delete Change Pointers [CFP4]: ECC • Logistics • Central Functions • Supply Chain Planning Interface • Core Interface Advanced Planner and Optimizer

• Integration Model • Change Transfer • Production Process Model • Delete Change Pointers

Change Transfer of Production Data Structure (PDS) — Transfer Production Data Structure (PDS) [CURTO_CREATE]: ECC • Logistics • Central Functions • Supply Chain Planning Interface • Core Interface Advanced Planner and Optimizer • Integration Model • Change Transfer • Production Data Structure (PDS) • Transfer Production Data Structure (PDS)

Change Transfer Production Data Structure (PDS) — Change Production Data Structure (PDS) [PDS_MAINT]: ECC • Logistics • Central Functions • Supply Chain Planning Interface • Core Interface Advanced Planner and Optimizer • Integration Model • Change Transfer • Production Data Structure (PDS) • Change Production Data Structure (PDS)

Change Transfer Production Data Structure (PDS) — Delete Additional Data for PDS [PDS_DEL]: ECC • Logistics • Central Functions • Supply Chain Planning Interface • Core Interface Advanced Planner and Optimizer • Integration Model • Change Transfer • Production Data Structure (PDS) • Delete Additional Data for PDS

Change Transfer Production Data Structure (PDS) — Transfer Bill of Material [CURTO_CREATE_BOM]: ECC • Logistics • Central Functions • Supply Chain Planning Interface • Core Interface Advanced Planner and Optimizer • Integration Model • Change Transfer • Production Data Structure (PDS) • Transfer Bill of Material

Change Transfer Production Data Structure (PDS) — Transfer Order BOM/WBS BOM [CURTO_CREATE_FOCUS]: ECC • Logistics • Central Functions • Supply Chain Planning Interface • Core Interface Advanced Planner and Optimizer • Integration Model • Change Transfer • Production Data Structure (PDS) • Transfer Order BOM/WBS BOM

Integration Model – Filter Object Search [CFM5]: ECC • Logistics • Central Functions • Supply Chain Planning Interface • Core Interface Advanced Planner and Optimizer • Integration Model • Filter Object Search

A.2   ECC Customizing

Customizing [SPRO]: ECC • Tools • Customizing • IMG • Execute Project

Name Logical System: [SPRO] • SAP Customizing Implementation Guide • Integration with Other mySAP.com Components • Advanced Planning and Optimization • Basic Settings for Setting Up the System Landscape • Name Logical System

Assign Logical System to a Client: [SPRO] • SAP Customizing Implementation Guide • Integration with Other mySAP.com Components • Advanced Planning and Optimization • Basic Settings for Setting Up the System Landscape • Assign Logical System to a Client

Specify SAP APO Release: [SPRO] • SAP Customizing Implementation Guide • Integration with Other mySAP.com Components • Advanced Planning and Optimization • Basic Settings for Setting Up the System Landscape • Specify SAP APO Release

Set Up RFC Destination: [SPRO] • SAP Customizing Implementation Guide • Integration with Other mySAP.com Components • Advanced Planning and Optimization • Basic Settings for Setting Up the System Landscape • Set Up RFC Destination

Assign RFC Destinations to Different Application Cases: [SPRO] • SAP Customizing Implementation Guide • Integration with Other mySAP.com Components • Advanced Planning and Optimization • Basic Settings for Setting Up the System Landscape • Assign RFC Destinations to Different Application Cases

Set Target System and Queue Type: [SPRO] • SAP Customizing Implementation Guide • Integration with Other mySAP.com Components • Advanced Planning and Optimization • Basic Settings for Setting Up the System Landscape • Set Target System and Queue Type

Set User Parameters: [SPRO] • SAP Customizing Implementation Guide • Integration with Other mySAP.com Components • Advanced Planning and Optimization • Basic Settings for the Data Transfer • Set User Parameters

Configure Application Log: [SPRO] • SAP Customizing Implementation Guide • Integration with Other mySAP.com Components • Advanced Planning and Optimization • Basic Settings for the Data Transfer • Configure Application Log

Initial Data Transfer: [SPRO] • SAP Customizing Implementation Guide • Integration with Other mySAP.com Components • Advanced Planning and Optimization • Basic Settings for the Data Transfer • Initial Data Transfer

Change Transfer: [SPRO] • SAP Customizing Implementation Guide • Integration with Other mySAP.com Components • Advanced Planning and Optimization • Basic Settings for the Data Transfer • Change Transfer

A.3   APO-PP/DS Master Data

Model and Version Management [/SAPAPO/MVM]: SCM • Advanced Planning and Optimization • Master Data • Planning Version Management • Model and Version Management

Location [/SAPAPO/LOC3]: SCM • Advanced Planning and Optimization • Master Data • Location • Location

Product [/SAPAPO/MAT1]: SCM • Advanced Planning and Optimization • Master Data • Product • Product

Resource [/SAPAPO/RES01]: SCM • Advanced Planning and Optimization • Master Data • Resource • Resource

Transportation Lane [/SAPAPO/SCC_TL1]: SCM • Advanced Planning and Optimization • Master Data • Transportation Lane • Transportation Lane

Quota Arrangement [/SAPAPO/SCC_TQ1]: SCM • Advanced Planning and Optimization • Master Data • Quota Arrangement • Quota Arrangement

Display Production Data Structure (PDS) [/SAPAPO/CURTO_SIMU]: SCM • Advanced Planning and Optimization • Master Data • Production Data Structure (PDS) • Display Production Data Structure

Delete Production Data Structure (PDS) [/SAPAPO/CULL_RTO_DEL]: SCM • Advanced Planning and Optimization • Master Data • Production Data Structure (PDS) • Delete Production Data Structure

Production Process Model [/SAPAPO/SCC03]: SCM • Advanced Planning and Optimization • Master Data • Production Process Model • Production Process Model

Mass Deletion of Plans and PPMs [/SAPAPO/PPM_DEL]: SCM • Advanced Planning and Optimization • Master Data • Production Process Model • Mass Deletion of Plans and PPMs

Supply Chain Engineer [/SAPAPO/SCC07]: SCM • Advanced Planning and Optimization • Master Data • Supply Chain Engineer • Maintain Model

Mass Maintenance [MASSD]: SCM • Advanced Planning and Optimization • Master Data • General Master Data Functions • Mass Maintenance

Maintain Interchangeability Group [/INCMD/UI]: SCM • Advanced Planning and Optimization • Master Data • Application-Specific Master Data • Product and Location Interchangeability • Maintain Interchangeability Group

Assign Interchangeability Group to a Model [SAPAPO/INCMD_MODEL]: SCM • Advanced Planning and Optimization • Master Data • Application-Specific Master Data • Product and Location Interchangeability • Assign Interchangeability Group to a Model

Procurement Relationships [/SAPAPO/PWBSRC1]: SCM • Advanced Planning and Optimization • Master Data • Application-Specific Master Data • Procurement • Procurement Relationships

Sales Scheduling Agreement Processing [/SAPAPO/CMDS_SCO1]: SCM • Advanced Planning and Optimization • Master Data • Application-Specific Master Data • Sales Scheduling Agreement Processing • Maintain Sales Scheduling Agreement

Maintain Setup Group [/SAPAPO/CDPSC6]: SCM • Advanced Planning and Optimization • Master Data • Application-Specific Master Data • Production Planning • Setup Group/Setup Matrix • Maintain Setup Groups

Maintain Setup Matrix [/SAPAPO/CDPSC7]: SCM • Advanced Planning and Optimization • Master Data • Application-Specific Master Data • Production Planning • Setup Group/Setup Matrix • Maintain Setup Matrix

A.4   APO-PP/DS Planning

Production Planning Run [/SAPAPO/CDPSB0]: SCM • Advanced Planning and Optimization • Production Planning • Automated Production Planning and Optimization • Production Planning Run

Production Planning Run in the Background [/SAPAPO/CDPSB1]: SCM • Advanced Planning and Optimization • Production Planning • Automated Production Planning and Optimization • Production Planning Run in the Background

Product View [/SAPAPO/RRP3]: SCM • Advanced Planning and Optimization • Production Planning • Interactive Production Planning • Product View

Receipts View [/SAPAPO/RRP4]: SCM • Advanced Planning and Optimization • Production Planning • Interactive Production Planning • Receipts View

Requirements View [/SAPAPO/RRP1]: SCM • Advanced Planning and Optimization • Production Planning • Interactive Production Planning • Requirements View

Order Processing [/SAPAPO/RRP2]: SCM • Advanced Planning and Optimization • Production Planning • Interactive Production Planning • Order Processing

Product Planning Table [/SAPAPO/PPT1]: SCM • Advanced Planning and Optimization • Production Planning • Interactive Production Planning • Product Planning Table

Product Overview [/SAPAPO/POV1]: SCM • Advanced Planning and Optimization • Production Planning • Interactive Production Planning • Product Overview

Pegging Overview [/SAPAPO/PEG1]: SCM • Advanced Planning and Optimization • Production Planning • Interactive Production Planning • Pegging Overview

Detailed Scheduling Planning Board—Variable View [/SAPAPO/CDPS0]: SCM • Advanced Planning and Optimization • Production Planning • Interactive Production Planning • Detailed Scheduling • Detailed Scheduling Planning Board – Variable View

Resource Planning Table [/SAPAPO/RPT]: SCM • Advanced Planning and Optimization • Production Planning • Interactive Production Planning • Detailed Scheduling • Resource Planning Table

Conversion of Orders/Purchase Requisitions [/SAPAPO/RRP7]: SCM • Advanced Planning and Optimization • Production Planning • Manufacturing Execution • Conversion of Orders/Purchase Requisitions

Display Logs [/SAPAPO/RRPLOG1]: SCM • Advanced Planning and Optimization • Production Planning • Reporting • Logs • Display Logs

Order and Resource Reporting [/SAPAPO/CDPS_REPT]: SCM • Advanced Planning and Optimization • Production Planning • Reporting • Order and Resource Reporting

Display Planning File Entries [/SAPAPO/RRP_NETCH]: SCM • Advanced Planning and Optimization • Production Planning • Reporting • Display Planning File Entries

Conversion SNP • PP/DS [/SAPAPO/RRP_SNP2PPDS]: SCM • Advanced Planning and Optimization • Production Planning • Environment • Conversion Supply Network Planning • Production Planning

Conversion SNP • PP/DS in Background [/SAPAPO/SNP2PPDS]: SCM • Advanced Planning and Optimization • Production Planning • Environment • Conversion Supply Network Planning • Production Planning in Background

A.5 APO Monitoring

Supply Chain Cockpit [/SAPAPO/SCC02]: SCM • Advanced Planning and Optimization • Supply Chain Monitoring • Supply Chain Cockpit

Alert Monitor [/SAPAPO/AMON1]: SCM • Advanced Planning and Optimization • Supply Chain Monitoring • Alert Monitor • Alert Monitor

A.6   APO Administration

Publish Orders [/SAPAPO/C5]: SCM • Advanced Planning and Optimization • APO Administration • Integration • Publication • Publish Orders

CIF Cockpit [/SAPAPO/CC]: SCM • Advanced Planning and Optimization • APO Administration • Integration • Monitor • CIF Cockpit

QRFC Monitor (Outbound Queues) [SMQ1]: SCM • Advanced Planning and Optimization • APO Administration • Integration • Monitor • QRFC Monitor (Outbound Queues)

QRFC Monitor (Inbound Queues) [SMQ2]: SCM • Advanced Planning and Optimization • APO Administration • Integration • Monitor • QRFC Monitor (Inbound Queues)

SCM Queue Manager [/SAPAPO/CQ]: SCM • Advanced Planning and Optimization • APO Administration • Integration • Monitor • SCM Queue Manager

Activate Application Log [/SAPAPO/C41]: SCM • Advanced Planning and Optimization • APO Administration • Integration • Monitor • Application Log • Activate Logging

Display Entries of Application Log [/SAPAPO/C3]: SCM • Advanced Planning and Optimization • APO Administration • Integration • Monitor • Application Log • Display Entries

CIF Comparison/Reconciliation [/SAPAPO/CCR]: SCM • Advanced Planning and Optimization • APO Administration • Integration • CIF Comparison/Reconciliation of Transaction Data • Execute Comparison/Reconciliation

Comparison of PP/DS Production Data Structure [/SAPAPO/RTO_ORD_COMP]: SCM • Advanced Planning and Optimization • APO Administration • Integration • Comparison of Master Data • Comparison of PP/DS Production Data Structure

CIF Error Handling—Postprocessing [/SAPAPO/CPP]: SCM • Advanced Planning and Optimization • APO Administration • Integration • CIF Error Handling • CIF Postprocessing

Settings [/SAPAPO/C4]: SCM • Advanced Planning and Optimization • APO Administration • Integration • Settings • User Settings

LiveCache Monitor [LC10]: SCM • Advanced Planning and Optimization • APO Administration • liveCache/LCA Routines • Monitor

Consistency Checks LiveCache [/SAPAPO/OM17]: SCM • Advanced Planning and Optimization • APO Administration • Consistency Checks • liveCache Consistency Check

A.7 APO Customizing

Customizing [SPRO]: SCM • Tools • Customizing • IMG • Execute Project

Alert Monitor: [SPRO] • SAP SCM – Implementation Guide • SCM Basis • Alert Monitor

Maintain Factory Calendar: [SPRO] • SAP SCM – Implementation Guide • Advanced Planning and Optimization • Master Data • Calendar

Product: [SPRO] • SAP SCM – Implementation Guide • Advanced Planning and Optimization • Master Data • Product

Resource: [SPRO] • SAP SCM – Implementation Guide • Advanced Planning and Optimization • Master Data • Resource

Transportation Lane: [SPRO] • SAP SCM – Implementation Guide • Advanced Planning and Optimization • Master Data • Transportation Lane

BAdI for Source Determination: [SPRO] • SAP SCM – Implementation Guide • Advanced Planning and Optimization • Master Data • Business Add-In (BAdI) for Source Determination

Production Data Structure: [SPRO] • SAP SCM – Implementation Guide • Advanced Planning and Optimization • Master Data • Production Data Structure (PDS)

Production Process Model: [SPRO] • SAP SCM – Implementation Guide • Advanced Planning and Optimization • Master Data • Production Process Model

Product and Location Interchangeability: [SPRO] • SAP SCM – Implementation Guide • Advanced Planning and Optimization • Master Data • Product and Location Interchangeability

Global Settings: [SPRO] • SAP SCM – Implementation Guide • Advanced Planning and Optimization • Supply Chain Planning • Production Planning and Detailed Scheduling (PP/DS) • Global Settings

Maintain Planning Procedures: [SPRO] • SAP SCM – Implementation Guide • Advanced Planning and Optimization • Supply Chain Planning • Production Planning and Detailed Scheduling (PP/DS) • Maintain Planning Procedures

MRP Planning Run: [SPRO] • SAP SCM – Implementation Guide • Advanced Planning and Optimization • Supply Chain Planning • Production Planning and Detailed Scheduling (PP/DS) • MRP Planning Run

Heuristics: [SPRO] • SAP SCM – Implementation Guide • Advanced Planning and Optimization • Supply Chain Planning • Production Planning and Detailed Scheduling (PP/DS) • Heuristics

Product View: [SPRO] • SAP SCM – Implementation Guide • Advanced Planning and Optimization • Supply Chain Planning • Production Planning and Detailed Scheduling (PP/DS) • Order View

Product Planning Table: [SPRO] • SAP SCM – Implementation Guide • Advanced Planning and Optimization • Supply Chain Planning • Production Planning and Detailed Scheduling (PP/DS) • Product Planning Table

Detailed Scheduling: [SPRO] • SAP SCM – Implementation Guide • Advanced Planning and Optimization • Supply Chain Planning • Production Planning and Detailed Scheduling (PP/DS) • Detailed Scheduling

Application Logs for PP/DS: [SPRO] • SAP SCM – Implementation Guide • Advanced Planning and Optimization • Supply Chain Planning • Production Planning and Detailed Scheduling (PP/DS) • Application Logs for PP/DS

BAdIs for PP/DS: [SPRO] • SAP SCM – Implementation Guide • Advanced Planning and Optimization • Supply Chain Planning • Production Planning and Detailed Scheduling (PP/DS) • Business Add-Ins (BAdIs) for PP/DS

Check Mode: [SPRO] • SAP SCM – Implementation Guide • Advanced Planning and Optimization • Global Available-to-Promise (Global ATP) • General Settings • Maintain Check Mode

Check Instructions: [SPRO] • SAP SCM – Implementation Guide • Advanced Planning and Optimization • Global Available-to-Promise (Global ATP) • General Settings • Maintain Check Instructions

Check Control: [SPRO] • SAP SCM – Implementation Guide • Advanced Planning and Optimization • Global Available-to-Promise (Global ATP) • Product Availability Check • Maintain Check Control

Name Logical Systems: [SPRO] • SAP SCM – Implementation Guide • Integration with SAP Components • Integration via APO Core Interface (CIF) • Basic Settings for Setting Up the System Landscape • Name Logical Systems

Assign Logical Systems to a Client: [SPRO] • SAP SCM – Implementation Guide • Integration with SAP Components • Integration via APO Core Interface (CIF) • Basic Settings for Setting Up the System Landscape • Assign Logical Systems to a Client

Set Up RFC Destination: [SPRO] • SAP SCM – Implementation Guide • Integration with SAP Components • Integration via APO Core Interface (CIF) • Basic Settings for Setting Up the System Landscape • Set Up RFC Destination

Assign RFC Destinations to Various Application Cases: [SPRO] • SAP SCM – Implementation Guide • Integration with SAP Components • Integration via APO Core Interface (CIF) • Basic Settings for Setting Up the System Landscape • Assign RFC Destinations to Various Application Cases

Maintain Business System Group: [SPRO] • SAP SCM – Implementation Guide • Integration with SAP Components • Integration via APO Core Interface (CIF) • Basic Settings for Setting Up the System Landscape • Maintain Business System Group

Assign Logical System and Queue Type: [SPRO] • SAP SCM – Implementation Guide • Integration with SAP Components • Integration via APO Core Interface (CIF) • Basic Settings for Setting Up the System Landscape • Assign Logical System and Queue Type

Set User Parameters: [SPRO] • SAP SCM – Implementation Guide • Integration with SAP Components • Integration via APO Core Interface (CIF) • Basic Settings for the Data Transfer • Set User Parameters

CIF Comparison/Match for Transaction Data: [SPRO] • SAP SCM – Implementation Guide • Integration with SAP Components • Integration via APO Core Interface (CIF) • Basic Settings for the Data Transfer • CIF Comparison/Match for Transaction Data

CIF Error Handling: [SPRO] • SAP SCM – Implementation Guide • Integration with SAP Components • Integration via APO Core Interface (CIF) • Basic Settings for the Data Transfer • CIF Error Handling

Various developer notes exist for APO-PP/DS, some of which are listed here.

B   SAP Notes on APO-PP/DS

B.1   PP/DS in General

426705   Guidelines for note searching in APO-PPS

654312   Release Restrictions for SCM 4.0

832393   Release Restrictions for SCM 5.0

B.2   Master Data in General

385602   Validity in APO (Documentation)

390850   Scrap in APO and R/3 (documentation)

331664   APO PP/DS: Material status

520561   Maintaining product master in R/3 or in APO

619976   Special procurement types in APO (documentation)

418995   Calendar resource

B.3   Production Process Model, Runtime Object and Production Data Structure

411733   PPM-transfer: Functionality with changes

485231   Explosion of PPM of reference product for product variant

323884   PPM Conversion: Description PPM conversion PP/DS-SNP

516260   PPM generation: Functionality description (II)

494486   PPM: Bucket consumption calculation during generation

525433   PPM generation with lot size margin: consumption det.

641876   Use of parallel sequences in PP/DS runtime object

610873   SCM: Using reference characteristics in PP/DS-PDS

357178   Examples for customer enhancements in runtime object

507025   Examples of customer enhancements II

705018   Change from PPM to PDS (documentation)

709884   Consulting notes for PDS and ERP-PDS

644403   Changing the validity mode during the planned explosion

B.4   MRP Areas

628739   APO 3.x Release restrictions for MRP areas

B.5   Product Interchangeability

617283   Migration of discontinuation data: SAP_BASIS 46C and below

617281   Migration of discontinuation data: SAP_BASIS 610 and above

B.6   Integration

619973   R/3-APO integration and Customizing changes (document)

481906   SNP-PP/DS integration (documentation)

492591   FAQ: Stock forwarding

307336   Object locked by user

B.7   Production Planning in General

448960   Net requirements calculation (documentation)

439596   Notes on Customizing planning processes

565972   FAQ: External procurement in PP/DS

441740   Planning time fence in APO: Documentation

577158   Withdrawal from alternative plant in APO (documentation)

575624   Locking concept in APO-PP/DS (documentation)

519070   Planning without final assembly (documentation)

861795   Incorrect rescheduling of confirmed orders

B.8   Production Planning Run, Heuristics, MRP

518556   Using heuristics in the production planning run

513827   Settings/parallel processing in the PP/DS planning run

457723   Planning period with PP heuristics

551124   APO: Finite Scheduling with MRP heuristic (documentation)

538201   Groff reorder procedure/part period balancing

584204   Planning standard lots for continuous I/O (SAP_PP_C001)

560969   Rescheduling: Bottom-Up (SAP_PP_009)

584051   Multiresource planning (primary resource) (documentation)

557731   Planning file entry + reuse mode (documentation)

431171   Quota heuristic: planning of shortage/excess quantities

B.9   Product View and Product Planning Table

531821   Date change in product view and detailed scheduling

607428   Product planning table – FAQs

330153   PPT: Explanation – quantity display in periods

439379   PPT: Explanation: Days' supply in periodic view

851298   Order view: Deleting a phantom assembly

B.10 Pegging

393437   Pegging in APO: background information (documentation)

458996   Fixed Pegging in SAP APO (documentation)

601990   External relationships (documentation)

696199   Including fixed pegging in the MRP run

698427   Fixed pegging: Supported document changes and replacements

601813   FAQ: Characteristic evaluation in ATP check mode

663137   R/3 MM-IM core extension for APO fixed pegging

704583   Fixed pegging in APO: Symptoms and restrictions

390151   Deleting unnecessary planning sections (pegging areas)

B.11 CTP, Multilevel ATP

455421   Comparing multilevel ATP and CTP (documentation)

426563   CTP: Settings, system behavior and performance (documentation)

459694   Finite scheduling with CTP or SAP_MRP_002 (documentation)

480292   Multilevel ATP (documentation)

744400   CTP: Bucket-oriented capacity check in APO

B.12 Conversion of Orders

358833   APO planned order conversion: Check on material statuses

435366 BAdI for additional checks when converting orders

862652 Unwanted transfer after you set and delete conversion indicator

862076 Incorrect message during conversion and repetitive manu-facturing

B.13 Safety Stock

517898 PP: Standard methods for safety stock planning

413822 Safety stock in APO-PP/DS (documentation)

B.14 Characteristic Dependent Planning/ Block Planning

449565 Integration with CDP in APO (Characteristic Dependent Planning)

526883 CDP: Unspecified characteristics in planning and pegging

528189 Additional information about block planning

B.15 Special Planning Processes

582212 External planning (documentation)

619898 Production in another location (documentation)

594982 Push Production (documentation)

B.16 Detailed Scheduling—Integration

392712 SNP orders in PP/DS detailed planning

B.17 Detailed Scheduling Planning Board

592465 Tips for using the detailed scheduling planning board

374307   Object display in the detailed scheduling planning board

374819   Not all graphical objects are displayed

460431   More objects in network view after rescheduling

538894   Scaling the axis for the curve view

312578   Display problem with pegging relationships

571265   Receipts/requirements are displayed incorrectly

525175   Problems with segmented retroactive loading in planning board

492747   Display of PI-operations an PI-phases in DS planning board

532700   Non-work times do not hide

523663   Displaying activities in the product chart

559785   Product repeatedly in the product chart

351508   Incorrect operation chart display in planning board

410567   Hiding unrequired lines in product chart

B.18   Scheduling

397989   PP/DS: Scheduling (Documentation)

445899   Problems in planning with sequence-dependent setup times

542779   Problems when planning with alternative resources (modes)

511084   Planning with alternative strategies

450761   Problems when planning with the "Compact planning" strategy

549205   Problems when planning with negative relationships

498223   Planning on resources with storage characteristics

362208   Creating deallocated orders in APO

B.19 Customer-specific Heuristics

590649 Rules for customer-specific DS heuristics

613189 Documenting heuristics

339576 Shelf life R/3 → APO, Settings in R/3

395321 Planning with shelf life in APO 3.0

563863 Planning with shelf life as of APO 3.1

599717 Shelf life of batch stocks without production date

B.20 Optimization

532979 Pegging in optimization

517178 Relationship violations

560683 Resource selection for the PP/DS optimization

517426 Planning time fence in optimization

B.21 Alert Monitor

495166 Tips and Tricks for Handling Alert Monitor

The standard version contains a multitude of heuristics that can be used in the context of PP/DS planning. The following selection is simply an overview of the overall list of available heuristics.

C   Heuristics

Heuristics are a central planning element in PP/DS. The list contained in this appendix provides an overview of the pool of heuristics that comes with the standard version of the different SAP APO releases.

Each heuristic is briefly described. For a more detailed description, you should refer to the comprehensive documentation in Transaction **/SAPAPO/CDPSC11**.

Note that some of the heuristics listed here are only relevant to industry-specific processes such as campaign planning, length-oriented planning, or model mix.

If, in addition to that, you want to program your own heuristic based on specific requirements, you should use the *Heuristic Framework*:

You can write your own algorithm by using the function group **/SAPAPO/RRP_HEUR_TEMPLATE** as a template. It contains the following modules:

▶ **/SAPAPO/HEU_TEMPLATE** as a template for the algorithm

▶ **/SAPAPO/HEU_TEMPLATE_DATAGET** as a Get module for parameterization

▶ **/SAPAPO/HEU_TEMPLATE_DATASET** as a Set module for parameterization

Then you can define the settings for the heuristic in customizing and assign your heuristic to the required heuristic profile.

The following list is sorted by APO releases.

C.1   Heuristics for APO 3.0

SAP001—Schedule Sequence
Planning of operations based on specific criteria in a freely definable scheduling sequence. This heuristic is suited for automated and interactive planning.

SAP002—Remove Backlog
Rescheduling of backlog operations to selected resources. This heuristic is suited for automated and interactive planning.

SAP003—Schedule Sequence Manually
Creation of a manual scheduling sequence via drag-and-drop from the detailed scheduling planning board.

SAP004—Minimize Runtime
Reduction of runtime for orders that own operations on the selected resources (the purpose of which is to make time intervals between the individual operations of the order as small as possible). This heuristic is suited for automated and interactive planning.

SAP005—Schedule Operations
Scheduling of operations with status "deallocated" under consideration of strategy settings.

SAP_MMP_HFW1—Model Mix Planning Run 1
Creation of a sequence for configurable products; it can be integrated in the total planning run.

SAP_PI_001—Merge Orders (Container Resources)
Previously marked (planned) orders are merged into one order. Pegging relationships are transferred to the extended order.

SAP_PP_001—Change Order Manually
Algorithm to change receipts manually in the order views or in the product planning table.

SAP_PP_002—Planning of Standard Lots
Procurement planning according to the standard lot-sizing procedure. This heuristic is suited for automated and interactive planning.

SAP_PP_003 — Planning of Shortage Quantities
Heuristic for the Capable-to-Promise (CTP) process. This heuristic is used in the context of an immediate automatic demand fulfillment. See also **SAP_PP_CTP**.

SAP_PP_004 — Planning of Standard Lots in Three Horizons
The planning is performed in three different time horizons using different lot-sizing procedures.

SAP_PP_005 — Part Period Balancing
Optimizing lot-sizing procedure in which requirement quantities are constantly added to a lot until the storage costs exceed the setup costs.

SAP_PP_006 — Least-Unit Cost Process: External Procurement
Schedules externally procured quantities under consideration of requirements, storage costs, and suppliers (delivery periods, scale prices).

SAP_PP_007 — Reorder Point Planning
Consumption-driven planning for products planned on APO resources (B and C parts).

SAP_PP_008 — Rescheduling: Bottom-Up for Continuous I/O
Bottom-up (forward) scheduling for the production of a demand fulfillment, starting from the time-critical element in the lower part of the Bill of Materials (BOM) structure. Supports continuous input and output.

SAP_PP_009 — Rescheduling: Bottom Up
Bottom-up (forward) scheduling with the purpose of keeping the shortage for dependent requirements and stock transfer requirements as small as possible.

SAP_PP_010 — Rescheduling: Top Down
Backward scheduling with the purpose of rescheduling receipts in such a way that existing demands can be fulfilled.

SAP_PP_011—Delete Fixed Pegging Relationships

Deletion of fixed pegging relationships. This heuristic is suited for the production planning run. You can also use this heuristic to fix pegging up to and including SAP APO 3.1.

SAP_PP_012—Change Order Priorities

The priorities of receipt elements that have been changed due to a specific planning are adjusted to the priorities of the different requirements.

SAP_PP_013—Groff Procedure

Optimizing lot-sizing procedure in which additional costs that have incurred due to the storage of large quantities of procured materials are compared to cost savings in the associated order costs.

SAP_PP_020—Stage-Numbering Algorithm

Adjustment of low-level codes that is required when changes occur in the production data structure or production process model, which may result in changes of the low-level codes.

SAP_PP_C001—Planning of Standard Lots for Continuous I/O

Product planning for products with continuous requirements or receipts based on the lot-sizing procedure that is set.

SAP_REM_001—Multiresource Planning (Equal)

Simple basic algorithm for equal line utilization planning of several production lines with several products. Can be used as a template for your own algorithms.

SAP_REM_002—Multiresource Planning (Primary Resource)

Wave algorithm for line utilization planning of several production lines, one of which is preferred. Can be used for interactive planning and the planning run.

C.2   New Heuristics Introduced in APO 3.1

SAP_CDPBP_01—Reschedule Blocks
Rescheduling of activities in which block planning is carried out (for example, when changing block properties). Can be entered as a follow-up activity in **SAP_CDPBP_02**.

SAP_CDPBP_0—Adjust and Reschedule Block Limits
Adjustment of block limits to the workload situation (extend blocks with overloads, shorten blocks with free capacity).

SAP_PCM_CRT—Create Production Campaigns
Creates production campaigns and assigns orders to them;
1. Activities on campaign resources are sorted chronologically.
2. Creation of campaigns under consideration of the campaign requirements and the campaign profile.

SAP_PCM_DIS—Dissolve Production Campaigns
Dissolves production campaigns or removes as many orders from them as possible. If campaigns are to be used and PP/DS optimization is employed (without campaign optimization), you must use this heuristic; if all orders of a campaign can be deleted, the campaign header is also deleted.

SAP_PCM_ODEL—Delete Setup/Clean-Out Orders
Deletes orders from production campaigns, particularly setup and clean-out orders. Setup orders must be deleted if you want the PP/DS Optimizer to perform a subsequent setup optimization (without campaign optimization).

SAP_PCM_SRVA—Create Setup/Clean-Out Orders
Deletes setup and clean-out orders and creates new ones, especially for campaigns (see adjustment option in detailed scheduling planning board). In other words, this heuristic deletes setup orders, ignores sequence-dependent setup transitions, and creates a setup order at the beginning of the campaign or at the end of the previous campaign.

SAP_PP_014—Ascertaining Planned Independent Requirements

Helps to identify planned independent requirements that are not yet assigned to sales orders. If quantities are scheduled for specific sales orders, customers who are late placing their orders can be requested to place their orders within a certain period, which is based on the result of the heuristic; then, the preliminary requirements are adjusted (see **SAP_PP_015**).

SAP_PP_015—Adjusting Orders and Planned Independent Requirements

Deletes open, unconsumed planned independent requirements for selected products.

SAP_PP_016—Adjusting Special Orders

Deletes open, unconsumed planned independent requirements for selected planned orders and purchase requisitions.

SAP_PP_SL001—Planning of Standard Lots with Shelf Life

Corresponds to **SAP_PP_002**, but under consideration of maturation time and shelf life (indicator is set in heuristic).

C.3 New Heuristics Introduced in SCM 4.0

SAP_CDS_A01—Admissibility OK without Check

Change of all selected sales scheduling agreement items to status "Admissibility OK" without having explicitly checked those items.

SAP_CDS_A02—Tolerance Check

Admissibility check for sales scheduling agreement items. Current dates and quantities requested by the customer are compared to preferred dates and quantities that were valid at the last confirmation. The comparison is based on a defined tolerance schema. The status of the sales scheduling agreement item is set accordingly. In the event of non-confirmations, additional alerts are triggered.

SAP_CDS_F01—Confirm Compliance Without Check

Quantities and dates in sales scheduling agreements requested by the customer are confirmed as being "compliant" without carrying out a feasibility check.

SAP_CDS_F02—Days' Supply Check

Quantities and dates in sales scheduling agreements requested by the customer are checked against the stored days' supply and are confirmed accordingly.

SAP_CDS_F03—Product Heuristic with Days' Supply Check

Quantities and dates in sales scheduling agreements requested by the customer are first planned using the product heuristic, and then checked against the stored days' supply and confirmed accordingly.

SAP_CDS_F04—Planning Standard Lots for Confirmed Quantity

Supply planning using standard lot-sizing procedures for sales scheduling agreement releases. This heuristic always uses the quantities requested by the customer.

SAP_PP_I001—Heuristic for Supersession Chains

Appropriate common planning for products of a supersession chain (product interchangeability). Must be called via Materials Requirements Planning (MRP) heuristic.

SAP_LEN_001—Length-Based Heuristic

Supports a length-based planning of materials. This heuristic creates new receipt elements to fulfill product requirements. It contains a cutting functionality that allows the requirements to be covered by cutting longer stocks and receipts and in so doing can be used to reduce material quantities. It can be carried out using planned or production orders or without orders.

SAP_MOP_001—Multiple Output Planning Heuristic

Creates new receipt elements to fulfill product requirements. The receipt elements are created via Multiple Output Planning (MOP). This involves co-items.

SAP_PP_017—Plan Standard Lots for Co-Products

This heuristic supports the planning of co-products using standard lot-sizing procedures.

SAP_PP_018—Create Safety Stock in SAP liveCache
Creation of a requirements element for the safety stock (to be confirmed in Planning Version Management) against which dynamic pegging can develop.

SAP_PP_019—Fix Pegging Relationships
Deletes fixed pegging relationships or converts dynamic pegging relationships into fixed ones (should not be used for subcontracting).

SAP_SNP_MULT– SNP-PP/DS—Conversion for Many Products
Conversion of SNP planned orders into PP/DS planned orders (here: for several products; refers to individual conversion, **SAP_SNP_SNGL**).

SAP_SNP_SNGL—Individual Conversion SNP-PP/DS
Conversion of SNP planned orders (or CTM planned orders) into PP/DS planned orders according to set selection conditions.

C.4 New Heuristics Introduced in SCM 4.1

SAP_CDPBP_03—Enhanced Block Maintenance
This heuristic can be used to create and modify blocks in the context of a block planning.

SAP_DS_01—Stable Forward Scheduling
This heuristic is used to eliminate planning-related malfunctions across several BOM levels (finite).

SAP_LEN_002—Manual Creation of LOP Order
In the context of length-based planning, a planned order is created containing several output nodes for several requirements (to be selected manually).

SAP_MOP_002—Manual Creation of MOP Order
In the context of multiple output planning, a planned order (or several planned orders) is created for several requirements (to be selected manually).

SAP_PP_CTP—Planning Shortage Quantities for CTP
This heuristic was specifically developed for the Capable-to-Promise (CTP) scenario and is used to take into account retroactive changes to the sales order quantity.

SAP_PP_STOWC—Restore Requests for Contract Release Orders
Restores automatically fixed pegging relationships between pegged requirement and stock transfer document.

C.5   New Heuristics Introduced in SCM 5.0

SAP_CDP_BP_04—Block Maintenance, Called Interactively
Maintenance function used for block planning based on interactive detailed scheduling.

SAP_CHECK_01—Check PDS
Enables the creation of orders for all change statuses of the production data structures (PDS) for a product. This enables a consistency check to be carried out for a newly transferred PDS.

SAP_DS_02—Enhanced Backward Scheduling
This heuristic implements a multilevel finite planning based on dates requested by the customer and with backward scheduling direction.

SAP_DS_03—Change Fixing/Planning Intervals
Fixing and planning intervals can be defined in relation to the current date. In addition, sequence-dependent setup activities can be deactivated in this context.

SAP_DS_04—Activate Sequence-Dependent Setup Activities
The sequence-dependent setup activities deactivated using **SAP_DS_03** can be reactivated here.

SAP_MLO_BU—Multilevel, Order-Related: Bottom-Up
Multilevel top-down planning is enabled using a single-level heuristic (here: the order-related heuristic **Bottom-Up Rescheduling**) to be deposed in this multilevel heuristic. This heuristic can be called interactively. Prerequisite: the low-level codes must be up-to-date.

SAP_MLO_TD—Multilevel, Order-Related: Top-Down

Multilevel planning using the heuristic contained in this heuristic (here: the order-related heuristic **Top-Down Rescheduling**). This heuristic can be called interactively. Prerequisite: the low-level codes must be up-to-date.

SAP_PMAN_001—Critical Path

Determination of the critical path in engineer-to-order or make-to-order production. The "critical path" contains all operations of an order in which a reduction results in the reduction of the overall lead time of the order.

SAP_PMAN_002—Infinite Forward Scheduling

Compact forward scheduling in case of delays in engineer-to-order or make-to-order production based on the current or specified date.

SAP_PMAN_003—Infinite Backward Scheduling

Compact backward scheduling in engineer-to-order or make-to-order production based on the final date. Is carried out after a reduction of the critical path.

SAP_PP_021—New Explosion

Forces a new explosion (for instance, after master data changes). This heuristic is preferably used in interactive planning as specific orders can be preliminarily marked here.

SAP_PP_CDOC—Capacity-Driven Order Creation

Interactive planning in detailed scheduling tools: Creation or adjustment of planned orders (forward/backward extension) in order to obtain an optimal utilization for the selected period and resource.

D   Authors

Dr. Jochen Balla teaches Applied Mathematics and Physics, as well as the Fundamentals of Computer Science at the University of Applied Sciences Bochum, Germany. From 1998 to 2004, he worked for SAP Deutschland GmbH & Co. KG as a training consultant for customer and partner trainings in the areas of SAP PP, APO-PP/DS, and APO CIF.

Dr. Frank Layer is a graduate engineer and works as a training consultant in the area of customer and partner trainings at SAP Deutschland AG & Co. KG. The primary focus of his work is with production planning (SAP SCM-APO-PP/DS and SAP ECC-MRP).

Index

Q

R

Interested in reading more?

Please visit our Web site for all
new book releases from SAP PRESS.

www.sap-press.com